Labour Managed Firms and Post-Capitalism

Marx claims that unselfishness is a child of (workplace) culture, whereas the gene is selfish. If Marx is right then the prerequisite for overthrowing capitalism is a system which both leverages selfishness and creates solidarity between workers. This book illustrates and discusses the major points of the economic theory of producer cooperatives, its evolution since the 1950s, and links with Marxian theory.

Labour Managed Firms and Post-Capitalism, most importantly, demonstrates that a system of producer cooperatives offers a wealth of advantages compared to capitalism. There is general agreement that the main benefit of this form of economic democracy is that people who are allowed to freely pursue their interests are happier than those acting on somebody else's instruction. The author argues that a system of democratic firms would eradicate classical (high-wage) unemployment and scale down both Keynesian and structural unemployment levels. He also shows that a system of producer cooperatives literally reverses the capital-labour relationship typical of capitalism and that its establishment can consequently be looked upon as a revolution.

This volume is of great interest to academics, lecturers and researchers with an interest in Marxism, political economy and industrial economics, as well as economic theory and philosophy.

Bruno Jossa has held teaching posts at the Universities of Pescara, Messina, Venice and Naples. He is a co-founder of the Associazione italiana per lo studio dei sistemi economici comparati, an association which he chaired in 1992-93. From 1994 to 2005 he was Chairman of the Associazione per la collaborazione tra gli economisti di lingue neolatine. Prizes received by Professor Jossa include the V ISTECOR European Culture Award (1991), the 'Saint Vincent' Award (1998) and, in 2011, the F. Nitti gold medal of the Accademia dei Lincei.

Routledge Frontiers of Political Economy

Labour Managed Firms and Post-Capitalism

Bruno Jossa

Routledge
Taylor & Francis Group

LONDON AND NEW YORK

First published 2017 by Routledge

2 Park Square, Milton Park, Abingdon, Oxfordshire OX14 4RN

52 Vanderbilt Avenue, New York, NY 10017

Routledge is an imprint of the Taylor & Francis Group, an informa business

First issued in paperback 2020

Copyright © 2017 Bruno Jossa

British Library Cataloguing in Publication Data
A catalogue record for this book is available from the British Library

Library of Congress Cataloging in Publication Data
A catalog record for this book has been requested

ISBN: 978-1-138-23756-8 (hbk)
ISBN: 978-0-367-59553-1 (pbk)

Typeset in Times New Roman
by diacriTech, Chennai

Contents

vi *Contents*

Introduction

1. The argument that both Marx's writings on the economic system of the future and his overall approach offer fragmentary suggestions rather than a full-fledged theoretical edifice is anything but new (and is actually consistent with Marx's claim that methodology only is what really matters). As early as 1899, Bernstein wrote that Marx and Engels's writings could be used to demonstrate everything and Kautsky warned that it was impossible to absolutely rely on every one of Marx's words because his sayings were often mutually contradictory (Kautsky 1960, p. 437).[1]

With reference to the social order of the transitional period, Marxists fall into two groups: those who assume that a truly Marxist socialist economy is one where firms are run by the workers themselves and those who think of socialism as a centrally planned command economy.[2] In point of fact there is no decisive textual evidence in support of either view. Marx once wrote: "If cooperative production is not to remain a sham and a snare; if it is to supersede the capitalist system; if the united co-operative societies are to regulate national production upon a common plan, thus taking it under their control, and putting an end to the constant anarchy and periodical convulsions which are the fatality of Capitalist production – what else, gentlemen, would it be but Communism, 'possible' Communism?" (Marx 1871a, p. 335). Irrespective of this, there is no clear consensus over the assumption that Marx looked upon a system of producer cooperatives as the new production mode destined to take the place of capitalism (see, *inter alia*, Marcuse 2015).

Leaving aside the issue of the existence of any such textual evidence, in this book I will try to answer the question whether a system of democratic firms operating in a market economy can actually be said to generate a new mode of production. A convinced socialist such as Walras did not believe that cooperation would give rise to a socialist order. In 1900, he wrote (Walras 1990b, vol. IX, p. 66): "Chercher la reforme sociale dans l'association coopérative, c'est exactement comme si on la cherchait dans l'assurance mutuelle. C'est à la fois diminuer sinon méconnaître la réforme sociale, et exagérer, pour la compromettre, l'association coopérative."

It is widely held that things stand differently today. In this connection, Gibson-Graham argued that "once it was the vision of socialism or communism and the experiments of the soviets in the Eastern Bloc that configured the foreground of the Left's economic imaginary," but that "today, at least for some, it is the original 'third way' communitarianism or a revitalized social democracy that occupies this otherwise vacated space" (see Gibson-Graham 2003). Describing the Soviet system as a mix of socialism and state capitalism, Andreani (2001b, p. 175) argues that the first alternative that comes to mind is a system of producer cooperatives.[3]

In *Antidühring* (p. 281), Engels categorised cooperatives as "transition measures to the complete communistic organisation of society": like him, I am persuaded that a feasible model of socialism is worker control of firms, the proposal of workers' councils that Oskar Lange (1957, p. 159) rated as "a springboard for pressing the working class into positive action" (for an earlier study suggesting that such a system realises socialism, see Jossa 1978). Taking the cue from Anweiler (1958, p. 472), let me add that nowadays the original idea of workers' councils as "the primary goal of Marxism" (Garaudy, undated, p. 187) is as topical as ever[4] and that due to the burgeoning role of markets in a globalised economy it is possible to argue that a system of worker-controlled firms operating in a market economy is the only council model that can be implemented in practice in our day.[5]

Ideologically speaking, economic democracy and political democracy are two facets of one and the same founding principle. According to Robert Dahl (1989, p. 331), "if democracy is justified in governing the state, then it must also be justified in governing economic enterprises; and to say that it is not justified in governing economic enterprises is to imply that it is not justified in governing the state."[6]

The idea that socialism may come in two forms is closely associated with the two main contradictions that Marx pointed up in capitalism: the capital-labour conflict and the mismatch between planned production and anarchical distribution. Anyone emphasising the latter contradiction will think of socialism as a centrally planned economy (see, e.g., Godelier 1966 and Mileikovsky 1969, pp. 306–07), while those prioritising the capital-labour conflict will argue that socialism arises when the functions of the 'primary factors of production' (labour and capital) are reversed upon the establishment of a system of producer cooperatives of the LMF type (see Jossa 2010b, pp. 262–63 and Jossa 2011), where labour switches roles with capital in running business enterprises.

According to Korsch (1923, p. 91), in bourgeois society the dead accumulated labour of past generations rules as 'capital' over present living labour (in practical and theoretical terms), whereas a proletarian economy and, hence, the Marxist economic system which is its theoretical counterpart envisages the control of society over its aggregate output; in other words, in such a society it is living work that rules over the dead labour accumulated in the past, i.e. 'capital.'[7]

As is well known, while the aim of capitalistic firms is to maximise profit in the interests of capitalists, the self-managed firms theorised by Ward (1958) and Vanek (1970) make it their task to maximise average worker income or, even more appropriately, the benefits accruing to the workers (specifically, to those majority workers who have authority to pass resolutions). As a result, as soon as economic activity is made to pursue a different goal, the system also (or, more correctly, the mode of production) will change as a matter of course. The well-known Italian philosopher Emanuele Severino has argued (2012, p. 94) that "within a logic which postulates goals and means (as has been prevailing over the entire course of human history), there is little doubt (though the consequence is less dominant than the starting assumption) that whenever an action – in this case the capitalistic mode of operation – is made to deflect from its original goal and to pursue a different one, this same logic determines that the action itself will turn into something different in content, rhythm, intensity, relevance and configuration."

Inasmuch as it is true that Marx's method is a combination of two procedures, namely the identification of aspects common to all production processes and the combination of such processes in such a way as to account for the specificity of individual modes of production and for the passage from one production mode to the next one at different stages of social evolution (see La Grassa 1972, p. 15), there are reasons for arguing that the transition from capitalism to self-management gives rise to a new mode of production because it identifies the aspects that the previous and new production modes have in common and combines them with the specific aspect of the new mode of production, namely the substitution of labour for capital as the sovereign power within the business enterprise.[8]

Nonetheless, the idea that a socialist revolution can take form in the two different ways discussed above is rejected by a great many Marxists who do not equate socialism with democratic firm control and are cynical about the possibilities for worker cooperatives.[9] Among them, analysts of peer production (PP) hold that this new production model has much in common with Marxian communism and may consequently offer a feasible alternative to capitalism (see Rigi 2013).

2. Additional points worth discussing are the reasons why firm management is assumed to mark a major advancement in the evolution of humankind and the rationale behind the claim that Soviet-type planning is a faulty model of socialism.

One major advantage of democratic firms (or producer cooperatives or worker-controlled firms) is the substitution of the 'one head, one vote' principle for the non-democratic 'one share, one vote' principle of bourgeois democracy. The suppression of hired labour acts as an enabler of democracy since it puts an end to the coercion of workers by their employers – an evil that turns useful thinking individuals into lifeless tools for the attainment of another's ends.[10]

In Cerroni (1973, p. 45), according to Marx, we read: "if the ultimate effect of capitalism is to turn the subject into an object and the object into a subject (i.e. to reify living individuals and humanise inanimate things), the tendency that the expropriation of the expropriators will set in motion is the creation of truly personalised (humanised) interpersonal relations and fully reified relations between things (effectively subject to the control of social man)."

One way to contrast socialism with capitalism is to liken socialism to Christianity and to argue that, while capitalism is grounded in egoism and characterised by "the reciprocal and all-sided dependence of individuals who are indifferent to one another," socialism is based on the need of individuals to entertain meaningful relationships with their fellow-beings (Marx 1857–58, p. 97). It is often argued that individuals are moved on by self-love and love for others, both of which are instincts that further the survival of the species, and – let this be repeated – capitalism is said to differ from socialism because the former is an outgrowth of self-love and the latter is mainly based on harmonious relationships with our fellow-beings. It is widely held that "an expansion in the scope of cooperation facilitates the diffusion of norms of generalized morality," but on closer analysis "generalized morality is hurt if external enforcement of morality is mainly local, whereas it is encouraged by strong enforcement of more distant transactions" (Tabellini 2008, p. 908).

These views are endorsed by a number of intellectuals who look upon morals as a reflection of the instinct for survival of the human species (see, *inter alia*, Scalfari 1995, pp. 836–47).[11] However, considering that gene selfishness theorists reject this view, it is worth adopting the line of reasoning of those modern biologists who contend that genes are selfish, that the behaviour of living beings is principally governed by their genes and that the survival instinct is not an inborn characteristic of the species. Starting out from their propositions, it is possible to argue that capitalism is antithetical to socialism since the former is the product of gene selfishness, while the latter is a worldview whose special attention for culture leads to prioritisation of all such organisational forms as may result in a favourable terrain for feelings of solidarity (Rifkin 2009).[12]

The reader is likely to wonder what bearing these reflections have on the claim that socialism can be established through the creation of a system of self-managed firms. The answer to this query is that modern producer cooperative theory, whose roots are in a culture supportive of altruism, is a realistic approach because it is founded on the awareness that individuals are selfish, while a centrally planned system will never function effectively since it fails to leverage either the profit motive or cultural interests.

In the light of the above-mentioned view of selfishness as a connotation of genes, rather than individuals, the terms of the issue can be stated as follows: if the gene selfishness theory is correct and Marx and Dawkins are right when they claim that unselfishness is a child of culture (specifically of interpersonal relations established in the workplace), the prerequisite for overthrowing capitalism is a system which leverages selfishness and creates solidarity between individual producers by the same token. These requirements are met by a system of producer cooperatives which both leverages the personal motive thanks to the apportionment of corporate profits among the partners and fosters mutual feelings of solidarity.[13]

At the other end of the spectrum is a centrally planned system, which puts selfish drives out of count and where individual producers, far from being bound to each other by solidarity, feel hatred for the planning board which monitors their work inputs. On all accounts, in a centrally planned system it is hardly realistic to assume that a correct appreciation of the benefits accruing to the community as a whole from the work of its members may act as a seedbed for generating dedication to work and inter-worker solidarity.

Truth to tell, Engels proclaimed that "in communist society, where the interests of individuals are not opposed to one another, but, on the contrary, are united, competition is eliminated … Private gain, the aim of the individual to enrich himself on his own, disappears" (Engels 1845, p. 566), but this statement is likely to sound somewhat unrealistic. Even if we should take it for granted that the Soviet-type planning model may help stifle the selfish drives that reign supreme in a capitalistic society, if genes are selfish, what breeding ground would be available for nourishing the germs from which solidarity feelings are supposed to sprout in the population? And what, if not their selfish genes, may induce individuals to engage in production?

Bearing in mind that revolutionary enthusiasm tends to be short-lived, it is difficult to argue that the desire for interpersonal relationships that culture tends to breed can justify centralised planning. Let me repeat that it is worker control, not planning, that generates solidarity by its very nature and satisfies the need to entertain harmonious interpersonal relationships. As is well known, in worker-run firms all the members are equally interested in the efficient management of their business and decisions are made jointly, often following in-depth discussion and exchanges of opinions. And it is hard to think of anything capable of generating more solidarity than the joint discussion of the means that will best help achieve shared goals.[14]

In an interesting book, Dunn (2005) contends that markets are antithetical to democracy since the former are driven on by egoistic drives, while the latter requires equality. For my part, I am persuaded that regardless of the fact that it is a market system, a worker-controlled economy would dampen both egoism and the confrontational climate prevailing in capitalistic societies.

In an analysis of socialist society, Gramsci went so far as to argue that "the average proletarian psychology will quickly lose all the mythological, utopian, religious, petit-bourgeois ideologies: the communist psychology will quickly and permanently be consolidated, constantly roused by revolutionary enthusiasm" (Gramsci 1919–1920, p. 30) and that it was possible to imagine "the coercive element of the State withering away by degrees, as ever more conspicuous elements of regulated society (ethical State or civil society) make their appearance" (Gramsci 1975, vol. II, p. 764).[15]

However, apart from the fact that these reflections are unrelated to the gene selfishness thesis, there can be little doubt that before they can be brought to bear on the centralisation issue it would be necessary to provide evidence that planning would actually generate solidarity feelings (which Gramsci failed to do). Ultimately, it is fair to say that the course of events recorded in countries organised in line with the system we term 'state socialism' have irremediably proved Gramsci's claim wrong.

3. The idea that production carried on in association is a means of emancipating workers was shared by John Stuart Mill, who went so far as to describe cooperatives as "a course of education in those moral and active qualities by which alone success can be either deserved or attained" (Mill 1871, p. 716). If workers are joined into cooperatives (where they become 'their own masters') – he argued – the productiveness of labour tends to increase thanks to "the vast stimulus given to productive energies" by the awareness of the members that their increased effort goes to boost their incomes. Yet, he added, this material

benefit "is as nothing compared with the moral revolution in society that would accompany it" thanks to the potential of cooperation for furthering "the transformation of human life, from a conflict of classes struggling for opposite interests, to a friendly rivalry in the pursuit of a good common to all, the elevation of the dignity of labour, a new sense of security and independence in the labouring class; and the conversion of each human being's daily occupation into a school of the social sympathies and the practical intelligence" (Mill 1871, p. 744).[16]

Much to the same effect, Marshall argued that cooperation "does rest in a great measure on ethical motives" and "has a special charm for those in whose tempers the social element is stronger" (see Marshall 1890, p. 292). The true co-operator, he wrote, "combines a keen business intellect with a spirit full of an earnest faith" and the cooperative movement "makes it its task to develop the spontaneous energies of individuals by educating them to collective action and teaching them to use collective resources for the attainment of shared goals." Although he did not deny affinities between cooperation and other movements, he spelt out in bold letters that no other movement was as directly aimed to improve the quality of man himself (see Marshall 1889, p. 227); and he put "the production of fine human beings" at the top of the list of the primary goals of this movement (*op. cit.*, p. 228).

This line of reasoning may explain why I strongly disagree with all those Marxists who declare an interest in cooperation, but hold on to the view that centralised planning is a necessary constituent of socialism. These authors think that it was their strong aversion to markets that led Marx and Engels to structure socialism as a planned system, and this aversion can, quite naturally, be traced to their Aristotelian view of man as a social animal. An acute Marx commentator such as Cornu points out that Feuerbach and Hess thought of economic and social contradictions as generated by an ethical conflict between egoism and altruism (see Cornu 1948 and 1955). Dealing with this conflict in the *Introduction* to the *Critique of Hegel's Philosophy of Right* (which dates from 1843) – Cornu argues – Marx translated it into a social conflict proper and by so doing he turned communism into a doctrine of action, transferred the social problem to the ethical plain (as Feuerbach, too, had done) and postulated its possible solution through altruism and love (Cornu 1948, pp. 154–55). Accordingly, considering that Marx had been thinking of man as a social animal since his early youth, his asserted identification of socialism with a planned, rather than democratically managed system can be traced to the fact that the former assumes individuals to be unselfish, while the latter builds on human egoism. In fact, if selfishness is a characteristic inherent in genes – as mentioned above – no economic system can thrive unless it comes to terms with markets and human instincts.

Marx's view of human nature is the subject of an extensive body of literature (including studies by myself, for instance Jossa 2005b, pp. 200–05 and Jossa 2010b, pp. 93ff.). Here, it is interesting to point out that both his choice of communism and its asserted identification with centralised planning date back to 1943, his twenty-fifth year of age, and that youthful decisions, especially if prompted by strong emotions, tend to remain pervasive influences throughout a man's life.

4. In *Life of Lenin*, Fischer (1964, vol. II, p. 957) reports that after the introduction of the NEP (as a response to the libertarian rebellion in Kronstadt), Lenin read a great many books on the cooperative movement and used the resulting insight to dictate an article (*On Cooperation*) which appeared in the Pravda on 26 and 27 January 1923 and proved to be "so innovative as to take the whole party by surprise" (Boffa and Martinet 1976, p. 240). Concerning this article, Lunacârskij commented that many of the slogans launched by Lenin were at first received with puzzlement and rated as absurd, though later on they were found to be rich in valuable implications (see Strada 1980, p. 117).[17]

Following the advent of Stalin, Lenin's article on cooperation fell into oblivion both inside and outside the USSR and although it marks a turning point in Lenin's political thinking it is little known even today.[18] As this article includes the conclusion that "we have no way out but to admit that all our opinions on socialism have radically changed" and the straightforward equation of socialism with cooperation, it is interesting to appraise the correct place this article has in the evolution of Lenin's thought, i.e. to establish if this statement is to be construed as a sign that late in life Lenin lost faith in central planning and came to identify socialism with cooperation straightaway.

The burgeoning role of the cooperative movement within the framework of the 'New Economic Policy' – Lenin remarked – was a clear indication that the task, at once simple and complex, lying before them was to organise the bulk of the population into cooperatives. In essence, he wrote, what we actually need "is to organize the population of Russia in cooperative societies on a sufficiently large-scale, for we have now found the degree of coordination of private interest, of private commercial interest, with state supervision and control of this interest, that degree of its subordination to the common interests which was formerly the stumbling block for very many socialists" (see Lenin 1923a, pp. 1797–98). And as the core idea behind the NEP was the need to leverage the private profit motive in the construction of a socialist system,[19] there can be little doubt that Lenin was pre-figuring a strong impulse to cooperation. Let it be specified, though, that in his mind the establishment of a socialist system was dependent on two preconditions, the public ownership of cooperatives and a party-controlled state organisation acting in the interests of the working class.

On reaching this conclusion, however, Lenin realised that his understanding of the true nature of socialism had undergone radical change. Now – he argued – "we are entitled to say that the mere growth of cooperation ... is identical with the growth of socialism," and "at the same time, we have to admit that there has been a radical modification of our whole outlook on socialism" (*ibid.*, p. 1802).

Cooperation, he continued, "which we formerly ridiculed as huckstering," constitutes the social regime we have to support by any means. As soon as those advocating a transition to communism seize power, "cooperation under our conditions nearly always coincides fully with socialism" (see Lenin 1923a, pp. 1797–1803).

These quotes are clear evidence that by 1923 Lenin had come to think of cooperation, not as a component of the NEP, but as the regime that better than any other could help establish a genuine socialist order.[20] We look at cooperation – he wrote – from a perspective which has so far been underrated, i.e. "the standpoint of transition to the new system by means that are the simplest, easiest and most acceptable to the peasant" (*ibid.*, p. 1798). "But this again is of fundamental importance. It is one thing to draw out fantastic plans for building socialism through all sorts of workers' associations, and quite another to learn to build socialism in practice in such a way that every small peasant could take part in it. That is the very stage we have now reached" (*ibid.*, p. 1798). As cooperation "is adjustable to the level of the most ordinary peasant," at last we are in a position to argue that "there are no other devices needed to advance to socialism" (*ibid.*, p. 1799). Consequently, there can be little doubt that late in life Lenin came to think of cooperation as the highroad to the edification of socialism – at last discovered.[21] "Owing to the special features of our political system" – he wrote – "cooperation acquires an altogether exceptional significance," so much so that it is possible to say – let this be repeated – that "it coincides fully with socialism" (*ibid.*, pp. 1801–02).[22]

According to Sartori (2015, p. 27), Lenin's seizure of power in 1918 bears witness to his ability to lead the revolutionaries to victory, but as he had no inkling of the way to keep it going, his successful revolution soon fell prey to the 'logic of things.' This, he adds, explains why Lenin came to conceive of cooperation as "the proper road to socialism, finally discovered" (see Lenin 1923a).

5. This book is a forward step in the author's research on the subject of socialism and further develops the findings of articles and essays published over the span of about thirty years, of which it reproduces many pages.[23]

Despite a minimum use of technical jargon, this book caters primarily to a readership of economists, rather than the general public, because I share Hayek's view that the precondition for circulating ideas effectively is pressing them on intellectuals.[24] A few points, for instance the financing difficulties of cooperatives, would probably have deserved being analysed in greater depth, but have just been touched upon since they were addressed at sufficient length in previous writings (to which readers are referred).

In this book, the terms democratic firm, labour-managed firm, worker-controlled firm and cooperative are used as synonyms.

6. To conclude this introduction, I must give a very deep thanks to Prof. Gaetano Cuomo for his attentive reading of my book and for the valuable help he has given me.

Notes

1 In this connection, an authority on Marx such as Roberto Finelli has argued that the collapse of 'state socialism' can by no means affect the validity of Marx's analysis since Marx "just provided generic indications on the society of the future and not even the rough draft of a theoretical approach" (see Fineschi 2007, p. 189).
   An attentive Marx commentator such as Rubel went so far as to argue that terms such as 'Marxian' or 'Marxist' lacked any sound basis (see Rubel 1974, pp. 20–21).

2 Zolo (1974) maintains that the dirigiste model founded on centralisation was of Engels's, rather than Marx's making.

3 In point of fact, in a different study (2008, p. 247), Andreani suggested that Marx stood for a combination of producer cooperatives and central planning.

4 The movement for worker control in enterprises – Garson wrote in 1973 (p. 469) – "is the central issue of class struggle in our generation."

5 The idea of two different socialist revolutionary models was implicitly refuted by Bernstein (1901, p. 234) in a well-known saying which runs: "I am singularly uninterested in understanding what people commonly mean by 'the final goal of socialism.' This goal, whatever it may be, means nothing to me; it is the movement itself which is everything."

6 "The concept of economic democracy seeks to extend democracy from the political arena to the domain of production. This, of course, directly contradicts the logic of capitalism" (Gunn 2012, p. 5).

7 In this connection, Gonnard remarks (1930, p. 437): "le socialism est une doctrine qui affirme la primauté du social sur l'individual – la réalité superieure de la societé par rapport à l'individu."

8 This line of reasoning goes to disprove Peyrelavade's claim that "Marx died for want of a precisely identifiable enemy" (Peyrelavade 2005, p. 91).

9 Whereas the General National Consolidated Trade Union (GNCTU), the nation-wide general union for the protection of workers established in England in February 1834, had a correct appreciation of the importance of producer cooperatives "as a key factor for the prompt establishment of a completely new social order" (see Cole 1953a, p. 136), few Marxists held this view in later years (see, among others, Turati 1897, Mondolfo 1923, p. 93, Labriola 1970, pp. 271–72, Quarter 1992, Westra 2002, McMurtry 2004 and Gunn 2006, p. 345).

10 Rejecting Rawls's claim that the principle of equal freedom is only applicable in the domains of civil and political affairs (see Rawls 1958), I hold that this principle is equally applicable to economic and social phenomena. There are reasons to argue that just as the equal rights principle includes the right to participate in political matters, so it should include the right to participate in the decision-making processes of a firm, especially when it comes to appointing managers (see Gould 1985, p. 204).
This means I share Gould's view (see Gould 1985, p. 204) that "Rawls fails to take clearly into account that equality with respect to certain social and economic conditions is necessary for political freedom."

11 In a well-known book, Singer (1980) provides an exhaustive analysis of the ethical foundations of Marx's theoretical approach and concludes that all Marx's propositions reflect the wish to get rid of a system in which individuals behave selfishly without the least regard to the needs of their fellow-beings.

12 Commenting on Marx's critique of the individualistic view of man, Cornu argues that the materialistic conception of history evokes a novel form of society which realises the true essence of man and illustrates how man can humanise nature by adapting it to his needs and organising society in line with humane principles (Cornu 1948, p. 186). In point of fact, this view is barely acceptable since it seems to descend from the Rousseauistic assumption that man is by nature unselfish.
Neither is it acceptable to argue, as Cornu does, that by assigning communism the mission to reinstate humane and collective values within society, Marx emphasised the dialectical nature of social development and vested in the proletariat the role of the antagonist expected to work towards progress (*op. cit.*, p. 155).

13 Lange described this opinion as the expression of a lower-middle class view of capitalism (see Lange 1958b, pp. 299–300).

14 In an early paper entitled "The Role of the State in State Monopoly Capitalism," Oskar Lange further developed Hilferding's and Lenin's analyses of state monopoly capitalism in the light of the theories of a number of Austrian Marxist thinkers who were critical

of the political platforms developed by the Social-Democrats of the time especially in Germany and Austria. Indeed, whereas these kept identifying socialism with a centralized economy, Adler, Bauer and Lange in their wake thought that the circumstances typical of state monopoly capitalism prevailing in those years would be the ideal *springboard* for a socialist revolution. An interesting remark by Lange runs that during a state monopolistic stage the class of capitalists is actually split into two groups and that the state, while enforcing laws that play into the hands of large monopolistic concerns, leaves smaller capitalistic businesses to stand up to competition and put up with much smaller earnings. This state of affairs has little to do with *laissez faire* politics, which does envisage government measures to protect private ownership, but no measures which would interfere with income distribution or provisions favouring one group of capitalists to the detriment of others. At this stage, it is the issue of democracy that takes centre stage. In an attempt to retain control of the state, economic oligarchies become ever more mistrustful of democratic practices, while petty peasants, the lower middle classes and intellectuals tend to join forces with the proletariat and form a large opposition group in defence of democracy. Hence, advocates of political democracy face two options: living under state monopoly capitalism right to the end or acting as tools for the dictatorship of the proletariat (see Lange 1932, p. 28).

15 An additional interesting passage runs as follows: "Worker solidarity which in the union developed in the struggle against capitalism, in suffering and sacrifice, in the council is positive, is permanent, is made flesh even in the most negligible of moments of industrial production, is contained in the glorious consciousness of being an organic whole, a homogeneous and compact system which, by working usefully and *disinterestedly* producing social wealth, affirms its sovereignty and its power and freedom to create history" (Gramsci 1919–20, pp. 36–37; italics added).

16 As argued by Vanek (1971a, p. 107), the fact that every week a man spends no fewer than forty of the most active hours of his life in a working environment where conflict is endemic must necessarily have an adverse impact on his whole life.

17 Strada's comment (1980, p. 125) is also interesting in this connection: "Lenin often strikes us as being an experimenter who does not adopt a rigid plan, but proceeds by subsequent adjustments."

18 It is neither mentioned in Lukàcs' *Lenin* (1924) or Meyer's *Leninism* (1957), nor in Tonini's *Cosa ha detto veramente Lenin* (1967), Deutscher's *Lenin* (1970), the collection of Lenin's articles about *The Construction of Socialism* published in Italy in 1972 or the history of Marxian economics by Howard & King (1989).

19 "Egoism is too essential to human nature to be uprooted from it – however desirable that might be," Durkheim wrote (1928, pp. 38–39). "When, therefore, one inquires under what circumstances it could be extirpated, one cannot but be aware that he places himself outside reality, and that he can produce only an idyll whose poetry can be pleasing to the imagination, but which cannot pretend to be in the realm of fact."

20 As is well known, Lenin described the NEP as 'State capitalism' and held it to be superior to war communism (see Lenin 1921a, 1921b, pp. 200–201, 1922a and 1922b, pp. 1745–46). It is also for this reason that cooperation is superior to the NEP and amounts to socialism.

21 Accordingly, we cannot agree with Hegedüs when he claims (1980, pp. 538–39) that in Lenin's theoretical approach cooperatives "carry a lesser weight, in terms of their contribution to the implementation of the values of socialism, than state-owned firms."

22 Stalin (1940, p. 10) described Leninism as "Marxism of the era of imperialism," but this definition referred to the time when Lenin thought that socialism would be a natural outgrowth of monopoly capitalism and imperialism, not the time when he wrote his 1923 article.

23 My previous books and articles of which specifically I reproduce some pages in what follows are: "Historical Materialism and Democratic Firm Management," published in the *Review of Political Economy*, 2015, vol. 27, n. 4; "A Few Advantages of

Cooperative Firms," which appeared in *Studi Economici* in 2010 (no. 65); the eleventh chapter of N. Salvadori, A. Opocher, *Long-run Growth, Social Institutions and Living Standards*, a book published by Edward Elgar, Cheltenham, in 2009; "Qualche considerazione perché le imprese democratiche non si affermano," which appeared in the August 2007 issue of *Economia politica;* "Producer Cooperatives and Socialism," a paper which appeared in *International Critical Thought;* "The Joint-Stock Company as a Springboard for Socialism," which appeared in the January-March 2014 issue of the *Rivista internazionale di Scienze Sociali* (vol. CXXII); "The Democratic Firm and 'Passive Revolution,'" a paper published in the *Rivista Internazionale di Scienze Sociali* in 2014 (issue no. 3); "A System of Self-managed Firms as a New Perspective on Marxism," which appeared in *Cambridge Journal of Economics*, vol. 36, no. 4, July 2012; "Marx, Lenin and the Cooperative Movement," in *Review of Political Economy*, 2014, vol. 26, no. 2; "The Key Contradiction in Capitalism," in *Review of Radical Political Economics*, vol. 46, issue 1, March 2014; and "An Innovative Approach to Marx," published in *Rivista Italiana degli Economisti*, 2014, December, no. 3.

24 Initially, Keynes strove to circulate his ideas by addressing a general readership, but starting from the 1930s, when he fleshed out the most original part of his approach, he followed in the steps of Hayek in terms of catering primarily to a readership of economists (see Backhouse and Bateman 2013, pp. 86–87).

1 Historical materialism and democratic firm management

Introduction

The core idea behind historical materialism – and, according to Korsch (1923, p. 96), the true underpinning of Marxism – is that the true underpinning of every social order is the mode of production. In other words, a historical materialist contends that the organisational model of production shapes the minds of human beings and, consequently, the legal and political systems, religion and all the aspects of society that Marx subsumed within the notion of the political and social superstructure. Put differently, in the mind of a historical materialist the socio-political structure of society, the ideals and policies of nations and – in brief – all the distinctive facets of a civilisation are ultimately determined by the structural conditions under which production is carried on (for an excellent paper on this subject, see Schumpeter 1941).

Bernstein 1899a (p. 30) holds that the mainstay of Marxism is the idea of historical materialism – materialism in sociology – which Vygodskij (1967, p. 5) describes as the brilliant formula with which Marx and Engels made their debut on the scene of social science in the early half of the 1840s (viz., well before Marx developed his theory of value and surplus value).[1] Plechanov (1911, p. 2) described it as "one of the greatest discoveries of our century, so rich in scientific discoveries," and Godelier (1982, p. 332) highlighted a contrast between the approaches of pre-Marxian historians and Marx: whereas the former used to deal mainly with political events or religious and philosophical ideas, the primary focus points of the latter's innovative approach to political history (or the history of ideas) were prime causes and the agents behind them, as well as interrelations between man, nature and a horde of actors grouped into castes, orders and classes.[2]

Both Engels and Lenin endorsed the materialistic conception of history as the true core of Marxism (Engels 1859a, pp. 202–03) and "a great achievement in scientific thinking" (Lenin 1913, p. 477); and Aron wrote (1970, p. 178) that the theory of the capitalistic mode of production, which is grounded in historical materialism, was the very gist of Marxism (for a comparable view, see Rodinson 1969, pp. 13–18).[3]

One of the key points of the materialist conception of history is the notion of modes of production. In Marx's approach a mode of production is a social organisational form in which a single prevailing production model – viz. a compound of productive forces and production relations – confers significance on the entire system (see Luporini 1966, p. 170). This is how the relevance of this notion is explained by Engels in his review of *A Contribution to the Critique of Political Economy*: "The proposition that 'the process of social, political and intellectual life is altogether necessitated by the mode of production of material life' … was a revolutionary discovery not only for economics but also for all historical sciences – and all branches of science which are not natural sciences are historical" (see Marx 1859a, p. 203).[4]

Corradi 2007 (p. 25) has argued that production modes and production relations, "ignored in classical, neoclassical and Keynesian economic theory and in functionalist and systemic approaches to sociology, provide preferential focus on social relationships and are able to bring to the fore, in capitalistic processes, a dynamic of subordination that social theories adopting a mercantilist, legal or political vantage point or emphasising individual requirements are unable to reveal."

The idea that the key assumption behind historical materialism is the existence of different modes of production is also emphasised by those who underscore the importance of Marx's unitary approach to history as a totality.[5]

In Marx's own words (1845, p. 228): "Mankind always sets itself only such problems as it can solve, since, looking at the matter more closely, it will always be found that the task itself arises only when the material conditions for its solution already exists or are at least in the process of formulation." Due to the claim that perception and awareness arise after the material conditions have changed, this passage might be mistaken for a simple application of the materialist conception of history. Actually, it enriches this conception by underscoring the fact that identifying an existing problem and realising that a task is to be undertaken entail a measure of assurance that this task can actually be performed (see Catephores 1989, p. 207). On closer analysis, it points to a link between historical materialism and the notion of production mode which was first highlighted by Althusser: the idea that as soon as this production mode is equated with socialism and ascribed certain characteristics, we automatically assume that it can become reality at some point in time.[6]

The close link between historical materialism and the concept of modes of production is the starting point for this chapter, in which I argue that the precondition for the unreserved acceptance of historical materialism and, therefore, Marxism as such is the firm belief that the collapse of capitalism will give rise to a new mode of production; and in my opinion, the new mode of production expected to rise from the ashes of capitalism is not Soviet-type centralised planning, but democratic firm management. Hence, the question to be answered is whether or not the widely held views that markets cannot be abolished and that central planning does not work are, in themselves, enough to justify the conclusion that revolution is but myth.

In economics, the term 'revolution' (in the way a society is organised) designates a change in the production mode. This was certainly the view held by Marx, the great theoretician of production modes and the way they arise, grow and pass away, but it is also shared by anyone prepared to admit that there are a variety of different modes of production and, specifically, that socialism is a social organisation form which differs from capitalism and is consequently a potentially new production mode.

Starting out from these reflections, in this chapter I wish to argue that historical materialism, conceived of as a theory of modes of production and, hence, of a feasible anti-capitalistic revolution, will be perceived as fully viable even today if we accept the idea that what is meant by 'socialist revolution' is actually the introduction of democratic worker control of firms.

Is the rise of a new mode of production a realistic assumption?

Quoting Norberto Bobbio (1990, p. 130), "while it is true that historical communism has proved abortive, the problems that communist utopian thought brought to the forefront of attention and attempted to tackle are not only still there, but bound to further escalate and be magnified to world scale in a fairly near future." This poses a need to inquire into the true causes of the crisis of communism, which reached its acme upon the fall of the Berlin Wall, the rise of market economies in Eastern European countries and the inception of the globalisation process.

Historical experience and economic theory have taught that the command economy model collapsed both because of the negative response of the population to its non-democratic nature and authoritarianism, and because of the poor performance of an economic system where the main spring of human action was not the private profit motive. An author with considerable experience in the Soviet planned system has argued that even such a trifle as a workshop order for repairing a piece of machinery would get lost in the meanders of the regime bureaucracy (see Wheeler 1973, p. 87). The belief that the centrally planned model is no viable prospect for the future must be traced not only to the insight that a planned economy cannot work without allowing markets more scope than they were given in Eastern bloc countries, but also to the theoretical and experiential conclusion of academics that central planning is hardly compatible with markets.

There is general agreement that after the death of Lenin Marxism experienced a downward spiral throughout the twentieth century and fell to an all-time low upon the dismantlement of the Berlin wall. In the estimation of Sève (2004, pp. 151–55) and others the true cause of this eclipse was the use of Marxism as a justification for the pro-USSR policies of communist parties,[7] whereas a most complete line of reasoning would suggest that Marxism faces a crisis when no new mode of production is in sight; in other words, that the crisis of Marxism originates both from the awareness that markets cannot be abolished and from the unwarranted belief that socialism cannot be realised in practice.[8]

This begs the question: can worker control of firms become the new polar star for the Left?[9]

As mentioned above, I think that worker control of firms is an effective alternative option to centralised planning and that firm management is tantamount to socialism.[10]

Let me add that there are two basic contradictions affecting capitalism: (a) the mismatch between socialised production and private appropriation, and (b) the capital-labour opposition. And whereas those endorsing the overriding importance of the former will theorise the role of centralised planning as an antidote to the evils of markets, anyone prioritising the latter will emphasise the prospects offered by a new mode of production capable of reversing the present-day relation between wage-labour and capital.

As argued by Bidet, Marx tends to look upon market relationships as a phenomenic element – contrasted with class relationships, which is constitutive of the essence; this is why he describes the capitalistic mode of production as a socio-political notion with special focus on class relations (Bidet 1990, p. 155). This prompts the conclusion that just as the system termed capitalism is one where firms are managed by capitalists, so socialism is a system where firms are run by workers.

A functionalist approach to historical materialism

The foregoing reflections have made it clear that due to the existence of an alternative to the capitalistic production mode historical materialism is still acceptable today, after the collapse of the Soviet system. Hence, at this point it is worth discussing different interpretative approaches and objections to the materialist conception of history and examining at least the most important of these criticisms.

On account of its multifarious nature, historical materialism has been described as an 'intellectual Proteus' (see Smith 1984, p. 316). One of these interpretations, which is referred to as 'fundamentalist,' is based on the works of Plekhanov, Kautsky and Bukharin and is endorsed by Cohen (1978 and 2000), Cohen (1983) and Abbagnano (2006, appendix) because of its extensive use of the technique of causal explanation.

Broadly speaking, it can be explained as follows.

By general agreement, anyone approaching historical materialism is likely to come up against two main queries, i.e. the 'central puzzle' of Marxism (see van Parijs 1984, pp. 88–89): (a) How can we argue that productive forces determine production relations and, by the same token, admit that productive forces are affected by production relations? (b) How is it possible to say that production relations are the base which determines the superstructure and, subsequently, admit that the superstructure influences the structural base?[11] Faced with this puzzle, many scholars resolved to reject historical materialism altogether. In a well-known study, Cohen (1978 and 2000, chap. X) suggested that the solution is at hand if Marx's explanations are rated as functional in nature, i.e. as pointing to a propensity to generate certain effects, but Cohen's solution in turn raises the question whether Marx can correctly be termed a functionalist.

The nature of historical materialism and, specifically, the question whether it offered a functionalist explanation of historical evolution were the main points of an interesting debate which involved van Parijs (1984), Noble (1984), Elster (1985) and Brenner (1986) and will be briefly outlined here below.

The connection between productive forces and production relations in historical materialism may be explained in two ways: (a) production relations tend to adjust to the level reached by productive forces; (b) the production relations that tend to prevail are those that *impress the most forceful impulse* on productive forces; and in the estimation of van Parijs the correct explanation is the latter, which conveys a clear sense of Marx's dynamic worldview.[12] As is well known, the central concern of capitalism according to Marx is capital accumulation. "Accumulate, Accumulate! This is Moses and the prophets!" one of his celebrated sayings runs. And whoever has experience of capitalism will endorse the view that the moment a capitalistic economy proves unable to continue accumulating capital at a brisk pace it will find itself in the middle of a crisis. As reported by Shaw (1984, p. 12), Marx made it clear that internal economic problems are magnified at the same pace that capitalism comes to maturity and that this inevitably determines a loss of efficiency within the system.

A functionalist explanation is a particular type of causal explanation. As theorised by Cohen (1978 and 2000, p. 260), if a type E event produces a type F event, the F event must tend to further, rather than avert, the event from which it originates; consequently, if the development of productive forces furthers production relations of a given type and these act themselves out in combination with a given type of superstructure, it is to be assumed that all such effects as are produced on the productive forces by the superstructure must tend to produce a growth of these forces; otherwise, the relations of production would be doomed to decay. Consequently, if historical materialists contend that the production relations that tend to prevail are those that further the growth of the production forces, the description of the explanation as 'functionalist' is correct since the aspect which is highlighted is the above-mentioned propensity of a phenomenon to generate given effects.

An additional reflection in support of a functionalist interpretation of historical materialism is the fact that overpopulation furthers capital accumulation and that capital accumulation is in turn one of the causes of overpopulation.

In fact, a functionalist explanation will only apply on condition that the productive forces are driven on by something, for example technical progress, which is independent of social relationships at least to a certain extent. Indeed, "if there is no asocially based (autonomous) tendency to productive growth – no underlying tendency to progress – then the functionalist argument is irrelevant" (Cohen 1982, p. 24).

Cohen's approach has been criticised for combining functional explanations with structural functionalism. The structural functionalists engaged in this debate went so far as to contend that Marxism and functionalism are like night and day (see Noble 1984, p. 105). Specifically, it has been criticised for conflicting with the central Marxist tenet that capitalistic societies are divided into classes (*ibid.*).

In point of fact, this is barely the case, since in capitalistic societies decisions are invariably made by the class – capitalists – whose aim in life is to accumulate capital as rapidly as possible and which would be weakened by any slowdown in accumulation. Hence, it is possible to argue that functionalism is in keeping with the view of society as split into classes.[13]

There is little denying that these short notes on the 'central puzzle' of Marxism do not offer an exhaustive analysis of historical materialism; and indeed, their only aim is to controvert the main objection usually raised against it. Additional reflections on the materialist conception of history, however, will be developed in the next two sections.

Is history heading in a precise direction?

To answer the query raised in this chapter, it is necessary to establish if history will necessarily head in a given direction and what this direction is.

Marx describes history as a process, governed by laws, which entails an uninterrupted chain of changes in the structure of social interrelations. In *The German Ideology*, he wrote (see Marx & Engels 1845–46, p. 27): "History is nothing but the succession of the separate generations, each of which exploits the materials, the capital funds, the productive forces handed down to it by all preceding generations; and thus, on the one hand, continues the traditional activity in completely changed circumstances and, on the other, modifies the old circumstances with a completely changed activity."[14] Further on, he and Engels specified (*op. cit.*, p. 59) that history is "at the same time, the history of the evolving productive forces taken over by each new generation, and is therefore the history of the development of the forces of the individuals themselves."[15]

Hence, *The German Ideology* offers the demonstration that the main purpose behind Marx's approach to history, i.e. historical materialism, is expounding the real process of production and comprehending the form of intercourse created by this mode of production, i.e. civic society in its various stages as the basis of all history, describing it in its action as the state, and also explaining how all the different forms of consciousness, as religion and philosophy, arise from it.

As is well known, right to his maturity Marx held on to the belief that the true foundation of the historical process was material production. In 1859, he wrote (Marx 1859b, p. 5): "In the real production of their existence men inevitably enter into definite relations, which are independent of their will, namely relations of production appropriate to a given stage in the development of their material forces of production." "In historical materialism" – Elster puts it (1985, p. 267) – "productive forces hold the centre of the stage."[16]

Emphasising the originality of Marx's approach to history, the Italian philosopher Giovanni Gentile defined it (1974, p. 10) as "a new perspective for approaching history from an unprecedented angle of view and a new method and a new system dictating the need to take a step back and try to offer a different elucidation of human experience, a new perspective on the essence of life and, in short, a new philosophical approach."[17]

Yet, Marx did not deny the importance of the subject, i.e. of man, in history. "Men" – he wrote – "make their own history" (Marx 1852b, p. 103).

Our reflections so far beg the question: is there progress in history?

In the wake of Marx,[18] Gramsci argued that history, the chronicle of man's struggle for freedom, has always been able to dismantle and break up the ponderous repressive machinery put in place by the power structure (see Gramsci 1984, p. 601); and Lukàcs (1968, p. 34) remarked that Marx's conception of world history "as a unitary process and the highroad to liberation" was actually in line with the approaches of German philosophers and chiefly Hegel. This view goes as far back as Kant, who described history as steady progress (see Kant 1784, p. 174).

It is hardly to be doubted that the long-term (not year-after-year) effect of a growth of productive forces is a rising trend in per capita incomes and that higher income levels are usually associated with an upward trend in education. In turn, scientific advancements and higher education levels help the population master their environment ever more effectively. Man is the only rational being in the universe and it is thanks to reason that he controls the environment. Provided it is true that the domain of knowledge is constantly widening and that people are ever better educated, there is good ground for believing that society will develop the ability to exercise ever tighter control over production activities as well. Hence, it is possible to argue that any Marxist will "classify existing societies by reference to an intrinsic criterion: their respective degrees of socialisation, i.e. the extent to which individuals are collectively able to control the conditions of their existence" (Balibar 1993, p. 131).[19]

The idea that man tends to make himself master of the environment in which he lives goes to reinforce the statement of Naomi Klein (2014) that the only way to halt the global warming process across the planet is overthrowing capitalism, a system in which the economy has a stranglehold over politics. In Klein's view, the relentless quest for economic growth is killing the planet, which means that revolution "is no longer a matter of mere ideological preference, but rather one of species-wide existential necessity."

An additional point to be discussed at some length is the tendency to absolute control that Marx extolled as the logic inherent in the economic process. Whereas Marx expected this tendency to impress momentum on the progress towards socialism, Horkheimer thought it to be fraught with danger. In Horkheimer's own words, this assumption was the aspect of Marx's approach that had induced him to distance himself from Marxism. Far from paving the way for the advent of socialism, he argued, each piecemeal extension of control over economic activity by compact industrial groups organised in line with unitary criteria would inevitably lead to a downward spiral in freedom. And a society where the totality of production establishments in existence obey the will of one and the same entity may, admittedly, become fairer and safe from the fear of the future – he argued – but will doubtless stifle autonomy and free expression in its members. Whereas Marx correctly predicted the progress of human societies towards an ever more tightly regulated world, Horkheimer added, due to his optimism he did not realise that subterranean forces were stifling fantasy and inventiveness in human beings and failed to conclude that all such freedom as had been made possible by bourgeois society was to be protected against the dangers stemming from total control. And this, he concluded, explains Marx's opposition to the growing centralisation of societies (see Horkheimer 1972, pp. 30–31, 44–47 and 52).

In my estimation, Horkheimer's conclusion betrays the misconception that socialism is to be equated with a system characterised by Soviet-type centralised planning – an idea that Marx would not have subscribed to.

From a different perspective, Marx's conception of history has been criticised for underrating the risks associated with prolonged periods of regression comparable to those recorded after the collapse of the Roman Empire or before Hitler's rise to power in Germany. The understatement of regression risks may either generate the delusion that the present circumstances being criticised are the worst possible or the equally misleading idea that revolution will not expose the masses involved to prolonged periods of misery – belief which is contradicted by the record of events in Russia and China (see Sowell 1985, pp. 205–09).

The idea that the ultimate goal of the historical process is the full emancipation of humankind has been called into question by many theorists, including Max Weber,[20] Lucio Colletti (in the 1977 interview printed in Colletti 1979) and Hodgson (2000, pp. 302–05), who have strongly criticised the finalistic, teleological component of Marxism, but have erroneously extended it from individual Marxist thinkers to Marxism overall.

Engels himself forcefully denied that his approach could be described as teleological (see Engels 1859a, p. 372, Marx 1860, p. 131, Marx 1861, p. 578, Marx 1867a, p. 114). In this connection, it is worth repeating that Marx certainly took it for granted that humankind would manage to master the environment ever more thoroughly, but he never contended that the future held in store a chain of piecemeal day-by-day gains in freedom. As is well known, he rather held that the ultimate effect of the development of productive forces under capitalism would be the growing subjection of workers to the oppressive power of capital. As he himself put it, "at the same pace that mankind masters nature, man seems to become enslaved to other men or to his own infamy. Even the pure light of science seems unable to shine but on the dark background of ignorance. All our invention and progress seem to result in endowing material forces with intellectual life, and in stultifying human life into a material force" (quoted in Ojzerman 1969, p. 270).

Regarding this point, it is worth mentioning that Lukàcs divided the history of *Kultur* into a pre-capitalistic stage, a capitalistic stage and a third, classless stage. And whereas in capitalistic societies, where everything that is produced is turned into a commodity, he saw culture stripped of its autonomy and ultimately nullified, he predicted that thanks to the abolition of mercantile relationships communistic societies would provide fresh scope for meaningful work and help mankind wield "its inner mastery over the external reality," i.e. *Kultur* (see Lukàcs 1971 and the comment by Cases quoted there).

Hence, it is possible to conclude that the description of history as the record of man's gradual attainment of ever greater control over the environment is a keystone of Marxism.[21] In the words of Bensaïd, the novelty of Marx's approach to history lies in its ability to decipher "tendencies that do not have the force of law," but are already powerfully under way (Bensaïd 2002, p. 14).

The overall validity of historical materialism

A 1978 book by Corrigan, Ramsay and Sawyer (CRS) and two well-known contributions by Sweezy (1981) and Brenner (1986) reject Althusser's claim that Marx's contribution was the formulation of a *general law* accounting for the way production modes arise, take ground and pass away. Marx and Engels's laws – they argue – have a bearing on the capitalistic production mode only and there are no *a priori* reasons for assuming that change necessarily originates or receives impetus from production in all ages.[22] Neither the well-known base-superstructure relation, nor historical materialism as such – they conclude – are necessarily relevant to all production modes and the gist of historical materialism boils down to the bare notions that each society has to produce what it consumes and that consumption is a necessary prerequisite for any social order to reproduce itself (Sweezy 1981, p. 16a). A similar idea is implicit both in Max Weber's claim that capitalism has its roots in the Protestant ethic and in Harold Lasky's argument that prior to the rise of capitalism State and Church used to judge the economic order by reference to their own principles, did not rate the private profit motive as particularly important and, unlike what happened later on, managed to regulate economic life through a body of laws prioritising considerations of social well-being over economic interest (in other words, in Lasky's view, self-interest was not the driving force of economic and social life in the Middle Ages – see Laski 1947, pp. 11–13).[23]

In point of fact, it is doubtful whether these reflections are compatible with a correct interpretation of Marx's theoretical approach. On page 31 in *The German Ideology*, Marx and Engels argued that "by producing their means of subsistence" "men are indirectly producing their material life" and on pp. 8–9 in the same book they added that "what they are, therefore, coincides with their production, both with what they produce and how they produce." Analysing the feudal era further on (pp. 36–37), they maintained that "the production of ideas, of conceptions, of consciousness is at first directly interwoven with the material activity and the material intercourse of men" and that "morality, religion, metaphysics and all the rest of ideology as well as the forms of consciousness corresponding to these no longer retain the semblance of independence" because "it is not consciousness that determines life, but life that determines consciousness."[24] In *Capital* also, Marx made it clear that the materialist conception of history was applicable to pre-capitalistic modes of production as well (see Marx 1867a, pp. 113–14, note 33; see, also, Balibar 1965, p. 234), and it strikes me as surprising that the relevant passage has never been mentioned either by Sweezy or by the authors mentioned above.

However, CRS's methodological approach is relevant to our analysis because it leads up to the argument that free will would have much more scope in a democratic firm system than it has ever been given in a capital-managed economy to this day.[25] And if this is true, then the one production mode to which historical materialism would not be fully applicable is a democratic firm system, where the combined effects of reduced insolvency risks and less aggressive competition would revitalise the role of conscience in human life and leave the working class free to restyle the organisational lines of the social context in which they live.[26]

According to Marx and Engels (1845–46, p. 438), in a capitalistic society "the domination of material relations over individuals and the suppression of individuality by fortuitous circumstances has assumed its sharpest and most universal form, thereby setting existing individuals a very definite task: ... replacing the domination of circumstances and of chance over individuals by the domination of individuals over chance and circumstances." And the reversed capital-labour relation in economic democracy is a fair proxy for this type of replacement.

Due to the lesser relevance of economics in social life, a declining trend in the volumes of commodities produced for their exchange value will be matched by an upward trend in those produced for the sake of their use value.[27]

As long as there are markets, the working of the invisible hand is sure to result in economic crises, but I daresay that in markets where capitalists wield no power unwanted turns of the economy, though still possible, would be less frequent than they are in a capitalistic system.[28]

These reflections are of help in commenting on the propositions of Etzioni, who has spearheaded a new socioeconomic approach which sees mankind split into two groups: individuals acting in line with the typical economic principle of self-interest and individuals driven by ethical motives, including the desire to work towards the well-being of their fellow beings. Etzioni specifies that many people within either group often act inconsistently because they are unable to solve the conflict between the need to pursue pleasure on the one hand and the need to obey ethical imperatives on the other. In the estimation of Etzioni, the awareness that people act inconsistently and in zigzag fashion because of two contrasting drives at war within them would greatly add to our understanding of human behaviour. He describes these 'divided' individuals as subject to what he terms the 'We paradigm' and the 'I paradigm' (see Etzioni 1992) and one of his basic ideas is that the economy is 'embedded in society' since economic conduct is conditioned by social norms and ethical values. In his opinion, firms are like communities whose members entertain relationships shaped by ethical considerations (Etzioni 1999).

What are we to think of Etzioni's line of reasoning?

From my perspective, his approach is marred by a failure to distinguish between human behaviour in capitalistic systems and the prospective behaviour of humans in a system of worker-controlled firms. In capitalistic systems, purely economic behaviour is doubtless prevailing. Despite the awareness that it is at odds with ethical imperatives, it is self-interest that tends to prevail over the interests of society because the risk of losing out in the competitive race under way is so strong as to discourage altruism. As a result, firms in capitalistic systems have nothing in common with communities whose members entertain relationships shaped by ethical considerations. The situation would be different in a system of worker-controlled firms to which the materialist conception of history is not fully applicable – as mentioned before. As a result of less tight competition and a lesser pressure of insolvency risks, in such a system workers would have full control of their choices and would be free to decide how society should be organised. In other words, whereas in capitalistic societies the economic system is not 'embedded in society' in the manner suggested by Etzioni, it is highly likely to become 'embedded in society' in a system of democratic firms.

In a democratic firm system, business firms would be partly organised as communities since the solidarity binding worker to worker and the socioeconomic circumstances mentioned above would allow workers to have regard to the interests of their fellow beings and let ethical imperatives prevail over economic interest.

Does this necessitate the conclusion that the neoclassical analytical approach, which assumes human behaviour to be rational throughout, is actually unsuited to describe the dynamic of cooperatives where decisions are often inspired by feelings of solidarity? As this question cannot be answered with certainty without a preliminary in-depth analysis, let me say that at this stage it is probably enough to remark that economic rationality is not necessarily synonymous with egoism and that the conduct of the member of a cooperative who has regard to the interests of his fellow members is not irrational as a matter of course. In this connection, it is interesting to remark that despite his emphasis on the frequent lateral and zig-zag movements caused by the contrast between economic and ethical behaviour, Etzioni does support the rational choice theory of neoclassical economics (Etzioni 1991, p. 66).

As a result, provided it is true that rational behaviour is not always antithetical to altruism, there is doubtless scope for arguing that the materialist conception is applicable to a (neoclassical) theory of cooperation which assumes that behaviour is rational.

Are markets at odds with democracy?

Our line of reasoning leads up to the conclusion that capitalism is unredeemably antithetical to democracy (see Egan 1990).

Branco, for instance, puts the matter in this way: "In mainstream economics there is only one best solution for each economic problem and thus the purpose of policy consists in finding out that solution and not in confronting collective preferences; in other words, in engaging in political debate. In the realm of politics transformed into economics, pluralism is, therefore, crowded out.... The conflict between economics and democracy does not result, therefore, from any moral weakness of economic actors, but from an intrinsic incompatibility between the logic of economics and that of democracy; between the institutions of economics, such as the market, and the institutions of democracy." If economics can present an optimal solution for a particular problem affecting the economy – he argues further on – then by definition that solution is the only one which, rationally, society should adopt. In other words, "in a world in which for each problem there is only one corresponding solution, pluralism and democratic debate are senseless ... economic decisions should be exempted from people's judgment, because economic laws and economic decisions do not belong to the same domain as democracy" (2012, p. 23).

This begs the question: is democracy irreconcilable with economic institutions such as markets or – as was suggested above – with capitalism itself?

To answer this question, it is convenient to start from the shared view that the precondition for fully democratic decision-making is absence of external conditionings (see, *inter alia*, Dahl 1997). If this is true – and provided the rationale behind historical materialism is correct – it follows that capitalism is antithetical to democracy because political choices, being influenced by an undemocratic institution such as its economic system, will necessarily be undemocratic themselves. At the other end of the spectrum – one may argue – is a worker-controlled system, in which decisions are freely made by workers without interference from external conditions.

With reference to markets, Fitoussi (2004, p. 49) goes so far as to argue that markets and democracy are actually complementary for two main reasons: firstly, being founded on free choices made by individuals, markets confer legitimacy on the system and, secondly, by reducing political control over such choices they contribute to the full implementation of democracy.

On closer analysis, however, this is only true of democratic – viz. non-capitalistic – markets, because it is only in a worker-managed firm system that political action can be shaped in line with fully democratic criteria able to prevent conflicts between markets and democracy. In the words of Stiglitz (2012, p. xxiii), "unfettered markets do not work well.... For markets to work the way markets are supposed to work, there has to be appropriate government regulation. But for that to occur, we have to have a democracy that reflects the general interests – not the interests of just those at the top."

A democratic firm system requires both production and distribution to be democratically organised. In such a system, even income distribution can be devised in line with democratic criteria, for instance by means of democratic resolutions passed at the central level to assign a pre-fixed income coefficient to each category of workers. In such a system, within-firm differences between the pay rates of different workers would exclusively be determined by the application of such coefficients.

In point of fact, the members of different worker-controlled firms would earn different pays in consequence of competition, but I do not see why the practice of using democratic procedures to fix different pay rates by due regard to the greater of lesser abilities of individuals and different competitiveness levels of firms should be rated as non-democratic.

All these reflections go to back up our conclusion that democracy is certainly in stark conflict with capitalism, but not with markets. Quite naturally, this does not entail that the State should abstain from regulating a system of democratic firms. Markets, even though democratically organised, do generate both crises and unemployment, and very often they work in accordance with circular and cumulative mechanisms. As a result, government intervention in such a system may well be massive, but will never be determined by the non-democratic nature of the economy.

In conclusion, let me spell out that a system of worker-controlled firms operating in a market economy is fully democratic since it is managed in line with the 'one head, one vote' principle.

The reflections developed in this section are consistent with the main point of this book because those who believe, like the author, that full-fledged democracy can only be achieved in a socialist system have to provide evidence that a system of democratic firms implements democracy to the full although it is a form of market economy. As a result, it is possible to maintain that the equation of socialism with democratic firm management can be endorsed both by historical materialists and by Marxists.

Is Marxism still viable?

In a very interesting paper, Kliman (2010) tries to account for the causes of a long-drawn process of disintegration of the Marxist school and to suggest possible solutions.

According to this commentator on Marxism, the dissolution of the Marxian school is associated with the endless debate on the transformation of values into prices, but the labour theory of value, which he rates as a theory of the crisis of capitalism, has become ever more topical since the inception of the disastrous economic-financial crisis in 2008. For over two decades after the publication of Sraffa's 1960 book, he argues, even Marxists admitted that the transformation of values into prices was unfeasible,[29] but within the framework of the so-called "new interpretation process" some scholars maintain that this transformation is possible and that the times are ripe for rehabilitating the labour theory of value as a price theory and thereby halting the disintegration of Marxism.

In point of fact, Kliman concludes, this is not occurring and it is worth asking ourselves why this is so.

While it is true that the current disintegration of the Marxian school was sparked off by the transformation issue – he argues – it is also due to problems which arose within the Marxist movement itself: internal divisions, the proliferation of different Marxist schools and the inability of Marxists to come together and solve theoretical issues collaboratively. The collapse of the Soviet system and globalisation, the seeming triumph of capitalism, doubtless played a role in accelerating a crisis which, however, did start well before these momentous events occurred: Steedman's *Marx after Sraffa*, which dates from 1977, is sure evidence that the dissolution process was already under way at that time. In support of the claim that Marxism had lost its common standards and criteria of justification and the ability to take strides forward even before the inception of globalisation, Kliman mentions Kuhn's argument that any major internal divisions within a school instantly become manifest to third parties looking at it from outside.

In other words, from Kliman's perspective the cleft within the movement caused by the difficulty to solve the transformation problem gave rise to a plurality of different Marxist schools which subsequently proved unable to reach agreement.

Kliman's ultimate conclusion is that the disintegration of the Marxian school can doubtless be halted and reversed, but that the success of any such attempt is strictly dependent on the will of Marxists to stop 'academising' Marxian theory and re-establish the genuinely cooperative spirit which is the precondition for a widely shared approach to the essence of Marxism.

How should we rate Kliman's well-reasoned approach?

In my opinion, Kliman's view that the present crisis of Marxism is to be partly blamed on Marxists themselves is sure to be endorsed. Twenty years after the collapse of the Berlin Wall it was high time for Marxists to inquire into the true causes of their failure and they were given this opportunity but failed to seize it (Freeman 2010, p. 85). To begin with, it is not true that the labour theory of value is basically a theory of the crisis of capitalism. Crisis theories come in a variety of different forms, and neither Marx's or Keynes's crisis theories, nor underconsumption theory or the theories of the disproportionality school are necessarily associated with the labour theory of value.[30] Secondly, under certain respects academisation is certainly a cultural vice, but there is no way of eradicating it. We do not see why political passion should be incompatible with academisation. A measure of political partisanship is in place even in academic debates.

However, our main criticism of Kliman's approach is the following. We share Kliman's call for a unifying grand idea to reverse the dissolution process, but we think that this idea should not be associated with the labour theory of value. A much more effective unifying element would be the renewed revolutionary thrust that might be generated by a concern with democratic firm management theory. If Marcuse was right when he argued that Marx changed political economy into a science of the necessary conditions for the communist revolution (see Marcuse 1932, p. 65), if, in other words, it is true that the core idea of Marxian theory is the need for an anti-capitalistic revolution, it follows that the 'grand idea' that Kliman expects to restore unity to the Marxian school and halt the dissolution of Marxism must necessarily be the prospect of a feasible revolution.[31]

Departing from the widespread belief that Marxism is doomed to decline, we think that the realistic prospect of a democratic revolution will give Marxism a fresh topicality and that the abandonment of the labour theory as a price theory will far from determine the breakdown of Marx's theoretical edifice. On the contrary, from the present-day re-elaboration process Marxism will draw both more theoretical strength than it used to have in the glorious days of the New Left and greater political relevance (see Wright 1995, p. 12).[32] As argued by Vygodskij (1967, p. 168), Marx did serve a good cause and the fact that he inextricably tied up the destiny of his theory to the fate of the working class will ultimately decree its immortality.

Inasmuch as it is true that historical materialism and the notion of production modes are Marx's primary contributions to social science and that the establishment of a system of producer cooperatives would amount to a revolution which is both feasible, in agreement with Marxian thought and forthcoming, Marxism today is as viable as ever and may retain its unity. The true core of Marx's theoretical approach – Sève wrote (2004, p. 12) – is his call for a transformation of the world capable of creating a classless society. And – let this be re-emphasised – provided that this transformation is still feasible today in manners in keeping with Marx's thought, Marxism will become more alive than ever.[33] Hence, we endorse Colletti's argument (1974, pp. 43–44) that the feasibility of a fully Marxian revolution is a test for the validity of Marx's entire theoretical approach. And this is also the reason why we think that today, after the collapse of the Soviet system, the importance of the prospect of a feasible revolution can hardly be overrated.[34]

Hence, Kliman's mistake is to assume that the central core of all Marxist approaches is the labour theory of value. Unlike him, we think that Marxist approaches have in common the materialist conception of history as their unifying thread and that, as a result, historical materialism and Marxism retain all their validity and may be unified around the core idea that the anticapitalistic revolution boils down to introducing worker control of firms.

Conclusion

In the opinion of Lukàcs, the crucial role of the notion of revolution in Marx's overall approach necessitates accepting the description of Marxism as a theory of revolution (see Lukàcs 1923, p. 320; see, also, Roberts 2006).[35] In a memorial speech delivered upon the death of Marx, Engels remarked that Marx was first and foremost a revolutionary and that his mission in life had been to work towards dismantling capitalistic society and emancipating the proletariat (see Mehring 1918, p. 530). The gist of this eulogy is proved true by quite a wealth of passages from Marx's works. For example, inquiring into the errors of reformists, he argued that wage increases would be nothing but better payment for the slave and would neither raise the human status of individual workers nor confer dignity on labour (see Marx 1844b, p. 84). In other words, the ultimate message emerging from Marx's economic approach is that that the precondition for substituting the communist mode of production for the capitalistic one is a successful socialist proletarian revolution.

It is worth repeating that the main aim of this book is to show that the only type of revolution still feasible today, after the collapse of the Soviet system, is the transition to a system of worker-controlled firm and that this is the perspective from which Marxism has to be rethought today. In recent years economists have been critically investigating and weighing every single aspect of a system of democratic firms in an effort to provide evidence that it would both work efficiently and offer considerable advantages over capitalism. As a result, it is possible to endorse Sartre's saying that "it is obvious that workers' councils are a democratic institution" and that to predict its role as the mainstay of the future socialist society is hardly an overstatement (Sartre 1960, p. 29). Ralph Tawney (1918, p. 103) holds that freedom will never be complete unless it is associated not only with absence of repression, but also with opportunities for self-organisation.

Economic freedom – he wrote – requires of necessity the extension of representative institutions to industry.

For our part, we have spelt out in bold letters that democratic firm management, not Soviet-type planning, is the organisational form that will realise socialism in practice. Accordingly, now that the globalised world is nearing a crisis comparable to that of socialism in 1989 it is no longer admissible to contend that capitalism has no alternatives. The great Marxist historian Wallerstein expects capitalism to enter its final crisis within the next twenty or thirty years (Wallerstein 2003, pp. 53–60). However, regardless of whether we do or do not believe that the final collapse of capitalism is impending, it is a fact that an alternative option to capitalism does exist and is feasible.

Quoting Pannekoek (1950, p. 391): "For the working class in the present time the real issue is between council organization, the true democracy of labor, and the apparent, deceitful middle-class democracy of formal rights. In proclaiming council democracy the workers transfer the fight from political form to economic contents. Or rather – since politics is only form and means for economy – for the sounding political slogan they substitute the revolutionizing political deed, the seizure of the means of production. The slogan of political democracy serves to detract the attention of the workers from their true goal. It must be the concern of the workers, by putting up the principle of council organization, of actual democracy of labor, to give true expression to the great issue now moving society."

Notes

1 By general agreement (see, *inter alia*, Buchanan 1982, p. 27), the earliest systematic attempt at theorising a materialist conception of history dates back to *The German Ideology* (1946).

2 The following quote shows that, for all the criticisms he came in for this reason (see Godelier 1975, p. 9), Lèvi-Strauss fully accepted the rationale behind historical materialism. "I do not at all mean to suggest" – he wrote – "that ideological transformations give rise to social change. *Only the reverse is in fact true.* Men's conception of the relations between nature and culture is a function of modifications of their own social relations" (Lévi Strauss 1962, p. 102).

   In contrast, Lazonick (1978) and others have appropriately emphasised the attention to political and cultural factors entailed in historical materialism.

3 In Orfei 1970 (p. 271) we read that Antonio Labriola described the materialist conception of history as "an effective means of splitting the huge and extremely complex working mechanism of society into its simplest constituent parts." In the opinion of Kautsky, for instance, the key ideas of Marxism were the materialist conception of history and the role of the proletariat as the driving force behind the socialist revolution (see Geary 1974, p. 85). Unlike them, Croce categorised historical materialism as "neither a philosophy of history nor a philosophical approach proper, but rather as an empirical interpretative canon, a recommendation to historians for them to focus on economic activity and give it the attention its major place in human life entitles it to" (see Croce 1896, pp. 1–19 and Labriola 1942, p. 292).

   According to the renowned Russian Marxist scholar P. Struve, the assumption that production relations are gradually adjusted to the existing production forces does not descend from the idea of economics as the cause and legal relations as the effect, but rather from the fact that they are closely correlated in terms of form and content and that it is simply impossible to conceive of the former independently of the latter. Struve endorses Marx's view that the legal system is the end result of piecemeal adjustments to the economy, and not vice versa, viz. the idea that the ultimate shaping force of a society is the country's economy. For this reason, he extols historical materialism as a theoretical approach which for all its simplicity is to be categorised as 'great' (1899, p. 126).

4 In the opinion of Bloom (1943, p. 58), Marx's most pregnant finding is the idea that society is shaped by its modes of production. In agreement with him, Stedman Jones (1978, p. 341) wrote that the mode of production is the core notion based on which the new theory of the materialist conception of history was fleshed out between 1845 and 1847.

In contrast, some authors maintain that economic approaches to history pre-date Marxism since the relevance of the economic factor in human affairs was emphasised by Swift, Mandeville, Turgot, Smith and a wealth of Enlightenment thinkers well before Marx (see, for instance, Bloom 1943, p. 55).

5 Balibar (1965, p. 222) holds that the overriding importance of the notion of modes of production is apparent to any Marxist. "In order to periodize the history of mankind" – he writes – "we must approach it from the side of *economic science* rather than from that of art, politics, science or law."

6 This quote would suggest that the materialist conception of history is a socialist or proletarian notion. As argued by Kautsky, the progress and discoveries made in the 1940s were in line with the basic tenets of the materialist conception of history, but "despite their genius and despite the preparatory work which the new sciences had achieved" even in the 1840s Marx and Engels would not have been able to discover it if, as socialists, "they had not stood on the standpoint of the proletariat" (see Kautsky 1906, p. 97). In Kautsky's celebrated definition – Haupt writes (1978a, p. 310) – Marxism is the scientific study of history from the vantage point of the proletariat.

7 In the opinion of Ragionieri (1965, pp. 129 ff.), socialism was equated with central planning due to the powerful influence of Engels and his *Antidühring* on the Second International. Similarly, Aron (1965, p. 2) holds that the main source of classical Marxism is Engels's *Antidühring*, though he emphasises that despite his appreciative reading of this book, Marx was hardly aware of the problems associated with centralised planning (see *op. cit.*, p. 3). It goes without saying that the association of Marxism with planning is to be mainly traced to the success of the 1917 Bolshevik revolution and the adoption of centralised planning in the USSR for over seventy years running. In this connection, Bertrand Russel (1935, p. 263) remarked that far from catching on immediately in political practice, socialism remained the creed of a minority with no noticeable bearing on reality until 1917. Considering that socialism has usually been implemented in centrally planned systems, it can hardly come as a surprise that Marxism, the offshoot of scientific socialism, has invariably been associated with planning.

8 For the claim that the decline of Marxism was caused by the failure of the centrally planned Soviet system, see, *inter alia*, Sartori 1969, pp. 316–17, Fukuyama 1989, Marga 1995, p. 85 and Longxi 1995, p. 70. For different views, see Kellner 1995, Stone 1998, Livorsi 2009 and, above all, Cohen 1978 and 2000, who argues (p. 389) that the failure of the Soviet system is actually a triumph of Marxism.

9 According to Chomsky, whether and to what extent State tyranny in Russia was caused by the Bolshevik doctrine or the circumstances under which the State arose and developed remains a matter for debate, but it is simply outrageous to describe that system as socialist (see Chomsky 1971, p. 79).

Gunn (2011), for his part, has remarked that in between worker participation in decision-making and full worker management there are a great many intermediate steps.

10 An equally relevant quote from Trower (1973, p. 138) runs: "If freedom is our goal, industry will only become democratic when it is governed by those working in it." Trower argued that the pendulum of democracy was finally swinging back from the opposite extreme in the direction of economic democracy (*op. cit.*, p. 138).

11 In the opinion of Bloch (1968, p. 98), the point is that "the material base in every society is again activated by the superstructure of consciousness."

12 This view is shared by Habermas, who writes: "crisis arises when the structure of the system allows for fewer problem-solving options than are necessary to the existence of the system" (Habermas 1975, p. 5).

13 Concerning this debate, see, also, Elster 1985, pp. 167–72, who dissents from Cohen.

14 In *An Idea for a Universal History from a Cosmopolitan Perspective*, written in 1784, Kant also described history as a process governed by laws. "Whatever concept of the *freedom of the will* one may develop in the context of metaphysics" – he wrote – "the *appearances* of the will, human actions, are determined, like every other natural event, in accordance with universal natural laws" (see Kant 1784, p. 123). The "grandiose ideas constituting Kant's philosophy of history" – so Adler wrote (1904, p. 196) – "show an extraordinary, at first glance surprising affinity with the basic ideas of the materialistic conception of history." And Kant's conception of history is an integral part of his overall conception – as is Marx's (see Adler 1904, p. 190).
The idea that history progresses towards the full emancipation of humankind has been called into question by numerous commentators including Colletti, who has strongly criticised the finalist and teleological component of Marxism (see the 1979 interview reported in Colletti 1979). And an expert of Marx such as Fineschi has claimed that Marx "just provided generic indications on the society of the future and not even the rough draft of a theoretical approach" (Fineschi 2007, p. 189; see, also, Fineschi 2006, p. 9).

15 As Hicks (1969, p. 2) puts the matter, it is reasonable to deduce from the social sciences – particularly economics – a number of overall ideas that can help historians "streamline their material." In his opinion, this is exactly what Marx endeavoured to do. The description of historical materialism as a one-directional approach is endorsed by Abbagnano (2006, vol. 9, appendix), according to whom the basic assumption for this doctrine of history is the technique of causal explanation.

16 This quote would suggest that the materialistic conception of history is a socialist or proletarian notion. According to Kautsky, the progress and discoveries made in the 1940s were in line with the basic tenets of the materialistic conception of history, but Engels and Marx, "despite their genius and despite the preparatory work which the new sciences had achieved, would not have been able, even in the time of the forties in the nineteenth century, to discover it, if they had not stood on the standpoint of the proletariat, and were thus socialists" (see Kautsky 1906, p. 97).

17 Merleau-Ponty traces the deterministic overtones of Marxism to the central place of the productive forces in Marx's approach. Marx – he argued (1955, pp. 292–93) – consistently emphasised the importance of objective factors in history, and it is this that induced him to drop the fascinating parallel between the advancement of philosophy and the progress towards socialism which he used to draw as a young man.

18 In the opinion of Agnes Heller, although history in Marx is presented as the record of the birth and piecemeal extension of freedom, it is fair to say that men have, admittedly, taken great strides in an effort to counteract fatality, but have failed to extirpate it completely (see Heller 1969, p. 325). Marx saw revolution as the upshot of evolving work processes. In *Capital* – J. P. Burke remarks (1981, p. 93) – Marx "shows how revolution can come about in practical life, i.e. in work processes and revolutionary activities, as well in the self-managed firms that carry on business in post-capitalistic societies. The driving forces behind evolution are not only the ever greater skills developed by mankind over the ages, but also certain traits of capitalism which go to expedite this evolution. Put squarely, this is tantamount to saying that in capitalistic societies the working class is trained in revolution and communism right on the job."

19 The idea that history is not the record of piecemeal gains in freedom is widely shared. Fukuyama, for instance, has written (1992, p. 13) that that advances in industrialisation levels far from generate political liberty as a matter of course.

20 Concerning this aspect of Weber's approach, see Jaspers (1958, chap. II).
21 Until the 1850s, Proudhon himself looked upon revolution as the 'fatal' offshoot of social evolution. Conversely, in the years of his maturity he came to believe that history, far from evolving in accordance with strict laws, was actually shaped by human initiative (see Ansart 1967, pp. 24ff.).
22 This is what Lange (1958b, p. 111) had in mind when he wrote that the economic theory of a social form "exists in a fully developed form only as far as the capitalistic mode of production is concerned."
23 Much to the same effect, Carandini has remarked that historical materialism is of help only in analysing capitalistic societies (see Carandini 2005, p. 24).
24 A comparable criticism of historical materialism is implied in Giddens's argument (1981) that class conflict is unable to account for the emergence of all forms of social organisation and that its effects in capitalism were much less pervasive than was suggested by Marx. In support of this argument, Giddens mentions forms of social organisation, including capitalism, in which the social structure was characterised by forms of exploitation and oppression which were unrelated to the conflict between opposed classes.

Carling re-echoes Sweezy when he remarks (1995, pp. 36–38) that Marx's works abound in ideas, but include just two theoretical approaches proper: the rough draft of a general theory of historical materialism and a specific theoretical approach applying the insights of the materialist conception of history to capitalism.

Vacca (1969b, pp. 105–06) correctly remarked that Korsch conceived of the principles underlying Marx's analysis (i.e. his critique of political economy) not as "more or less arbitrary research hypotheses, but as *realities* on a par with the social relations they connote" and that consequently each social organisation mode was to be consistently approached with focus on its dominant production mode.

Engels, too (1890), specified that the materialist conception of history starts from the proposition that the production of the means to support human life and the exchange of things produced, are the basis of all social structures.
25 Analysing the notion of historical materialism, Korsch (1891) remarked that it was not necessarily a faithful or exhaustive reflection of truth. Although Marx had identified all of the interconnections between the relations and ideas underpinning a given social order and had correctly traced each such order to its historical period and social organisation mode – he argued – his theoretical approach was nothing but a historical construct linked to a precise step in social evolution and a specific social class. In his opinion, this conclusion was perfectly in keeping with the 'critical and materialist' essence of Marx and Engels's theoretical approach.
26 L. Bruni (2006, pp. 77–78) remarks that both Adam Smith and Antonio Genovesi rated markets as a necessary precondition for free and disinterested interpersonal relations and that both of them held that such free interplay would be greatly enhanced in an economic system freed from the oppression of capital.
27 Commenting on Snow's well-known book on 'the two cultures' (1959 and 1963), G. O. Longo (2005, p. 122) pointed to humanities as a powerful antidote to all such homologation processes as are caused by a excessive impact of the economy on human life. The two criteria – he wrote – by which man reconstructs the world by reference to economic or even subsistence criteria make for uniformity, whereas the strong subjective components that arise during poetical and artistic work in connection with emotional, expressive, ethical and aesthetic needs have a potential for counteracting homologation. If our approach so far has been correct, it follows that the homologating power is capitalism, an economic system which is still under the iron grip of capital, whereas a fully democratic system would create the assumptions for the free development of poetry and the arts, effective antidotes to homologation.
28 "The multitude" – we read in Bull (2006, p. 5) – "acts either as one or as many, and becomes a political agent either through the unity of the will or through the workings of

the invisible hand." But the unity of the will that is expressed through political majority resolutions is much less forcefully counteracted by the action of markets (the invisible hand), which have ceased being conditioned by the requirements of capital.

29 In 1977, the review named *Capital & Class* was founded with the specific aim to vindicate the validity of the labour theory of value and open a forum on it (see Freeman 2010, p. 87).

30 As argued by Habermas, "crisis arises when the structure of a social system offers fewer opportunities for solving problems than would required for the system to survive" (see Habermas 1975, p. 5). What link is there between this and the labour theory of value?

31 It goes without saying that Marxists who associate the feasibility of socialism with the labour theory of value will hardly accept this conclusion (see Becker 1977, pp. 263–54).

32 As has repeatedly been observed, criticising capitalism without simultaneously making positive proposals is like combating capitalism with its own weapons: in the end, you will be on the losing side even though you seen to have been victorious (see, *inter alia*, Holloway 2005, p. 213). This is why we maintain that, provided Marxists devise an effective proposal for the establishment of a new kind of society, Marxism will gain strength and will be more alive than ever.

33 In the words of Tronti (1966, p. 33), Marx's critique of political economy amounts to "the utter condemnation of everything that exists" (Tronti 1966, p. 33).

34 The overriding importance of the prospect of a feasible revolution is confirmed by the fact that following the criticisms raised against the Soviet model and its serious crisis, some Marxists went so far as to rehabilitate utopian thought (see Marcuse 1967, p. 10).

35 The categorisation of Marxism as a theory of revolution is accepted, at least implicitly, even by those who term it a 'gospel' or 'creed' of sorts (see, *inter alia*, Keynes 1966, pp. 54–65 and Schumpeter 1942, p. 5).

2 A system of producer cooperatives

Marx's concept of revolution

In a celebrated passage Marx wrote: "In the real production of their existence men inevitably enter into definite relations, which are independent of their will, namely relations of production appropriate to a given stage in the development of their material forces of production. The totality of these relations of production constitutes the economic structure of society, the real foundation on which arises a legal and political superstructure, and to which correspond definite forms of social consciousness.... At a certain stage of development, the material productive forces of society come in conflict with existing relations or production or – this merely expresses the same thing in legal terms – with the property relations within the framework of which they have operated hitherto. From forms of development of the productive forces these relations turn into their fetters. Then begins an era of social revolution" (Marx 1859a, p. 263).

Accordingly, for Marx, to argue that the current production relations are no longer consistent with the existing productive forces and predict the rise of a new production mode is tantamount to acknowledging that the existing social order is at a transitional stage because the current production mode is in the process of becoming obsolete due to changes in the productive forces. These reflections support the claim of the equation of revolution with a change in the production mode.[1]

The productive forces constitute the material basis of a production mode, but as they can only act themselves out within the corresponding relations of production, it is the relation between production and the productive forces concerned that play a decisive role. In the opinion of Althusser, this major point has often received insufficient attention from Marxists.

As the equation of revolution with a change in the production mode takes centre stage in Marx's approach, Marxism must be defined as a 'theory of revolution' (Lukàcs 1923). From this, it follows (a) that the criterion against which the validity of Marxist theory is to be tested is the extent to which the establishment of a genuine socialist system will prove to be practicable (see, *inter alia*, Panaccione 1974, p. 4 and De Giovanni 1976, pp. 8–9) and (b) that the qualification of Marxists should be restricted to those who take it for granted that a socialist or communistic order can be established in practice (in accordance with Marx's thought), and, conversely, denied to all those who are inimical to the idea of revolution. As was correctly observed (Buchanan 1982, p. 26), "without reference to life in communism, Marx's criticisms lose their radical character." In this connection, Bloom (1943, p. 54) has argued that Marx is the only major intellectual whose importance "is judged in terms of events rather than ideas" (1943, p. 54).

Abendroth (1958, p. 77) holds that the key issue with which Marx and Engels strove to come to grips is the fact that most actions, though autonomously devised, evolve in directions other than those that were and could be anticipated and end up by shaping human behaviour. And as this is an irreversible situation, he concludes, the hoped-for aim to enable men to become masters of their destinies will never be attained. According to him, it is the concern with this core issue that makes Marxist thought as topical as ever (*op. cit.*, pp. 78–79).

Colletti's argument that Marx's theoretical edifice can only be classed as consistent if a genuinely Marxist revolution ultimately proves to be practicable (see Colletti 1974, pp. 43–44) can be underscored and further reinforced by stating that the feasibility issue is of paramount importance especially today, following the collapse of the Soviet system.

Scholars who reject the categorisation of Marxism as a theory of revolution include Elster, who maintains that Marxism offers an effective critique of capitalism, but proves ineffectual when it comes to modifying it (see Elster 1985).

In a well-known 1976 study, Anderson wrote that during the heyday of Stalinism and Fascism the fairly moderate post-WWI revolutionary wave of the 1920s started to trend down as a result of a counter-revolutionary phase which caused the decline of Marxism as a mass movement. Marxist intellectuals found themselves cut off from the mainstream of Western politics and responded to this change in circumstances by giving themselves up to rhetorical exercise and abstaining from practical action – a clear sign that they had become pessimistic about the prospect of realising socialism in practice (see Anderson 1976, pp. 35 ff.). During this process, Blackledge adds, Western Marxism turned from an economic into a prevailingly philosophical movement (see Blackledge 2004, p. 60).

By 1980, even Anderson's faith in the final advent of socialism had been badly shaken. Some authors claim that this retreat into philosophysing had a dual impact on the American Left: on the one hand, it led to the development of a specialist theoretical jargon which proved impenetrable to non-academics; on the other, it produced a wealth of speculative studies which had little, if any bearing on the crucial political and social events of the time (see Jacoby 1987, p. 158 and Blackledge 2004, p. 147).

Let me repeat that Marxist thought is rightly said to draw strength from the prospect of social change. Consequently, "if the twenty-first century turns out to be a time of long-term social stability, all Marxist movements are likely to be perceived as irrelevant and, hence, to wither away. In contrast, if stability is not achieved, specifically Marxist ideals and other associated approaches are sure to exert a notable influence on social thought" (Mayer 1994, p. 317).

It is widely held (see, *inter alia*, Sherman 1995 and Sève 2004, pp. 151–55) that throughout the twentieth century, ever since the death of Lenin, Marxism experienced a decline that Sève traces to two main causes. On the one hand, he argues, over the greater part of the past century Marxism was used to justify the pro-Soviet policies of the communist parties; on the other, and even more so, revolutions proclaimed in the name of Marx did not break out in advanced capitalistic systems, as Marx had predicted, but in backward economies.

Today, the Left overall, not only Marxist parties, have difficulty standing their ground. Due to the disintegration of the Soviet system, the globalisation of the economy and, generally, a distrust of theoretical orthodoxy, major theorists and even the general public have realised that there is little sense in clinging to their long-standing statist principles and the Left, deprived of its traditional polar star, is as yet striving to flesh out an inspiring principle other than the generic mission of speaking out for the disadvantaged. And, as experience has shown that the State is hardly in a position to provide effective support to the needy, the Left is still in search of a new beacon to guide it on its way.

Is socialism still viable?

Now that history has proved centralised planning wrong, it is highly unlikely that anybody should attempt to revive it notwithstanding its failure to stand the test of time. Contrary to popular belief, however, this does not necessitate proclaiming the death of socialism or Marxism. As soon as we flesh out an alternative option to capitalism which proves to be unrelated to central planning, Marx's name will cease being associated to an oppressive bureaucratic system and his approach will be 'rediscovered' after a period of near-hibernation (see Bensaïd 2002, p. xi). Within Marxism, there is a clear-cut distinction between socialism and communism and even Marx and Engels spelt it out in bold letters that markets would have to be retained for a long time following the demise of capitalism. To the extent this is true, it goes to support our claim that a system of democratic firms which vests sovereign power over production in workers and strips capital of all its sway would be fully consistent with Marx's thought even though it should fail to suppress markets.

All the same, it is widely held that socialism and markets are not reconcilable. Andreani (2001a, p. 133), for instance, has gone so far as to argue that "market socialism has long been looked upon as a contradiction in terms." For the rationale behind this persuasion we may refer to Westra (2002), where socialism is described as connoted by equality, democracy, meaningful interpersonal relations and control over economic activities, and then set against the tendency of markets to create inequality, encroach on democracy and prevent the launch of goal-directed actions aimed to keep the economy in check. From our perspective, this line of reasoning points to scant attention for the already mentioned distinction that Marx and Engels drew between different stages of the hoped-for new social order and their emphasis on the necessary long-term retention of markets following the demise of capitalism.

Moreover, we do not see why a system of producer cooperatives which has stripped capital of all its power should oppose state intervention in the economy;

in fact, there are reasons to assume that it would call for state intervention in all such cases in which this is deemed to be expedient.

Although it seems safe to conclude that a system of producer cooperatives is consistent with Marx's thought, it is worth bearing in mind Sève's warning that today we have to "think with Marx," rather than "attempt a return to Marx" and that watchwords such as "the seizure of power through revolution," the mission of "spokesman for the proletariat," "the socialisation of large-scale means of production of exchange" or other associated political programmes will hardly inflame hearts and minds as they used to do in the past (see Sève 2004, pp. 101–02 and p. 106). Notwithstanding this, Marxism is far from dead. Since Marxism is nextricably bound up with the disastrous crisis of Soviet socialism, it is only the prospect of a new production mode to take the place of the Soviet-type centralised planning model that may justify the claim that Marx is still alive.

Assuming that the new polar star for the Left will be the search for a feasible mode of production that even orthodox theoreticians might rate as capable of outperforming capitalism, it is necessary to specify that cooperatives will not gain a firm foothold unless they adopt the model developed by economic theorists after Ward's (1958) paper. Indeed, there can be little doubt that cooperative firms that stick to their traditional operation modes are bound to face defeat. To perform their mission to the full, however, they have to adopt strategies and tools comparable to those of their privately owned competitors and, at the same time, hold on to the ethical principles that led to their establishment and have inspired their conduct to this day (Bauer 1963, p 38).

The basic characteristics of a system of worker-controlled firms

There is general agreement that a system of cooperative – or worker-controlled – firms must necessarily operate in a market economy. And this entails that the main magnitudes with which economists concern themselves, i.e. output volumes, levels of demand for the relevant products and their prices, have to be determined in line with the 'law of demand and supply' or 'the rules of the production of commodities by means of commodities,' as would say a Ricardian economist today. From the perspective of traditional economists holding that market forces are vehicles for individual choices, the statement that a system of self-managed firms is a market system means that it gives producers and consumers ample scope for making their choices in freedom, in line with their private utility calculations.

Yet, whoever has subjected the present-day economic system to critical scrutiny is sure to ask himself what sort of 'freedom' we are talking about.

As Marx put it, "competition is nothing more than the way in which many capitals force the inherent determinants of capital upon one another and upon themselves" (Marx 1857–58, pp. 333–34).

If this is true, we must ask ourselves if the irrational nature and alienating effects of the economic system in which we live are actually caused by its mercantile (rather than capitalistic) essence and if markets and competition can be rearranged in such a way as to have them meet social needs. As "the market economy is a genus, whereas capitalism is one of its species" (see Zamagni & Zamagni 2008, p. 12), it can be assumed – as most advocates of democratic management do – that the path towards communism includes a preliminary intermediate station, the abolition of hired labour, which has to be reached before we can head towards our final goal and extinguish market relations by degrees. This conclusion necessitates inquiring into the working mechanism of a system which initially will have to be described as a non-capitalistic market economy.

A worker-controlled firm system operating in the market must ensure ample scope for personal utility calculations, which by general agreement are the main-spring of all human actions, but within each of its individual producer coopera-tives the workers pursue, at least in part, a shared goal. Hence, it is argued, besides offering all the benefits flowing from competition, such a system must convert the distinctly capitalistic form of competition between individuals into a differ-ent form of competition between groups. The result is held to be a radical change in human behaviour, i.e. a marked attenuation of typically capitalistic attitudes such as individualism and, conversely, more intense feelings of brotherhood and solidarity (though the extent to which this is feasible and ways to achieve this goal should be the object of careful analysis). Private utility calculations include choos-ing a job. In a system of cooperative firms workers must be free to switch from job to job, i.e. to leave a work position and look for a different one. As for the firms of such a system, as a rule they are free to dismiss their workers.[2]

The second characteristic of a system of worker-controlled firms is that the obligation to adopt democratic forms of management would apply to medium-large enterprises only (specifically, firms with over ten members). Indeed, it seems reasonable to assume that such a system may still include a certain amount of small-size capital-managed firms and that the straightforward abolition of hired labour would not be an absolute necessity: there are circumstances under which the retention of hired labour may appear expedient for a number of reasons, for instance the need to provide jobs to people with minimum or no professional qualifications.

The third characteristic of this system is the public ownership of means of pro-duction, which justifies its characterisation as a form of socialism. As mentioned above, in the market socialism model we have in mind the State performs a major role in rectifying market dysfunctions and working towards the interests of the general public.

In what was once the Socialist Federalist Republic of Yugoslavia, self-management was introduced following the nationalisation of the bulk of existing firms. And as the socialist nature of that country was never called into question, the issue of the true ownership of those firms (i.e. whether they belonged to the State or the working partners) was at first not raised: in the early post-war period the communist governments declared that all firms (except very small ones, in practice one-man firms only) were the property of the State and by 1952, upon the launch of the economic decentralisation programme and self-management experiment, the process had been completed. This explains why the point that first came up for discussion upon completion of the self-management experiment was not the kind of ownership that was best suited for a system of self-managed firms, but clarifying the way workers could materially self-run those firms although they were employing capital goods they did not own. Yugoslav theoreticians solved the problem by describing the position of the workers as that of 'usufructuaries.' Today, it is more appropriate to say that the firms would be owned by the collective of the workers, as mentioned above. (The ownership issue is addressed in a considerable body of literature on worker-control whose analysis, even through cursory, falls outside the scope of this book; see, *inter alia*, Pejovich 1966, chap. 1, Horvat 1976, chap. 4).

In this connection, Levine argues (1984 and 1988, p. 6) that "where existing capitalistic enterprises should be turned into collectively owned cooperatives (regardless of the procedure adopted and even in the absence of any further changes), the resulting economic order would still be a capitalistic one. When we say that something is publicly owned, we mean it is owned by the general public, not just by part of it." In the firms of a self-managed system, though, the transfer of the ownership title is accompanied by two more major processes of change: (a) the suppression of hired labour as a basic rule of cooperatives, and (b) the assignment of the entire surplus to workers; and that is why a system of cooperative firms cannot be categorised as a capitalistic economy.

During the proceedings of the Italian Constituent Assembly, it became clear that it was exactly the plan to vest title in firms in the State that induced the Catholic and Liberal parties to distance themselves from the cooperative movement. As things stand, this reflection goes to confirm that the transfer of firm ownership to workers' collectives is a matter of policy. During the debate at the Assembly, Catholic and Liberal deputies voted against the State ownership motion for fear that the assignment of supervisory powers to the State might lead to the nationalisation of the cooperative movement. The parties represented in the Assembly reached an agreement when it was made clear that the sole aim of State control was preventing the rise of 'sham' cooperatives set up for the exclusive purpose of securing the benefits that the Constitution was about to grant to cooperative firms. In an address to the Assembly, the Christian Democrat Cimenti declared that the cooperative movement would have to pay too high a price if this, i.e. the main incentive to establish sham cooperatives, should induce the State to exercise direct control over cooperative firms.

In the *Manifesto of the Communist Party* we read (1848, pp. 73–74): "All the preceding classes that got the upper hand sought to fortify their already acquired status by subjecting society at large to their conditions of appropriation. The proletarians cannot become masters of the productive forces of society, except by abolishing their own previous mode of appropriation, and thereby also every other previous mode of appropriation. They have nothing of their own to secure and to fortify; their mission is to destroy all previous securities for, and insurances of, individual property."

Lukàcs's comment on this quote from Marx (1923, p. 94) was: "The revolutionary victory of the proletariat does not imply, as with former classes, the immediate realisation of the socially-given existence of the class, but, as the young Marx clearly saw and defined, its self-annihilation."

For our part, we deem it reasonable to argue that the very first revolutionary move should be vesting all power in workers in order to have them switch places with capitalists. In this connection, Bettelheim wrote that the progress towards socialism is nothing but "the domination by the immediate producers over their conditions of existence and, therefore, in the first instance, over their means of production and their products" (Bettelheim 1971, p. 289).

The core idea that prompted anti-liberalists to theorise a system of cooperative firms is that liberalism is no truthful reflection of social reality. Despite the tendency of capitalism to destroy social links, a lot of people today still have a correct appreciation of the importance of interpersonal bonds and shared values and do not pursue their interests irrespective of the needs of their fellow beings.

A like way to criticise advocates of the existing world order is to argue that they hold up a social model, capitalism, which tends to destroy all bonds other than contractual relations, and support present-day market mechanisms without regard to the fact that actions inspired by private utility calculations destroy family ties and bonds of friendship, feelings of love and the interests of the community at large (see Walzer 1995). Danner (2002) has described our society as governed by the *homo homini lupus* rationale, i.e. as a context in which boundless greed for money makes us insensitive to the needs of our fellow beings, dissolves social bonds and destroys community feelings. Under capitalism – Gramsci wrote – "society is cut loose from any kind of collective bonds and reduced to its primordial element, the citizen-individual. And society begins to dissolve, eaten away by the corrosive acids of competition: Dragons' teeth are sown amongst men and frenetic passions, unquenchable hatreds, implacable enmities spring up. Every citizen is a gladiator, who sees in others enemies to be destroyed or made subservient to his own interests. All the higher bonds of love and solidarity are dissolved: from those of the craftsmen's guilds and social castes, to those of religion and the family" (Gramsci 1919–20, p. 4).

Hence, a possible preliminary conclusion is that the aim of a system of producer cooperatives is to bring about a form of society capable, if nothing else, of attenuating the individualism that markets tend to generate.

It is worth noting, however, that due to its communitarian matrix, a system of cooperatives is difficult to place on the left-right political spectrum. As argued by Lasch (1995, p. 86): "We can now begin to appreciate the appeal of populism and communitarianism. They reject both the market and the welfare state in pursuit of a third way. This is why they are so difficult to classify on the conventional spectrum of political opinion. Their opposition to free-market ideologies seems to align them with the left, but their criticism of the welfare state (whenever this criticism becomes open and explicit) makes them sound right-wing." In point of fact, to account for this assumed political neutrality we have to adopt a somewhat different perspective: the solidarity principles by which it is shaped and the assumption that markets will function more effectively when capital is stripped of its power would seem to align it with the left, whereas the critical view of statism which prompted its first theorisation might induce us to classify it as right-wing despite the major role we assign to the State in rectifying market dysfunctions.

An additional point to be touched upon is the dimensional issue, i.e. the widespread and unsubstantiated misconception that the cooperative form fits small-size firms mainly (see, *inter alia*, Wolff 2012, pp. 160–61).

The self-management principle

Information, agency and game theory studies have recently made a major contribution to the development of farming cooperative theory (see Cook *et al.* 2003). On closer analysis, the function of these studies parallels the role of Ward's 1958 pioneer study with respect to the development of non-agricultural producer cooperative theory.

At this point, it is worth defining the true essence of a producer cooperative.

The main characteristic of the worker-controlled firm, i.e. its management in accordance with the 'one head, one vote' principle, marks it out as a genuinely socialist entity. Thanks to this thoroughly democratic principle, workers are in a position to decide what kind of commodities are to be produced and the relevant processes, and this prevents them from making purely economistic choices.

In a worker-controlled system, therefore, it is the workers themselves that run the firms for which they work. As a result, they qualify, not as the owners, but as the tenants of the firm. However, as a firm is, by its very nature, an entity requiring a hierarchical structure, it is reasonable to assume that worker-controlled firms will choose their managers in democratic elections and, where necessary, replace them.

Both Marshall and Paley Marshall (1881) and Zanotti (2014, p. 58) are agreed that the management issue is by far the main difficulty cooperatives are bound to come up against. The Marshalls (see *op. cit.* p. 275) emphasise that these firms are unable to retain the services of a first-rate manager "unless he is so much under the influence of the Cooperative Faith as to be willing to work for the Cause at a lesser salary than he could get in the open market."

As far as I can see, this remark is hardly applicable to the cooperative firm model discussed in this chapter. Indeed, regardless of whether these firms operate in an all-cooperatives system or have to compete with other forms of business enterprise in the open market, in consequence of their choice to operate in the open market these firms will have no way out but to carry on business in line with the laws of this market and will consequently have to adjust their internal income distribution criteria to the mechanisms of the system in which they have resolved to operate.

Control over the manager's actions is ensured by the workers' right to appoint their managers and replace them with others whenever the need should arise. Their managers may, but do not necessarily have to be chosen from among the partners of the firm and their powers and duties may either be laid down by law or in the firm's by-laws or purposely fixed by the workers' collective from time to time. All major functions, including hires and major investments, are to be vested in the worker-members, who will be free to dismiss a manager who fails to work towards their interests.

This does not mean that worker-appointed managers should have authority to make all or nearly all 'entrepreneurial' decisions or that the by-laws of these firms should grant them full autonomy. Fully autonomous managers are at odds with the very idea of self-management. "It is against the natural order that the majority govern and the minority be governed" Rousseau wrote. And Screpanti has argued (2007a, p. 167): "provided a manager acts in accordance with the instructions received from the workers and the latter are able to exercise close control over his actions, the firm will be democratically self-managed and the freedom of the workers will by no means be curtailed"; and by general agreement, the supervisory authority of the workers is part and parcel of their right to appoint and dismiss their managers. Dissenting from this view, however, I wish to claim that the main functions impinging on production should be retained by the workers.

A system of producer cooperatives is a model of direct democracy whose political advantages and benefits in terms of awareness-building can only be fully appreciated by those who have critically weighed the limits of what is known as 'bourgeois democracy.' On the one hand, democracy may be the offshoot of a certain level of growth of the productive forces that the more advanced capitalistic countries doubtless reached at a certain stage of their development. On the other, in synch with Marx's approach democracy may be said to increase thanks to the changes that capitalism undergoes in time as a result of the so-called 'long waves of growth' or the dynamics postulated by the theory of 'systemic cycles of accumulation' (Arrighi 1994). The first and clearest sign of this development is the ever more negligible part that capitalists are seen to play in advanced capitalistic systems.

The most striking effect of self-management, though, is its potential for ending class struggle and the separation of labour from means of production. And this is why its extension to the system as a whole (even though only in the most important sector of the modern economic system, industry, in agriculture or any other sector where this need should be felt) would result in superseding capitalism.

Maximising worker benefits as the guiding principle of the self-managed firm

In democratic firms, workers run production by themselves and appropriate the surplus earned by their firm. This surplus is the balance between the firm's total sales and its aggregate expenditure, i.e. the sum of the cost of the raw materials and semi-finished products it employs, the interest payable to providers of funds and the taxes levied by the State. It is clear that the shares of the surplus accruing to the workers cannot be categorised as income from employment because the workers are not hired by third parties. And as the relevant amounts are strictly dependent on the firm's financial performance, they constitute a variable income.

The workers participate in the surplus in accordance with the pro-rata criterion, in terms that each worker is allotted a pre-fixed percent rate of the profit reported by the firm. To prevent frictions within the firm, these rates must obviously be fixed before the firm is started up and the relevant procedure will either be provided for by law or fixed in collective agreements. Although a system of producer cooperatives is not expected to achieve a fully egalitarian distribution of the surplus, whenever the applicable distribution criteria are democratically fixed, the resulting pattern will prove to be more egalitarian than those prevailing today.

These reflections may help define the principle that is to govern the running of a producer cooperative (which does not reject methodological individualism).

As is well known, the core aim of a capitalistic economy is profit maximisation. In capitalistic systems, Marx wrote, "the expansion or contraction of production are determined by the appropriation of unpaid labour and the proportion of this unpaid labour to materialised labour in general, or, to speak the language the capitalists, by profit and the proportion of this profit to the capital employed, and thus by a definite rate of profit" (Marx 1867a, p. 312). In other words, as the decision-makers of capitalistic systems, i.e. capitalists, work towards maximising profit, they will tend to transfer productive resources, i.e. capital and labour, from activities yielding lower rates of profit to those capable of ensuring higher rates.

What criterion would be paramount in a system of producer cooperatives?

When workers are allowed to run their firms on their own and to apportion the resulting earnings among them, they will tend to maximise the income accruing to each of them. Hence, provided it is assumed, as mentioned before, that the firm's earnings are distributed to workers based on accrual rates negotiated between them beforehand, the goal of the cooperative firm can be described as maximising the average income levels of the workers. As a first approximation, it is possible to say that the basic operational principle which governs the working of a system of producer cooperatives and the entrepreneurial choices of its constituent firms is the criterion of maximising average worker income.

On closer analysis, though, while it is true that this criterion is at the basis of producer cooperative theory, the findings of any analyses that should be performed by exclusive reference to it would hardly ensure a faithful picture of the real situation because this criterion is just one of a variety of different guiding principles of worker-controlled firms.

Today, the 1958 paper in which Ward's per capita income maximisation principle was first enunciated is regarded as the founding stone of producer cooperative theory and the basic rule that is to govern the conduct of worker-controlled firms. Based on this principle, a producer cooperative will find it convenient to take on more workers on the condition that the marginal productivity of labour, i.e. the productivity of its latest hire, exceeds the average income of the firm's existing workers. Indeed, so long as the output of the latest hire exceeds the average labour output level of the pre-existing workers, the average income from work will tend to increase to everyone's benefit, and vice versa.[3]

This rule turns a spotlight on one major difference that marks out the LMF from the WMF cooperative. The net income of the former, which segregates labour incomes from capital incomes and rates capital charges as a cost, falls short of the net income of the latter (since the income allotted to the firm's partners is inclusive of its savings). This is the reason why LMF cooperatives will usually hire a larger number of workers than WMF cooperatives would do under comparable circumstances.

One major point which is still to be touched upon is whether these firms may dismiss their workers in cases of need. This query is of major relevance since job stability is not only a major aim towards which workers can be assumed to work, but probably an even more important one than the above-mentioned principle of maximising average worker income. If this is true and if the right to dismiss workers is taken for granted, it is worth noting that job stability will be at odds with the per capita income maximisation criterion since the former requires maximising the firm's total sales and, hence, its long-and short-term financial performance.

This takes us back to the problem whether the findings of analyses exclusively based on the per capita income maximisation criterion are actually cogent. Indeed, an analysis conducted on the assumption that dismissals should be allowed would fail to provide focus on the fact that the partners, in an effort to avert dismissals, may find it expedient to prioritise actions designed to further the growth of the worker-managed firm over measures aimed to maximise average worker income.

At this point, a provisional overall conclusion may be that the guiding principle of the cooperative firm is the criterion of maximising the well-being workers, i.e. a compound of wages per worker, job stability and a number of additional non-pecuniary benefits such as pleasant working conditions (see, *inter alia*, Vanek 1971c, pp. 12–14). This criterion, i.e. maximising well-being rather than pecuniary benefits, is an aspect which marks out democratic from capitalistic firm management since capitalistic enterprises not only carry on business in the exclusive interests of capitalists, but tend to maximise pecuniary gains only.

The different principles and criteria highlighted above support the view that the establishment of a system of worker-managed firms amounts to the rise of a new mode of production.[4]

Competition in a system of democratic firms

As far as competition is concerned, the Scottish eighteenth-century economists that were the first to underscore its power argued that thanks to the 'magic' effects of competition, those actively pursuing their own interests would actually end up promoting other people's interests and that, hence, the benefits of their effort would accrue to society as a whole. This idea is reflected in Adam Smith's well-known saying that "it is not from the benevolence of the butcher, the brewer, or the baker that we expect our dinner, but from their regard to their own interests. We address ourselves, not to their humanity, but to their self-love, and never talk to them of our own necessities, but of their advantages" (Smith 1776, p. 17).

The degree to which competition will prove more of less stiff or soft depends on ethical, social and government-driven mechanisms. It is well known that Max Weber traced competition to the Calvinistic ethic and that the general public are more supportive of the competitive race in the United States than anywhere else.

Marx (1857–58, p. 333) defined competition as "the free development of the mode of production based upon capital; the free development of its conditions and of its process as constantly reproducing these conditions." In free competition – he argued – "it is capital that is set free, not the individuals. As long as production resting on capital is the necessary, hence the fittest form for the development of the force of social production, the movement of individuals within the pure conditions of capital appears as their freedom."

Further on (1857–58, p. 335) he concluded: "thence, on the other hand, the absurdity of regarding free competition as the ultimate development of human freedom, and the negation of free competition as equivalent to the negation of individual freedom and of social production based upon individual freedom. It is merely the kind of free development possible on the limited basis of the domination of capital. This kind of individual freedom is therefore at the same time the most complete suspension of all individual freedom, and the most complete subjugation of individuality under social conditions which assume the form of objective powers, even of overpowering objects – of things independent of the relations among individuals themselves."

In the wake of Marx, it is possible to argue that the crux of the issue is not so much overly tough competition, as the fact that competition today appears as "the free development of the mode of production based upon capital." In other words, insofar as it is true that competition in the service of capital is one thing and competition in the best interests of consumers and workers quite another, where a system of democratic firms should practice the latter type, competition would be a valuable mechanism and, as such, deserve effective protection.

Accordingly there are grounds for arguing that one of the advantages offered by a system of producer cooperatives is the potential for generating a softer type of competition than that that typifying capitalism. As I will argue in greater detail in Chapter 6, the main reason why competition would be softer in such a system is the fact that cooperatives face lesser insolvency risks. A firm whose managers are tolerably safe from risks of bankruptcy are free to opt for less stiff competition. For instance, they may grant the partners more free time, shorten the working day and, hence, prioritise reduced workloads over increases in earnings. Competition under these circumstances, however keen, would not be an ill, since individuals would be in a position to handle its effects by freely deciding if they wish to stand up to it or opt for lower earnings.

An additional reason why competition can be assumed to be softer in this system is the fact that the surplus earned by a cooperative is apportioned among all the partners. As a rule, in capitalistic systems the greater earnings associated with the successful performance of a business enterprise accrue to a single individual. In contrast, cooperatives apportion both earnings and losses among all the partners by definition. And this, too, helps make competition less tough.

An additional factor accounting for the softer competitive regime prevailing in worker-controlled firm systems is the rule providing that the pay rates of partners providing equal work inputs do not tend to level out (see Montias 1976, pp. 255–56). As the aim of cooperatives is to maximise *per capita* incomes, these firms have no incentive to recruit workers prepared to accept wage rates below the average pay rate accruing to the existing partners. It is a well-known fact that cooperatives are only interested in recruiting partners whose prospective marginal productivities are above the level corresponding to its average pay rate.

This is why workers in cooperatives enjoy a greater and, even more importantly, a different freedom to choose between work and non-work. To clarify this point, it is worth considering that a firm which does not deem it worthwhile to hire workers willing to accept lower pay rates is one which knows all too well that it is not at risk of losing its existing workforce if its pay rates should fall below those of other firms. The partners, in turn, will use this circumstance to their advantage by freely opting for more free time and reduced hours of work.

On closer analysis, however, the situation just described is not devoid of drawbacks. Rothschild (1986, p. 190) has argued that an individual who has reached the status of a capitalist and wishes to protract this newly acquired status in time has no way out but to accumulate. He is compelled to do so by the rules of competition inherent in the historically determined mode of production which prompts him into action. Accordingly, one adverse effect of a softer competitive regime is to interfere with the dynamic of the economic system and, probably, reduce its potential for growth.[5]

Notes

1   Marx's definition of revolution is a clear and simple notion. With occasional exceptions (see, for instance, Kautsky 1892, pp. 65–70), Kautsky himself admitted that he did not think that the decisive difference between reformism and revolution was the reformists' rejection of violence and its acceptance by revolutionaries (see Kautsky 1902, p. 168). In his opinion, the essence of revolution was the takeover of political power by a different class (*ibid.*, p. 169).
Notwithstanding the evidence that Marx and Kautsky did propose clear, simple and ultimately concordant definitions of the notion of revolution, Simone Weil argued that "among all those who still persist in talking about revolution, there are perhaps not two who attach the same content to the term" (see Weil 1955, p. 32). The definition of revolution which is proposed and discussed in Sartori 2015 (pp. 15–35) is antithetical to mine.
2   Due to the market orientation of the firms constituting it, this system will be affected by all the usual shortcomings of market economies, viz. regional imbalances, gender inequalities and varying environment protection levels.
3   For a critique of the use of the Ward's model for theorising the cooperative firms cf. Cuomo 2003, Cuomo, 2010, chap. II and Cuomo 2016.
4   On the motivational complexity in producer cooperatives cf., e.g., Sacchetti and Tortia, 2015.
5   In Antoni (1952, p. 127) we read that Weber ceased his advocacy of historical materialism when he realised the major influence of irrational thought processes and utopian dreams on economic action and even on the course of history at large. The line of reasoning developed in this chapter goes to support this view with respect to democratic firms.

3 Democratic firm management and socialism

Two cooperative firm models

The distinction between 'internally' and 'externally' financed democratic firms was first drawn by one of the most renowned theoreticians of democratic firm control, Jaroslav Vanek (1971a and 1971b), and is oft read as contrasting self-financing firms with those funding investments with third-party capital. In point of fact, the distinction that really matters is that between (a) LMFs, i.e. cooperatives that remunerate capital separately from labour and use publicly owned means of production on the one hand and, (b) WMFs, i.e. cooperatives which allocate all their revenues (labour and capital incomes) to the partners (specifically, those engaged in production in the period of time concerned from time to time), do not remunerate capital owners as such and use privately owned means of production.[1]

The type of self-managed firm which is analysed in this book is one which operates solely with borrowed funds. It is widely held that in self-managed firms (a) all the decisions concerning production overall, the product mix and investment choices are made by the workers or their representatives, and that (b) due to the fact that the balance between the firm's aggregate revenues and operating costs is cashed by the workers, labour performs the role of an 'entrepreneurial input' (see Dubravcic 1970). A worker-controlled firm operating solely with loan capital can therefore be described as an enterprise whose workers 'hire' capital, remunerate it at a pre-fixed rate of interest and apportion the firm's earnings among themselves.

Basically, the differences between these two firm models can be summed up as follows: whereas in capitalistic enterprises the owners (or their representatives) carry on business solely in their own interests and, for this purpose, hire workers, pay them fixed wages or salaries and retain the residual earned (profit), in democratic (cooperative or self-managed) firms, the workers (or their representatives) carry on business in the interests of all the partners and, hence, borrow third-party capital, pay debt holders a fixed income (interest) and cash the residual themselves.[2]

Hence, democratic firms can be described as non-capitalistic enterprises which literally capsize the capital-labour relation specific to entrepreneurial firms (this point will be dealt with at length in Chapter 10). It is this characteristic, rather than other aspects, that justifies the claim (discussed in detail in the section "A system of self-managed firms from the perspective of scientific socialism" below) that the establishment of a system of democratic firms amounts to the rise of a new mode of production. A struggle for a meaningful control of workers over production – Mattick writes (1969, p. 152) – "is clearly equivalent to the overthrow of the capitalist system."

Self-managed firms reverse the typical capital-labour for two main reasons: (a) because decisions are made by workers instead of capitalists, and (b) because capitalists switch places with workers: the former become fixed-income earners, while the latter are turned into variable-income entrepreneurs who are accountable for the business resolutions they pass.[3]

In open contrast with the thesis advanced in this book, Marshall warned his readers: "it is not true that under competition labour is hired by capital; it is hired by business ability in command of capital; and it is not true that in co-operation capital is hired by labour; it may be hired by the business ability that lives in the heads that the working men have on their shoulders" (Marshall 1889, p. 245).

In this connection, Zanotti has appropriately remarked that this line of reasoning is actually at odds with an earlier statement of Marshall's in which cooperation and certain practices of profit sharing were categorised as means of implementing socialism at its best (see Zanotti 2014, p. 41).

Marshall's statement should be read in the light of an analysis of producer and consumer cooperatives in which he concluded that since a great many production and business activities were at odds with the cooperative management mode, cooperation was unlikely to give rise to a new mode of production.

The Italian patriot Giuseppe Mazzini wrote: "The right to the fruits of one's labour is the goal that lies ahead and it is our duty to work towards its attainment. The benefits of pooling capital and production in the same hands will be great indeed and will be reaped not only by workers, but by Society as a whole, because its effects include more solidarity, as well as higher outputs and consumption levels" (Mazzini 1935, p. 489). In Mazzini's opinion, "ever more numerous producer cooperatives are bound to arise and their inalienable capital will be used to provide opportunities for collective work to a growing amount of workers" (*ibid.*).

A cursory review of the literature on the potential of LMFs to generate a new mode of production shows that this thesis has been called into question by numerous authors. Some authors have objected that LMFs struggling to solve their financing difficulties might be induced to pay interest rates by far exceeding the average market rate. In such a situation, they argue, the surplus earned by them would accrue at least in part to capitalists in place of the partners. On closer analysis, this objection is unsubstantiated. Indeed, whereas decisions in capital-managed firms are the exclusive prerogative of capitalists (in line with the 'one share, one vote' criterion), in LMFs they are solely vested in the partners (based on the 'one head, one vote' principle). Accordingly, if some providers of substantial loans to cooperatives were found to cash interest at disproportionately high rates, they would be doing so on the basis of resolutions that were freely passed by the workers' collectives under the pressure of the failure to raise funds by other means.

To argue that financers might turn such a situation to their advantage, claim for themselves the functions of managers with far-reaching decision powers and use this position to pursue their own interests will hardly make sense. In the section "The self-management principle" in Chapter 2, it has been spelt out that the functions that the partners of a cooperative have to retain for themselves include both the power to make hires and major investment decisions, and authority to dismiss a manager who fails to serve their interests effectively.

However, although it is doubtless true that a firm allowing its financers to cash disproportionate earnings might be categorised as an 'improper' cooperative, I do not think that this objection is forceful enough to cancel the socialist essence of cooperative firms even under such circumstances.

These reflections are a suitable starting point for a comparative analysis of the LMF and the WSDE, i.e. the *workers' self-directed enterprise* which was theorised by Richard D. Wolff, probably the best-known Marxist academic equating socialism with democratic management. The WSDE is a worker-controlled firm in which decisions in matters of product mix, suitable technological processes and marketing procedures and the like are made by the workers and investment expenses may be financed by external shareholders. In it – Wolff writes – "all the workers who produce the surplus generated inside the enterprise function collectively to appropriate and distribute it" (Wolff 2012, p. 118). In Wolff's WSDE, "no separate group of persons – no individual who does not participate in the productive work of the enterprise – can be a member of the board of directors. Even if there were to be shareholders of the WSDE, they would not have the power to elect the directors" (*ibid.*). "Two facts define WSDEs," Wolff specifies (p. 122): "the appropriation and distribution of the surplus are done cooperatively" and "the workers who cooperatively produce the surplus and those who cooperatively appropriate and distribute it are identical."

Hence, factors common to the LMF and WSDE are the right of the workers to elect their managers and to retain the most important functions, including the appropriation and distribution of the surplus. According to Wolff, the fact that managers are only empowered to run the firm's ordinary business is both a distinctive characteristic of the WSDE and a major difference with respect to existing cooperatives (see Wolff 2012, pp. 120–21). In my opinion, the same applies to LMFs.

One difference between the LMF and the WSDE which I do not rule out has to do with estimated headcounts. Whereas I do not deny that the LMF may employ a limited number of workers, Wolff excludes this hypothesis for surplus producing workers, though not for the category of enabler workers (which includes, by way of example, secretaries, office personnel, receptionists, security guards, cleaning staff, managers, lawyers, counsellors and the like).

An additional difference between a system of LMF cooperatives and WSDEs is that the former has to operate in markets in accordance with utility calculations, while Wolff's WSDEs "can coexist with planning or markets or a combination of both" (*op. cit.*, p. 143).

Concluding, I do not see any noticeable differences between Wolff's WSDE and the LMF cooperative analysed in this book.

Democratic firm control strips capitalists of much of their power

By far the greatest advantage of democratic firm management is the substitution of the 'one head, one vote' principle for the 'one share, one vote' criterion. As workers would both derive great satisfaction from the exercise of decision-making powers (i.e. sovereignty) and wrest themselves free from the need to obey third-party commands, it is they that would come off best from the introduction of the 'one head, one vote' principle.[4] Even more importantly, since the disempowerment of capitalists would provide a major impetus for political democracy, there would be comparable benefits for society as a whole.[5] One of the authors thanks to whom the term 'capitalism' came into general use, W. Sombart, was the first to describe worker control of firms as a mode of production and a social order founded on the antithesis between those in command and those supposed to obey (see Sombart 1902 and 1916, chap. 19). Ever since that time, critics of capitalism have been pressing the view that the despotism with which capitalists impose their laws not only on workers, but also on politics and culture is part and parcel of the essence of the capitalistic organisation mode of society.

Capitalism is typified by economic inequalities, which in turn breed political inequality. While it is true that most political systems vest voting rights in all the citizens, there can be little doubt that high-income individuals wield more political power both through their control of the media and by bribing politicians into acting in their favour.

As argued by Marx and Engels (1845–46, pp. 35–36): "The ideas of the ruling class are in every epoch the ruling ideas, i.e. the class which is the ruling *material* force of society is, at the same time, its ruling *intellectual* force. The class which has the means of material production at its disposal, has control at the same time over the means of mental production, so that thereby, generally speaking, the ideas of those who lack the means of mental production are subject to it."

In an analysis of capitalism, Huberman and Sweezy raised a set of questions concerning the degree of freedom we actually enjoy: "Do we really tolerate all political and economic dissenting opinions? In ordinary times, it is true that we do not clap liberals or radicals in jail. But, isn't it also true" – he continued – "that jobs, power and prestige almost always go to those who do not dissent, those who are 'sound' and 'safe'?" (see Huberman & Sweezy 1968, p. 74). Categorising democracy as just the form and political rights as the substance of politics, the well-known Italian political commentator Gustav Zagrebelsky has argued (2014, p. 29) that when the substance is destroyed what remains is just an empty shell, a deceiving simulacrum.

In an analysis of lobbying in Italy in his time, Sraffa denounced the "enormous financial and political power of lobbies and the use of this power to influence both the foreign and home policy of the government in favour of their own interests" (1922, p. 198). In a 2010 book entitled *Freefall,* Stiglitz discussed the continuing impact of financial markets on US politics to argue that even after the crisis of 2008 corporations active in financial markets had been financing the electoral campaigns of either party with contributions in a total of hundreds of millions of dollars and had consequently been influencing political agendas in the United States both directly and indirectly (p. 60).

In capitalistic systems, even social security ultimately plays into the hands of capitalists. On the one hand, Offe and Lenhardt argue (1979, p. 36), social security schemes reduce the labour costs incurred by capitalistic firms; on the other, they help increase demand for labour. To understand the above-mentioned cuts on costs we have to bear in mind that without the benefits accruing to workers from these schemes "levels of wage demands would arguably be much higher than they are at present." Hence it is possible to argue that the mission of the State is to prevent individual capitalists from 'overusing' the labour force, i.e. shield the workers from a myopic form of exploitation (see Böhle & Sauer 1975).

This explains why the aspect of a worker-controlled firm system on which I intend to provide preferential focus is its potential for preventing capitalists from imposing their will and interests on society.[6] A major advantage of a democratic firm system is its ability to help workers gain freedom and the status of full-fledged members of society – i.e. its ability to satisfy those aspirations that according to Marx were antithetical to the capitalistic mode of production and would only be met at the stage where "the next leap forward in the material conditions of social labour and, hence, in the materiality of the productive attributes of the labourers, becomes incompatible with the capitalist social form of the production process of human life" (see Kiciloff & Starosta 2007, pp. 26–27). "Nothing" – Wolff writes (2012, p. 146) – "will more effectively inspire and activate workers to become informed, competent and full participants in democratic government of the communities in which they reside that functioning in that way inside their workplaces."

"Why has democracy difficulty entering the factory?" Vittorio Foa asked himself (1962, p. 10). "Whoever you may ask, whether manual worker or office clerk, the answer will invariably be that those in command *inside* are also in command *outside,* so that democracy is stifled by the power system." This means that "representational democracy, viewed as an instrument for wielding public power, will not become effective unless it wrests itself free from its paralysing encumbrances. And the setting within which the necessary struggle for freedom – a long-drawn-out attempt to conquer worker power – will have to act itself out is prevailingly, though not exclusively, the workplace."

The benefits stemming from the disempowerment of capital will become palpably clear if we focus on an economic system imagined to have become mainly formed of democratic firms. Compared to the circumstances prevailing today, as a result of the partial disempowerment of capital owners, such a system can be assumed to have developed political democracy to the highest possible degree. Whoever has given some thought to the insoluble conflict between true democracy and the power of wealth will clearly appraise the crucial role that democratic firm control may play. The media, including the press and television, would cease being subservient to the interests of their owners and would no longer be monopolised by anybody (if nothing else, not by a single individual). This is the idea behind M. Adler's distinction between 'political democracy' and 'social democracy.' Although the former is described as a democratic firm, he argues, in actual fact it resembles a dictatorship of sorts since the 'general will' it is said to express is actually a reflection of the specific interests of the power class and the underlying rationale is the liberalist principle of the atomisation of society into abstract individuals. As for the latter, it is truly and fully democratic, but can only become a reality in a classless society (cf. Marramao 1980, p. 292).

Simone Weil's is an even more radical view (1959, p. 171): "All the laws guaranteeing freedom and equality in the Republic are illusions" – she argued – "because the state is not controlled, nor could it be. It is impossible to bring about a reform of the state unless one first of all changes the system of production."

To claim that democratic firm governance would bridge the cleavage between civil society and political society is but to cast the same argument in different words.

This line of reasoning goes to support the claim that markets cannot be blamed for shortcomings which are actually inherent in the mechanisms governing capitalism (see Bidet 2004, p. 82). Capital, not the market, is the enemy that the Left is expected to overthrow.

The importance of disempowering capitalists is emphasised by Habermas, Offe and O'Connor, who share the view that the phase-out of liberalist democracy is the effect of the growing mismatch between increasing demand for welfare services from citizens and the inability of capitalistic economies to meet such demand in consequence of the opposition of firms to State intervention in the present globalised era. Insofar as it is true (as we will show further on) that no such opposition would come from companies operating in a democratic firm system, this bare fact goes to support the need to strip capitalists of their power.[7]

Democratic firm control enhances and magnifies political democracy in many respects, not only by disempowering capitalists. It is a well-known fact that democracy is superior to other forms of government due to a variety of different reasons, but primarily because its gradual expansion furthers the development of the human dimension and makes for a more effective use of human capabilities. In addition to this, democracy requires equality under many respects and the democratic process is desirable not only because democracy is a value in itself, but also thanks to its potential for ensuring distributive justice. And distributive justice is, in turn, a means of accelerating economic growth.

While it is true that interest groups might work towards redressing these imbalances and that the impoverished classes of society might join forces and attempt to dismantle the power positions of industry tycoons and bankers, in fact, since the financial resources available to the poorer classes of society, albeit organised, are bound to come short of those owned by the wealthy, the poor will hardly emerge victorious from their combat against political inequality.

Further reflections on the links between political power and economic democracy

In an analysis of the benefits of democracy at large, Dahl (1989, pp. 311–13) also mentions major strengths he holds to be specific to democracy, namely:

1 A tendency to expand its range and promote ever greater levels of freedom
2 The development of a great many human skills that freedom of choice tends to further
3 The availability of mechanisms capable of effectively protecting the property and interests of the citizens

Norberto Bobbio, for his part, discussing the distinction between representative and direct democracy in contemporary society, remarked that "the domain of democracy widens both under the dual impulse of representative and direct democracy and, even more so, as a result of increasing levels of democratisation, that is to say thanks to processes which enable individuals to play an active part in the decision-making processes of a rich array of non-political collective bodies" (see Bobbio 1985, p. 147).

Moreover, since the task of running firms should continue to be vested in managers, the extension of democracy we are thinking of does not boil down to the making of collective decisions. The partners will be called upon to state their opinions on major issues which do not impinge on efficiency and, above all, will be in a position to meet whenever they deem it appropriate in order to discuss inconveniencies associated with their work and make recommendations to the managers. And decisions supported by exchanges of opinion are fruitful in several respects. First and foremost, preferences which would have remained concealed are brought to the fore and can be properly weighed; secondly, as reflection is stimulated by debate and each participant may build on the insight flowing from the opinions of his fellow partners, consultations can lead to solutions that would not have occurred to the participants individually. Let me add that group discussion offers scope for stating wishes and raising issues which the speakers have as yet not fully pondered and on which they will probably wish to hear the opinions of others. Thirdly, resolutions passed following in-depth discussion gain added legitimacy and a moral authority which individual decisions necessarily lack, and will consequently be implemented with greater sense of purpose (see Fearon 1998).

Inasmuch as it is true that capitalism is often praised for guaranteeing freedom and democracy, but never in its own right (see Levine 1984 and 1988, p. 2), a democratic firm system (that is to say socialism) will outperform capitalism in terms of ensuring even higher levels of democracy.

Discussing similarities between pre-Marxian socialism and capitalistic democracy, MacPherson (1984) argued that both were based on non-scientific and non-democratic tenets since they acknowledged the right of individuals to a variety of political rights, but not to full-fledged democracy. In a much praised study entitled *Development of Socialism from Utopia to Science*, Engels remarked that utopian theories were those which, though designed to pursue lofty aims, were unrealistic and ineffectual. Engels's description reflects the typical mindset of advocates of capitalistic democracy who deny the very possibility of a turn to the better (see Macpherson 1984, p. 141).

As argued by Branco (2012, p. 23), in mainstream economics there is only one best solution for each economic problem and thus the purpose of policy is finding out that solution rather than weighing collective preferences or, in other words, engaging in political debate. In the realm of politics transformed into economics, he concludes, there is no place for pluralism: "The conflict between economics and democracy does not result, therefore, from any moral weakness of economic actors but from an intrinsic incompatibility between the logic of economics and that of democracy." In fact, this widely shared view is barely convincing since the antithesis is not between democracy and markets, but between democracy and capitalism. Thanks to the application of the 'one head, one vote' principle, a democratic firm system would be fully democratic notwithstanding the retention of markets.[8]

And since I am confident that the shortcomings of formal democracy would be swept away upon the establishment of a system of democratic firms, I dissent from Lindblom's argument that despite the need for alternative models of democracy for the very survival of polyarchy, no such models have been devised so far or are likely to be fleshed out in the future (see Lindblom 1977).

My reliance on the potential of economic democracy does not spring from an optimistic view of human nature or the belief that human beings tend to make rational decisions. As is well known, the theory that man is by nature good was propounded by Jean-Jacques Rousseau and was taken up by a wealth of left-ist thinkers. Yet, even advocates of this view will barely assume that collective decisions are, for the most part, made based on rational considerations. For our part, paraphrasing Friedrich Schiller, we wish to argue that people endowed with reason are exceptions and that most collective decisions are emotionally determined. This means that the desire to establish economic democracy is not only associated with the need to wrest power from capitalists, but also, and primarily, with a goal that is far beyond the reach of a society split into classes, namely educating individuals for social responsibility.

In the words of Stiglitz (2012, p. xxiii), "unfettered markets do not work well.... For markets to work the way markets are supposed to work, there has to be appropriate government regulation. But for that to occur, we have to have a democracy that reflects the general interests – not the interests of just those at the top."

A system of self-managed firms from the perspective of scientific socialism

Whereas there seems to be sufficient evidence that a system of producer cooperatives does give rise to a new production mode replacing capitalism in full keeping with Marx's theoretical approach, it still remains a matter for debate whether the current stage of producer cooperative theory can be rated as Marxist despite its use of methodological individualism, an approach which is usually held to be at odds with Marxism (see, *inter alia*, Callinicos 2005, p. 370). In a well-known book by Elster (1985), this query is answered in the affirmative, while Antonio Labriola, arguing from a socialist perspective, criticised cooperation as an illusory, even deceitful solution (see Labriola 1970, pp. 271–72).

According to Marx and Engels, the mission of a socialist/communist order was substituting "the domination of individuals over chance and circumstances" for "the dominance of circumstances and of chance over individuals" (see Marx & Engels 1845–46, p. 430). Such a change in the direction of society, they argued, would become feasible thanks to a reversal of the current relation between capital and labour. In Marx's view, the capital-labour opposition in capitalism was to be traced, not to the diverging interests of different social classes, but to the fact that man, far from exercising control over things, is actually under the sway of inanimate things (specifically, of capital looked upon as the bulk of production means). As a result, by suppressing the sway of capital and enabling workers to manage production activities, the reversed capital-labour relation simultaneously breaks the dominion of things over man. Discussing this point, Dunayevskaya (1951) has mentioned Marx's forceful argument that only when *cooperative* labour replaces *private* labour from the ground up will *social control* become the natural attribute of individuals who cooperate in labour and thereby become truly *social individuals*.

In Marxian theory, the capital-labour opposition is by far the most glaring contradiction in capitalism. As a result, inasmuch as it is true that a producer cooperative system reverses the respective positions of capital and labour and, hence, ends (or dampens down considerably) the opposition between capital and labour, from the perspective of a Marxist it follows that the rise of such a system boils down to establishing socialism and, hence, requires the concerted efforts of forces determined to work towards the achievement of this goal.[9]

From the perspective of Tronti, the more capitalist production takes root and, by extension, invades the bulk of social relations, the more society appears to be a totality shaped by production. Yet, he argues, this is just what appears, because at the acme of capitalism society as a whole becomes an appendix of production, society as a whole is reduced to the factory and, consequently, it is up to science to point up the basic relation (see Tronti 1966, pp. 49–52). If this is true, the reversal of the capital-labour relation will spark off a process capable of ridding society of the sway of capital and scaling down the present dominance of production in social life.

This begs the question: is it true that the 'one head, one vote' principle and the reversed capital-labour relation strip capitalists of their power and – as argued above – help workers gain their freedom?

This prospect is forcefully denied by Holloway, who argues that "to break away from capital it is not enough to flee" because capitalism "is an active process which separates us from the means of doing" and this separation is inevitable as long as capital exists. And as long as capital exists, he contends, the system obeys the laws of capital. In his opinion, it is not means of production that are owned by capitalists: to argue that production means are the property of capitalists is just a euphemism for the fact that capital infringes on our daily actions and deprives us of what we have produced. This – he concludes – is why the aim of the battle we have to fight is not to seize means of production, but to dismantle ownership rights and means of production at one token (Holloway 2005, pp. 208–10).

In a similar vein, Basso (2008, p. 132) writes: "To break away from the current situation, it is not enough to reverse the circumstances prevailing today and leave the underlying logic unaltered. Inasmuch as it is true that the subjection of the individual to an abstract social power is caused by the existence of a dominant structure embodied by one specific class, the reversal of the respective positions of the factors of this relation to the detriment of the class (previously) in power will not be enough to put an end to this subjection."

The line of reasoning adopted in this chapter has provided sufficient evidence that Holloway's and Basso's arguments are not only extreme, but wrong.

Two main requirements have to be met before the capital-labour relation can be reversed: (a) democratic firms must be prohibited from employing hired labour; and (b) borrowed capital must be remunerated at fixed rates of interest irrespective of the bottom-line results reported by the firms concerned.

In the light of the ideal principles of cooperation, (a) is all-important since it is only the abolition of hired labour that may spark off a true revolution reversing the current capital-labour relation, suppressing the sway of 'things' over man and restoring the mastery of man over means of production.[10]

In practice, the absence of wage labour would not seem to be an essential aspect of the 'ideal' social organisation model expected to take the place of capitalism. In point of fact, just as entrepreneurial firms borrowing third-party capital are specific to a social organisation model in which capitalists hire labour, take over third-party capital, reserve decision-making powers entirely for themselves and retain the whole of the 'residual,' so worker-controlled firms might be described as business firms in which a number of workers borrow capital and *labour* while reserving all the decision-making power and the 'residual' for themselves.[11]

It is worth re-emphasising that the main conclusion prompted by these reflections is that the characteristic of a system of producer cooperatives that leads to the establishment of a genuine socialist system is its potential for solving the contradictions between wage-labour and capitalists.[12]

Although the above-mentioned Marxist theorist Richard D. Wolff does not distinguish between LMF and WMF cooperatives, he defines socialism in terms which closely recall our own, namely as a system in which "it is the surplus-producing workers that appropriate and distribute the surplus themselves" (2012, p. 105).

Wolff is adamant that a centrally planned system where firms are prevented from carrying on business autonomously must be categorised as State capitalism, rather than socialism (see Wolff 2012, chap. 5).

Fineschi is one of the academics who raised the question whether Marx had actually provided a detailed picture of the future society and the way it would be organised. His analysis of the Paris Commune and the *Critique of the Gotha*

Programme actually touch on this point, but it is doubtful whether these writings can be rated as organic parts of his theory of capital. Fineschi's concluding argument is that there are missing links in Marx's work, in terms that Marx failed to complete his overall theoretical approach with clear indications concerning its practical implementation (see Fineschi 2008, p. 132). Further on, however, Fineschi specifies that this does not mean that the resulting gap cannot be filled and that Marx himself, in an effort to operate politically even in the absence of the required theoretical instruments, proceeded as follows: "through the doctrine of surplus value, in *Capital* he demonstrated that the working class was being exploited and that capital and labour were the opposite extremes of a relation which in essence defines the capitalistic mode of production" (*ibid.*).

On closer analysis, Fineschi's line of reasoning supports my view that socialism boils down to worker control of firms, i.e. to a social model that puts an end to worker exploitation by definition and brings about a new mode of production typified by a reversed relation between capital and labour.[13]

The most forceful argument against democratic firm management

A great many market socialism models have been theorised over the past years (see, *inter alia*, Stauber 1987, Roemer 1993 and 1994b, Yunker 1992 and 1995, Schweickart 1993 and 2002 and Burczak 2006) and even more can be expected to be fleshed out in future. Among them, the system in which workers run firms themselves – the one upheld in this book – is both the simplest to prefigure and the most widely discussed. The question is: can such a system be categorised as a new production mode?

As mentioned above, the claim that the transfer of management powers from capitalist entrepreneurs to workers does not amount to a full-fledged revolution has been refuted by numerous Marxist theorists. Among them, Sweezy has argued that to assume that a free market system with state-owned production means and firms run by non-capitalistic entrepreneurs realises socialism is to mistake legal relations for production relations. In point of fact, he specifies, a system where firms are run by groups of workers striving to maximise profits by manufacturing goods and placing them on the market is a very near proxy for capitalistic production relations (see, *inter alia*, Sweezy 1968). This opinion is shared by Mandel (1973, p. 8), who points out that "there have been many examples of workers' cooperatives that went wrong; there have even been some that have 'succeeded' – in capitalist terms that is! All that they have succeeded in, however, has been to transform themselves into profitable capitalist enterprises, operating in the same way as other capitalist firms."

With reference to worker-controlled firms, Althusser wrote: "As for buyers', sellers' or producers' cooperatives (the last named are extremely rare), they are incontestably part of the capitalist mode of production, constituting a direct 'anticipation' of the socialist mode of production only in the fancy of a handful opportunists or superannuated utopian thinkers" (1969 and 1995, pp. 14, 67 and 94). Much to the same effect, Mészàros 1995 (p. 981) argued: "Capital is a controlling force. You cannot control capital. You can do away with it only through the transformation of the whole complex of metabolic relationships of society; you cannot just fiddle with it. It either controls you or you do away with it, there is no halfway house between; and that is why the idea of market socialism could not conceivably function from the very beginning."[14]

The extent to which these statements are beside the point becomes evident if we bear in mind that in Marx's dialectical or relational approach capital would no longer exist if wage labour should disappear, that is to say, if the workers' connection to capital were found to change radically (see Ollman 2003, p. 26). And as Marx held capital to be embodied by the capitalist (see the *Grundrisse*), the abolition of wage labour leads to the suppression of capitalism as a matter of course.

To bring this point into better focus it is convenient to recall the distinction between two types of cooperative firms. As mentioned before, Vanek was adamant that only the establishment of LMFs (and not the creation of other forms of cooperatives) would result in reversing the relation between capital and labour. Hence, firms are either owned and managed by capitalists – in which case the system is capitalism – or they are neither the property of the owners of the capital factor nor run by them – in which case the system cannot, by definition, be a capitalistic one.

As is well known, Marx held that the sway of capital over labour in capitalism gives rise to a form of fetishistic dominion in the production process; and in Marx's mind fetishism is the process which reifies interpersonal relations to the point of making them resemble connections between things. In other words, according to Marx fetishism originates from the fact that the control of things (capital goods) over man in capitalism reverses the 'natural' relationship between man and things. "Yet it is obvious" – Marx argues (1857–58, p. 576) – "that this process of inversion is a merely historical necessity, a necessity for the development of the productive forces from a definite historical point of departure, or base, but in no way an absolute necessity. [...] The property-lessness of the worker and the property of objectified labour in living labour, or the appropriation of alien labour by capital – both merely expressing the same relation at two opposite poles – are basic conditions of the bourgeois mode of production, by no means indifferent accidental features."

An additional argument against democratic firm management

To all appearances, due to the fact that the triumph of financial capital has relegated the traditional capital-labour opposition to the back rows of the political scenario, democratic firm management might seem to have been proved wrong by history. From the mid-1930s onwards, the size of the manual working class started describing a descending parabola first in the United States, and then, gradually, in Great Britain, Scandinavia and the rest of the world; and a rising trend in labour productivity as well as the generalised growth of the service industry and the sector of administrative support services determined a fall in industrial employment. This is how the manual working class ceased to be "the future battering on the door": in the early twentieth century "it represented the collective interest in an age damaged by individualism," but by the end of the century "it represented history's losers" (Crouch 2003, pp. 64–65). This was the beginning of a phase, in social development, which today is known as post-democracy.

The span of historical development which was characterised by the confrontation of capital and labour, i.e. industrialism, is by now a thing of the past. The present is marked by the eclipse of social classes and even of democracy itself in its traditional form, so that it is possible to speak of post-democracy.

In most Western European countries and the United States, democracy arose in the mid-twentieth century and was characterised by widespread trust in the power of policy, by a significant role of trade unions, by Keynesian policies of State intervention in the economy, by the rise of the *welfare state*, Fordism and mass production cycles, as well as by the idea that governmental power was called upon to combat concentrations of private power through taxation. The core of political life was the confrontation between capital and labour, and the prevailing idea was that the mission of the State was to reduce the gap dividing the wealthy from the poor. And the central role of trade unions was closely associated with the emphasis on the importance of democracy in those years.

In industrial societies, "a certain social compromise was reached between capitalist business interests and working people. In exchange for the survival of the capitalist system and the general quieting of social protest [...] business interests learned to accept certain limitations on their capacity to use their power" (Crouch 2003, p. 11). This trend amounted to "a creative compromise between a vigorous capitalism and highly wealthy elites, on the one hand, and egalitarian values, strong trade unions, and the welfare policies of the New Deal, on the other" (*op. cit.*, p. 15). One basic feature of industrial society was the perception that the mass of manual workers were heading towards a great future (*op. cit.*, p. 63).

In point of fact – Crouch himself makes this clear – democracy can only thrive when the masses actively participate in public life and elites are prevented from keeping them in check. Democracy, he argues, describes both an ascending and a descending curve and today we are experiencing post-democracy, a system where a powerful minority bends the political system to its own interests, where political elites manipulate the interests of people, where deference to government collapses and where the welfare state is being dismantled and governments have stopped combating concentrations of power, unions have been pushed to the margins of the social scene, taxation is ever more rarely used for income redistribution purposes and politicians strive to elicit electoral consensus through the promise of tax cuts. At this stage, parties tend to frame ever more vague agendas, electoral claims (for instance Berlusconi's in Italy and Pim Fortuyn's in Holland) are growingly personalised, people are becoming more and more disappointed with politics, politicians are likened to shopkeepers and people have stopped going to the polls.

Today, liberalism has taken the place of democracy, and while it is true that democracy cannot grow without a certain dose of liberalism, it is a fact that democracy differs from liberalism in many respects and is, at least to a certain extent, even in conflict with it. Interest groups and lobbies are part and parcel of the liberal scene, just as unchecked party financing obeys a liberalist, rather than democratic rationale. As is well known, the idea that the citizens can do without the State is of liberalist making and the more State intervention shrinks, the more multinational corporations are able to prosper.

Crouch's basic argument (p. 4) is that "we are increasingly moving towards a post-democratic social model and that this may explain why in many, if not most, advanced democracies the masses are growingly disillusioned and dissatisfied with the limited scope there are given for participation and with the relationship between the political class and themselves."

In post-democratic societies, he adds, it is elites that are experiencing their heyday. Lobbying groups are multiplying, whereas politicans and governments alike are losing ground. Especially in richer countries with blatant distributive inequalities, for instance the United States, the effect of the globalisation of business interests and fragmentation of the rest of the population is to minimise welfare allowances, marginalise trade unions and widen the gap between rich and poor to an extent comparable to that of the pre-industrial scene. In a post-democratic society, he argues, there is a highly diverse growth of self-help groups which make it their task to fill the void produced by the dismantlement of the welfare state, but as these groups are characterised by a turning away from politics, they are not "an indication of the health of democracy."

In a globalised world, production proper is losing most of its previous importance because leading enterprises tend to externalise everything except financial decision-making, a function which is invariably retained by the headquarters of companies. As Gallino (2005) has appropriately argued, the globalised world is under the sway of financial capital and business success is strictly dependent on the ability of companies to maximise the value of their shareholders' equity, rather than their levels of productivity. At the same time, globalisation encroaches upon democracy, which has hardly any place in international relations.

Moreover, Crouch points out that there are two forms of citizenship. One is a positive citizenship which is typical of democracy, "when groups and organisations of people together develop collective identities, perceive the interests of these identities and autonomously formulate demands based on them"; the other is a negative attitude and is widespread at the post-democratic stage, "when the main aim of political controversy is to see politicians called to account, their heads placed on blocks, and their public and private integrity held up to intimate scrutiny" (Crouch 2003, p. 18).

This description of today's advanced societies provides fresh focus on the already mentioned assumption that democratic firm management is a thing of the past, i.e. that the confrontation between capitalists and workers is specific to industrial societies and that the call for reversing the relation between capital and wage-labour hardly makes sense in countries governed by financial capital. But is it true that democratic firm management is an outworn institution?

As far as I can see, such a claim is unsubstantiated, because the moment the relation between capital and labour should actually be reversed and capitalists were stripped of their power, it is the overwhelming weight of financial capital that would come to an end as a matter of course and democracy would triumph over liberalism in modern societies. There is little denying that, today, the manual working class is "a numerically declining and increasingly disorganized grouping being marginalized within political life" (Crouch 2003, p. 8), but this is not enough to take it for granted, as Crouch does, that "given the difficulty of sustaining anything approaching maximal democracy, declines from democratic moments must be accepted as inevitable" (*op. cit.*, p. 17). The difficulties standing in the way of sustaining some form of democracy even today will not appear unsurmountable to those convinced that a parliamentary majority is in a position to expedite the passage from capitalism to a system of self-managed firms.

Conclusion

Concluding this chapter, let me argue that provided democratic firm management is structured in such a way as to segregate labour incomes from capital incomes, it will effectively reverse the current relation between capital and labour and give rise to a genuine socialist system depriving capitalists of (the greater part) of their power. Thanks to the disempowerment of capital, economic democracy magnifies political democracy and sheds light on the contradictoriness of bourgeois policies, that is to say on the fact that the opposition of this class to economic democracy is actually at odds with its very principles, as we shall see better in Chapter 12.

Notes

1 As pointed out by Pejovich (1982, p. 240), the findings of modern theoretical studies are in line with Marx's claim that ownership rights have a major bearing on the way economic life is organised.
2 It is worth bearing in mind that in large-size industrial firms decisions are usually made by managers (rather than the capital-owners themselves) and that in trading companies decision-making powers are often vested in individuals who operate with borrowed funds (that is to say, not capitalists proper).
3 For an interesting debate on this point, see Wolff and Resnick (1982, 1983), Lindsey (1983), Houston (1983) and, especially, Poulantzas (1974), who has made valuable critical contributions to the traditional theoretical approach to social classes.
4 According to Tronti, the only way to "subvert bourgeois society from within capitalistic production" is "to reverse social production relations right within the social relations in factories" (see Tronti 1962, pp. 24 and 30).
5 Rejecting Rawls's allegation that the principle of equal freedom is only applicable in the domains of civil and political affairs (see Rawls 1958), I hold that this principle is equally applicable to economic and social phenomena. Indeed, there are reasons to argue that just as the equal rights principle entitles the citizens to exercise their political rights, so it should include the right to participate in the decision-making processes of a firm, especially when it comes to appointing managers (see Gould 1985, p. 204).

6 Hence, we agree with Gould that "Rawls fails to point up that equal social and economic conditions are a prerequisite for political freedom" (see Gould 1985, p. 204).

7 For a comparable view, see also Cohen and Rogers (1983) and Bowles and Gintis (1986).

8 The idea that "economic freedom is the prerequisite for the attainment of political freedom" (Hayek 1982, p. 7) is a mainstay of liberalist thought. Strangely enough, Hayek and liberalists in general reject the view that the 'one share, one vote' principle is not part and parcel of liberalism.

9 Further on in Chapter 7, we will expatiate on the need that both production and distribution in a democratic firm system have to be democratically organised. In the same chapter, it will also be specified that the fairest income distribution system is one in which each category of workers is assigned an income coefficient fixed in resolutions democratically passed at the central level. In such a system, within-firm differences between the payrates of different workers would only be determined by the application of such coefficients. As a consequence, payroll inequalities between the workers or partners of a cooperative are usually less pronounced than they are in capitalistic enterprises (see Adams 1963, Goodman 1974 and von Siemens 2011).

10 Several authors find it surprising that Marshall, though sharing Owen's view that cooperation and socialism arose simultaneously, failed to dwell on the process that led them to drift apart with the passing of time. In the opinion of Zanotti (2014, pp. 10–12), this is explained by the fact that Marshall equated cooperation with socialism straightaway.

11 The idea of contracts of employment as a distinctive feature of capitalism is discussed in Offe (1985) and in even further depth in Screpanti (2001). In 2007, this author went so far as to contend that "inasmuch as it is true that hired labour is a basic institution of capitalism, the only way to establish communism is to suppress hired labour." Weitzman, for his part, has argued (1984, p. 147) that, as wage labour is neither necessitated by universal norms or decrees of diving powers or natural laws, nor inherent in human nature, but was created by humans under the pressure of historical forces, it is humans themselves only that can replace the wage system with a more suitable system by their free will.

12 Even the stoutest advocates of democratic firm government are prepared to admit that a certain number of wage earners are compatible with the nature of the employee-managed firm (see, *inter alia*, Schweickart 1992, p. 40).

13 Oakeshott (1978) maintains that this model has its roots in the socialist traditions of the Italian and French cooperative movements.

14 For comparable opinions, see, also Turati (1897), Mondolfo (1923, p. 93), Labriola (1970, pp. 271–72), Quarter (1992) and McMurtry (2004). Sylos Labini denies both links between democratic firm management models and Marxism and the equation of the establishment of a system of cooperatives with a real and proper revolution (see Sylos Labini 2006).

4 More advantages of a system of democratic firms

Introduction

This chapter offers a review of the main advantages of a system of employee-managed firms. There is general agreement that one major benefit of economic democracy is the fact that people who can freely pursue their personal interests are happier than those obliged to act on somebody else's instructions. Indeed, since business decisions must be made by few persons in any firm, this is certainly a point which deserves major focus. In point of fact, the benefits associated with democratic firm management would accrue to the collectivity as a whole. Our analysis in this chapter will only cover those plus points which we look upon as the most important ones: positive effects on the development of human personality compared to capitalism, reduced alienation, a labour productivity edge on capitalistic businesses, the suppression of external firm control, slower monopoly-building, reduced bankruptcy risks, a socially determined income distribution and a reduced need for state intervention into the economy. The potential for depriving capitalists of their decision powers, which is probably the main advantage of a system of producer cooperatives, has been dealt with at some length in Chapter 3.[1] An additional advantage, reduced unemployment levels, will be discussed further on in Chapter 6.

In light of these reflections, it is also possible to decide whether, and to what extent, economic democracy is a public good proper or a 'merit good' (see Musgrave 1958). As will be shown in greater detail further on, economic democracy can be 'engineered' by a dual method: through a parliamentary act suppressing wage labour by operation of law or, better still, by enforcing policies targeted towards furthering a gradual but steady growth of the producer cooperative sector. In the former case, those holding that the benefits of a democratic firm system outnumber the corresponding drawbacks would be able to categorise it as a public good proper; in the latter case, they would rate each newly established cooperative firm as a merit good (see Jossa 2004d).

Marshall's idea of the cooperative firm as an agent moulding character

In an analysis of the impact of economic organisation on character, Alfred Marshall argued that more than by any other influences (unless it be the influence of his religious ideals), man's character is moulded by his everyday work and by the material resources which he thereby procures, and that consequently the two great forming agencies of the world's history have been the religious and the economic.

An excerpt from a work dated 1897 reads as follows (pp. 299–300): "Social science or the reasoned history of man, for the two things are the same, is working its way towards a fundamental unity; just as is being done by physical science, or, which is the same thing, by the reasoned history of natural phenomena. Physical science is seeking her hidden unity in the forces that govern molecular movement: social science is seeking her unity in the forces of human character."[2]

The idea that human character, rather than given from the outset, is thoroughly shaped by the environment and its economic structure, was advanced by Marshall in earlier writings as well. For example, in one of them we read that "we scarcely realise how subtle, all pervading and powerful may be the effect of the work of man's body in dwarfing the growth of man" (Marshall 1873, pp. 105–06). Discussing the relative importance of the main two factors in world history, in the *Principles* he states that, compared to religious factors, whose influence is more intense, economic factors act themselves out by the day and hour throughout the greater part of a man's life; for a man's mind is absorbed by matters associated with his business even when he stops working and, as often is the case, sets out to plan future actions (see Marshall 1890, p. 2).

The decisive part played by work in shaping man's character led Marshall to contend that the main task of a social thinker was to suggest institutional reforms that would enhance the best qualities in man, namely the 'high' motivations he equated with ethics. In Marshall's view, the shaping principles of capitalism were the profit motive and individualism, the mainsprings of "base motivations."

The foregoing may explain why Marshall praised the cooperative movement for its ethical motives and the main aim it pursued, namely "the production of fine human beings" (Marshall 1889, p. 228).

Marshall's approach underscores the potential of a genuinely democratic market system for generating positive externalities and a variety of other benefits accruing to the collectivity at large.

Alienation in a system of labour-managed firms

The different forms and levels of alienation that Marx theorised in his maturity were in part common to a variety of social organisation modes and in part specific to capitalism only. In general terms, he argued, the categories of work to be described as 'alienated' are production activities not primarily aimed to meet human needs, work done to earn our daily bread and, even more generally, activities conditioned by external constraints. And in all the societies of which we have knowledge, he added, labour and productive life itself appeared to man not as means of satisfying an inner urge, but only as means of satisfying other people's needs.

In this fairly wide meaning, any work done in a system characterised by productive specialisation – the division of labour – is alienated. In Marx's opinion, those who find pleasure in their work tend to diversify their activities, switch between jobs and eschew over-specialised occupations,[3] whereas the division of labour strips workmen of the intellectual potential inherent in any work process.

In an equally wide and comprehensive sense, alienation comes in association with the working of markets, where its roots are impersonal mechanisms whose effects can hardly ever be planned or wilfully contrived. The main alienation-generating market mechanism is competition, which impels people to behave in manners they would probably shun if they were not obliged to vie with competitors. Overall, market-related alienation is the effect of scarcity and the resulting need to renounce freedom of choice and act under compulsion.

These quotes suggest that any work that people undertake to earn a living is described as 'alienated' and that this characterisation is the core idea behind Marx's entire theoretical approach. Speaking of the worker, he raised the query: "Is this 12 hours' weaving, spinning, boring, turning, building, shovelling, stone-breaking, regarded by him as a manifestation of life, as life? Quite the contrary. Life for him begins where this activity ceases, at the table, at the tavern, in bed" (see Marx 1849, p. 34). And in the *Grundrisse*, with reference to a tradesman or professional, he argued that the exchange relation confronts us like a power which is external to producers and independent of them. "The social character of the activity, as also the social form of the product and the share of the individual in production" – he wrote – "appear here as something alien to and existing outside the individuals; not as their relationship to each other, but as their subordination to relationships existing independently of them and arising from the collision between indifferent individuals" (see Marx 1857–58, p. 94).

A less general, but even more compelling definition of alienation is 'work which is subject to the sway of capital.' In Marx's *Manuscripts of 1844* we read: "the more the worker exerts himself in his work, the more powerful the alien, objective world becomes which he brings into being over against himself, the poorer he and his inner world become, and the less they belong to him." "The alienation of the worker in his product means not only that his labour becomes an object, an external existence, but that it exists outside him, independently, as something alien to him, and that it becomes a power on its own confronting him. It means that the life which he has conferred on the object confronts him as something hostile and alien" (Marx 1844a, p. 211).

In the *Grundrisse* he further specifies: "No extraordinary intellectual power is needed to comprehend that, if the initial situation assumed is that of free labour arising from the dissolution of serfdom, or wage labour, the only way in which machines can originate is in opposition to living labour, as property alien to it and hostile power opposed to it, i.e., they must confront labour as capital" (Marx 1857–58, p. 577).

And elsewhere, Marx argued: "It is not the worker who buys the means of production and subsistence, but the means of production that buy the worker to incorporate him into the means of subsistence" (Marx 1863–66, p. 35). "Means of production confront living labour as capital and, at this stage, as the dominion of past dead labour over present living work" (see Marx 1863–66, p. 18).

In contrast to Althusser, Elster argued that the dominion of dead labour over living labour, the subjection of labour to capital and the idea that production means are an alien power holding workers in their sway are by far the most important points with which Marx concerned himself in his maturity (see Elster 1985, p. 102). The worker's estrangement from the commodities he has created – Elster wrote – is closely related to his spiritual alienation. To produce commodities is to create a need for them – a need which is often frustrated in the capitalistic production context. The link here is a fairly transparent one. In contrast, the reason why the estrangement of workers from production means should cause alienation is much less easy to grasp, since it is hardly possible to maintain that workers need production means in one way or other. Nonetheless, although this form of alienation is certainly less evident, it has even more far-reaching implications. It reflects the crucial structural fact that the worker is stripped of his claim on the entire value of his product and its effect is to further exacerbate the worker's commodities-related alienation. Dispossessed of production means, workers have no control over the work process as a whole and are consequently unable to realise their work potential to the full (see Elster 1985, p. 103). According to Elster, a major assumption of Marxism is the idea that life is rewarding when it is founded on self-realisation, rather than passive consumption. Indeed, from Marx's perspective the severest form of alienation originates from the estrangement of man from his creative faculties and may either magnify or stifle a desire for self-realisation; hence the ideal of self-realisation in work is an immensely valid guiding principle for industrial and political reform (see Elster 1998, p. 297).[4]

From the analysis of different levels of alienation we proceed to the central point of this chapter.

From Marx's argument that hired labour is the cornerstone of capitalism it follows that the suppression of hired labour in a system of self-managed firms would sweep away that particular form of alienation that stems from the formal subjection of work to capital. As mentioned above, a democratic firm system reverses the capitalistic capital-labour relation because workers become buyers of production means instead of being bought by them. As a result, democratic firms counteract that form of alienation that is related to the subordination of labour to capital:[5] "The worker actually treats the social character of his work, its combination with the work of others for a common purpose, as a power which is alien to him; the conditions in which this combination is realised are for him property of another. It is quite different in factories that belong to the workers themselves, as at Rochdale" (Marx 1894, p. 179).[6]

An additional reason why alienation is a lesser evil in a cooperative firm system is that the division of labour is, as a rule, less pronounced in cooperatives than it tends to be in capital-managed enterprises.

Moreover, Marx and Engels strove to account for the fact that alienation is specific to workers, rather than capitalists. "The propertied class and the class of the proletariat present the same human self-estrangement – they argued – but the former class feels at ease and strengthened in this estrangement, it recognises estrangement as its own power and has in it the semblance of a human existence" (see Marx & Engels 1845, p. 36).

The labour productivity edge on capitalistic businesses

According to Gramsci, for workers' councils to emerge, each worker "must have gained an awareness of his place within the economy. First of all, he must have felt part of an elementary unit or team and realised that technical upgrades to machinery and equipment reshape relationships with engineers: less and less dependent on the engineer, his one-time master, the worker must have gained in autonomy and acquired the ability to self-govern himself" (Gramsci 1919–20, p. 81).[7] It is also important, however, that labour productivity is not inferior to labour productivity in capitalistic businesses.

All the production modes that arose at various stages of world history, from slavery to capitalism, had one thing in common: they invariably stripped workers of the product of their labour by assigning them to tasks whose benefits were reaped by others. In other words, over the span of world history the best energies of workers have been 'wasted' for want of just those incentives that would have induced them to engage in work to the best of their abilities.

At the opposite end of the spectrum are the partners of a producer cooperative, since their title to the earnings from their work and their responsibility for the firm's operations are strong inducements to streamline production and increase output (see e.g. Grossman & Hart 1986, Borzaga *et al.*, 2011, Ben-Ner & Ellman, 2013 and Tortia *et al.*, 2015, pp. 141–43).[8]

Gintis writes (1976, p. 37), "the labour forthcoming from a worker depends, in addition to his/her biology and skill, on states of consciousness, degree of solidarity with other workers, labour market conditions and the social organization of the work process." Distinct characteristics of a system of cooperatives include a work organisation model which provides scope for the free pursuit of private utility calculations and, particularly, a major impulse to the development of solidarity feelings binding worker to worker.

Two additional reasons accounting for the higher labour productivity rates of cooperative firms include greater focus on human capital building and less frequent dismissals. Indeed, risks of dismissal act as a disincentive to working towards the success of the firm and interfere with interpersonal relations.

Despite this, several academics have emphasised the risk that a cooperative firm system may reduce incentives to work. Whereas in a capitalist-managed enterprise the proportional link between a worker's pay rate and his marginal work input acts as a powerful stimulus to work, they argue, the cooperative reduces this incentive since the income level of the workers depends on the way the surplus is apportioned among them (for this objection, see, *inter alia*, Williamson 1980).

Others have objected that the assumed higher productivity levels of cooperative firms have not been sufficiently proved. Pointing to promotion as a powerful stimulus to greater dedication and to earning the employer's esteem, these authors contrast this advantage of a capital-managed system with a major drawback of democratic firms: the strong incentive to shirk stemming from the awareness that hard-working partners will cash only part of the surplus revenue generated through their increased effort. In a cooperative of n members assigned to equal tasks this part is but $1/n$ – which means that incentives to production in labour-managed firms increase in an inverse proportion to firm size. Meade (1972, p. 403), Blumberg (1968) and Conte (1982) have argued that even in larger cooperatives worker involvement may generate benefits in terms of motivation.

Occasionally, the solidarity feelings binding worker to worker in labour-managed firms may produce the opposite effect of inducing hard-working staff members to slow down work inputs for fear of embarrassing their fellow workers (on this point, see the findings of Prandergast's 1999 overview of the literature on the perverse effects of incentives, as well as Tortia 2008a and 2008b, pp. 87–88).

As far as the effect of worker involvement in the firm's decisions on productivity is concerned, a well-known experimental project of the E. Mayo school with a long history in the sociological literature found that worker involvement may actually, and effectively, help boost productivity.

The labour productivity gains obtainable by involving workers in decision-making have recently been confirmed by a great many empirical research findings. Cases in point include Jones and Backus (1977), Bellas (1972), Thomas and Logan (1982), Zevi (1982), Defourny *et al*, (1985), Estrin *et al*. (1987), Weitzman and Kruse (1990), Levine and Tyson (1990), Sterner (1990), Estrin and Jones (1992), Defourny (1992), Bartlett *et al*. (1992), Doucouliagos (1995), Levine (1995), Craig and Pencavel (1995), Gui (1996), Ben-Ner *et al*. (1996), Tseo *et al*. (2004) and Tortia (2008a).

Conversely, the finding that capital-managed businesses tend to outperform cooperatives was reported in Hollas and Stansell (1988) and Faccioli and Fiorentini (1988).

For rather more ambiguous results, see Fitzroy and Kraft (1987) and Berman and Berman (1989). Similarly, a comparative analysis of capital- versus labour-managed firms conducted by Estrin (1991) reported conflicting results: a negligible productivity differential in surveys in which the measure of labour input used was headcount and a considerable underperformance of cooperatives when the measure of labour output used was the total hours worked by blue collars.

Two noticeable surveys of this same subject are those by Jones and Pliskin (1991) and by Bonin, Jones and Putterman (1993).

In point of fact, however, the findings of these surveys have little, if any bearing on our approach in this book because in the lead-up to the time when economists at last picked up employee management as a research goal, cooperatives had been organising themselves along lines which are at odds with the theoretical model to the point of impinging upon labour productivity.

Gramsci and Fordism

In the light of the productivity gains associated with labour-managed firms, it is worth asking ourselves if the scant fortune of Gramsci's workers' councils may have been caused by the spreading of Fordism and Taylorism.

Skilled labour forces are a necessary prerequisite for the success of a system of cooperative firms. From Gramsci's perspective, before the workers meaning to shed the capitalistic yoke can give rise to a worker-managed economy they have to gain a correct appreciation of their potential role in production and train themselves in the technical, financial and managerial functions they intend to take over in future. In other words, it is argued, Gramsci looked upon the working class as a 'political agent' striving to achieve its emancipation from capitalism while maturing a conscience as a 'civil producer' and thereby preparing the ground for its hegemony in society.

In early post-war Germany, a movement for workers' participation arose in advanced sectors of the engineering industry on the initiative of multi-skilled workers capable of vying with their managers in developing process innovations. At that time there were few assembly-line workers proper and the influence of trade unions on labour was still negligible. These conditions started changing from 1924 onward, when Fordist production and working modes spread rapidly across the country.

However, at least with respect to Italy there are academians who maintain that the factors that spurred on society in directions not anticipated by Gramsci were frictions in labour relations in large-size Northern factories and the rise of an entrepreneurial class in the part of the country named 'Third Italy.' Moreover, when workers faced with growing workloads resolved to prioritise the fight for better work conditions, the result was an increase of the unskilled labour force due to immigration from Italy's South.

A different explanation of the dynamics of Italian society is suggested by Bonazzi, who maintains that the progress of Taylorism (which is analysed at length in Braverman 1974) was not perceived as "a deterministic process entailing the debasement of labour in capitalistic societies as a matter of course" (Bonazzi 2002, p. 12) because the industrial conflict raging in Italy at that time had reached a level which seemed to justify the assumption that workers would manage to fend off its evils.

Bonazzi's line of reasoning may help identify the reasons why Gramsci's council movement ultimately failed to assert itself. If different cultural traditions had been in place, the radical changes observed in Italy (and elsewhere) in the 1970s might well have led to the rise of workers' councils. Concerning himself both with Fordism and Taylorism, Gramsci found fault with the deterministic worldview underlying the latter movement, but he never suggested that Fordism was at odds with his theory of workers' councils. As for Taylorism, he held it to have been responsible both for the rise of the corporatist movement (see Gramsci 1975, pp. 2156–58 and 2175–77) and "the so-called high wage" (Gramsci 1975, pp. 2166 and 2171–75) and described it as nothing but "the latest step in a long-term process whose inception dates back to the very birth of industrialism" (Gramsci 1975, p. 2165) and which might with equal probability have resulted in a cooperative movement. Just as Taylorism had generated the corporatist reaction of Fascism, he argued, so it might have produced a response in the socialist direction and, hence, the establishment of a system of workers' councils. From Gramsci's perspective, management skills could be acquired after the material establishment of workers' councils, for it is these that are the educational tool that will "radically change the minds of workers" and prepare them for the exercise of power (Gramsci 1919–20, pp. 89–90).

As a result, it is possible to conclude that both Taylorism and Fordism, far from conflicting with Gramsci's approach, have a place in his theory as factors capable of sparking off a socialist response to the degradation of labour in capitalistic societies.

Internal firm control and firm size in a democratic firm system

The 'one man, one vote' principle is a major advantage of a system of labour-managed firms because it determines a less systematic control of firms by other firms. The cross-holding structure of group companies is, indeed, both anti-democratic and extremely unfair because it enables holders of comparatively small stakes to control large business sectors and creates the assumption for the holding company to appropriate the profits of any of its subsidiaries by simply passing a majority resolution to this effect.

To a large extent, the substantial shadow cast over world politics by the business world is one of the effects of the proliferation of multinational corporations, and the growing political power of firms is the main driving force behind the advancement of post-democracy. Another advantage of lesser external firm control to be mentioned here, therefore, is its potential for sweeping away multinational corporations from an all-cooperatives system.[9]

Is it possible to argue, in even more general terms, that the less systematic control of firms by other firms mean that average firm size in an all-cooperatives system will exceed the average size of capitalistic businesses today?

Vanek emphasised the tendency of cooperatives to keep firm dimensions at levels commensurate with the size of the production establishment (see Vanek 1970, p. 273). As is well known, a capitalist-managed enterprise reaching the dimensional optimum of its production unit feels encouraged to implement an endless set of plant enlargements and upgrades on the assumption that this will generate comparable rises in profits; this is how monopolies arise. In contrast, a cooperative will make plant upgrades dependent upon the entry of new partners so as to leave *per capita* incomes roughly unaltered. This is a major factor accounting for the bigger average size of capitalistic firms compared to that of cooperative firms.

According to Gordon (1976), the main factor accounting for the high industrial concentration levels observed in capitalistic economies is not the prospect of securing economies of scale, but the process known as 'qualitative efficiency,' i.e. the aim of the ruling class to keep in check the working class and exercise full control over production. Indeed, capital concentration makes for tighter capitalistic control over production processes and leaves workers less and less scope for opposing employer decisions. It is the typical response of the ruling class to labour's struggle for fairer income distribution patterns.

Two benefits of lesser firm concentration in cooperative systems are a downward trend in expenditure for advertising (see Steinherr 1975) and an appreciable drop in transport costs: if nine firms operate in a given industrial sector in place of a single monopolist – Vanek computed (2006, p. 18) – the distance to be covered in supplying consumers assumed to be evenly distributed in space will decline by one-third of the previous total.

This means that labour-managed firms have much to gain from their smaller average size. And in Vanek's view, this is probably the most important winning edge of this system and, arguably, one whose scope is far from confined to the domain of economic theory (Vanek 1993, p. 90).

Greater focus on human capital investments

As decisions in cooperatives are passed by majority votes,[10] the individual workers have an incentive to commit themselves to the firm because any disutilities that can possibly arise are such that the worker of a cooperative, more than the worker of a capitalistic firm, can remove them through a sort of voice effect. Whereas the dissenting worker of a capitalistic firm just has the option of leaving, in a cooperative firm he can voice his dissatisfaction and participate in the decision-making process. If this is true, jobs in the cooperative firm will tend to be tailored to the partners' needs and this will clearly augment their commitment to the firm and reduce quits, i.e. the number of workers leaving voluntarily.

Inasmuch as this is correct, i.e. if quits are actually less frequent in cooperative firms, an important consequence for investment arises. It has long been recognised that the fear of quits may induce capitalistic firms to under-invest in human capital. And while it is true that an efficient outcome will only be reached if workers and the firm share the risks and benefits of investment in human capital, in point of fact neither of them can be sure that the relation will last long enough to make all the expected gains from the investment. In fact, even in the case of firm-specific human capital workers quitting their jobs will reduce the benefits the firm expects to draw from its investment in human capital.

To the extent quit rates depend, among other things, on working conditions, in cooperative firms which make decisions by a majority vote Hirschman's voice mechanism is likely to prevail.

In contrast, when the quit rates of a cooperative firm are lower for this particular reason, both the benefits expected from investment in human capital and, accordingly, investment in training will increase.

In short, the whole argument can be posed as follows. When deciding about an investment in human capital, both cooperatives and capitalistic firms will consider whether it is in their best interests to produce an asset over which the individual worker retains full property rights. As this particular aspect of the property rights regime can never be modified, the firm in discounting the benefits expected to flow from its investment will include the probability of unwelcome resignations. If the relevant interest rate is the same for both types of firms, but the quitting rate differs so that the quitting rate of a co-operative firm is lower than the quitting rate of a firm maximising profit, then, as a consequence, the cost of investment in human capital that a cooperative firm is willing to bear will be higher for a given time horizon and interest rate.

If the above argument holds, the tendency to under-invest is much reduced (or even eliminated) as investment can be considered as the sum of both investment in fixed assets and investment in human capital.

The greater propensity for investment in human capital may also have a different explanation. As it is difficult to see the purpose of pooling generic (i.e. non-specific) resources into a firm, some theorists today tend to assume that firm-specific resources are one explanation for the very existence of firms. Capital and labour resources are classed as firm-specific if they decrease in value on being moved from one firm to another.

The property-rights based model of the firm theorised by Grossman, Hart and Moore (GHM) is based on the starting idea that property is tantamount to control and on two additional assumptions: the idea that a firm is to be equated with the capital assets its owns (Grossman & Hart 1986, p. 692) and the argument that "ownership confers residual rights of control over the firm's assets" (Hart & Moore 1990, p. 1120). Moreover, considerable emphasis is laid on the insight that the owners of given assets are fully and exclusively entitled to prevent third parties from making any use of them and that the essence of ownership is the owners' title to dispose of the assets from which they draw the payoffs of their business. This exclusive disposition right may indirectly lead to control over human capital.

In GHM's theoretical model, the primary importance of rights of control is to determine the relative power positions of the parties to a labour relation and, accordingly, the distribution pattern of a firm's surplus and its incentives to invest in physical and human capital. This influence explains why business mergers may produce two antipodean results: a greater incentive for the purchaser of the other firm to invest in physical and human capital and, conversely, the loss of the right to invest on the part of the owner of the purchased firm. Workers, for their part, will give more consideration to the goals of an agent whom they know to be in control of the assets which are their work implements.

Commenting on this model, Stiglitz rightly concluded that the true essence of ownership was not the right to appropriate the residual, but the residual rights of control over the relevant assets: title to use assets of every kind and nature for any purposes not specifically provided for in a contract is only vested in the owner, which is tantamount to saying that an owner who is not contractually obliged to take specified actions is free to use all the assets of which he has control for the purposes he will deem most expedient from time to time (see Stiglitz 1994, p. 165).

This line of reasoning may help explain the basic difference between capitalistic and cooperative firms in matters of surplus and incentives. Upon the transformation of a capitalistic firm into a cooperative, the firm's control rights over the relevant capital assets are transferred from the one-time owners to the workers' collective with unpredictable results in terms of efficiency. And this is an explanation for the greater propensity for human capital investment observed in cooperatives (see McCain 1992, pp. 213–14, Jossa & Cuomo 1997, pp. 277–81).

Conclusion

According to Musgrave (1986, p. 453), the situation in which the concept of merit or demerit good is most clearly appropriate is one where the production of a given good is perceived as advantageous both by its direct users and in the light of prevailing community preferences. In line with his approach, therefore, each newly founded democratic firm can be rated as a merit good provided it generates benefits for its workers, uses the 'one man, one vote' principle to strip capitalists of part of their power, helps slow down inflation, improves the characters of its members or brings about any of the remaining advantages discussed in this chapter.

The classification of the democratic firm among merit goods explains why it would be a mistake to rely on spontaneous evolution, as mentioned above. In a 'free competition' context, cooperatives are at risk of losing out to the capital-managed corporation because they may prove less efficient than their capitalistic competitor and because businessmen have little incentive to opt for the cooperative form either when setting up new firms or when reorganising existing ones. If this is true and if democratic firms are actually merit goods, the task of furthering them cannot be left to private initiative. Deploring the narrow scope of so many economic policy decisions, Rawls commented that considerations of efficiency are but one basis of decision and often relatively minor at that, spoke out against the tendency of society to acquiesce without thinking in the moral and political conception implicit in the *status quo* or leave things to be settled by how contending social and economic forces happen to work themselves out, and expressed the hope that economic policy specialists would at long last broaden their horizons (see Rawls 1971).

With our classification of cooperatives as merit goods, it follows that any government, regardless of political-economic orientation, should take on the task of supporting the growth of democratic firms by enforcing tax or credit benefits in their favour. Considering the advantages highlighted above, it is possible to argue, in the wake of Marshall, that the firm model we should strive to expand and strengthen by all means is the producer cooperative operating autonomously in a non-centrally planned system (Marshall 1889, p. 153).

On this subject, though, Dow (2003, p. 75) has objected that nothing can prevent sceptics from arguing that the social benefits stemming from a growth of the cooperative sector are not such as to justify the (government) expenditure required to further it.[11]

Notes

1　A dozen advantages of cooperatives are mentioned in Vanek (1969) and Vanek (1970). Five additional ones are discussed in a study by Horvat dating from 1975 (pp. 77–78). For my part, I covered this point in Jossa and Cuomo (1997, chaps 6 and 13), and again in Jossa (2010a) and Jossa (2010b, sect. 1).

2　Since personality is the result of the interpersonal relations entertained by an individual in society (Heller 1980, p. 51), it seems fairly obvious that the main focus point of social science must be the agents that shape human personality.

3　The idea that work in systems organised in line with the principle of the division of labour becomes degrading was shared by a large number of eighteenth-century writers including Smith, Ferguson, Millar and Wallace (see West 1969, p. 137).

4　A well-known study of alienation theory (see Mészàros 1970, chap. 4) includes the largely unwarranted claim that alienated labour in Marx is to be equated with wage labour straightaway.

5　For an interesting and exhaustive analysis of this point, see Reich and Devine (1981).

6　In an outline of different levels of alienation, Sobel (2008) contends that alienation would outlast the demise of capitalism and extend right into the early phase of the new social order.

7　In Gramsci's mind, a social group aspiring to power must develop leadership abilities well before taking control (see Gramsci 1975, p. 2010).

8　The fact that a rich treasure of artistic and scientific inventiveness may harbour in the minds of a myriad poor chaps and might bear rich fruit under favourable social circumstances – Becattini has argued (see Becattini 1989, p. 209) – was appropriately highlighted by Marshall, but is generally overlooked by mainstream economists today.

9　Hence the comment in Crouch (2003) that this insight would have induced first-generation revolutionaries to campaign for the abolition of capitalism.

10　For the benefits to the production process coming from implementing voting procedures, see Drèze (1989), pp. 31–35.

11　Jacobsson, Johannesson and Borgquist (2007, p. 762) have made it clear that the concept of merit good, though well-established within economic science, lacks any sound theoretical basis.

5 Unemployment in a system of producer cooperatives

Introduction

Proceeding to discuss what is probably the most interesting plus point of cooperatives – the unemployment issue – it is possible to argue that a system of producer cooperatives would help cancel unemployment.

Bearing in mind that the main rule of conduct of cooperatives according to Ward and Vanek is maximising average worker incomes, it follows that a cooperative will not deem it in its interests to hire fresh workers unless the marginal labour productivity levels of the prospective newcomers are assumed to exceed the level corresponding to the firm's average income. It is well known that this principle marks out LMF from WMF cooperatives, in terms that income levels in the former, which segregate labour incomes from capital incomes, tend to come short of those prevailing in the latter. As a result, in comparable situations an LMF-type firm will tend to hire more workers than a WMF cooperative.

Now that this point has been made clear, it is time to analyse the causes of unemployment in a system of worker-managed firms.

Classical and Keynesian unemployment

As is well known, in neo-classical mainstream economics involuntary unemployment is mainly traced to high wages. The best-known theoretical approaches to high-wage unemployment are efficiency wage theory, insider-outsider theory and path-dependence theory and it is widely held that since worker-controlled firms incur, by definition, zero labour costs, none of the forms of unemployment that are theorised in these approaches can exist in a system of democratic firms.

As far as Keynesian unemployment is concerned, let me preliminarily state that Keynes categorised the 'cooperative system' as a 'natural economy,' and that while it is true that his analysis of this subject is somewhat obscure, the way he defines a cooperative economy does not substantially depart from the way modern theorists define a system of producer cooperatives or worker-controlled firms.

In the 1933 draft of what was subsequently to develop into *The General Theory* he discussed the differences between a 'cooperative' and an 'entrepreneurial' economy and argued that the former system was not subject to fluctuations in aggregate demand and was governed by Say's law, while involuntary unemployment was, in any case, specific to market economies founded on hired labour. According to Keynes, in a cooperative economy the factors of production are rewarded by dividing up the actual output of their cooperative effort in agreed proportions. As a result, the second postulate of classical theory applies and workers will choose to work so long as the marginal productivity of labour exceeds its marginal disutility level.

Keynes accepted Marx's weighty argument that the nature of production in the actual world is not, as 'classical' economists assumed, a case of C-M-C', that is of exchanging commodities for money in order to obtain another commodity, but an instance of M-C-M', that is, a situation in which money is exchanged for commodities with a view to obtaining more money. And the belief that the second postulate of classical theory is valid in a cooperative economy induced Keynes to state that a cooperative economy differs from an entrepreneurial economy because, unlike the latter, it is an instance of C-M-C', that is, an instance of exchanging commodities or effort for money in order to obtain another commodity.

This is one of the reasons why Keynes held that overproduction crises were specific to capitalistic economies and simply impossible in economies which have production systems of the C-M-C' type, for instance barter economies or cooperative economies.

Can this approach be classed as cogent?

In my opinion, considering that the investment function of a democratic firm does not substantially differ from that of a capitalistic enterprise, Say's law is not applicable to a labour-managed economy and aggregate demand can well be subject to fluctuations (see Jossa & Cuomo 1997, chap. 10). On the contrary, as the second postulate of classical theory is certainly valid in a system of democratic firms, involuntary Keynesian unemployment will be inexistent in such a system.

The second postulate is applicable to a system of cooperatives since workers organising their work freely tend to work a number of hours that will maximise their satisfaction, i.e. at which the income they derive from the last hour of work will equate the marginal disutility entailed in the effort required by it (as stated in the postulate). It is worth noting that this postulate is fully applicable both to a firm whose partners are assumed to have the same preferences and to a single worker whose preferences are assumed to be representative of those of all the firm's partners.

The question now is: what would happen in a scenario where the partners have different preferences? In such a case, the firm may either leave the workers free to fix their individual working days or oblige all the partners to work the same amount of hours. And as the former resolution would cause much inconvenience to the firm, it is reasonable to assume that firms will opt for an equal working day for the whole workforce regardless of the fact that the second postulate would only be applicable to a partner representative of the average workforce preferences.

The next question to be raised is what would happen in a system of democratic firms which is subject to the second postulate (in the way clarified above), but not to Say's law. How would a cooperative firm respond to a fall in aggregate demand?

In a system to which Say's law is not applicable and where the national income is determined in Keynesian terms, each fall in aggregate demand will reduce the aggregate number of hours worked. In this case, however, provided layoff decisions are adopted by the workers' collective or, more generally, in the interests of the workers, it is barely to be assumed that the partners will be prepared to fire their fellow workers. Indeed, especially in situations where the partners to be laid off are selected by drawing lots, the fear of being drawn might induce a majority of the members of the workers' collective to vote against the layoff resolution. Consequently, it is likely that instead of dismissing any workers, a democratic firm will opt for a shorter working week. No involuntary unemployment will ensue wherever this happens: all the workers already in employment will retain their jobs, though all of them will work fewer hours.

Hence, it comes as no surprise that the analyses of layoff decisions in cooperatives conducted by Vanek (1969), Steinherr and Thisse (1979a and 1979b) and Brewer and Browning (1982) concordantly concluded that the workers of democratic firms would tend not to authorise any layoffs and that this finding was reached although none of these authors had addressed the subject of worker solidarity.[1]

Reduced bankruptcy risks in democratic firms

A major advantage with a significant bearing on the issue of unemployment is a relatively small number of insolvencies. As is well known, companies face bankruptcy when their costs exceed revenues. Hence, the absence of a substantial cost item such as wages and salaries would greatly help reduce insolvency risks in a democratic firm system.

An additional reflection acquires relevance in this connection: if the pay rates accruing to the members of a firm fall below the average for the system, the members will tend to leave the firm. However, due to the aversion of theoretical model cooperatives to the entry of newcomers they will find it difficult to get better paying jobs elsewhere. This means that, while risks of insolvency can generally be ruled out in an all-cooperatives system, those workers whose pay levels are below the system's average will face the major disadvantage of having to put up with meagre incomes.

In other words, the downward trend in insolvencies is the result of a major difference between capital- and employee-managed firms: in the former, workers take precedence over capital providers since they cash their wages and salaries on a monthly basis; in the latter, the members participate in the 'residual' and although this may be paid out in monthly instalments, it is in any case determined after the whole of the firm's costs, including capital charges, have been duly settled.

Let me add that my arguments in support of low bankruptcy frequency are chiefly relevant to the theoretical cooperative model in which workers earn variable incomes. In actual fact, in most existing cooperatives the members are paid fixed wages and salaries.[2]

In a system where incomes may be zeroed workers must evidently enjoy some measure of protection, but this goal calls for state intervention in the economy, a point which falls outside the scope of this chapter.

Remote bankruptcy risks are mutually inter-related with lower probability of dismissal, which is also typical of cooperatives. As we have said, a cooperative may respond to declining demand by reducing the working hours of the members instead of laying off part of the workforce; and this is because democratic firms seldom face bankruptcy even in situations of excess headcount and/or drops in income. On the other hand, it is thanks to such reduced insolvency risks that cooperatives are hardly ever obliged to dismiss their excess workforce: an advantage of the reduced insolvency risks of an employee-managed firm is thus to make jobs in cooperatives safer and stabler.

Structural unemployment and producer cooperatives

The reflections just developed have provided ample proof that structural unemployment only is an option in a system of democratic firms. At this point, the question is: would structural unemployment be higher than it is today? It is widely held that a system of democratic firms would increase structural unemployment to levels above those recorded in capitalism. This argument is based on the difficulties that democratic firms tend to face when it comes to raising investment funds.

Economists have long been arguing that the severest obstacle to the self-driven growth of an employee-managed firm system in a capitalistic economy is the so-called 'collateral dilemma' (Vanek 1970, p. 318). But is this objection really as cogent as mainstream economists tend to suggest today?

Before this question is answered, it is convenient to clarify one major preliminary issue. The members of a democratic firm are usually held to make particularly risky investments because they are exclusively remunerated out of the firm's residual. Specifically, they are assumed to think that, while the success of a risky investment will step up their earnings, in the event of a failure they can leave the firm at any time without honouring their obligations to external creditors (see Drèze 1976, Schlicht & Weizsäcker 1977, Gui 1982 and 1985, Eswaran & Kotwal 1989, and Putterman *et al.* 1998, pp. 886–97). As a matter of fact, no such risk-proneness is observed in real-case scenarios, that is to say in existing cooperative firms.

In fact, since the worker-members of a cooperative are mainly concerned with making their incomes safe and stable, they can be assumed to be far less risk-prone than the shareholders of capitalistic public limited companies and, accordingly, to prioritise less hazardous investments (see Drèze 1976, 1989 and 1993). In capitalistic systems, investment decisions are generally made in the exclusive interests of the owners, without regard to the interests of workers, and hazardous projects may be prioritised irrespective of the risks for the firm's existing employment base. Things are different in the cooperatives described, since the managers who decide if a given investment should be made have been appointed by the workers of the firm and will consequently give equal consideration to prospective cash flows and the impact that each investment is likely to have on the firm's head-count. In this connection, it is possible to argue that functions such as employment protection and boosting, "far from being perceived as external constraints, should be looked upon as prerequisites for the specificity and growth of cooperatives" (Sapelli 1982, p. 70). And this is why the members of a cooperative will tend to prioritise less risky investments.

An additional factor accounting for the assumed lesser risk tolerance of coop-eratives is the antithesis between the sense of relative security associated with the awareness of a capitalist that he can diversify his investment portfolio and the acute risk perception of the partner of a cooperative who is aware that he can work for just one firm at a time.[3]

Coming to the subject of the greater funding difficulties that cooperatives are assumed to face compared to capital-managed enterprises,[4] let me start out from the fact that financers of the former are at a disadvantage since unlike the latter they cannot choose between shares or bonds (it is well known that cooperatives are denied the right to issue shares). However, provided the assumption of the com-paratively lesser risk tolerance level of democratic firms is found to be supported by sufficient real-case evidence, this would be outweighed by reduced investment risks. But this is just a first preliminary reflection.

As mentioned above, high net-worth individuals venturing into business tend to opt for a capital-managed enterprise, rather than a cooperative, in the awareness that this choice will enable them to retain all decision powers and the whole of the earnings from the operations of their firms. This reflection is at the basis of a study of the issues associated with the mix of entrepreneurial and worker-controlled firms in capitalistic economies: from the assumption that individuals are not equally risk-prone, but that risk propensity tends to increase in proportion to rises in income, Bowles and Gintis deduce that people with considerable financial means resolving to set up a business enterprise will opt for a capitalistic firm, while those owning no property will opt for a coopera-tive (see Bowles & Gintis 1994). And non-propertied individuals will doubtless come up against considerable difficulties when it comes to raising the financial means required to set up a cooperative firm. Indeed, to secure the repayment of their loans, potential providers of funds usually require some form of col-lateral that workers owning no property will seldom, if ever, be in a position to lodge. In this connection, Zafiris (1986, p. 37) appropriately argues "providers of funds who are remunerated out of the residual can be likened to 'insur-ers' of part of the risks taken by those who provide contractually remunerated resources."

Ben-Ner (1987), for his part, notes that the relative paucity of cooperatives should be traced not only to the fact that an able and rich businessman will hardly be prepared to share the prospective earnings from a newly founded firm with third parties, but also to the financing difficulties faced by non-propertied indi-viduals meaning to set up cooperatives.

In Drèze (1989, chap. IV) and (1993, pp. 257–62) we are told that self-managed firms with a fairly high capital-labour ratio and those intending to launch comparatively high-risk projects may find it particularly difficult to obtain credit and may hence be pressured into using risk capital. In this connection, it is interesting to mention that joint-stock companies were introduced and gained ground in capitalistic systems because they offered means of solving funding problems exactly in these delicate situations. In other words, worker-controlled firms with very high capital-labour ratios and those launching high-risk projects derive most of their earnings from capital, and if the loan capital they use has been borrowed at fixed interest rates and must be remunerated before the residual is determined, in situations of crisis the members' income from work will be greatly eroded, if not altogether nullified.

Drèze (1993, p. 254) holds that the funding issue is crucial to a correct understanding of the reasons why the cooperative sectors of capitalistic economies are comparatively undersized. In an exhaustive review of this point, Gui (1993) concluded that the relative paucity of cooperatives in economic systems today is to be mainly traced to difficulties in attracting capital and able managers.[5]

In the latest economic literature, the specific funding difficulties of LMFs are summed up as follows. As the use of self-owned resources is a sign of the firm's self-confidence, lenders tend to be particularly well-disposed towards firms which self-finance their investments. This explains why the interest rates charged by external providers of funds tend to increase in an inverse proportion to the self-funded portion of a firm's investments. Moreover, in line with Kalecki's 'increasing risk proposition' (see Kalecki 1937), the risks taken by workers remunerated out of the firm's residual escalate in proportion to the portion of the investments that is funded with borrowed resources (see, also, Baumol 1953–54 and Stiglitz 1969). As a result, if the self-managed firm is an LMF, a firm which funds its investments exclusively with loan capital, in the event of a failure the risks for the members will be maximised.

Compared to financers of public limited companies, providers of funds to LMFs take lesser risks also because cooperatives are under an obligation to remunerate loan capital prior to labour. In capitalistic firms, workers are paid on a fortnight or monthly basis, loan capital is remunerated at longer intervals of time and risk capital merely appropriates the residual; in cooperatives it is labour that bottoms the list. Hence, the residual earners of labour-managed firms can be likened to 'insurers' of some of the risks taken by those who provide the firm with contractually remunerated resources.

The need to allow LMFs to self-finance their investments (and the assumption that this will not turn them into WMFs)[6] shed light on a different method of providing security to external financers: the enforcement of the rule that interest on the members' bonds be paid out only after external financers have been remunerated. Under this rule, bonds issued by democratic firms would fall into two categories: (a) bonds for distribution to the members which are issued at the direction of the manager or based on a majority resolution to such effect; (b) bonds for subscription to third parties in general (external financers and members). And preference rights would only attach to those freely offered to the general public (see Cuomo 2003).

In conclusion, if cooperatives were to receive no aid at the formation stage and public support to medium-large firms were made conditional on the adoption of the cooperative firm, the assumption that the funding difficulties of such firms stifle the growth of the cooperative movement would barely apply (see Albanese 2003, Tortia 2007 and Jossa 2007).

The assumpton of the funding difficulties of the cooperative firm is generally contradicted also by practical evidence (see Hansmann 1996, p. 75). Specifically, it was proved wrong by the events in the Socialist Federal Republic of Yugoslavia, where unemployment levels started rising after the collapse of self-management.

Unemployment and State intervention in the economy

Two major points have to be touched upon before we can address the subject of this section, i.e. State intervention in support of full employment.

One of these is the non-applicability of the 'Phillips curve,' the well-known inverse relation between unemployment and the rate of increase in monetary wages, to a system of democratic firms, i.e. a system which is only typified by a different and less pronounced inverse relation between unemployment and the rate of inflation. This circumstance is held to enable the State to put in place employment-boosting policies without generating any wage hikes (see Vanek 1970, pp. 172–75 and 353–55; see, also, *inter alia*, Di Giacomo 1991, p. 269).

The second, even more significant point is discussed in Kalecki's 1943 analysis of obstacles to full employment. In this well-known paper, Kalecki argued that in state capitalistic systems the State is prevented from enforcing long-term employment-boosting policies by the awareness that jobs are readily available would produce the effect of undermining within-factory discipline.

In Kalecki's own words (1943, p. 168): "Under a regime of permanent full employment, the 'sack' would cease to play its role as a disciplinary measure. The social position of the boss would be undermined, and the self-assurance and class-consciousness of the working class would grow. Strikes for wage increases and improvements in conditions of work would create political tension."

In point of fact, although this argument has received considerable attention in recent studies of 'efficiency wages' it is hardly applicable to a system of democratic firms whose salient characteristic is the absence of masters likely to impose strict discipline on their subordinates.

Insofar as this is true, the State might enforce more effective employment- and income-boosting policies and these, due to the accelerator effect, would act as an enabler of investment and, consequently, reduce structural unemployment.

The conclusion suggested by these reflections is that this system would offer ample scope for the enforcement of Keynesian anti-cycle policies, and for the launch of public work projects for the establishment of new firms and (in line with a suggestion found in Vanek 1970, chap. XV) industrial sheds for assignment to cooperatives prepared to create jobs for people in search of employment.[7]

Producer cooperatives and unemployment in the current literature

Most modern labour management theorists hold that worker control tends to increase unemployment. This claim is supported by the seminal 1958 article in which Ward showed that short-term equilibrium requires higher capital-labour ratios in worker-managed firms than in capitalistic enterprises (see Ward 1958). In point of fact, this objection can be overruled by remarking that Ward's is the finding of a static analysis and, as such, somewhat less reliable than findings reached in dynamic analyses. The employment figures obtained in situations of equal capital accumulation are barely significant if it is possible to demonstrate that capital is being accumulated at different rates in the situations being compared.

An additional argument in support of the same claim, i.e. Ward's suggestion that the supply curve of a cooperative operating in a perfect-competition environment may have a decreasing slope, was also introduced in Ward's 1958 article, but has since been challenged by a wealth of authors (see, *inter alia*, Domar 1966, Sen 1966, Berman 1977 and Miyazaki & Neary 1983).

The idea that every upsurge in demand generates fewer jobs in labour-managed firms compared to capital-managed enterprises has not been refuted in the literature, but is barely forceful enough to prove our line of reasoning wrong. Inasmuch as it is true that neither classical nor Keynesian unemployment may arise in a system of cooperative firms and that capital is accumulated more rapidly in such a system than in the one prevailing today, there seems to be good ground for assuming that unemployment levels would start trending down upon the transition to the new system.

The claim that the tendency of democratic firms to underinvest is an additional factor leading to rises in unemployment has been repeatedly raised (see, *inter alia*, Furubotn & Pejovich 1970 and 1972, Furubotn 1971, 1976 and 1980 and Vanek 1970, pp. 296–303),[8] but refuted by a great many authors with various arguments (see Zafiris 1986, p. 37, Drèze 1993, Bowles & Gintis 1993a, p. 95, Putterman *et al.* 1998, p. 886) and by myself in Jossa and Casavola (1993) and Jossa (2014a, chap. 4), where I argue that a democratic firm which does not use its retained earnings to fund investments will barely cause underinvestment.

Conclusion

In an effort to provide the evidence that Marshall omitted to offer, I have examined the three types of involuntary unemployment which have received preferential attention in the latest economic literature. My conclusions can be summed up as follows.

The first type of unemployment can be automatically excluded from a system of democratic firms by definition; the same is to be said of Keynesian unemployment because a labour-managed economy is subject to the second postulate of classical theory; as for structural unemployment, the main reason why this form of unemployment may be assumed to be higher in a system of democratic firms than in a capitalistic system is the fact that in the short run democratic firms tend to have a higher capital-labour ratio.

Dubravcic's objection that a democratic firm system, where workers are their own managers, may oust from the labour market exactly the poorest and 'less able' people, i.e. those lacking initiative or any proper training (see Dubravcic 1970) is certainly forceful, but can be countered by arguing that even this situation might be remedied by envisioning a small number of employment contracts proper, at least on a temporary basis/by authorising cooperatives to take on a limited number of hired workers on strictly short-term employment contracts.

One further observation is probably worth making here: in a system of self-managed firms, the Government is much more likely to perform the role of employer-of-last-resort. And this seems to be an additional and fairly weighty argument in favour of the idea that the democratic management of firms would tend to eradicate involuntary unemployment.[9] However, this is not the proper forum to dwell on this subject, which has been discussed at some length by other authors (see, for example, Aspromourgos 2000).

The foregoing suggests a very general, though fairly obvious, conclusion which I nevertheless wish to set forth here. If employment is a primary objective to be steadily and consistently pursued, and provided the train of reasoning adopted in this book is correct, it seems barely possible to argue that a capitalistic system approximating the ideal of perfect competition should be preferred to worker control (only because the latter system is far from achieving a Pareto optimal). This conclusion is prompted by the fact that the perfect-competition ideal is equally unrealised in a capitalistic economy and in a worker-controlled system. Insofar as it is true that a higher employment level is an ideal to be pursued by any means, a system which is capable of attaining this end in the real-case scenario of today's world is preferable to a system which may afford higher *per-capita* incomes under certain circumstances.

Notes

1 The claim that classical and Keynesian unemployment would be unknown in a system of cooperatives has been refuted by Roncaglia (2004, pp. 288–90) with arguments re-echoing those which are raised by the Neo-Ricardians.
2 At any rate, the assumption that insolvency cases are less frequent among cooperatives than among capitalistic firms is backed up by the findings of numerous empirical surveys (see, *inter alia*, Ben-Ner 1988a, Stauber 1989 and Dow 2003, pp. 226–28).
3 Meade (1972, pp. 426–27) suggests that this is one reason explaining why law firms and enterprises conducting business in labour-intensive sectors tend to opt for the cooperative form.
4 The idea that the right benchmark against which the efficiency of a socialistic firm should be tested is the public limited company (rather than the classical capitalistic firm) was first suggested by Lange (1936–37, pp. 108–10) and then dealt with at length by Meade (1972) and by Bardhan and Roemer (1993, pp. 106–07).
5 See, also, Mygind (1997). Unlike him, in a study of firm ownership and management Hansmann argued that the role of capital intensity and potential risk profiles in determining whether the firms prevailing in a given type of industry are, or are

not, investor-owned is less decisive than it is usually assumed to be (see Hansmann 1996, p. 4).

6 This is why I cannot subscribe to Baglioni's argument (1995, p. 93) that the distinction between members and providers of funds adds to the obstacles to fund-raising and makes LMFs even more "difficult to establish both in theory and in a practice."

7 In an analysis of Keynesian theory, Pivetti (2006, p. 83) argues that "the Ricardian foundations of Marxism that this new theoretical approach is intended to sweep away boil down to the theory denying the Keynesian postulate of insufficient aggregate demand." Inasmuch as this is true, a system with a Marxist matrix such as self-management socialism is indeed a new mode of production (see Chapter 7) which rules out constraints on demand for business output.

8 Authors endorsing the idea that unemployment would actually increase in a system of self-managed firms include Lepage (1978, chap. 2).

9 This idea is shared, *inter alia*, by Wolff (2012), who has theorised a system of worker-managed firms and has argued that one of the main advantages of such a system would be the cancellation of unemployment thanks to the action of agencies spefically created for this purpose (p. 126).

Democratic socialism and income distribution

Introduction

It is clear that dramatic wealth and income disparities are a major characteristic of all capitalistic economies. A few findings from surveys conducted at various points in time may help state the terms of the problem. A 46-country survey froma 1999 showed that the part of the aggregate national income accruing to the bottom 30 per cent of the population in 1992 was but one per cent, while the top 20 per cent of the population received a 90 per cent slice of the pie. An income distribution study of 45 large countries throughout the world found that the share of the national income earned by the poorest population decile was 0.5 per cent of the total, whilst that of the richest decile stood at 54.3 per cent. In 2003, Bill Gates alone owned assets in a total amount equal to the GDP of the whole of Norway and one per cent of the US population was reckoned to own about 40 per cent of the nation's entire wealth (see Albert 2003, pp. 17 and 28). In 2008, the aggregate wealth of the highest-income families, one per cent of the US population, equalled the aggregate incomes of the lowest-income families, compounding a 40 per cent share of that country's entire population. In pre-2009 years, the wealthiest families in the top slice of the world population owned, in the aggregate, more assets than those owned by the bottom 50 per cent slice (as reported in the Credit Suisse 2010 Global Wealth Report).[1] One of the most striking findings in Piketty's recent bestseller (2013, pp. 47–48) is that the 30–35 per cent share of the national income earned by the top decile of the US population in the 1940s spiked to 45–50 per cent between 2000 and 2010.[2] In 2014, the jobless rates of Greece and Spain stood at 27 per cent and 14.4 per cent respectively.

The question is: would the situation be the same in a system of labour-managed firms? The aim of this chapter is to develop the income distribution scenario expected to arise in a system of democratic firms and to provide evidence that one of the major plus points of such a system is to vouchsafe much fairer income and wealth distribution patterns than those prevailing at the present day. The section "Labour as the sole 'source' of value" deals with labour as the sole 'source' of value; the section "Income distribution in market socialism" sketches the way income would be distributed under market socialism; the section "Mill's approach to income distribution" reports and discusses a well-known statement by John Stuart Mill on the subject of income distribution; the section "Should the State provide support to cooperatives?" raises the question whether the State should provide support to cooperatives; and the "Conclusion" states the author's conclusions.

Labour as the sole 'source' of value

Our starting point is the claim that the only viable part of the labour theory of value is the criterion of labour as the 'sole' source of value.[3] The Ricardian socialists were prompt to realise that this criterion was not the simple enunciation of a vague ideal, but entailed the weighty implication that workers were to have title to the whole surplus from production (an implication that even Marx himself rated as 'utopian' in capitalism – see Marx 1847, pp. 67–68 and Engels 1884, p. 13). And as it is apparent that the acknowledgment of this title is just a hopeful prospect for the future, there is little denying that the Ricardians were deluding themselves when they postulated the applicability of this principle even in their own day.[4]

To clarify our point, it is worth specifying that Marx defined value as the amount of labour which is socially necessary for producing an article and that the magnitude of such value – he argued – is determined by the labour-time that is socially necessary to produce it (Marx 1867a, p. 71).[5] In other words, Marx looked upon values as 'crystals' of a social substance that is common to them all (Marx 1867a, p. 70).

An additional distinction relevant in Marx is that between exchange value and price.[6] In Marx's own words, the former is an invisible, hence, unknown essence, whereas the latter is appearance, a "phenomenal form" (see Marx 1867a, p. 70).[7] Engels, for his part, made it clear that the categorisation of capitalist appropriation of value as an iniquity had, admittedly, nothing to do with economics (see Engels 1884, p. 13), but was probably correct "from the point of view of world history." "If mass moral consciousness declares an economic fact to be unjust – he specified – that is proof that other economic facts have made their appearance due to which the former has become unbearable and untenable" (*ibid*.).[8]

These reflections explain our contention that Marx's notion of value as the amount of labour which is socially necessary for producing an article, rather than a simple definition, is a full-fledged labour theory of value which postulates that (a) value is solely and entirely generated by labour, with the implication that capitalist appropriation of interest and profit has no theoretical justification,[9] and that (b) it is necessary to create a social order in which the revenue flowing from everything that is produced will be assigned to workers.[10]

The idea of value as generated by labour prompts the conclusion that a social order in which the surplus from production activities is not entirely assigned to workers is an exploitative one. In other words, inasmuch as it is true that the notion of value is much more than a simple definition, it follows that the capitalism=exploitation equation, far from being true *by definition*, requires the support of a demonstration (which indeed was offered by Garegnani). And since the claim that value is solely generated by labour is supported by the demonstration that the accrual of profits to capitalists is not justified by any economic theory, there are reasons for arguing that, far from being tautological, the claim that value is solely generated by labour is validated by this demonstration.

Both the view of labour as the sole source of value and its corollary, i.e. the assumed title of workers to the whole of the surplus from production activities (a claim, let this be repeated, which was first laid in by Ricardian socialists) are generally criticised for their 'ethical' implications (and the resulting conflict with Marx's scientific criticisms of capitalism).[11] In point of fact, although there is no denying that value judgments have no place in science,[12] so long as the failure to assign all such surplus to workers is not used as a pretext for categorising capitalism as iniquitous or theorising the title of workers to such revenue even at the capitalistic stage of an economy (an utterly senseless statement), there is good ground for arguing that it is no ethical proposition. Its scientific validity is sure to become apparent as soon as, paraphrasing Engels, it is interpreted as suggesting that the ultimate goal of historical evolution is superseding capitalism and vesting in workers title to the whole of the surplus. And while it is true that this is a Hegelian approach to history, i.e. the vision of an Idea that materialises within the world, it is also Marx's idea of history as a process marked by the gradual but continuous supersession of existing contradictions.[13]

The true reason why I tend to endorse Garegnani's theory of exploitation is that it affords a correct perspective on the socialist revolution. Indeed, in the light of the assumptions that capital generates no value and that the accrual of profit to capitalists is not supported by any valid economic theory, the goal of a socialist revolution will be cancelling this contradiction by transferring title to profits from capitalists to workers – as would be the case in a system of producer cooperatives.[14]

In other words, it is the 'seed of revolution' implied in the notion of value as the product of human labour that confers relevance on the labour theory of value (Deutscher 1970, p. 214);[15] and it is a well-known fact that ever since Marx's day a great many scholars striving to account for the advent of marginalism have been emphasising the dangers associated with the fact that classical economic theory is based on the labour theory of value.[16]

Viewed as an attempt to restore momentum to revolution as a process which puts an end to the undue appropriation of profit by capital through the establishment of a labour-managed system, the claim that labour is the sole source of value is consequently a far from negligible statement.[17] Moreover, as soon as it is looked upon, not as a theory of prices, but as one containing the 'seed of revolution,' it will even magnify, rather than scale down, the cognitive potential of the labour theory of value. In the opinion of Mayer (1994, p. 2), before we can reject the labour theory of value as a theory of prices we have to face the formidable task of reformulating the whole of Marxist economics on sound logical foundations that will not impair its theoretical and critical vigour. Endorsing this view, we can observe that the first material steps in this direction were taken by Roemer when he offered the demonstration that the theory of value was aimed to spotlight the sheer magnitude of worker exploitation under capitalism and ended his analysis with the concluding remark that "although the theory of labour is false, I think the conclusion is true" (see Roemer 1988, p. 2).[18]

To dispel the perplexing impression that these reflections may be surreptitiously re-introducing ethical overtones into our analysis, it is possible to mention the view of analytical Marxists that occasional normative notations can hardly impair the scientific standing of any discipline, including Marxist thought, provided the overall line of reasoning is otherwise compliant with the canons of scientific research (in this connection, see, specifically, Mayer 1994, p. 21).

In Benedetto Croce 1899 (pp. 57–59) we read that the validity of the labour theory of value as a theory of prices was initially challenged by Sombart on grounds that Marx's law of value was not an empirical fact, but a category of thought (see Sombart 1894, pp. 555–94), and that a comparable argument was later set forth by Labriola. Specifically, Labriola argued (1902, p. 191) that the theory of value "does not represent an empirical fact drawn from vulgar induction, nor a simple category of logic, as some have chronicled it. It is rather the *typical premise* without which all the rest of the work is unthinkable." To endorse – or simply explain – Labriola's remark, Croce added that Marx's approach to value was "the function of a term of comparison, of a standard, of a type" (Croce 1899, p. 59) and that this interpretation had led many scholars to describe the equation of value with labour as "an ideal of social ethics, a moral ideal" (*op. cit.*, p. 60).

Income distribution in market socialism

Inasmuch as it is true that all surplus from production should accrue to workers, it is reasonable to ask ourselves if the resulting optimal income distribution model would actually become a reality in a system of worker-managed firms, i.e. in a regime which is usually termed 'market socialism.'

A well-known Italian cooperation specialist wrote: "Cooperative societies are economic institutions designed to redress the greater part of the natural imbalances typifying the distribution of wealth in the present-day free-market system" (Valenti 1901, p. 516). But is this true?

Before we attempt an answer to this query it is necessary to spend a few words on the notion of classes. "What makes a class?" – Marx asked himself at the end of the 3rd volume of *Capital* (pp. 1025–26). At first sight, he answered, "the identity of revenues and revenue sources" (as Ricardo's analysis of the relations between workers, capitalists and landowners would seem to suggest), but if this were true, then "the same would hold true for the infinite fragmentation of interests and positions into which the division of social labour splits not only workers but also capitalists and land-owners" (e.g. for doctors and government officials).

Dissenting from Marx on this point, Mattick argues (2002, pp. 31–32): "It is to illuminate not the existence of conflicting social interests, which are indeed legion, but the question of fundamental social transformation that Marx's analysis abstracts from the myriad occupational groupings and income levels to focus attention on the distinction between producers and appropriators of surplus-value."

Accordingly, it is a fact that Marx looked on society as split into just two classes: workers and masters. This is why he wrote (Marx 1867a, p. 874): "In themselves, money and commodities are no more capital than the means of production and subsistence are. They need to be transformed into capital. But this transformation can itself only take place under particular circumstances, which meet together at this point: The confrontation of, and the contact between, two very different kinds of commodity owners; on the one hand, the owners of money, means of production, means of subsistence, who are eager to valorize the sum of values they have appropriated by buying the labour-power of others; on the other hand, free workers, the sellers of their own labour-power, and therefore the sellers of labour.... With the polarization of the commodity-market into these two classes, the fundamental conditions of capitalistic production are present."

Reverting to the subject of income distribution in a system of producer cooperatives, economic theorists – and primarily Ward in his 1958 article – have made it clear that the workers of democratic firms should earn pay rates based on 'coefficients,' i.e. pre-fixed per cent shares of the firm's surplus. In particular, the coefficients applicable to entire categories of workers would have to be centrally fixed for the system as a whole, while those applicable to individual workers might be fixed at firm level. If Aristotle was right when he claimed that "sensations are always true" (see Castoriadis 1975), there are reasons to assume that the socially determined distribution pattern that would be substituted for the current market-determined criterion would vouchsafe a juster social order. The 'sacrifice-based criterion' is a socially determined distribution method which was theorised by Albert and Hahnel and then analysed and discussed by other authors, including Panayotakis (2009).

However, to avoid drawing rash conclusions it is worth specifying that the different production capabilities of the individual members of each group are likely to induce firms to alter the centrally fixed coefficient pattern in line with firm-specific criteria and that this raises the question of whether distribution can be said to be 'socially determined' notwithstanding this specification.

In a system of cooperative firms, differences in worker incomes exist both within one and the same firm and between different firms. By definition, the former are socially determined when they depend on centrally fixed coefficients, but in this case – let this be repeated – the different abilities and skills of individual workers of the same category may lead firms to award some of them higher coefficients than those centrally fixed. Whenever such firm-level coefficients are fixed by the workers themselves in collective resolutions passed at meetings, these, too, will be socially determined by definition, but as the relevant choices are to be made by reference to the prevailing market conditions it is possible to claim that they are socially determined only in part.

In point of fact, the external market constraint does not nullify the social essence of the relevant decisions since these are made partly by the State and partly by the partners at general meetings. Significantly enough, in real-world cooperatives the highest pay rate is rarely set at a coefficient being more than three or four times the lowest.

In contrast with the neo-classical rule that in every market economy all prices, including those of the factors of production, are determined by the law of supply and demand, there are reasons to argue that socially determined distribution coefficients will tend to reduce inequalities. Indeed, supply and demand are governed by different mechanisms: unlike demand for labour, which depends on a firm's short-term needs and considerations, supply of labour is not exclusively determined by market factors and, consequently, tends to fluctuate over considerably longer time-spans. As firms are in a position to hire fresh workers whenever they need, demand for labour fluctuates in sync with the conditions prevailing in markets from time to time. In contrast, labour supply is not only far less volatile, but is mainly determined by the professional qualifications that workers have been able to acquire in training programmes. As a result, it is strongly conditioned by social choices, especially the structure of the educational system. This leads to the conclusion that the prices of production factors, unlike those of commodities, are in many respects unrelated to the law of supply and demand. "This strongly suggests" – Nobel laureate Krugman wrote (2007, p. 7) – "that institutions, norms and the political environment matter a lot more for the distribution of income – and that impersonal market forces matter less – than Economics might lead you to believe" (on this point, see, also Fleetwood 2006).

To clarify our point, let us assume that distribution coefficients are determined by social choices made in parliament and by the partners at the meetings of their firms and that in either case the decisions made are unrelated to the conditions prevailing in markets. *A priori*, there are no reasons to assume that demand for one or the other category of workers will equal the corresponding supply level within the resulting socially determined distribution pattern. What would happen in the event of disequilibrium in a single labour market?

When supply for a given job description exceeds the corresponding demand, it is clear that firms will be in a position to select workers with optimal qualifications, whereas those who fail to find jobs for a long time will have no way out but to switch to different job descriptions. Above all, based on an analysis of the trends under way in various labour markets, young people preparing for their entry into the labour market will tend to shun those qualifications for which supply systematically exceeds demand. In contrast, when demand exceeds supply, for some time firms will have difficulty finding workers with the required qualifications. In the long run, however, the market will develop its natural response, in terms of inducing new entrants to choose those job descriptions for which prospects of employment are greatest.

In point of fact, thanks to the crucial role played by the educational system and the practice of hiring personnel based on competitive examinations, the socially determined nature of distribution will not be entirely neutralised by such spontaneous market responses. In essence, competitive examinations act as a tool capable of balancing out labour supply and demand and it is hardly necessary to specify that ancillary services such as career counselling and vocational guidance are integral parts of the mission of any educational system. As is well known, it is even possible to say that the educational system and recruitment by competitive examination are ultimately designed to attain convergent goals.[19]

Both of them may help streamline labour supply in such a way as to bring the pay rates of different worker categories into line with the desires of society.

In other words, if the public hand works towards streamlining labour supply in manners apt to produce the required adjustments to demand, the pay rates for the individual factors can be set at levels that social conscience will perceive as fair.[20]

An additional major point worth discussing is the coefficients that would be applicable to managers. Considering that in a labour-managed system workers are expected to be better paid than they are in capitalistic systems, some authors have suggested that managers – the sole surviving representatives of the class of capitalists – are likely to suffer cuts on their incomes. Marshall, for instance, argued that "the hardest work of business management is generally that which makes the least outward show" and his realistic view of human nature induced him to believe that those working with their hands would generally underrate the intensity of the strain involved in the superior work of engineering a business and, consequently, "to grudge its being paid for at anything like as high a rate as it could earn elsewhere" (1890, p. 292). These reflections, combining with a clear appreciation of reality in his day, led him to argue that no cooperative firms had so far been able to offer salaries capable of attracting first-rate managers, excepting only cases of excellent men who for the sake of the cooperative faith in them accepted a lower pay than they might have secured by offering their services in the free market.

Refuting this assumption, Korsch argued that as the greater part of the surplus generated in capitalistic systems tends to accrue to the private owners of capital goods, rather than managers, there were reasons to assume that the moment capitalists ceased appropriating such earnings, managers would probably be in a position to negotiate higher pay rates for themselves. On closer analysis, he concluded, this was in full keeping with the characteristics of business enterprises which are managed by their workers in legal terms, but whose efficient running is actually dependent on the abilities of their managers (Korsch 1922, pp. 33–34).

To complete our analysis of income distribution, we have to examine an additional major objection raised by some authors, including Ben-Ner (1987 and 1988a, pp. 295–96), who argue that it is highly unlikely that workers expected to take all the risks entailed in the business carried on by democratic firms should be satisfied with the volatile incomes associated with the varying fortunes of their firms. To clear the field of this objection, it is worth specifying that the optimal corporate organisation model of a worker-controlled firm is one in which the aggregate fixed payroll expense of a firm would be kept well below its anticipated average bottom-line result and all excess amounts would be allocated to a reserve whose proceeds could then be used to offset falls in the partners' revenues in the event of a downturn in business. An alternative option would be using corporate tax receipts to create a social fund that the State might use to supplement the meagre distributions likely to be made by firms in temporary financial distress (a solution which, understandably, tends to be met with fierce opposition).

The last, and fairly obvious, remark to be set forth at this point is that even in situations where distribution is socially determined the State will be called upon to work towards redressing excessive inequalities, for instance by using tax receipts to award subsidies and putting in place employment-boosting policies (just as happens in capitalistic systems).

In this connection, it is worth remarking that liberalists have always (though often unconsciously) looked upon liberty and equality as antithetical. The former, they argue, is characterised by that emphasis upon individual action for which they are always zealous; the latter, by "the outcome of authoritarian intervention" which results in "a cramping of individual personality" (see Laski 1947, p. 5). And the reason is that freedom in capitalist markets quite obviously creates imbalances which State intervention in the economy is called upon to redress. In their opinion, the same is not applicable to self-managed systems, in which freedom and equality are not in antithesis. As mentioned above, in a system of democratic firms equality is vouchsafed by the coefficient-linked income distribution model which is largely the result of collective decisions, so that people are given ample scope for making their choices in utter freedom.

Mill's approach to income distribution

The idea that distribution is socially determined goes back to John Stuart Mill, specifically his statement that the laws governing production differ from those of distribution. The former, he argued, were imposed by nature and were consequently objective and mechanistic; the latter, in that they depended "on the laws and customs of society," could be altered and controlled by legislators (see Mill 1871, p. 196). In other words, in Mill's estimation "the laws and conditions of the production of wealth partake of the character of physical truths" and are therefore neither optional nor arbitrary; conversely, since the criteria governing the distribution of wealth are solely devised by the decisions of human institutions, once the things have been produced, "mankind, individually or collectively, can do with them as they like" (Mill 1871, pp. 195–96). This idea of Mill's has recently been brought to the forefront of public attention by Piketty's categorisation of the distribution of wealth as a distinctively political process (see Piketty 2013, p. 43).

At the time when Marx wrote *The Misery of Philosophy* (1847), his position on this point was antithetical to Mill's, but later on he adopted a different line of reasoning. Specifically, refuting the arguments of a citizen named Weston, in the 1865 pamphlet entitled *Value, Price, Profit* he argued that an immense scale of variations is possible between the limits of the rate of profit and that "the fixation of its actual degree is only settled by the continuous struggle between capital and labour" (Marx 1865, p. 108).

The claim that wages and profit are socially determined was also laid in by Engels, whose letter to Bebel includes the following statement: "the laws governing wages are very complex ... and are by no means iron, but, on the contrary, exceedingly elastic" (see Engels 1875, p. 982).

Our reflections so far prompt the following conclusion: considering that distribution is often socially determined even under capitalism, a system where democracy is apparent rather than real, there is ample scope for arguing that a truly democratic social order such as a system of worker-controlled firms can well be assumed to take effective strides in the direction of distributive justice (for the opposite view, see Nozick 1974, p. 251).[21]

Concluding, we cannot but forcefully endorse Zamagni's dictum that "the most effective and least costly way to reduce inequality is [...] creating the assumptions for the proliferation of cooperative firms and/or social service enterprises in markets" (see Zamagni 2006, p. 228).

Should the State provide support to cooperatives?

The fact that spontaneous evolution is unlikely to lead to the emergence of an all-cooperatives system is confirmed by historical experience. Such individual cooperatives, or groups of cooperative firms, as have spontaneously arisen so far have failed to free the masses from capitalist oppression because of their inability to trounce competition from capitalist monopolies. This would suggest that State intervention is a must.

Although there is little doubt that the rise of a nationwide state-supported system of cooperative firms requires of necessity the seizure of State power by the enemies of capitalism, nothing in Marx's work rules out the possibility that a working-class majority should take power by peaceful means and put in place policies designed to promote the growth of the cooperative sector on a national scale.

In the *Inaugural Address* of 1864 Marx explicitly states that "co-operative labour ought to be developed to national dimensions, and, consequently, to be fostered by national means." In the *Critique of the Gotha Programme*, however, he rejected both Lassalle's idea of the State and his belief that worker emancipation could be attained via a state-subsidised system of producer cooperatives. The platform of the *Gotha Programme* envisaged solving social problems by establishing producer cooperatives through State aid and placing them under the democratic control of workers. Marx objected to this platform on grounds that "the workers' desire to establish the conditions for cooperative production on a social scale, and first of all on a national scale, in their own country, only means that they are working to transform the present conditions of production, and it has nothing in common with the foundation of co-operative societies with state aid" (Marx 1875a, pp. 93–94). Otherwise – and this is the gist of Marx's argument – socialism would come about through State action, and this would conflict with the central idea of scientific socialism that workers were to achieve their emancipation by their own means. If workers were to demand State support for their revolutionary movement – he argued – they would only be providing evidence of "their full consciousness that they neither rule nor are ripe for rule!" (see Marx 1875a, p. 93).[22]

Consequently, Marx concludes, "as far as the present co-operative societies are concerned, they are of value *only* insofar as they are the independent creations of workers and not protégés either of the governments or of the bourgeoisie" (Marx 1875a, p. 94).

Elsewhere, Marx seems to adopt a different approach. The prerequisite for inducing the State to further the growth of the cooperative movement on a national scale, he writes, is, quite obviously, the takeover of power by the enemies of capitalism. In this case, Marx says, a majority of workers coming to power could be expected to provide all the aid that would be necessary for the cooperative movement to achieve national scale and he expressly wrote that "to convert social production into a large and harmonious system for free and co-operative labour, general social changes are wanted [...], never to be realised save by the transfer of [...] state power from capitalists and landlords to the producers themselves."[23] Engels also was not averse to the idea of proletarians seizing state power and suppressing the capitalistic state apparatus (see Negt 1978, p. 140). Actually, Marx thought that the primary task of the working class was conquering political power.[24]

The necessary conclusion that flows from the above is as follows: on the one hand, Marx took it for granted that a piecemeal progress of the cooperative movement "fostered by national means" would only become possible *after* the takeover of the working class; on the other, he did envisage the possibility that this aim should be achieved by peaceful means, i.e. through the vote of a parliament mostly composed of representatives of the interests of workers.[25]

In fact, I doubt that any Marxists will be prepared to subscribe to this conclusion. To account for this aversion, Thomas went so far as to argue that the very idea that gradual changes in the political organisation structure of society should be brought about by promoting the emergence of alternative economic and social forms right within capitalism is anathema to most of them (Thomas 1985, p. 872). All the same, let us repeat that this aversion can only be understood if we bear in mind that they do not envisage the possibility that a parliament mostly composed of representatives of the working class would doubtless be able to reverse the present rules governing capitalistic society and there are hardly any reasons to assume that the resistance of capitalists to such a policy and illegal outflows of capital – which would doubtless be massive – will reach a scale where they would rule out the prospects of success of such a revolution (for possible objections to this view, see Jossa 2010b, pp. 282–85).

From these reflections it clearly follows that the stepwise substitution of financial capital for industrial capital in capitalist-managed companies is clearing the way for the advent of democratic firm management in full keeping with Marx's idea that the new social order would come to maturity in piecemeal fashion *right within* the older order. In short, this is also the reason why the subject of Chapter 12 is an analysis of the role of limited companies as a possible springboard for socialism.

Conclusion

In this chapter, I have endeavoured to show that one of the greatest plus points of a system of worker-controlled firms is its potential for making income distribution much more egalitarian than it is to date. An additional major point dealt with at some length is the greater scope for employment-boosting policies that the State would be allowed in such a system.

Notes

1 From Fetscher (1979) we learn that Bernstein developed his revisionist approach based on statistical data that seemed to provide evidence that the future of capitalism would not be marked by a progressive concentration of wealth. The findings just reported prove Bernstein wrong.

2 In this connection, let us mention that the considerable pre-1929 crisis income distribution imbalances recorded in the United States narrowed in the era of Keynes and widened again beyond 1929 levels after the introduction of monetarist policies in the 1980s (see, in particular, Krugman 2007, tab. 1, p. 15).

3 The phrase 'labour theory of value' may either designate a method for determining the exchange prices of commodities or the investigation into the origin of their values. In a valuable study, Screpanti defines the claim that labour is the sole source of value as "*the value substance axiom*" (see Screpanti 2003, p. 157).

4 From Perri (1998, pp. 213–14) we learn that Marx rated as 'just' all the actions that do not stand in the way of the advancement of society.

5 Dussel (1999, p. 104) has called attention to the fact that Marx defined value as the 'source,' not the 'foundation,' of value. In his opinion, this distinction is of major consequence since it contrasts an 'ontological' notion (the foundation) with a 'metaphysical' notion (the source).

6 Dunayevskaya (1988, p. 100) has emphasised that in earlier years (at least up to 1859) Marx did not distinguish between value and exchange value (see also Rubin 1928, pp. 102–03 and Kliman 1998).

7 In the estimation of Wennerlind (2002, p. 3) the theory of value "is neither an alternative economic theory of exchange, nor just a theory of economic exploitation, but a theory of the social constitution of value."

8 In the estimation of Joan Robinson (1942, p. 20), the theory of value, looked upon as a theory of relative prices, is not the core of Marx's system and, consequently, "no point of substance in Marx's argument" can be said to descend from it. Inasmuch as this is true, it is possible to conclude that the validity of Marx's overall theoretical approach is by no means undermined by the labour theory of value. In the light of the fact that to categorise the partial appropriation of value by capitalists as iniquitous may be correct from the point of view of world history, this conclusion will sound all the more convincing.

9 According to Robinson, to claim that capital is productive or that its existence is the prerequisite for making labour productive is a matter of no great consequence; what really matters is "to say that *owning* property is not productive" (1942, p. 16). However, this claim would only be admissible if it were possible to show that saving entails no sacrifice.

The idea that value is solely and entirely created by labour is unscathed by a criticism that Adam Smith levelled against Epicurus, the charge that he "indulged a propensity which is natural to all men, but which philosophers in particular are apt to cultivate with a peculiar fondness, as the great means of displaying their ingenuity, the propensity to account for all appearances from as few principles as possible" (Smith 1790, p. 567).

10 Even in its 'new interpretation,' value is no simple definition, but "a complex notion: value is the abstract labour unit (its subsistence) and money (its form) is consequently connoted both by an immanent or intrinsic magnitude (socially necessary labour) and by an extrinsic magnitude (exchange value or price)" (see Ramos-Martinez & Rodriguez-Herrera 1996, p. 51).

11 Hodges (1965 and 1970) rejects Marx's notion of 'value' because he rates it as a subjective value judgment and, as such, incompatible with a scientific discipline such as political economy. Conversely, it has rightly been emphasised that to say that a thing or a human being has a value is tantamount to stating that human beings are strong or virtuous and that Marx took his concept of value from earlier classical economists discussing this concept in their scientific analyses (see Morris 1966). In the opinion of others, value (unlike use value) is the characteristic that commodities have in common and thanks to which they become comparable (Duffield 1970).

12 Authors who do not consider value judgments as antithetical to science include, among others, Bush (2009).

13 Hence, we dissent (cfr. Jossa 2010b, pp. 273–77 and 2014a, chap. 13) from authors such as Hess, Grun and others, who called for the advent of socialism as an act of justice, rather than a historically inevitable development (see Berlin 1963, p. 149, note).

14 As Murray put it (2002, pp. 250–52), to claim that work is the only source of value and to call for the conversion of all firms into worker-owned cooperatives one need not be a Marxist, since Ricardian socialists did so no less than Marx.

15 See, also, Lippi 1976, p. 151.

16 Antonio Labriola, for instance, wrote (1895, p. 50, note 2) that certain critics, including Wieser, "propose to abandon Ricardo's theory of value because it leads to socialism."

17 "The essential discovery of Marxism" – Sartre wrote (1960, p. 225) – is that the real foundation of the organisation of social relations is "labour as a historical reality and as the utilisation of particular tools in an already determined social and material situation."

18 Van Parijs has argued that Marx principally rejected capitalism because of its inability, from a certain stage forward, to promote the advancement of the productive forces, rather than because it entailed the exploitation and oppression of workers (1993, p. 234). For our part, dissenting from this view we rather believe that the idea of capitalism as founded on worker exploitation is far more central to Marx's approach than the claim that capitalism slows down development.

The extent to which Marxists are concerned with the issue of exploitation is emphasised by Balibar (who forcefully rejects the description of Marxism as an economic discipline proper) when he writes: "due to the ideological struggle endlessly raging within the Marxist tradition, every – more or less conscious – attempt to reformulate it on a sound political-economic basis (and, hence, reverse the double break inaugurated by Marx) is frustrated by a misinterpretation of the notion of surplus value" (Balibar 1974, pp. 111–12).

19 The idea that distribution may be socially determined is at the basis of the movement for participatory economics promoted by Albert (see Albert 2003).

20 In contrast, with reference to self-managed firm systems Miller (1989, chaps 6 and 7) argues that distribution is determined by market mechanisms, but that purposeful corrective actions put in place by the State might raise social acceptability well beyond its level in capitalistic systems.

21 Hayek has gone so far as to describe egalitarianism as the most destructive of the constructivist morals (Hayek 1982, p. 552).

22 Further on, Marx writes that the Programme "shows that its socialist ideas are not even skin-deep, in that, instead of treating existing society … as the *basis* of the existing *state* …, it treats the state rather as an independent entity that possesses its own *intellectual, ethical and libertarian bases*."

23 This quotation appears in Thomas (1985, p. 275).

24 In the *Manifesto* he wrote that "the first step in the revolution by the working class is to raise the proletariat to the position of ruling class, to win the battle of democracy" (Marx & Engels 1848, p. 504).

25 For a comparable explanation of Marx's position concerning this point, see Egan (1990, pp. 73–76).

7 Cooperative firms as a new mode of production

Introduction

In a 1935 paper weighing the benefits and shortcomings of Marxian political economy against those of mainstream economic theory, Oskar Lange (1935) argued that the former, while admittedly falling short of the latter in areas such as pricing and resource allocation, offered a number of additional major advantages: specifically, besides bringing to the foreground economic organisation patterns, class divisions in society and different modes of production, it mainly aimed to reveal the laws governing the evolution of human society in a long-term perspective.

Gramsci argued that it is not from scientific advances that we are to expect solutions to the problems traditionally explored by philosophers and economists. Philosophical and economics insights have instead come from notions such as 'social production relations' and 'mode of production.' This means that also for Gramsci the strong points of Marxian theory can be summed up as follows: it highlights a sequence of different production modes in history (the mode of the ancients, feudalism, capitalism, etc), suggesting that capitalism can hardly be the last link in this chain; and it makes clear that the mechanisms and evolution of each production mode obey specific laws and rules and that individual behaviour is greatly affected by the way production activities are organised.

Those who rate Marx's 'history-as-totality' conception as the true core of his theory of society attach major importance to the concept of 'mode of production.' In Marxian theory, production, distribution, exchange and consumption are different links of a single chain, i.e. different facets of one unit. Commenting on this point in a youthful work on historical evolution, Lukàcs (1968, p. 34) remarked that Marx, much like the German philosophers and chiefly Hegel, conceived of world history as a unitary process and an everlasting revolutionary avenue towards liberation, and that the uniqueness of his approach lay in the way he consistently prioritised a comprehensive global approach.

In the light of these ideas the point to be analysed in this chapter is whether an all-cooperatives system would give rise to a new mode of production and whether this new production mode is socialism. The chapter is concerned with Marxism, but not with a correct interpretation of Marx's thought. It defines capital in orthodox terms as the goods of production.

The chapter assumes the reader has some familiarity with the economic theory of producer cooperatives (see Vanek 1970; Jossa & Cuomo 1997). In the chapter the terms cooperative firms, labour-managed firms and democratic firms are used as synonyms. In a cooperative firm, therefore, (a) all decisions about production are made by managers elected by the workers, (b) the firm uses private loan capital only, and (c) the workers appropriate the balance between the firm's total revenues and total production costs.

Early theorists of the idea of cooperatives as a new mode of production

When cooperatives arose and took hold in the latter half of the nineteenth century, there was widespread agreement that they did implement a new mode of production.[1]

Robert Owen is widely held to be the true founding father of the cooperative movement. Based on firsthand knowledge of industrial life in Manchester, the ruthless conduct of industrialists and the race for wealth triggered by the ongoing Industrial Revolution in his day, Owen concluded that free competition and the factory system were bound to breed greed, inhumanity and moral decay. On this assumption, he planned new forms of social organisation to do away with competition-based profit. First, he set up 'unity and cooperation villages' that provided jobs to the unemployed; but he eventually came to look upon these communities as a universal regeneration tool and a springboard for freeing the world from competition-based profit systems. He soon found himself the leader of a large movement, but on realising that more and more members of newly established cooperatives and most of the union representatives listening to his speeches had in mind a democratic organisation aimed at helping workers throw off the capitalistic yoke and see to their interests directly, he had to bring his propaganda into tune with their expectations (see Cole 1953a).

Another well-known theorist of cooperation was Charles Fourier (1772–1837). In *Theory of the Four Movements* (1808) he suggested organising social life along cooperative lines founded on principles of universal harmony. He imagined society to be divided into 'phalanges': communities of about 1,600 people each which were to adopt modes of organisation founded on generally accepted rules: communal life, extensive use of jointly owned assets, competence-based distribution of tasks, and so forth.

Pioneers of cooperation include William Thompson, a strong advocate of trade unionism as a tool for cutting the profits of capitalists and furthering the gradual rise of a system of cooperatives to replace existing capitalistic firms. Convinced of the superiority of the cooperative production mode over the capitalistic mode, Thompson (1827) strongly advocated the establishment of a system of producer cooperatives aimed to oust capitalists from the production process.

A major impetus to the growth of the cooperative movement in Italy came from Giuseppe Mazzini, a champion of the country's unification process who encouraged workers to get rid of the 'wage yoke' and become 'self-standing producers appropriating the full value of production.' To Mazzini, capital was the arbiter of a production system to which it is alien. As a result, its role was to be taken over by associated labour: associations of workers called upon to see that all their members were given equal voting rights in the election of pro-tempore (i.e. revocable) managers and were paid profits commensurate with the quantity and quality of the work input contributed by each of them. This, he argued (1935, pp. 109, 132), would be "the ideal revolution," since its effect would be to make labour "the economic basis of human society."

All this is clear evidence that Owen, Fourier, Thompson and Mazzini, no less than some classical economists (such as J. S. Mill and J. E. Cairnes), looked upon the cooperative movement both as an option to capitalism and as a new mode of production (see Pesciarelli 1981, pp. 9–11).[2] Their idea was shared by Proudhon, who was probably the most powerful voice speaking in favour of the cooperative ideal and whose 'theory of an anti-authoritarian non-statist type of socialism ... opens up a new course in the evolution of socialism' (Ansart 1978, p. 29). Proudhon described capitalism as a close-meshed web of contradictions, the most glaring of which is the oppositional relation between capital and labour. And as he held that these contradictions could not be wiped out within a capitalistic system, it followed that capitalism was beyond reform and had to be overthrown altogether. The watchword ringing through all of Proudhon's writings is revolution. He called for a socialist order enabling workers to organise production activities autonomously in the workplace. A recurring slogan in his work, *destruam et aedificabo*, suggests that dismantling the private ownership regime and establishing a form of emancipatory libertarian socialism were to him the prime goals of any revolutionary movement. Discussing labour appropriation mechanisms, he argued that capitalism was grounded on the opposition between the haves and the have-nots, and on the struggle between capital and labour, and that privately owned means of production were nothing but loot plundered from workers by rapacious capitalists. Capitalism could not be reformed because the precondition for any reform was the straightforward abolition of hired labour and the exploitation it entailed. Proudhon strongly argued for 'industrial democracy' or 'mutualism' as desirable forms of social organisation, but rejected 'state capitalism' as a system in which means of production are entirely appropriated by the State instead of being assigned to workers as their joint and indivisible property (see Proudhon 1851; Ansart 1978).

The reversed capital-labour relationship in the Vanek-type labour-managed firm

To account for the claim that a producer cooperative system organised in accordance with the rules of economic science amounts to a new production mode it is necessary to start from Jaroslav Vanek's distinction between two kinds of cooperatives. Worker-managed firms (WMFs) are firms that self-finance their investments without strictly segregating labour incomes from capital incomes; labour-managed firms (LMFs) are firms which finance their investments with borrowed funds (see Vanek 1971a, 1971b).

As Vanek himself has made clear, WMFs suffer from a number of shortcomings. One of these is the tendency of majority members to oust minority members in an attempt to appropriate earnings on previous investments. The second major short-coming of WMFs is under-investment, a subject addressed in depth in a wide body of academic literature (see, for example, Furubotn 1976 and 1980, Furubotn & Pejovich 1973). The most relevant point for our analysis is the third shortcom-ing of WMFs, i.e. the fact that capitalistic capital-labour relations are reversed in LMFs, but not in WMFs, because the idea of a firm in which labour hires capital (by borrowing investment resources), runs production activities and cashes the surplus is only applicable to a cooperative that separates labour incomes from capital incomes (see Dubravcic 1970; Jossa 1986; Srinivasan & Phansalkar 2003). In other words, as this description does not apply to WMFs, an anti-capitalistic revolution can only be triggered by a system comprised of LMFs, which are firms that do reverse the capital-labour relation.

The anti-capitalistic firm proper is thus the LMF, and the fact that existing cooperatives are mostly of the WMF type may explain why those wishing to estab-lish a new mode of production are seldom attracted to the cooperative form.

An 1865 study by Walras on cooperatives in his day (the time of Marx) may shed further light on this point. Starting from the conventional supposition that land, capital and labour are the three main sources of wealth, Walras argued that individuals strive to accumulate ever greater amounts of all three types of wealth. This led him to define economic progress as the piecemeal expansion of every individual's access to all these categories of wealth and, specifically, as the expan-sion of capital ownership by workers (Walras 1865, p. 14). Moreover, he con-cluded that the formation of cooperatives was ultimately aimed at helping workers to acquire capital through their savings (*ibid.*, p. 7).

Walras's approach may explain why Marxists seldom concerned themselves with cooperative.[3] Moreover, his account of the perception of cooperation in his day reveals why Marx categorised cooperatives as firms where workers are "their own capitalists" and why later Marxists endorsed Karl Korsch's definition of an all-cooperatives system as "producer capitalism."[4] A system of firms which ultimately breeds nothing but a different form of capitalism is barely worth battling for.

A short glance at the history of the cooperative movement will confirm the relevance of these reflections. The proceedings of the earliest meetings of the First International reached markedly pro-cooperation conclusions, and the 1868 Brussels Congress sustained a pro-cooperation motion which had been put for-ward with specific reference to the long-standing 'machinery issue.' On the ques-tion of who was to own the means of production, many of the delegates argued that capital goods had always been used to exploit and enslave labour and that it was high time they were turned to the benefit of the working class by giving them to workers as their property.

However, whereas some saw producer cooperatives as the tool to attain this goal, others objected that the appropriation of the means of production by the working class was likely to breed a new form of capitalism. At the Brussels Congress, a committee appointed to probe more deeply into the matter of producer cooperatives denounced interest-bearing capital accumulation and dividend distribution as practices which would perpetuate capitalism to the exclusive advantage of a portion of the working class and give rise to a sort of 'fourth estate' with bourgeois characteristics (Cole 1954).

A 'querelle' between Godelier and Sève

The idea that reversing the existing capital-labour relation is tantamount to changing the means of production is consistent with the assumption that this relation is the crucial contradiction behind capitalism. A dispute between Lucien Sève and Maurice Godelier may be here recalled.

Starting from the strict separation of economic science from ideology in Marx's scientific approach to the contradictions of capitalism, Godelier argued that the need to identify the main contradiction inherent in capitalism arose in connection with Marx's claim that a new mode of production would arise the moment this main contradiction was superseded.

To a structuralist theorist of capitalism such as Godelier, the most glaring of all contradictions was the conflict of interests between capitalists as a class and workers as a class, whose origin he traced to two main causes: capital ownership was vested in capitalists as a monopoly and denied to workers, and the profits earned by the former amounted to the value of the work for which the latter were not remunerated (see Godelier 1966, p. 29). And as this state of affairs is intrinsic to capitalistic production relations and specific to capitalism, he argued, the resulting conflict is bound to last as long as capitalism itself.

On closer analysis, though, in Godelier's approach the crucial contradiction of capitalism is not so much the labour-capital antagonism proper, as a mismatch between the social character of productive forces and the private nature of the means of production, which he held to be external (not internal) to the mode of production and to result from the structural contradiction between increasingly socialised productive forces and persistently private production relations. In Godelier's opinion, this additional contradiction was not coeval with capitalism: it arose at a given stage in the evolution of productive forces, specifically upon the rise of industry.

Sève (1967, p. 66) found parallels between Godelier's approach and Marx's writings, where the mismatch between productive forces and production relations is said to have arisen at a given stage of history, and revolution is described as the clear sign that the threshold of tolerance had been overstepped. Despite these similarities, though, Sève rejected Godelier's approach. He objected that downscaling the capitalist-worker antagonism to a non-crucial contradiction was tantamount to downgrading the role of class struggle as the main driving force behind revolutionary change. Far from assuming that the evolution of productive forces would solve this crucial contradiction as a matter of course, Sève argued, Marx emphasised the crucial role of the revolutionary efforts of the working class and its allies; the dynamics behind such antithetic production relations were central to Marx's analysis (see Sève 1967, p. 67). And as Marx thought of class struggle as the only way out of this contradiction, from a strictly Marxian vantage point Sève rejected the implication that the intrinsic contradictions of capitalism would not themselves generate the conditions for their solution (*ibid.*). In Marx, he added, the dynamics behind the evolution of productive forces would clash with production relations from within, rather than from without, because they self-generated the external and internal prerequisites for superseding class antagonism.

Sève's closing argument was that Godelier had failed to put the basic concept of the mode of production into the right perspective. In Marxian theory, a mode of production is not a loose aggregation of elements 'entirely distinct' from one other. It is a compound of productive forces and production relations generating a close-meshed web of inter-connected contradictions. Concluding, Sève saw the main contradiction of capitalism as internal to the mode of production itself, rather than as an external opposition between distinct and independent structures.

Revolution as the reversal of the capital-labour relation

In Marx, the subversion of the traditional capital-labour opposition triggers a revolution proper, and provided we accept his claim that the severest contradiction in capitalism is the capital-labour antithesis, we will realise that revolution is a radical change in production relations (not only in legal forms, as argued by Sweezy): by reversing the roles of capital and labour within it, revolution sets off the instantaneous collapse of the existing mode of production. In a capitalistic system, the rules governing production and the motive to maximise profits are outgrowths of capital. The moment the capital-labour relation is capsized and capital starts being managed in accordance with rules set by labour, man will acquire control of the conditions of production and regain mastery over what he himself has created.

If we think of capital as a thing, and not as a social relation, the 'capitalism as an upside-down world' view and the description of revolution as reversing the capitalistic capital-labour relation will be recognised for what they are: truly scientific propositions. Indeed, the view of capitalism as a reversed world has the same scientific standing as the distinction between living individuals and inanimate objects. In terms of scientific standing, it is on a par with Keynesian underconsumption, the separation of ownership and control, the scientific revolution and other notions which today are widely accepted in mainstream economics.

The same scientific standing adheres to the claim that reversing the capitalistic capital-labour relation amounts to carrying through a real and proper socialist revolution. What we term 'revolution' is, we repeat, a change of the existing mode of production and, provided we hold the notion of the 'mode of production' to be scientifically grounded, the idea that the establishment of a system of producer cooperatives brings about a socialist order because it reverses the capitalistic capital-labour relation must be categorised as a scientific proposition.

One of Marx's major teachings is that those who control production control men's lives because they own the tools men need to pursue whatever aim they have in mind. On closer analysis, the idea that revolution is nothing but the handover of means of production from capitalists to workers and the concomitant disempowerment of capital receives further confirmation from this notion. In Gramsci's words (1921, pp. 148–149), "the control issue is the issue of industrial power, of deciding whether industrial planning is to play into the hands of bankers and stock gamblers or serve the interests of the masses; in other words, whether planning tasks are to be vested in the servants of capitalists or the trustees of the working class."

This conclusion is called into question by those who hold that the most glaring contradiction in capitalism is the antithesis between the private essence of appropriation (the very basis of privately owned means of production) and the socialised essence of production in large-size factories (where hundreds and even thousands of workers see to their jobs side by side) (see Marx 1894, pp. 373, 375, 567ff). The fact that the contradiction 'between socialised production and capitalistic appropriation' was first described by Engels in *Antidühring* (1878, pp. 260–261) as "an antagonism between the organisation of production in the individual workshop and the anarchy of production in the society as a whole" offers scope for arguing that an anti-capitalistic revolution can be looked upon as the transition from anarchical markets to organised planning.[5]

A different, though equally broad approach to the contradictions of capitalism is suggested by Bettelheim (1971), who thinks of progress towards socialism as a process marked by increasing worker control over production and over living conditions in general, and of planning as a tool for attaining such control. Terms such as 'plan' and 'market,' he argues, are empirical, rather than scientifically argued notions, and what really matters is not so much if the economy is governed by plans or markets, but rather the true nature of the class holding power.[6] And, we emphasise once again, if the capital-labour conflict is actually the main contradiction in capitalism, triggering the reversal of this relation amounts to a revolution proper.[7]

While theorists who distinguish between revisionists and revolutionaries based on whether they think of the State as an even-handed institution or as a power structure to be overthrown with the turn to socialism tend to reject this conclusion, to me it seems clear that the moment revolution is equated with a change in the mode of production, a system of producer cooperatives which reverses the capital-labour relation will result in a revolution even if it should fail to overthrow the State.[8]

Competition in a system of producer cooperatives

The opinion that a system of producer cooperatives is a new mode of production is confirmed by the stark differences between the cooperative and capitalistic modes of work. One such difference is related to unemployment. Two main types of unemployment would be unknown in an all-cooperatives system: high labour-costs unemployment (because wages in cooperatives are nought by definition) and Keynesian unemployment (since the response of workers empowered to make decisions in the face of an impending crisis would be to reduce their working hours instead of leaving themselves or their fellow workers jobless); see Jossa (2003 and 2009b).

Another major difference between the working modes of these two systems has to do with competition. In a capitalistic system, competition is closely associated with what Marxists term the laws of capitalist production. Free competition, we read in the *Grundrisse* (Marx 1857–58, vol. II, p. 38), "is the relation of capital to itself as another capital, i.e. the real behaviour of capital as capital ... the free development of the mode of production based on capital, the free development of its conditions and of its process as constantly reproducing these conditions. In free competition, it is capital that is set free, not the individual." From this follows "the absurdity of regarding free competition as the ultimate development of human freedom, and the negation of individual freedom as equivalent to the affirmation of individual freedom and of social production based upon individual freedom. It is merely the kind of free development possible on the limited basis of the domination of capital" (*ibid.*, p. 40).

For those who share these views (which are unobjectionable even from a non-Marxist vantage point), there arise two interesting questions: (i) whether a system of producer cooperatives will tend to be more or less competition-based than capitalism; and (ii) which of the two systems will perform better. Vanek suggested that competition in an all-cooperatives system would hardly be less efficient than in capitalism, though it would certainly be less aggressive. The gist of his argument was that capitalist firms and cooperative firms would head in different directions on reaching optimal size: the former were likely to pursue further expansion and set up ever more new workshops in an effort to maximise profits; the latter would not deem such expansion expedient because it does not maximise the *per capita* incomes of their members. Unlike other forms of market systems, Vanek (1971c, p. 27) concluded, a participative economy would quite naturally tend to adopt the 'live and let live' principle and suffer no appreciable losses in the process.

Neither Vanek nor other theorists, though, have touched upon the one subject that has the greatest bearing on the point of the present paper. As is well known, competition in capitalistic markets is much more of the nature of a stick than a carrot, where the stick is the risk of insolvency faced by firms unable to cope with competition: in our present social order, insolvency is the way out of a trap in which weaker firms are caught when they see their bottom-line results eroded by escalating costs and falling competitor prices. Conversely, as cooperatives do not pay wages proper, they are in a position to avert excessive cost pressures: the reason cooperatives face lower insolvency risks is that they can make up for competition-related losses by reducing the earnings of their members. And because the members of a cooperative have the option of boosting their incomes by increasing their work inputs or reducing work hours and incomes, they will not contemplate winding up their firm as long as the downward trend in incomes is tolerable (for further discussion of this issue, see Jossa & Cuomo 1997, pp. 246–253).

In other words, in a system of cooperative firms competition would continue to act as a carrot but hardly ever as a stick, and markets, no longer conditioned by the laws of capital, would allow greater freedom of choice in decision-making. Moreover, when bankruptcy is a minor risk, coercion also loses its grip and choices can be made in more freedom.

This may explain why Lenin was a stout advocate of competition in a social order freed from the conditionings of capital and why he wrote: "Bourgeois writers have been filling pages and pages with slogans in praise of competition, private initiative and a variety of supposed virtues of capitalists and capitalistic regimes. Socialists are disparagingly described as unreceptive to such virtues and wanting in awareness of the 'true essence of humankind.' But ... socialism, far from stifling competition, offers the unprecedented opportunity of clearing the way towards large-scale and even *mass* competition" (Lenin 1917b, p. 1027).

"Competition must be carefully organised among practical operators, workmen and peasants, while the tendency to standardise articles by casting them in the same mould or enforce uniformity by virtue of top-down commands should be discouraged by any means.... All 'communes,' workshops, villages, consumer cooperatives and procurement committees are expected to engage in competition with one another" (Lenin 1917b, pp. 1033–34).

Lenin's line of reasoning has one obvious implication: as markets in a system of democratic firms would be freed from the conditionings of oppressive forces, they would allow more freedom of choice, and this is enough to refute both the criticisms of radical Marxists and Sweezy's and Althusser's opinion that capitalism and market are two facets of the same coin.

Marcuse (1964) distinguished between true and false needs. 'False' needs are those that perpetuate toil, misery and injustice. In essence, they are socially determined since they arise under the pressure of external forces outside the control of individuals and still are what they used to be right from the start: outgrowths of a society whose ruling forces call for repression. However, the moment capital is disempowered, the external forces man is unable to control will simply vanish. Modes of competition which perpetuate fatigue, aggressiveness or misery will be discarded and men and women will be free to decide if they wish to work harder and boost their earnings or, conversely, reduce their work effort and put up with the cuts in incomes that this necessarily entails. Competition will not be wiped out altogether, but its grip will be loosened since the penalty for those losing ground in the competitive race is no longer the spectre of bankruptcy.

Notes

1 The earliest worker-managed cooperatives date back to the times of Guild Socialism, a movement which drew inspiration from ancient medieval guilds and whose prominent supporters included Bertrand Russell and R. H. Tawney.
2 Max Adler (1919, p 10) reports that Saint Simon, Fourier, Owen and other pioneers of modern socialism thought that political change alone was unable to improve the conditions of life of the masses appreciably.
3 Many theorists of cooperation hold that in cooperative systems capital and labour are still overlapping (see, *inter alia*, Stefanelli 1975).

4 In some of his writings, Marx (e.g., 1894, pp. 178–179) claimed that the ultimate goal of the working members of cooperatives was to become owners of means of production.

5 Panzieri (1962, pp. 346, 362) points to a conflict between Book I of *Capital* and other works by Marx. In *Capital*, the opposition between "despotism (planning) in factories and anarchy in society" is described as "the general form of the law of value"; elsewhere, we can detect the germs of a different approach.

6 For a comparable, though earlier, approach see Lenin (1921a); for Kautsky's idea of the capital-labour opposition as the main contradiction in capitalism see Panaccione (1974).

7 Authors reluctant to accept the idea that a system of producer cooperatives amounts to a new production mode include Robbins. In 1952, Robbins wrote (1952, p. XXXI) that following his enduring concern with the most challenging revolutionary schemes of the British guild socialists he realised that a system of functional groups was much more congenial to the spirit of man than an individualistic or collectivist system. However, he added, when the hope to see this vision materialise induced him to take up economics he realised that this aim was just an illusion, an *ignis fatuus* which leads to a morass of misery, injustice and conflict, and that men and women of good will had no option but to choose either collectivism or liberalism.

8 The claim that revolutionists should not take over the power positions they have just dismantled is endorsed by those who think of revolution as enhancing democracy in the firm, i.e. as a movement which disempowers capital without establishing a new power structure, but the approach we are discussing has been rejected by many theorists (see, *inter alia*, Dinerstein 2005, Löwy 2005) on the assumption that it fails to mention such a crucial goal as democracy.

8   An in-depth analysis of the links between producer cooperatives and socialism

Marx's approach to producer cooperatives

Marx defined the production mode as a combination of given productive forces and the relations of production existing between them. The more we go back into history, he wrote, the more clearly we will see man as part of a greater whole: the family first, the clan later on and, subsequently, the various forms of communal society. The standpoint of the isolated individual acquired relevance no earlier than the eighteenth century, the time when social relations reached an acme. This means that man is a gregarious animal and, as such, carries on social production activities whose laws are summed up in this well-known passage: "In the real production of their existence men inevitably enter into definite relations, which are independent of their will, namely relations of production appropriate to a given stage in the development of their material forces of production. The totality of these relations of production constitutes the economic structure of society, the real foundation on which arises a legal and political superstructure, and to which correspond definite forms of social consciousness.... At a certain stage of development, the material productive forces of society come in conflict with existing relations or production or – this merely expresses the same thing in legal terms – with the property relations within the framework of which they have operated hitherto. From forms of development of the productive forces these relations turn into their fetters. Then begins an era of social revolution" (Marx 1859a, p. 263).

Thanks to his theorisation of the notion of production modes, Marx opened up the 'Continent of History' to scientific knowledge and thereby created the assumptions for the further evolution of all human sciences, from sociology and psychology to any other scientific discipline concerned with investigating society and man (Althusser 1995). Although Marx held each material societal structure to be primarily shaped by the dominant production mode, he also attached great importance to non-dominant production modes: the older production mode that has yet not been completely outgrown and the future one just arising within the existing social order. Accordingly, to argue that the current production relations are no longer consistent with the existing productive forces and, hence, to predict the emergence of a new production mode is tantamount to acknowledging that the existing social order is at a transitional stage because the current production mode is in the process of becoming obsolete due to changes under way in productive forces. In the light of these reflections, to equate a revolution with a change in the relevant production mode is a correct approach from the perspective of both economic science and Marxism.

The productive forces constitute the material basis of a production mode, but as they can only act themselves out within the corresponding relations of production, it is the connection between the relations of production and the productive forces concerned that must be said to play a decisive role. In the opinion of Althusser, this major point has often received insufficient attention from Marxists.

From the centrality of the revolution/change in production mode equation in Marx's thought it follows that Marxism must be defined as a 'theory of revolution' (Lukàcs 1922). And this determines (a) that the criterion against which Marxism should be tested is the extent to which it is able to foretell the transition to socialism (see, *inter alia*, Panaccione 1974, p. 4 and De Giovanni 1976, pp. 8–9) and (b) that the qualification of Marxists should be restricted to those who are confident in the possibility to realise a socialist or communist order (consistent with Marx's thought) in practice, and, conversely, denied to all those who are averse to the idea of revolution. Buchanan (1982, p. 26) has correctly observed that "without reference to life in communism, Marx's criticisms lose their radical character," while Bloom (1943, p. 54) has described Marx as the only major intellectual whose importance "is judged in terms of events rather than ideas" (1943, p. 54).

Discussing Marx's approach to cooperation, a preliminary observation to be made is that Marx emphasised the tendency of firms in advanced capitalistic systems to keep ownership separated from control. In *Capital* (vol. I, pp. 448–49), he wrote:_"All directly social or communal labour on a large scale requires, to a greater or lesser degree, a directing authority, in order to secure the harmonious co-operation of the activities of individuals, and to perform the general functions that have their origin in the motion of the total productive organism, as distinguished from the motion of separate organs. A single violin player is his own conductor; an orchestra requires a separate one. The work of directing, superintending and adjusting becomes one of the functions of capital, from the moment that the labour under capital's control becomes co-operative."

The same idea underlies a passage from the third volume of *Capital* which runs as follows: "Capitalist production has itself brought it about that the work of supervision is readily available, quite independent of the ownership of capital. It has therefore become superfluous for this work of supervision to be performed by the capitalist. A musical conductor need in no way be the owner of the instruments in his orchestra, nor does it form part of his function as a conductor that he should have any part in paying the 'wages' of other musicians. Cooperative factories provide the proof that the capitalist has become just as superlous as a functionary in production as he himself, from his superior vantage-point, finds the large landlord."

Thanks to the separation of ownership from control, Marx argues, the control functions can be performed either by the workers themselves or by their representatives. In Book III of *Capital* we read (p. 512) that in the cooperative factory, "the antithetical character of the supervisory work disappears, since the manager is paid by the workers instead of representing capital in opposition to them" and that since "the mere manager, who does not possess capital under any title … takes care of all real functions that fall to the functioning capitalist as such, there remains only the functionary, and the capitalist vanishes from the production process as someone superfluous."

These passages make it absolutely clear that the system of producer cooperatives envisaged by Marx was a market system that makes workers "their own masters" (Mill 1871, p. 739) and deprives capital owners of the power to make decisions in matters of production.[1]

In the third volume of *Capital* Marx also argued: "With the development of co-operatives on the workers' part, and joint-stock companies on the part of the bourgeoisie, the last pretext for confusing profit of enterprise with the wages of management was removed, and profit came to appear in practice as what is undeniably was in theory, mere surplus-value, value for which no equivalent was paid" (Marx 1894, pp. 513–14).

Further on, Marx goes so far as to suggest that the transfer of management powers from capitalists to workers will result in the emergence of a new mode of production.

In the *Inaugural Address* (1864), Marx wrote: "But there was in store a still greater victory of the political economy of labour over the political economy of property. We speak of the co-operative movement, especially of the co-operative factories raised by the unassisted efforts of a few bold 'hands.' The value of these great social experiments cannot be over-rated. By deed, instead of by argument, they have shown that production on a large scale, and in accord with the behest of modern science, may be carried on without the existence of a class of masters employing a class of hands; that to bear fruit, the means of labour need not be monopolised as a means of dominion over, and of extortion against, the labouring man himself; and that, like slave labour, like serf labour, hired labour is but a transitory and inferior form, destined to disappear before associated labour plying its toil with a willing hand, a ready mind, and a joyous heart" (Marx 1864, p. 11).[2]

All of this justifies the statement that Marx's position on worker cooperatives was nuanced and, in general, enthusiastic.

An additional relevant passage from Book III of *Capital* runs as follows: "The co-operative factories run by workers themselves are, within the old form, the first examples of the emergence of a new form, even though they naturally reproduce in all cases, in their present organization, all the defects of the existing system, and must reproduce them. But the opposition between capital and labour is abolished there, even if at first only in the form that the workers in association become their own capitalists, i.e. they use the means of production to valorise their labour. These factories show how, at a certain stage of development of the material forces of production, and of the social forms of production corresponding to them, a new mode of production develops and is formed naturally out of the old."

These quotes leave no doubt that Marx looked upon an all-cooperatives system not only as feasible, but as bound to assert itself in history, as a new mode of production which would wipe out hired labour and a system where privately owned means of production – capital – would cease being used to enslave workers. In Marx's opinion, this system is "in accord with the behest of modern science" and arising right within the older mode of production and supplanting it.[3] In such a system, he claimed, workers would no longer be exploited and, even more importantly, would be freely and willingly working for firms owned by them.

Both the equation of an all-cooperatives system with a new mode of production and its assumed potential for outperforming and superseding capitalism are underscored in numerous often-quoted passages from *Capital*. On pages 570–71, for instance, Marx describes joint-stock companies as firms that will lead to the abolition of the capitalist mode of production "within the capitalist mode of production itself" and further on, he also argues: "Capitalist joint-stock companies as much as cooperative factories should be viewed as transition forms from the capitalist mode of production to the associated one, simply that in one case the opposition is abolished in a negative way, and in the other in a positive way" (Marx 1894, pp. 571–72).

One of the reasons why Marx forcefully endorsed the introduction of cooperatives and the abolition of hired labour even in a system remaining purely mercantile in nature is that (from the perspective of a critic of capitalism) producer cooperatives realise such a basic component of political democracy as economic democracy. Indeed, Marx, Marxists and other critics of the existing social order concordantly rate political democracy as merely formal when power remains firmly in the hands of capitalists, i.e., in other words, when capital is still the economic power holding everything in its sway.[4]

Further reflections on producer cooperatives as a new production mode

As the idea that a system of cooperatives realises socialism was forcefully endorsed, among others, by Korsch (1922) and Max Adler (1919), but called into question by a wealth of other authors, it is worth delving deeper into the issue.

It is widely assumed that the roots of democratic firm control do not lie in Marxism. Suffice it to mention that the French trade union organisation which endorses self-management, C.F.D.T., forcefully denies its Marxist affiliation (see Rosanvallon 1976).[5]

This may explain why many Marxist authors challenge the view that the transfer of firm management powers from capitalists to workers would amount to a revolution proper. According to Sweezy, for instance, to assume that a free market system and firms not run by capitalists makes up a socialist order is to mistake legal relations for production relations, because a system where firms are run by groups of workers maximising profits by manufacturing goods and placing them on the market is a very near proxy for capitalistic production relations (see Sweezy 1968).

Sweezy's argument resonates in those of Althusser and Mészàros. Specifically, the former maintained that producer cooperatives are part of the capitalistic production mode and may prefigure a socialist production mode only in the minds of utopians or opportunists, while the latter argued that "capital is a metabolic system, a socio-economic metabolic system of control. You can overthrow the capitalist, but the factory system remains, the division of labour remains, nothing has changed in the metabolic function of society. The only way to evade the control of capital is to do away with it" (Mészàros 1995, p. 981; see, also, *inter alia*, Webb 1891, Weber 1918, pp. 171–74, Gibson-Graham 2003 and the other authors cited in the note).

Both of these comments miss the point. Within Marx's dialectical or relational approach, capital ceases to exist as soon as hired labour is suppressed, or, put differently, the moment when the relation between capital and labour is reversed (Ollman 2003, p. 26). And as capital entails of necessity the existence of the capitalist, the abolition of hired labour will result in the abolition of capitalism as a matter of course.

Clues for a better understanding of this point may come from the distinction between the two different types of cooperative firms, the LMF and the WMF. In modern producer cooperative theory (which defines capital consistently with our approach, i.e. as the bulk of production means), it is the so-called LMF cooperatives that reverse the existing capital-labour relation. Indeed, whereas in capitalistic systems it is the owners of capital that hire workers (either directly or through managers in their service), pay them a fixed income and appropriate the surplus, in LMF-type cooperatives it is the workers running their own firms that borrow capital, pay it a fixed income (interest) and appropriate the surplus themselves.

In other words, there are but two antithetical options: capital goods are either owned or not owned by capitalists; in the former case, the system concerned is capitalism; in the latter case, when firms are run by workers (and are the LMF type), the system is non-capitalistic by definition and reverses the capital-labour relation. And the change in the production mode entailed in this process triggers a revolution real and proper.

In Marx's approach, the reversal of the capitalistic capital-labour relation triggers a real and proper revolution because it entails changing actual production relations, instead of legal forms only. The moment we accept Marx's claim that the principal contradiction in capitalism is the capital-labour opposition, it quite naturally follows that the reversal of the respective roles of capital and labour triggers a radical change in the existing production mode which unquestionably amounts to a revolution (see Jossa 2012a and 2012b).

Marx held that those controlling production are also in control of men's lives in consequence of the ownership of the tools allowing them to pursue whatsoever aims they may have in mind; and this argument goes to reinforce the idea that revolution is to be understood as the handover of production means from capitalists to workers and the concomitant disempowerment of capital.

The potential of a system of producer cooperatives to spark off a socialist revolution is also called into question by those, including Pannekoek and Lukàcs, who distinguish between revolutionaries and revisionists based on whether they advocate the overthrow of the state or look upon it as a neutral institution. From our perspective, instead, the idea that revolution comes down to changing the existing production mode brings the conclusion that a system of producer cooperatives reversing the capital-labour relation does amount to a revolution even though the State is not overthrown.

Views to the contrary

A point of the Marxist line of reasoning which we hold to conflict with our approach to the transition is his view of the State as the 'lobbying group' of the bourgeoisie. From our perspective, however, this description reflects a fairly uncritical approach dating back to Kautskian Marxist orthodoxy, and this is why, far from presenting the State as a tool subservient to either the aims of capitalists or those of workers, we prefer to describe it as a system which simultaneously offers capitalists sufficient freedom of action and allows workers elbow room for gaining strength and, possibly, seizing power.

An additional point that may help us outline the present status of the capital-ism-versus-socialism debate is Elster and Moene's claim that an inferior mode of production may be stable and a superior one instable (see Elster & Moene 1989, p. 9). Let us assume – these authors argue – that the majority of the population should be in favour of a system of democratic firms on the assumption of its considerable advantages over capitalism, but that democratic firms should prove to be less efficient for some reason (e.g. financing difficulties). Under such circumstances – they argue – individual workers are likely to refuse to move to self-managed businesses and, hence, to impede the establishment of the superior production system. In the opinion of Elster and Moene, this is a case where the stability of the inferior mode of production is an obstacle to the establishment of a superior mode.

On closer analysis, Elster and Moene's scenario is objectionable for two reasons. Firstly, from a Marxist viewpoint a 'superior' mode of production is not one supported by the greater part of the population, but one with a potential for higher productivity and efficiency levels. Secondly, Elster and Moene fail to distinguish between the case where the majority pressing for the superior mode has a correct appreciation of all the implications of the issue and the case where it simply does not know that there exists a superior mode of production which, if well organised, might outperform the inferior one. To complete their scenario, let us assume that democratic firms operating in a capitalistic system are inefficient as long as they are outnumbered by capitalistic firms, but that the moment they gain the upper hand and outnumber capitalistic firms they will outdo all the others in terms of efficiency since their operating context has been adjusted to their needs. Would the inferior system be as stable as Elster and Moene hold it to be?

It is clear that workers who are aware that the few democratic firms in existence are inefficient will hardly think of creating new ones and that the end result would consequently be the retention of the inferior mode. At this point, we may ask ourselves if the community would be in a position to take action, for instance to pass majority resolutions to the effect of translating into action one of the above-mentioned transition scenarios. In our opinion, this question might be answered in the affirmative; but advocates of historical materialism might argue that the transition would not be implemented because the capitalist class controlling the media might impede the circulation of the relevant ideas and prevent the majority of the population from gaining an awareness of the superiority of a democratic firm system over capitalism. As we have just suggested, however, the idea that the capitalistic State is necessarily a class State is unacceptable even to many Marxists.

Another problem requiring discussion is this: who is likely to be the agent of the revolution we are suggesting? And how can the necessary parliamentary majority be secured? There is no denying that following the eradication of the misery of the proletarian class in developed capitalistic countries the issue of class consciousness has become an even more urgent one.[6]

Today, the working class no longer represents the negation of the existing order (Marcuse 1970);[7] and it is well known that in his convincing theorisation of *One-Dimensional Man* (1964) Marcuse depicted contemporary society as one where the concentration of economic and political power had reached an all-time high, where the individual was conditioned by public opinion at every stage of his/her existence and where public opinion was in turn shaped by existing monopolies. Does this mean that in due time a majority of the population will resolve to turn formal into full democracy by putting into practice one of the above-described scenarios and disempowering capital once and for all? As we have argued, there is a material prospect that this will happen.

The demise of capitalism

The Italian philosopher Emanuele Severino has recently argued that processes currently under way point to the impending death of capitalism. In the present age of brisk technological growth, he argues, capitalism is on the wane because the need to obey the imperatives of technology is obliging business enterprises to deflect from profit maximisation as their one-time overriding goal. According to Severino (2012, p. 94), "within a logic which postulates goals and means (and has been prevailing over the entire course of human history), there is little doubt (though the consequence is less dominant than the starting assumption) that whenever an action – in this case the capitalistic mode of operation – is made to deflect from its original goal and to pursue a different one, this same logic determines that the action itself will turn into something different in content, rhythm, intensity, relevance and configuration."

On page 23 in the same book, Severino clarifies that techno-scientific considerations and needs are ever more often taking precedence over those typifying capitalistic policies. As a result, he argues, it is not the inherent contradictions of capitalism highlighted by Marxists that are hastening this decline, but the gradual marginalisation of the pure capitalistic system by the techno-economic system. In his estimation, every human action is characterised by the goal it is designed to achieve. The goal is the master, and no one can serve two masters. It is the goal that makes an action what it is, and an action that is assigned a different goal changes into a different action. The individual's subjective aim is one thing – he continues – and the objective aim of the apparatus is another; and whenever the objective aim takes precedence over the subjective aim, it is technology that gains the upper hand to the detriment of capitalism (*op. cit.*, pp. 48–49). When technology is turned from a tool into a goal, he argues, "the result is a reversal of roles, in terms that part of the available tools are destroyed for the sake of increasing the global sway of the apparatus, viz., of the ability to devise fresh goals" (*op. cit.*, p. 105). Hence – he continues (p. 66) – capitalism enters a stage of decline when, in an effort to tackle head-on confrontations between workers and employers or fend off competition from other nations, it starts using the technological means under the direction of modern science.

On closer analysis, the decline of the system is expedited by the capitalistic mode of action itself "since business enterprises engaged in the competitive struggle make ever greater reliance on the latest technological breakthroughs and capitalists stop working towards profit maximisation as their ultimate goal and end up by magnifying the power of technology" (p. 35). In the end, the importance of a goal such as private profit maximisation is progressively eroded and eclipsed. Inasmuch as it is true that States (betraying their original mission) are ever more deeply involved in technology, they, too, will cease being masters of the techno-scientific apparatus and will become its servants (p. 63).

Further on (p. 77), Severino adds: "the true foundation of modern science is the rejection of the finalistic principle of nature." However, within the framework of a scientific approach to nature it is appropriate to argue that the tendency of men to assign goals to natural processes results in changing them into tools, i.e. something different from what they originally were. Despite human intervention, though, it lies in the nature of things that those processes invariably have a beginning and an end.

Capitalists – he argues (p. 73) – simultaneously further and employ technology, i.e. a tool which is designed to reduce scarcity and draws legitimisation from this ultimate goal.

For my part, I daresay that no economist will be prepared to subscribe to Severino's line of argument. Although it is evident that technology is achieving a burgeoning role in economic affairs, and that capitalism is ever more thoroughly dependent on it, it remains that capitalists make use of technology in an effort to achieve their prime aim, which is and remains profit maximisation. As a result, Severino's argument that the growing sway of technology is preventing business enterprises from pursuing profit maximisation is beside the point. The pursuit of profit maximisation by enterprises is still the main characteristic of capitalism.

The situation would be radically different if capitalistic businesses were replaced with a cooperative system of firms setting out to maximise, not profit, but the well-being and satisfaction of the majority of the workers making all the relevant decisions.

On page 68 of his book, Severino adds that capitalism "is its own enemy for two reasons: firstly, because it strives to destroy its own mainstay, competition, and, secondly, because *in essence*, due to its will to pursue profit through the use of technology, *it wages war against itself."* On closer analysis, the claim that the tendency of companies to form monopolies conflicts with the essence of capitalism has nowhere been raised and business enterprises keep employing technology for their own ends without undergoing a change of nature. Further on (pp. 61–62), Severino argues that the sole, specific and ultimate object of a business enterprise is to maximise profits, but that capitalism is obliged to deflect from this goal. Indeed, if the opponents of capitalism – for instance China or Islamic fundamentalists – should succeed in developing technological tools more efficiently and Western capitalists should suffer their adversaries to gain the upper hand, capitalistic countries would be doomed to extinction unless, in an effort to fend off this danger and gain supremacy, they resolved to drop the private profit maximisation goal. In point of fact, Severino's line of reasoning boils down to arguing that *governments* wishing to leverage business firms may make decisions, for instance, tax increases, that may jeopardise, if not altogether reduce, corporate bottom-line results. In no way – let this repeated – does it demonstrate that companies have stopped pursuing profit maximisation as their ultimate goal. And the distinctive characteristic of capitalism is and remains corporate business profit maximisation. "Even today" – Severino continues (p. 66) – "a great many economists hold that there is no economically relevant *difference* between building cars for the (sole) purpose of boosting private profit and building them for the (sole) purpose of providing jobs to workers (as Sylos Labini pointed out to me some time ago)." As a matter of fact, we do not know of automotive works building cars for the sole purpose of providing employment opportunities and where the State should resolve to establish publicly run motor car companies in an effort to create new jobs, this would not mark an end to capitalism unless such businesses were found to prevail in both quantitative and qualitative terms – which is definitely not the case today.

Concluding, although I do not deny that technology helps capitalistic countries combat scarcity, or that capitalism would cease to exist if the scarcity problem were finally brought to a satisfactory solution, I wish to emphasise that there is hardly an economist who is not fully aware that the scarcity problem will never be solved once and for all.

Sweezy, the proletariat and revolution

In a fine 1967 paper reviewing Marx's theory of revolution, Sweezy first expressed a number of ideas which in later years proved highly influential. The core assumption behind Sweezy's approach is the equation of the socialist revolution with the replacement of capitalism with central planning and is consequently antithetical to the line of argument adopted in this book.

In the opening section, Sweezy raises the question whether Marx's description of the proletariat as the principal agent of the socialist revolution is still valid today.

To answer this query, he starts out from the two phases of capitalism that Engels identified in the preface to the first complete English edition of the first volume of *Capital*, i.e. the distinction (rated as negligible by many Marxists) between the period of manufacture proper (which started with the introduction of Wyatt's first spinning machine in 1753) and the period of modern machine-based industry.

In the former period, he argues, technology was conservative in character and proletarians were no revolutionaries. The reason why Sweezy describes early technological developments as 'conservative' is that the new devices used were mostly extensions and adaptations of older handicraft working processes making a possibly rational use of existing techniques. The most innovative move, he argues, was increasing specialisation and labour productivity by gathering a great many craftsmen in a single workshop. In the estimation of Sweezy, this move was an innovation, rather than an invention, and inventions proper, though not entirely absent, were few indeed. The proletariat is described as non-revolutionary because it lacked class consciousness.

This state of affairs – Sweezy remarks – changed radically upon the advent of machinery. At that stage, technological progress was no longer brought about by ingenious individual workers or inventors, but by scientific research, and the effect of this was that the costly and time-consuming training programmes designed to develop the skills of craftsmen became redundant. Opening the way to the entry of women and children into the labour market, this produced a sky-rocketing surge in labour supply exactly at a stage when the rapid introduction of ever more new machinery was causing a rapid decline in demand. Wages tumbled down, while work paces started escalating (in order to keep pace with the growing speed of machinery) and labour became ever more dependent on capital. By the same token, however, the political power of the proletariat increased because "the nature of work in the modern factory requires the organization and disciplining of the workers, thereby preparing them for organized and disciplined action in other fields" (Sweezy 1967, p. 323). This prompts the conclusion that proletarians are turned into revolutionaries in consequence of poor standards of living, low wages and severe labour exploitation.

Yet – Sweezy argues further on – as revolution is often impeded by objective circumstances, here is an issue on which Marx failed to provide focus: will the proletariat retain its revolutionary spirit in situations where objective obstacles stand in the way of a revolution? To answer this question, Sweezy preliminarily remarks that the use of technology reduces the size of the industrial labour force and leads to generalised increases in worker incomes. Whereas this process does not turn workers into non-revolutionaries as a matter of course, he concludes, it is a fact that when workers become a minority, "their attitudes and ideology are not likely to be totally different from those of the non-revolutionary majority of the working class which surround them" (*op. cit.*, p. 328). Does this mean that today there are no revolutionary agents left?

Sweezy's answer is that within the capitalistic world system all the countries that proved able to complete their industrialisation process invariably took to exploiting less developed nations and thereby helped change the agricultural and industrial workers of the exploited countries into revolutionaries. In support of this contention he mentions the revolutions in Vietnam, China and Cuba.

Sweezy's conclusion is that the long-term effects of the industrial revolution do not substantially depart from its immediate effects: both of them change revolutionary agents in full keeping with Marx's claim that capitalism produces its own grave-diggers.

The question is: is Sweezy's analysis convincing?

In point of fact, it was accepted for many years running since its starting assumption was endorsed by most Marxists. Now that the socialism-central planning equation has been proved wrong by the collapse of the Soviet Union, the correct opinion is that socialism is tantamount to the democratic management of firms. And anyone holding this view can be said to come closer than Sweezy to Marx's original approach since he will also assume that revolution will break out in one of the more industrialised countries.

Hence the records of events in the USSR and in China are ultimately evidence of the truth of the following proposition: any revolutionary order that is established in a less developed country is found to be far from genuinely socialist and will lead up to a return to capitalism at some point in time.

Conclusion

Time and again, Marx and Engels argued the case for a transitional period to communism during which workers would be managing firms themselves. Considering the intrinsic advantages of self-management, however, such a system would be a major step forward on the road towards progress and democracy even if we should abstract from the opinions of these great classics.

Starting from these considerations, two main queries were raised in this chapter: (a) whether a form of market socialism would be consistent with Marx and Engels's thought; and (b) whether the transition to a new social order is possible. The basic premise for our line of reasoning is the awareness that Marx and Engels, far from theorising a sudden bound to communism, made it clear that the transition from one production mode to another was to be a long-term process.

Notes

1 In Marx's approach, in addition to challenging the capitalistic social order, workers perform a positive role: they work towards self-organising themselves in manners recalling those suggested in Flora Tristan's *L'Union Ouvrière*, a book which is mentioned by Engels in *The Holy Family* (1844, pp. 21–31) and which Marx himself had certainly read (see Massari 1974, pp. 82–83).
2 The *Inaugural Address* of 1864 has been described as the rough draft of a political economy of labour (see Balibar 1993). From Lichtheim (1965, pp. 114–59) we learn that Marx defined a nationwide system of producer cooperatives created with State de aid as basically socialist in nature despite the absence of such an essential component as the socialisations of means of production (a goal whose inclusion in the programme of the International would have been strongly opposed by the bulk of French delegates).
3 Numerous Marxist authors are agreed that this new mode of production will be a direct offshoot of capitalism. Among them, Offe points to a structural mismatch, within capitalist society, between new sub-systems and structural elements which are functionally at odds with the logic of capital valorisation (see Offe 1972a, chap. 3).

4 Although these passages bear witness to Marx's concern with cooperatives, several commentators have argued that the works from which they are taken are just descriptive in nature and do not reveal Marx's overall evaluation of the real potential of cooperation (see, for example, Lowit 1962, p. 79). Mellor (in Mellor, Hannah & Stirling 1988, p. 70) has emphasised Marx's ambivalence about cooperatives and few authors hold that Marx thought of a system of cooperative firms as the materialisation of socialism.

5 Similarly, Sylos Labini stands firm on the claim that democratic firm management models have little in common with Marxism (see Sylos Labini 2006).

6 The partial autonomy of political action implied in Gramsci's notion of hegemony doubtless makes the role of the working class less central and confers greater weight on the issue of alliances (see Forgacs 1995, pp. 66–67).
Clues for the identification of the agent of revolution may come from Ernst Bloch's pregnant reflection that hope, along with a project and a time horizon for its implementation is the strongest and by far the best reality we can conceive of (Bloch 1959b, p. 59). On this point, see, also, Genovese (2007).

7 Hobsbawm (1982, pp. 27–28) argued that while Marxism had its early social roots principally, if not exclusively, in movements and parties of manual workers, from the 1950s onwards it had especially caught on amongst intellectuals.

9   Self-driven economic growth and Darwinism

Introduction

One answer to the question raised in the previous chapter is probably the widely shared belief, in today's economic science, that anything of benefit to the community will come about unaided at some point in time and that anything failing to assert itself in its own right can barely be in the interests of society as a whole. Quite obviously this is the opinion of liberalists and advocates of 'Social Darwinism' (see, *inter alia*, Nozick 1974, pp. 314–17, Jensen & Meckling 1979, p. 473, Williamson 1975, 1980, p. 35 and 1985, pp. 265–68) or of authors such as Hansmann, who analyse social evolution by reference to the 'survivor-ship test' (see Hansmann 1996); but it is fair to say that a less extreme version of this view is widely shared even by economists who do not think of themselves as laissez-faire liberalists.[1] An important preliminary observation is that the central proposition behind the phrase 'survival of the fittest' is that the survivors are those best adapted to a given environment under the circumstances prevailing from time to time (see Hodgson 1996, p. 100).

Consequently, it seems appropriate to attempt a critical evaluation of the claim that modern economic theorists have come up with a considerable number of explanations for the failure of economic democracy to assert itself despite its considerable potential for adding to the well-being of the citizens at large.

A different way to approach this issue is to shed light on links between reformism and revolution. An interesting analysis by a Russian economist writing in the early years of the twentieth century, Peter Struve, will help us state the terms of the problem correctly.[2]

Darwin in the estimation of Marx and Engels

To begin with, let us clarify what Marx and Engels thought of Darwinism.

As for Marx, although he admired Darwin's work to the point of considering the possibility to dedicate *Capital* to him, he was convinced that Darwinism had no bearing on historical and political investigation. The same is true of Engels.

The first to bring up the matter of Darwinism was Engels in a letter to Marx dated 12 December 1859: "Darwin, by the way, whom I'm just reading now, is absolutely splendid. There was one aspect of teleology that had not yet been demolished, and that has now been done. Never before has so grandiose an attempt been made to demonstrate historical evolution in nature, and certainly never to such a good effect. One does, of course, have to put up with the crude English method."

One year later, comparable ideas were expressed in a letter written by Marx to Engels on 19 December (Marx 1860): "during the past four weeks I have read all manner of things. *Inter alia* Darwin's book on *Natural selection*. Although developed in the crude English fashion, this is the book which, in the field of natural history, provides the basis for our views."

In January 1861 Marx wrote to Lassalle (Marx 1861, p. 578): "Darwin's book is very significant, and I like it as a scientific-natural basis for the historic struggle of classes. Of course, one has to put up with the rough English manner of its development. In spite of all its shortcomings, it has for the first time dealt a death blow to the 'teleology' of natural science. Furthermore, its rational sense has been empirically explained."

Lastly, let us report a passage from the letter that Marx wrote to Engels on 7 December 1867 (Marx 1867b, p. 114): if one "demonstrates that the present society, economically considered, is pregnant with a new higher form, he is only showing, in the social context, the same gradual process of evolution that Darwin has demonstrated in natural history."

Based on these excerpts, the parallel between Marx's approach to the study of society and Darwin's theory of biological evolution is the acknowledgement that Darwin's evolutionism provides a biological support to Marx's theory of class struggle and controverts the 'teleological' interpretation of nature founded on the idea that the world originated from a divine act of creation.[3] In place of the long-held belief that the stupefying functionality of organs of the human body such as an eye could only be accounted for by assuming the intervention of a Supreme Creator, the Darwinian principle of the survival of the fittest offers an alternative explanation for the perfection of our world.

This leads us to ask ourselves if Schumpeter was right when he argued that while "Marx may have welcomed the emergence of Darwinian evolutionism," it is a fact that his approach "had nothing whatever to do with it, and neither lends support to the other" (see Schumpeter 1954, p. 445).

Although Schumpeter sees Darwin's evolutionism and Marx's vision of history as integral parts of a broader stream of thought that shaped a whole era, he contends that Marx and Darwin did not mutually influence each other. But there is more to this. In the opinion of Ureña, Schumpeter's view is to be shared because Marx's approach differs greatly from Darwinism. Whereas Marx likened the conduct of humans under capitalism to the behaviour prevailing in the animal kingdom, he also thought that they would drop their bestial attitudes in the pacified world that was to emerge from the communist revolution. This is confirmed by Marx's statement (1861, p. 578; see, also, Marx 1869, vol. 32, p. 592) that based on his analysis of the struggle for life in English society (described as "the competition of all with all, *bellum omnium contra omnes*"), Darwin made the discovery that the struggle for life was "the dominating law of animal and plant life" and held this to be "a decisive reason for human society never attaining emancipation from its bestial essence."[4]

Marxism, however, is wrong if it argues than under communism humankind will be free of its bestial essence. In the light of Dawkins's well-known argument that human beings are conditioned by selfish genes which generate self-love (see Dawkins 1992), socialism and communism can be expected to damp down, but not to eradicate egoism altogether; therefore, concerning the *bellum omnium contra omnes*, it is Darwin, rather than Marx, that is right.

All the same, although no one has so far been able to provide evidence that humankind is in a position to wrest itself free from its bestial essence, there are reasons to endorse Marx's view that socialism has a potential for greatly improving human nature.[5] At any rate, an in-depth analysis of this point lies outside the scope of this book, which is mainly concerned with establishing whether socialism is likely to assert itself spontaneously at some point in time.

As a result, bearing in mind Marx's own critique of Darwinism we cannot but conclude, in full agreement with Schumpeter, that Marx, though admiring Darwin for the light he shed on English society in the nineteenth century and the true essence of capitalism, was in no way influenced by his work and that Darwinism is consequently of no help in correctly understanding socialism.

Social evolution in Struve's approach

As mentioned above, a contribution by Struve (1899) may help us state the terms of the subject of this chapter.

The following instance of social evolution may illustrate Struve's line of reasoning. In an early capitalistic society, it may be assumed that all restaurants are run by capitalists and that it is these alone that decide what has to be produced and what kind of target customers are to be catered for. As the cooks and waiters working in these restaurants are fairly uneducated, they have to stick to the orders of their masters and do nothing on their own initiative. In due time, however, these cooks or waiters – as also the rest of the workers – are likely to set aside some savings, educate themselves and, hence, acquire the ability to see to their tasks autonomously. By degrees, they are likely to be involved in some of the owners' decision-making processes; for instance, they may be asked to make suggestions on materials to be purchased, on which dishes are to be served and the way they are to be prepared or how the restaurant itself should be furnished and arranged. As time drags on, they will inevitably conceive a desire to shed their status as hired workers and become self-employed entrepreneurs running a restaurant of their own,[6] and this desire will start a slow – as it were 'evolutionist' – advancement from the capitalistic to the socialist restaurant management mode. The process just described is in keeping with the general rule governing social evolution: the transition from capitalism to socialism is a stepwise, but incessant process comparable to the dynamic of natural phenomena.[7]

Inasmuch as it is true the above-reported sample case reflects the general rule of social evolution (as Struve contends), the new firm management mode will assert itself by degrees. According as hired workers manage to raise their educational levels and organise themselves effectively, they will also learn how to force through parliament a number of reforms that will put an end to their subjection to a master and enable them to take over the management of firms. The precondition for this to happen is, obviously, a parliamentary majority of representatives of the working class.

Although Struve does not equate socialism with worker management of firms, his approach will appear clearer and more convincing if we think of socialism in the manner suggested in this chapter, that is to say as a system in which the right to appropriate the surplus earned by a firm is allowed to workers. Let us repeat that this process is likely to come about in piecemeal fashion. The first step might be a small measure of profit sharing to be raised at subsequent steps, whereas the final leap, the 'expropriation of the expropriators' and the resulting implementation of self-management, would be the crowning achievement.

From Struve's perspective, change is an evolutionary process and social relationships evolve through successive adjustments to the existing productive forces. As a result, to speak of revolution would hardly make any sense.[8] In Struve's approach, the employer-employee relations connoting production relations in capitalism are directly shaped by the legal mechanisms in force from time to time and will consequently change in sync with the dynamic of productive forces, the economic phenomenon *par excellence*. In his opinion, this points up an error in Marx's revolutionary conception and orthodox Marxism. In Marx's approach, productive forces are looked upon as an economic factor, as the basis of social relations, and it is production relations that are the distinctively legal phenomenon; production forces undergo constant change and, while the social essence of production activities becomes more and more pronounced in proportion to rises in the average size of firms, production relations do not change. It is the escalation of the resulting tensions between economics and law, base and superstructure – he holds – that will inevitably spark off revolution. In contrast, Struve denies that social movements may come in two different forms, of which one evolves in full harmony with the existing social order, while the other aims to overthrow the established social order. In his opinion, "the only driving force behind the evolution of society is continual adjustment of laws in force to the socio-economic phenomena under way" (Struve 1899, p. 126).[9]

In Struve's thinking, the belief that production relations are brought into line with the existing production forces in piecemeal fashion does not descend from the idea of economics as the cause and legal relations as the effect, but rather from the fact that economic and legal relations are so closely interrelated in terms of form and content that it is simply impossible to conceive of the former independently of the latter.

Spontaneous change and social reform, he holds, combine in cooling off class antagonism since the victories won by the proletariat in society lead to the stepwise, though unstoppable establishment of socialism.[10] More often than not – he argues – leaps forward in society are made by breaking resistance gradually, without recourse to violence, rather than by dismantling exacerbated antagonisms through revolution (*op. cit.*, p. 128).

In Struve's approach, socialism is bound to become a reality as a matter of course because it is indissolubly linked to capitalism. It is a necessary development, he writes, which is driven on by the steady evolution of economic phenomena and the way they are legally regulated under capitalism. Where socialism, a real power, should not arise right within the existing order, that is to say within capitalism, he continues, we would have to conclude that it simply cannot exist in any form.

Specifically, he thinks of the transition to socialism as the inevitable effect of the growing power of the proletariat. As he puts it, anyone denying the gradual socialisation of capitalistic society must necessarily think of economic and political struggle as nothing but an intellectual sport which is designed to while away the time separating us from the all-out blow, namely social revolution proper and of the day-by-day confrontation between inimical classes as a preparatory process of sorts, devoid of any other content or living link with real life. In fact, the truth is that class struggle is the tool for and reflection of the growing power position of the proletariat. The idea of a stepwise socialisation of society is doubtless at odds with the belief that the transition from capitalism to socialism will be sparked off by a social revolution caused by escalating class antagonisms. The precondition for socialisation is cooling down and, finally, wiping out class antagonisms (*op. cit.*, pp. 143–44). From Struve's perspective, therefore, social evolution is a revolutionary process proper and this means that socialist reformism is, by its very nature, a revolutionary process: the phrase 'social revolution' is just a different way of designating the concept of social evolution.[11]

At this point, we may ask ourselves whether the transition to socialism requires of necessity the advent of the proletariat to power. The rise of the proletariat to political power, Struve writes, "is both the result and a sign of social upheaval.... To contend that the acquisition of law-making authority and the power to amend the legal system arise at different stages is simply absurd" (*op. cit.*, p. 137).

On closer analysis, Struve's line of reasoning is only partly convincing. The idea that reform and revolution are different ways of describing one and the same thing can barely be endorsed. Reforms of the welfare state, for instance, far from advancing socialism, strengthen capitalism by making it more acceptable, while the launch of profit-sharing schemes or the granting of co-determination rights to workers are designed to change the prevailing mode of production. In contrast, the contention that reform and revolution are not always antithetical is one we are prepared to endorse.

In other words, the weak point of Struve's approach is his failure to come to terms with such a crucial point of Marxian theory as 'modes of production' (see Jossa 2012b). In point of fact, there is no such thing as an intrinsically revolutionary reform. For a reform to be categorised as such it has to lead to a partial or total change in the current mode of production. All the same, Struve's approach is interesting because it emphasises the need for an evolutionary road to the establishment of socialism.[12]

Reflections on Social Darwinism

Struve is a theoretician of Social Darwinism, a discipline which has not gone unchallenged and will now be examined in the light of Marx's remarks on Darwin reported in a previous section.

Today, the extension of Darwin's approach to economics is advocated by a great many evolutionist theorists, including Veblen (see, e.g., Hamilton 1999, pp. 25–28). One point of Darwinism on which any economist can be expected to agree is the rejection of the teleological approach to history (see De Gregory 2003, pp. 19–20, and the works of Marx cited above), but the extension of the notion of natural selection to economic processes is objectionable for methodological reasons also, that is to say because of its markedly positivistic rationale. From Gramsci's (and Benedetto Croce's) perspective, this is a shortcoming of sociology at large. As Gramsci puts it, "Sociology represented an attempt to create a method for subordinating historical-political science to an existing philosophical system, namely evolutionistic positivism … an effort to describe and classify historical and political facts in accordance with the logic of natural sciences" (Gramsci 1964b, p. 125).

The idea that economic life is governed by natural selection is also rejected by Commons, who describes economic phenomena as the result of an artificially induced, not natural selection process (see Commons 1924, pp. 376 and 1934, pp. 636 and 657–58). In point of fact, several authors have emphasised that Darwin did envisage a measure of intentionality in the selection process, though he made it absolutely clear that the intentions, where any, had to be explained (see Copeland 1931 and 1936, pp. 343–44).

As a result, Commons's critique of Social Darwinism is to be unreservedly endorsed.[13] The rationale behind this critique is the persuasion that socio-economic and biological evolution are governed by different mechanisms.[14] In either case, evolution leads to the success of the strongest (and in economic selection processes the strongest are usually the most efficient players), but economic events are, at the same time, thoroughly shaped by issues associated with power; and organised forces are able to inhibit the progress of any firm, however efficient.[15] As worded above, this objection is not aimed at Darwinism as such – the principle of the survival of the fittest – but at a specific form of Social Darwinism which equates efficiency with economic power and holds that the economic organisations that will eventually prevail are surely those which are most efficient.

Indeed, there are solid reasons for arguing that economic selection mechanisms differ from those governing natural selection.[16] In economic matters to say that the strongest tend to prevail is just a tautology and, as such, will barely add much to our understanding. Things would stand differently if it were possible to say, as Social Darwinists mistakenly do, that in economic matters it is the best organisations that tend to gain the upper hand.[17]

The idea that the ultimate goal of the historical process is emancipating humankind to the full has been challenged by many authors. Among these, Colletti (in a 1977 interview printed in Colletti 1979) and Hodgson (2000, pp. 302–05) have concordantly highlighted in Marx a telelogical, i.e. finalistic strain which they categorise as strongly objectionable. In actual fact, this criticism is beside the point and let us re-emphasise that Engels and Marx unequivocally denied that teleology had a place in their approach to history. Although he was firmly persuaded that humankind would come to master the environment ever more effectively, Marx never thought of the future as a chain of piecemeal day-by-day gains in freedom. He rather held that the ultimate effect of the dynamic of productive forces under capitalism would be a growing subjection of workers to the oppressive power of capital.

Timing the socialist revolution that Marx had in mind is anything but easy. As is well known, Engels and Marx thought that the times were ripe and that revolution was at hand, but Henderson (1977, p. 21) points out that "Engels waited for the fulfilment of his gloomy prophecy" for years, and that "for years he waited in vain." Today, following the failure of the revolutions in Eastern European countries, there are some who doubt that a socialist revolution will ever materialise and, at any rate, there is no way of predicting whether it will be a short- or long-term process.

Corporate governance and economic democracy

In addition to inimical ideologies and vested interests, there are numerous other forces that tend to oppose a small and gradual transition from capitalism to economic democracy.

First and foremost, the legal framework within which economic actors operate is structured in manners apt to further the growth and permanence of capitalism. As Marxism, distinguishing between the base, i.e. the economic structure of society, and the legal, political and other aspects of society that constitute the so-called superstructure, assumes the latter to be conditioned by the former, this point is a mainstay of Marxist thought,[18] and quite a lot of non-Marxist economists are prepared to subscribe to this view. Quite obviously, laws and institutions tailored to the needs of capitalistic businesses are ill suited to support the growth of democratic firms and have been fleshed out in a centuries-long process of gradual adjustment to the requirements of societies formed of capitalistic businesses, rather than democratic firms. A great many authors (including Putterman 1982 and 1984, Hodgson 1993, pp. 91–93 and Gunn 2000, pp. 451–55) have argued that within a different context characterised by different institutions democratic firms would probably outnumber capitalistic businesses. In other words, the typical economic growth pattern of those societies ensures (in the fashion of a path-dependence process) that those systems that have gained the upper hand there for some reason will in turn breed an environment and institutions capable of perpetuating them to the detriment of any competing systems (see Arthur 1989, North 1990 and Pagano 1991a and 1991b).[19]

In an analysis of the cooperative movement, a well-known law expert has argued that throughout this century, most legislatures have been pursuing a sophisticated design: instead of obstructing the growth of the cooperative movement openly, they have sought means of 'sabotaging' it from within. Specifically, they have worked towards transferring the capitalistic logic of profit to cooperatives on the assumption that it would be comparatively easy to win over their members to this logic (Galgano 1974, p. 163).

One aspect of this issue is the theory which explains that firm control is closely linked to asset specificity and emphasises the tendency of economic systems to self-perpetuate themselves. The theorists concerned hold that business firms arise when a group of producers uses team-specific resources, i.e. resources which would suffer a decline in value if they were moved to a different team. From this basic idea they deduce that control is usually vested in the most significant firm-specific factor. In capitalistic systems, this factor is usually capital.

At this point, one may wonder if – in a vicious circle of sorts – there is a mechanism capable of ensuring that democratic firms will be mainly connoted by labour just as capitalistic businesses are mainly connoted by capital.

It is a well-known fact that an ownership title vests in the owner the right to prohibit third parties from using his property, and although it is inappropriate to speak of the ownership of a corporation (see Ellerman 1990 and 1992), it cannot be ruled out that the factor resolving to take over the control of a firm may be doing so in an effort to avoid being ousted from it. In the awareness than he can no longer be ousted from the firm, the individual who has taken over control will probably make increasing amounts of investments in 'human capital' and thereby become ever more specific to the firm in which he operates.

In other words, the relation between the ownership title in resources and the specifics of such resources can be said to evolve in either direction. Marx held relations of production and ownership rights to be determined by the level of growth of the productive forces, but he also emphasised the opposite causal link when he demonstrated that the effect of capitalistic ownership relations is to multiply obsessively repetitive jobs that can do without specialised skills.

A causality link between ownership rights and the characteristics of the resources used has recently been emphasised by some radical economists who have reversed the links highlighted by neo-institutionalists. From the starting assumption that control is either vested in firm-specific resources or in resources that are difficult to monitor, they have deduced that most of the workers employed in capitalistic businesses are both 'easily monitored' and 'non-firm-specific' since the owners of such businesses select them with this end in mind and will barely think of adding to the qualifications of workers not bound to their firms by per-manent ties. As is well known, an investor in human capital is not entitled to appropriate the future incomes of the staff members he has hired. This means that a firm investing in staff qualification programmes is at risk of wasting resources on workers who are free to leave the firm after they have completed their train-ing programmes. In other words, from the perspective of radical theorists, dif-ficult control of resources and their greater or lesser specificity are the effects, not the cause, of the existing structure of property rights (see Braverman 1974, Marglin 1974, Edwards 1979, Bowles 1985, Pagano 1991a, 1991b and Marginson 1993, pp. 149–53).

In even more general terms, it is possible to argue that growth obeys the same mechanism in democratic and capitalistic businesses: conditions favourable to their growth are more likely to arise in situations where firms of the category concerned outnumber other forms of business enterprise (see Levine & Tyson 1990).

Additional drags on the unaided growth of economic democracy

The road to economic democracy is obstructed by a number of additional obstacles. In the estimation of Meade (1972, p. 426), one of the main reasons why "we find risk-bearing capital hiring labour rather than risk-bearing labour hiring capital" is that "while property owners can spread their risks by putting small bits of their property into a large number of concerns, a worker cannot put small bits of his effort into a large number of different jobs" (see also, for example, Reich 1981, p. 198).

An additional obstacle has already been discussed above. As mentioned there, whoever has a mind to venture into business because he thinks he has the requisite qualifications will opt for the establishment of a capitalistic business because in such a firm he would retain the entire surplus and all decision-making powers. He will hardly think of setting up a cooperative firms, in which he would have to apportion powers and earnings among all the partners. Apparently a minor point, this is actually the crux of the matter. Inasmuch as it is true that managers prefer to see to their tasks in capitalistic businesses and that enterprises are set up by individuals who have developed managerial competences, it will hardly come as a surprise that cooperative firms have difficulty arising spontaneously or, whenever they do arise, are established by individuals who feel that their managerial skills come short of the level required to run a capitalistic business enterprise. From this, it follows that democratic firms will generally be set up by individuals with scant entrepreneurial skills and that few of them, where established at all, will actually prove viable.

The claim that the main drag on the successful performance of cooperatives is lack of entrepreneurial skills is also supported by additional arguments. Firstly, due to their small size and the egalitarian ideal dictating the need to minimise wage rate differences, these firms are not in a position to offer would-be managers income incentives on a par with those offered by capitalistic businesses; secondly, given the relative paucity of existing cooperatives, most managers are little, if at all, familiar with the specific circumstances under which cooperatives operate (see, also, Cornforth 1989, p. 44).

Vanek was also the first scholar to remark that self-financing cooperatives will hardly be viable enough because once they have been set up they tend to be dissolved regardless of whether or not they prove to be efficient.

The way a revolution can be followed through in practice

On several occasions, Marx and Engels made it clear that the revolution they had in mind could come about by democratic means and be enforced by a parliament. In *The Principles of Communism*, Engels emphasised that, once in power, the working class would enforce a democratic constitution, for "democracy would be quite useless to the proletariat if it were not immediately used as a means of carrying through further measures" (Engels 1847, p. 350). And many years later Engels wrote also (1891a, p. 226): "One can conceive that the old society may develop peacefully into the new one in countries where the representatives of the people concentrate all power in their hands, where, if one has the support of the majority of the people, one can do as one sees fit in a constitutional way: in democratic republics such as France and the U.S.A., in monarchies such as Britain."

Moreover, in Engels's Introduction to *The Class Struggles in France* we read: "The irony of world history turns everything upside down. We, the 'revolutionaries,' the 'overthrowers,' we are thriving far better on legal methods than on illegal methods and overthrow" (Engels 1895, p. 552).

In a number of works published in the last years of his life, Engels concerned himself with specific events in the economic and political lives of individual nations and expatiated on changes in political climate recorded over the years. As is known, the collapse of Bismarck's regime marked the eclipse of policies aimed at the outright suppression of socialist parties. Reviewing similar trends in other European nations, Engels remarked that on realising the changing scene, the socialist parties of the day found that legal methods served the interests of the working class much more effectively than the violent methods associated with insurrections could have done: "The attempt must be made to get along with the legal methods of struggle for the time being. Not only we are doing this, it is being done by all workers' parties in all countries where the workers have a certain measure of legal freedom of action, and this for the simple reason that it is the most productive method for them" (Engels 1890, p. 78).

In a polemical 1890–91 paper written in stark opposition to L. Brentano, Engels argued that the power of factory legislation and trade unions to improve the conditions of the working class (which was Brentano's contention) had been underscored by Marx and himself in a wealth of writings ranging from *The Condition of the Working Class in England* and *The Misery of Philosophy*, through *Capital* down to later ones.[20] However, he also added that this statement was to be taken with caution, since the positive effects of trade union action were confined to periods of thriving business and were bound to become erratic in times of stagnation and crisis. Moreover, he argued, neither labour legislation nor the opposition of trade unions could do away with the main obstacle to the freedom of workers: capitalistic relations (Engels 1890–91, pp. 97–98).

The most pregnant analysis of this subject is found in the Introduction to *The Class Struggles in France* written by Engels in 1895. The teachings of earlier revolutions, especially those in France in 1789 and 1830, he admitted, had exerted a strong influence on both of them, but later developments – he added – proved those approaches wrong and, moreover, the conditions under which the proletariat was expected to carry on its struggle had meanwhile undergone radical change. Each of those earlier revolutions had resulted in replacing one ruling class with another, but the ruling groups coming to power were all found to be small minorities compared to the mass of those ruled. Moreover, upon seizing power, each such minority group remodelled the state apparatus in accordance with its own needs and the majority of the governed did nothing but support that minority or, at any rate, show themselves acquiescent. In Engels's words, "if we disregard the concrete content in each case, the common form of all these revolutions was that they were minority revolutions" (Engels 1895, p. 510), and after each such minority revolution – he continued – the feelings of the masses always, and often presently so, changed from enthusiasm to utter disappointment and even despair.

From these reflections Engels drew the conviction that the times were not ripe for a socialist revolution; in fact, as a result of post-1844 developments and the introduction of universal suffrage in Germany in 1866, he had come to believe that a revolution was to be enacted by parliamentary means, through a real and proper majority resolution. From Engels's perspective, therefore, universal suffrage had laid the foundations for a new method of proletarian struggle, and from then on "the bourgeoisie and the government came to be much more afraid of the legal than of the illegal action of the workers' party, of the results of elections than of those of rebellion" (1895, p. 516).

However, Engels's confidence in a final victory was far from eroded by the prospect of a parliamentary road to socialism. The electoral successes of the proletariat and its new allies, he argued, were steady and irresistible and, though tranquil, as unavoidable as a natural process. For workers to win out in the end, they must "simply refuse to let themselves be lured into street fighting" (*op. cit.*, p. 523).

Marx, too, often declared himself in favour of a peaceful transition to communism. With reference to his description of universal suffrage as one of the primary goals that the proletariat was to pursue, a commentator has argued that he equated the takeover of the proletariat with a successful battle for democracy even in such an early work as the *Manifesto of the Communist Party* (Avineri 1968); and in *Capital*, Marx attached major importance to factory legislation and, generally, the role of assemblies returned in elections by universal suffrage, besides dwelling extensively (in hundreds of pages) on the fact that in parliaments the interests of the working class had often taken precedence over those of employers (see Sidoti 1987, p. 280).[21]

Conclusion

According to Eswaran and Kotwal (1989, p. 163), there is no way of determining the 'boss' of a modern company. In our opinion, instead, this claim might only be shared if the choice between capitalism and self-management (or, overall, between different economic systems) were just a question of pure logic, i.e. determined by a rational choice made by a majority. As things stand, the failure of workers to take control of business firms stems from two main reasons: the power of ideologies and vested interests to prevent pro-cooperation majorities from attaining their declared goal and the obstacles to the spontaneous emergence of a system of cooperatives in a capitalistic context. As argued by Wolff (2012, p. 158), the erroneous belief that worker-managed firms are less efficient than capitalistic firms has been purposely circulated by representatives of the dominant ideology with the aim of discouraging the belief that a system of democratic firms may be a viable alternative to capitalism.

Considering the overriding importance of democracy, it is possible to argue that political parties, far from waiting for a system of worker-controlled firms to arise without help from outside, should rather work towards framing political programmes envisaging public action in support of its emergence.

For our part, in this chapter we suggest the stepwise introduction of cooperative firms into the existing system either through the enforcement of suitable tax provisions and/or credit facilities or through the conversion of defaulting capitalistic companies into cooperatives. These solutions are similar to those suggested by other authors who recommend a major impulse to cooperation (see Oakeshott 1978, Cornforth *et al.* 1988, Ellerman 1990, chap. 7 and Bardhan & Roemer 1993).

More than in any other area, major breakthroughs in cooperation can only result from the synergic action of spontaneous evolution and focused political programs consistent with the recommendations of economic theorists. Ramsay (1983) has appropriately described the struggles for worker control of firms as a cyclical, rather than continuous process. In Italy and elsewhere, Visser also argues (1989, pp. 171–76), the cyclical attempts by the workers to seize factories between 1917 and 1921, from 1935 to 1937 and again in 1968–83 were sparked off not only by the political circumstances prevailing from time to time, but also by advancements in economic theory.

At this point, we will assume that Hayek is right when he argues that the prerequisite for a major political turn is persuading intellectuals and we will also assume that it is possible to share the view of intellectuals that Chekhov voiced through his 'black monk' in the passage reported here below: "Without you, who serve the higher principle and live in full understanding and freedom, mankind would be of little account: developing in a natural way, it would have to wait a long time for the end of its earthly history. You will lead it some thousands of years earlier into the kingdom of eternal truth – and therein lies your supreme service" (see Checov 1894a, p. 21). Those advocates of economic democracy who are of one mind with Hayek, then, will draw from him a determination to break the current stalemate by fuelling scientific debate as best they can.

For our part, despite our awareness of the serious implications of the objections that call into question the efficient working of democratic firms, we think it worthwhile to stress that the benefits flowing from the substitution of economic democracy for capitalism would be such as to call for a concerted action of intellectuals. In sync with our approach, Dahl (1989, p. 331) emphasises the need to ensure a favourable environment for democracy at both the national and corporate levels, but he also warns that these conditions do not lie in the nature of things and will therefore not arise as a matter of course.

Concluding, let us mention that despite the 150-year time lag separating us from the time when Marx and Engels launched their proposal and backed it up with scientific arguments, to call for a socialist revolution today is no rearguard action.

Notes

1 Authors who have extensively concerned themselves with self-management have gone so far as to argue that, given the absence of legal barriers to their establishment, self-managed firms will not assert themselves in market economies unless and until workers realise that their benefits exceed the relevant costs, as perceived by them (see, *inter alia*, Jensen & Meckling 1979, pp. 472–73, Putterman 1990, p. 161, Horvat 2000, p. 6 and Nuti 2001, pp. 22–25).

2 Chattopadhyay (2010, p. 30) has argued that the theoretical categories underlying twentieth-century socialism (TCS) were shaped originally and principally by Lenin and subsequently developed and perfected by Stalin. "The resulting conceptual framework – he specified – became, broadly speaking, the heritage of TCS. Indeed, the theoretical categories of TCS are only footnotes to Lenin (to paraphrase A.N. Whitehead on Western philosophy in relation to Plato). They had little relation with the categories that Marx (and Engels) had put forward in their own presentation of the future society. In fact, TCS's theoretical representation of the post-capitalist society shows a near complete revision (in Lenin's precise sense of the term) of Marx's ideas."

3 In contrast, Colletti has argued (see Colletti 1979, p. 147) that Marxism includes "a finalistic, teleological component tinged with overtones of an *eschatological* conception of history."

4 See Ureña 1977, pp. 182–83 and McQuarie & Amburgey 1978, pp. 207–11.

5 Expatiating on the influence of the environment on human nature, Bowles and Gintis have strongly criticised all those economists who condone the prominent role of the personal profit motive in economic life by tracing selfishness in individuals to their selfish genes and conclude their comprehensive analysis with the trenchant argument that "the idea that selfish genes must produce selfish individuals is false" (Bowles & Gintis 2011, p. 45).

6 It is interesting to note that even in the years immediately after the October Revolution, when Lenin did oppose the idea of having workers run firms on their own, he never as much as suggested that the reason for postponing worker control of firms was lack of entrepreneurial skills on the part of workers. The same is true of most Marxist historians and, generally, modern Marxists.

7 Struve's approach is intended to refute the widely shared view that "socialism is not a new social model which evolves (as did bourgeois society) right within the older society" (Magri 1977, p. 88).

8 In contrast, Marx wrote: "All *revolution* – the *overthrow* of the existing ruling power and the *dissolution* of the old order – is a *political act*. But without revolution *socialism* cannot be made possible. It stands in need of this political act just as it stands in need of *destruction* and *dissolution*. But as soon as its *organising functions* begin and *its goal*, its *soul* emerges, socialism throws its *political* mask aside" (Marx 1844b, vol. I, p. 409). As pointed out by Natoli (2008, p. 32), it is statements in this vein that are responsible for the development of Marxism into the "lexis of revolution" – specifically of revolution conceived of as the violent overthrow of the existing order.

9 The distinction between purposely established structures and structures which evolve spontaneously was first drawn by Sumner in 1906 and was extensively and repeatedly dealt with by Hayek (see, especially, Hayek 1982). Sumner's distinction was taken over by Strang and Sine (2002), who reformulated it as contrasting agent-determined

processes with naturalistic ones. Struve, for his part, denies he relevance of any such distinctions.

10 Similarly, Marcuse held that "the Marxian concept of revolution simultaneously implies continuity in change" (see Marcuse 1969, p. 180).

11 When Lenin reversed the concept of reformism in the last years of his life, he and Bukharin in his wake spelt out in bold letters that they conceived of evolution as "economic revolution, not by one stroke of the revolutionary sword, but by organic evolution" (see Cohen 1973, pp. 138–39).

12 Considering what has just been said, it is not possible to agree with Galasso that the link between democracy and reformism is a distinct characteristic which is common to liberal democracies and to any political forces accepting libertarian practices, that is to say the concordant belief that reform is the only high road to progress (see Galasso 2013, p. 35).

13 It has been remarked (Mueller 1992, p. 301) that Darwinian approaches to economics are more often grounded in a faith in the virtues of *laissez faire* policies than on a close scrutiny of factual reality.

14 Discussing Marx's argument that every society organises itself in such a way as to secure its survival without regard to any principles, but, rather, by making the most of the prevailing material conditions, Simone Weil (1955, p. 147) concludes that "this is exactly Darwin's idea." In contrast, Musto correctly remarks (2011, p. 139) that "while the traditional method of evolutionary theorists had been to proceed, as it were, along an ascending ladder of sorts in terms of describing simpler organisms first and then illustrating ever more complex ones, Marx chose a more complex logical method and ended up by developing a conception of history conceived of as a string of different modes of production."

15 Social Darwinism is rated as objectionable also by those who think (like Nietzsche) that whereas an economic system is governed by given laws, nature "is not a cosmos, i.e. a harmoniously ordered whole whose structure evolves consistently with timeless laws or finalistic aims; it is chaos, that is to say a temporal *continuum* without any enduring structures or laws and ordained by no intentions" (D'Iorio 2013, p. 15).

Critics of Social Darwinism include Bowles and Gintis, who hold that this argument is marred by the failure to distinguish between economic-financial performance and efficiency. In competitive markets – they write (1986, p. 84) – survival is a function of profit, which should not be mistaken for efficiency. The distinction between profit and efficiency, they add, will be clearly recognised if we bear in mind that – assuming equal pay rates – profit is determined both by the output per labour unit generated in one hour of work and by the amount of work performed in one hour. And while it is true that the productivity level of the work performed is a good measure of efficiency, they conclude, the amount of work accomplished in a single hour is mainly an indicator of the employer's ability to put in place effective control procedures. Accordingly, if the workers of a cooperative should outperform their capitalistic competitors in terms of managing to streamline production processes more effectively, they would attain higher efficiency levels even though they were to opt for a slower pace of work and decide to put up with lesser profits.

16 As argued by Hayek, neither biological nor cultural evolution is governed by the laws of necessity, but diversity is doubtless the effect of a non-genetically determined phenomenon such as cultural evolution (see Hayek 1982).

17 As argued by Ragionieri, Kautsky's opinions on the relations between Darwinism and socialism changed with the passing of years. At the time he was editing the *Neue Zeit*, he thought that such relations were material, but from 1890 onwards he started to deny them (see Ragionieri 1966, pp. 85–91). Dissenting from Ragionieri, other authors emphasise that Kautsky explicitly endorsed Social Darwinism even in *Ethics and the Materialist Conception of History*, a work written as late as 1906.

For an interesting analysis of Darwinism and economic evolution, see Colombatto (2002).

18 A well-known passage from Marx and Engels's *German Ideology* runs as follows: "the ideas of the ruling class are in every epoch the ruling ideas, i.e. the class which is the ruling material force of society is, at the same time, its ruling intellectual force [...] The ruling ideas are nothing more than the ideal expression of the dominant material relationships, the dominant material relationships grasped as ideas; hence of the relationships which make one class the ruling one, therefore, the ideas of its dominance" (see Marx & Engels 1845–46, pp. 35–36).

19 Concerning the conservative essence of institutions, see, also, Veblen 1899, pp. 190–98.

20 According to Engels, the enemy of trade unionism was Proudhon, "the socialist of the small peasant and master-craftsman" (Engels 1891a, p. 187).

21 The idea that Marx might have welcomed a peaceful transition from capitalism to a system of producer cooperatives necessitates rethinking numerous points of Marxist theory (see Jossa 2012c).

10 The democratic firm and the transition to socialism

Introduction

Considering the crucial importance of historical materialism within Marx's overall thought, in this chapter we will try to answer the question of whether it is actually a deterministic approach and whether or not this is an Achilles heel of Marxism. According to Plechanov (1895, p. 46), the course of history in Marxism "is ultimately determined, not by the human will, but by the evolution of material production forces"[1] and Bernstein, for his part (1899b, p. 31), makes it clear that "to be a materialist means first of all to trace all phenomena to the necessary movements of matter." And "as it is always the movement of matter which determines the form of ideas and the directions of the will" – he concludes – these also (and with them everything that happens in human reality) are inevitable."

Although these opinions have been severely criticised by more than one author, they are still widely shared and constantly resurgent: in recent times, many orthodox Marxists, of which G.A. Cohen is perhaps the most prominent example (see Cohen 1978 and 2000), maintain the *fundamentalist thesis*, as it is called, which amounts to a form of technological determinism.

The first of the classics who forcefully rejected the description of Marxism as 'technological determinism' was Kautsky (1899, pp. 1–34). Modern authors who share this view and appropriately classify Marxist dialectic as antithetical to determinism include, among others, Acton (1955, pp. 159–68), Plamenatz (1963, pp. 274 ff.), Sowell (1985, pp. 30–31) and Miller (1984).

In the opinion of several authors, economic determinism reflects the idea of a linear causality, i.e. of direct relations between a paramount cause and the effects that passively flow from it (see, for instance, Dunlap 1979, p. 313). As a result of such a linear notion of causality – they argue – the economic base is the necessary and, in itself, sufficient cause, whereas the superstructure is stripped of its autonomous role and production relations are the direct offshoot of the prevailing state of technology. In economics, the notion of determination, i.e. materialism, ultimately becomes economic fatalism, i.e. determinism. On closer analysis, however, this is the worldview behind mechanistic materialism, not Marxist materialism, and is a conception which tends to obliterate the part played by superstructural factors and is therefore unable to account for the rise of societies with a variety of different characteristics (see Karst 1974, pp. 120–24). From this perspective, it is also antithetical to Althusser's structuralist approach, in which the political and ideological aspects of a mode of production are seen to act themselves out in a fairly autonomous manner.

According to the conception of mechanistic materialists, Marx's determinism is the result of a particular form of dialectic which is interpreted as economic determinism and is antithetical to the non-deterministic dialectic method enabling Althusser to relate everything to notions such as totality and production mode, as well as to a concept of causality which he himself described as 'structural' (see Althusser 1965a, chap. VI).

As a rule, the charge of determinism is pressed against Lenin's assumption that the transition to socialism will follow upon the stage termed state monopoly capitalism. As is well known, in an attempt to provide an 'objective' description of the evolution of capitalism, Lenin argued that the growth of monopolies and ever more massive State intervention in the economy would pave the way for a centrally planned socialist system with large-size monopolistic concerns. In fairly advanced countries and in capitalistic economies straightaway – Lenin wrote – the assumptions for the takeover of the capitalistic economic apparatus by the mass of workers had been created by such a genuinely socialist measure as the extension of compulsory schooling to all citizens, by the subjection of workers to the discipline of industrial work and, lastly, by greatly simplified governance and administration procedures.[2]

Be that as it may, instead of expatiating on Althusser's far from consensus-based criticism, let us emphasise that as soon as we think of socialism, not as a centrally planned system, but as a mode of production typified by worker control of firms, the element of determinism inherent in the materialistic conception of history will promptly appear in a more appropriate perspective.

One more aim of this chapter is providing the demonstration that the socialism-worker control of firms equation offers the additional advantage of affording an entirely new perspective on Marxism overall (see Jossa 2012c).

Despite numerous references to Marx's and Engels's writings, this chapter is chiefly intended to provide the demonstration that *Marxism* need not necessarily be categorised as a deterministic approach. The aim of this chapter, let us repeat, is that, where socialism is equated with democratic firm control, the element of determinism behind Marx's materialistic conception of history is likely to appear acceptable.

The fundamental contradiction in capitalism

In orthodox Marxist terms, the fundamental contradiction is the mismatch between the socialised character of production in large-size industrial concerns (where hundreds and even thousands of workers see to their jobs side by side) and the private nature of appropriation (the very underpinning of privately owned production means) (see, *inter alia*, Engels 1878, part 3, II and Tsuru 1969, pp 364–65). According to Engels (1878, pp. 260–61), this contradiction gives rise to an additional one which he described as follows: "The contradiction between socialised production and capitalistic appropriation now presents itself as an antagonism between the organisation of production in the individual workshop and the anarchy of production in the society as a whole."[3] Consequently, in the opinion of Engels the second contradiction is the conflict between organised factory production and private anarchical production in society as a whole.[4]

This leads Engels to argue that an anti-capitalistic revolution would result in the transition from anarchical markets to organised planning.

In our opinion, the fundamental contradiction of capitalism is not the one mentioned by Engels. In Bettelheim's words, the road towards socialism is a process characterised by increasing worker control of production and of living conditions, and one of the tools for the attainment of this control is planning. However, as 'plan' and 'market' are descriptive and empirical, rather than scientific notions, he argues, the crux of the issue is not the market- or plan-based nature of the economy (and hence the State), but the nature of the class that wields power (see Bettelheim 1971, p. 9). In other words, this means that the basic contradiction of capitalism is the capital-labour opposition – as every genuine Marxist will confirm.[5] This was also the opinion of Vacca, according to whom "the qualifying aspect of socialism is not state planning, but the effort to create a social order characterised by self-government in every form" (Vacca 1985, p. 124). And inasmuch as it is true that the fundamental contradiction is the capital-labour opposition, it is obvious that a change of the kind suggested in this paper will reverse the relations of wage labour to capital and thereby spark off a revolution (see Jossa 2010b, pp. 60–62).[6]

In *Anti-Dühring*, Engels wrote (pp. 260–61): "The contradiction between socialised production and capitalistic appropriation now presents itself as an antagonism between the proletariat and the bourgeoisie."

These words seem to suggest that the two fundamental contradictions we are considering are nothing but two different ways of describing one and the same state of affairs. Commenting on this passage, Sève (1970, p. 145) appropriately objected that, as each of these contradictions obeys a different logic, it was not correct to assume that Engels intended to describe them as identical in purely abstract terms. Further on, however (p. 146), Sève added that it would be a mistake to look upon the production forces–production relations contradiction and the contradictions internal to production relations (the capital and labour polarity) as two completely different things.

In this connection, however, it is probably more interesting to remark that even those who rate the capital-labour opposition as the most glaring contradiction of capitalism and draw a clear-cut distinction between this contradiction and the mismatch between socialised production/private appropriation can hardly be assumed to deny that escalations in the latter contradiction will help ignite the former, i.e. the capital-labour conflict.[7]

Market socialism and transition scenarios

Coming to the way the transition from capitalism to a system of democratic firms can be achieved, one possible scenario is the decision to convert down-run capitalistic businesses into cooperative firms. Many countries have a track record of insolvent capitalistic firms turned into cooperatives. In capitalistic systems, Vanek wrote (1977b, p. 46), every corporate insolvency case may offer an excellent opportunity for setting up a self-managed firm.[8]

Corporate insolvencies may be caused by burgeoning wage claims that the firms may not be in a position to satisfy. This means that an alternative road towards the establishment of socialism may take the form of a generalised revolt against the system through insistent demands for ever higher pay rates and, finally, the demand for taking over the management of firms.

As a result, it is possible to argue that the revolution we have in mind can be implemented in piecemeal fashion and by democratic means, in manners that Gramsci predicted when he contrasted revolutions feasible in the West with the revolution in Russia.[9] A gradual transition is what Rosa Luxemburg had in mind when she wrote: "The conquest of power will not be effected with one blow. It will be a progression; we will progressively occupy all the positions of the capitalist state and defend them tooth and nail. ... It is a question of fighting step by step, hand-to-hand, in every province, in every city, in every village, in every munici-pality, in order to take and transfer all the powers of the state bit by bit from the bourgeoisie to the workers and soldiers councils" (Luxemburg 1918, p. 629).

Such an agenda would be consistent with Marx's approach, i.e. with his belief that cooperatives were to be the "independent creations of the workers" (Marx 1875a, p. 17). As has rightly been pointed out by more than one author, in the mind of Marx and any Marxist there is an indissoluble link between the progress of the cooperative movement and an active, militant worker movement (see Egan 1990, p. 74).

A third way to establish the *new order* is to secure the passing of an Act of Parliament to convert the shares of existing companies into bonds of equal value and outlaw hired labour to the extent and in manners deemed appropriate. By virtue of such an Act, capitalists would be deprived of all power and capitalistic companies would be turned into self-managed firms. The prerequisite for such a move is, obviously, a parliamentary majority formed of representatives of the working class.[10]

It is obvious that none of scenarios sketched are reconcilable with Lenin's claim that the transition would lead to the establishment of the dictatorship of the proletariat.

This leads us to say that where socialism is equated with democratic firm control and imagined to be implemented in one of the manners mentioned above, the element of determinism behind Marx's materialistic conception of history is likely to appear acceptable.[11]

On the dynamics of the plan-market contradiction

As mentioned above, according to orthodox Marxists the revolution sparked off by a mounting conflict between socialised production and private distribu-tion is the adoption of central planning. Lenin spelled this out in bold letters. In *The Impending Catastrophe and How to Combat It*, a pamphlet written on the eve of the October Revolution (Spring 1917), he clearly stated that the material preconditions for the transition to socialism were created during the state-controlled monopoly capitalism phase, which he termed "state capitalism" and described as the "ante-chamber" of socialism or "the rung on the ladder of history between which and the rung called socialism *there are no intermediate rungs*" (see Lenin 1917c, p. 341).

Capitalism differs from pre-capitalistic systems – Lenin wrote – because it is characterised by close interconnections between its production branches and, hence, by an increasing interdependence between production activities. At the monopoly capitalism stage, he argued, these interdependencies reach levels at which control over production is taken over by the banking system. As pointed out by Hilferding, in Lenin's approach the banking system plays a major role in this process and banks are the vital ganglia of modern capitalistic organisation. Thanks to the involvement of banks in trade and industry, Lenin argued, the banking system reaches a concentration level at which it appears as the trunk from which the bulk of business activities branch out and as a basic factor accelerating such interconnections and concentration.

In Lenin's approach, on the one hand the capitalistic state tends to exacerbate capitalistic exploitation due to these interconnections, the resulting interdependence of production activities, and increasing concentration levels, specifically by steering and controlling production in the interests of business magnates and the propertied class; on the other, the banking system paves the way for the advent of socialism, since "a large-scale capitalist economy, by its very technique, is socialised economy" (*ibid.*, p. 322). "If a huge capitalist undertaking becomes a monopoly, it means that it serves the whole nation" (*ibid.*, p. 340), because it works for millions of people and, even more importantly, whether directly or indirectly, it "unites by its operations thousands and tens of thousands families" (*ibid.*, p. 322). In Lenin's approach, therefore, socialism is "merely state-capitalist monopoly which is made to serve the interests of the whole people and has to that extent ceased to be capitalist monopoly" (*ibid.*, p. 340); as a result, it will be established as soon as the state of capitalists and landowners is replaced with a state intending to abolish all privileges and to introduce the fullest level of democracy.

In short, in the opinion of Lenin ever closer interconnections between industrial branches and central planning pave the way for the nationalisation of the production apparatus as a whole and set off a head-on clash with private appropriation. And at that stage, Lenin argued, the nationalisation of production means, while triggering the socialisation of production activities, turns distribution into a socialised activity (because it is decreed by the state) and thereby sweeps away the most glaring contradiction of capitalism. Both production and distribution turn into state-controlled activities.

What should we say of this approach? A close look at the contemporary scene is enough to show that it is no reliable proxy for the situation prevailing at the present day, when the competitive pressure of a globalised economy is obliging businesses to opt for more flexible and cost-effective organisational structures and is thereby generating a proliferation of smaller-size firms. Throughout the world, businesses are joining together to form 'network systems' founded on a key role of product-, transport-, and telecommunications-related links. One of many possible examples is Italy. From the mid-1960s onward, vertically integrated 'column-fashion' business groups have been gradually replaced by 'network system groups' where each firm specialises in one or a few production process steps and links up to the remaining network businesses along an 'assembly line' of sorts; and the effect of this process has been a marked increase in the number of comparatively small-size firms. In Italy, this business downsizing process was sparked off both by the transfer of part of the manufacturing processes of large-size concerns to smaller associated firms and by the creation of horizontally integrated chains of smaller firms which started exchanging finished and semi-finished articles as well as services.

Marx's idea of a "progressive decline in the variable capital in relation to the constant capital" and "a progressively rising organic composition, on the average, of the social capital as a whole" (Marx 1894, p. 518) is in full agreement with the view that the gap between the social nature of production activity and the private nature of appropriation is ever-widening. But the findings on the ratio of income from constant capital to income from variable capital have shown that, in the long Keynesian era, this has not been the case (see, e.g., Krugman 2007, chap. 3).

Moreover, in due time the service sector tends to expand to the detriment of the industrial sector and to become predominant; and service firms are usually fairly small in size. In the light of this, it can be denied that the discrepancy between socialised production and private distribution is always on the increase. In other words, the criticism most frequently levelled against the current interpretation of the main contradiction of capitalism is that even where the evidence for an increasing trend of average firm size (i.e. the ratio of large-size to small-size firms) is held to be non-conclusive, there is no way of producing any historical evidence in support of the opposite conclusion.

Is the capital-labour contradiction systematically escalating?

According to some, another weak point of Marx's approach is the idea that the conflict between the interests of capital and those of labour is bound to escalate in time. Actually, they argue, workers are seen to become less averse to capitalism in direct proportion to increases in their income levels.[12]

van Parijs & van der Veen contend (1986, see p. 159) that Marx nowhere offered any arguments to back up his claim that the growth of the productive forces (as distinct from their use) is fettered by capitalism and that – in line with historical materialism – the substitution of socialism for capitalism is necessitated by this fettering. In other words, in the opinion of these authors Marx did not provide evidence that the transition to socialism was a necessary development.

Dissenting from their view, we hold that Marx did provide arguments in support of his claim that the transition to socialism was in the nature of things. The most important of them is his argument that the contradictions inherent in capitalism (including the crucial conflict between the interests of capital and those of workers) tend to escalate over time until they spark off the collapse of capitalism. In Marx's estimation, the ultimate motive force of this collapse would be insurrections of the workers during ever more disastrous crises (not in periods of prosperity). As mentioned by Mattick (2002, p. 18), this thought occupied Marx's mind all his life. Engels, for his part, wrote that sooner or later "the proletariat will attain a level of power and insight at which it will no longer tolerate the pressure of the entire social structure bearing down on its shoulders, when it will demand a more even distribution of social burdens and rights; and then – unless human nature has changed by that time – a social revolution will be inevitable" (see Engels 1845, p. 577).

To account for Marx's and Engels's belief that the passing of time made revolution ever more probable we have to bear in mind that the progress of productive forces tends to magnify both the power of man over nature and the effectiveness of human actions designed to solve emerging social problems.

This point can be outlined as follows. It is a well-known fact that technological evolution is currently moving in the opposite direction to Fordism. As a result, at this stage the argument that the advent of economic democracy is being expedited by the degradation of human labour caused by Fordism and Taylorism is unwarranted. Does this validate the opposite assumption that the higher educational and expertise levels required by modern technology are expediting the transition to democratic firm management and, hence, restoring momentum to labour management theory? According to Laibman (2006, pp. 315–16), there is a stage, in the evolution of production processes, at which efficiency and productivity gains become strictly dependent on autonomy, creativity, critical discernment as well as modes of behaviour supported by sound criteria. From this, he argues, it follows that when this threshold is reached and people interiorise the idea that quality and productivity are inextricably interconnected, the highroad to socialism will be followed through as a matter of course.[13]

This idea is widely shared.[14] By general agreement (see, for instance, Ben-Ner 1987 and 1988b, pp. 295–96 and Bowles & Gintis 1996, p. 82), the living standard of workers is a major determinant of both the advantages granted to labour-managed firms and the difficulties they come up with. There is evidence that workers become less risk-averse and develop greater entrepreneurial skills according as their income levels increase and that this leads them to attach more and more importance to the contradiction between their personal interests and those of capital. As argued by Cunningham (1987), low-income people who are dependent on others tend to put up with their lot with resignation and may occasionally develop a cynical attitude towards the human condition (p. 161). Moreover, as higher income levels are usually associated both with higher educational levels and with professional qualifications, the greater a worker's educational levels, the less he will be prepared to work at the behest of another (see, for example, Mandel 1973, p. 349). Very often, workers in self-managed firms have the feeling that their incomes may be at risk and that they may prove unable to finance a decent standard of living for their families, but this feeling recedes in proportion to increases in income. Moreover, the abolition of hired labour in a labour-managed system gives rise to a more democratic system in which workers are no longer alienated because they cease being under coercion from employers.[15]

Accordingly, anyone thinking, like Marx, that mankind will gradually gain more and more freedom (even though via the most tortuous of paths) can hardly doubt that democratic firm management is bound to become a reality at some point in time. In the words of Lukàcs (1968, p. 34), "Marx, much like German philosophers and chiefly Hegel, conceived of world history as a unitary process and the highroad towards liberation."

In short, it is reasonable to assume that labour management is bound to make headway in history according as manual labour loses importance and workers acquire greater educational and professional qualifications.[16] According to van Parijs and van der Veen, "what is politically feasible depends largely on what has been shown to make economic and ethical sense" (1986, p. 156); and it is reasonable to assume that what makes economic and ethical sense will in due time come true.

The association emerges as a counterpart to the capitalist and the shopkeeper is matched by the cooperative, Gramsci wrote (1918c, p. 189), and he posed the question of the causes that might explain the increasing tendency of workers to be joined into cooperatives.

As pointed out by Harman (1977), "Gramsci often uses the bourgeois struggle for power against feudalism as a metaphor for the workers' struggle for power against capitalism. In point of fact, this comparison is highly misleading. As capitalistic production relations are closely associated with commodity production, which may arise within feudal society, the bourgeoisie can use its growing economic dominance to build up its ideological position within the framework of feudalism before seizing power. Conversely, the only way for the working class to become economically dominant is by taking collective control of means of production – an aim which requires rallying to arms in order to seize political power." On this point, however, it is Gramsci, not his critic, that is right.

It is interesting to mention that even in the years immediately after the October Revolution, when Lenin was averse to the idea of allowing workers to run their firms on their own, he never suggested that the reason for postponing worker control of firms was lack of entrepreneurial skills on the part of workers. The same is true of most Marxist historians and, generally, modern Marxists. An example is the Althusserian Karst (1974, p. 188), who argues that there are no technical requirements imposing the need that the users of means of production should be propertiless or deprived of the power to make decisions concerning the use of labour power. This state of things, he adds, is typical of most, though not all modes of production and principally connotes the development of productive forces within the capitalistic mode of production. Under capitalism, he concludes, the subjection of workers to the control of technicians and engineers reflects social needs associated with the particular configuration of the prevailing mode of production and a tendency to super-determine the technical requirements of the productive forces.

The need to raise the education levels of the working class was spelt out by Lenin in clear letters. In Lefebvre 1968 (p. 120), we read that around 1920, shortly after he had come to power, Lenin strongly recommended a real and proper cultural revolution geared towards enabling the working class to administer a huge country, manage industry, master technological resources and markets and assimilate – as well as instantly overstep – capitalistic rationality. His conclusion was that the revolutionary forces had to work towards elevating the educational levels of the population. Today, this view is concordantly endorsed by all those who advocate a transition to socialism. Consequently, we agree with Zamagni (2006, p. 60) that "as soon as we realise that the strategic role of human and social capital is far superior to that of physical and financial capital, we will also have a correct appreciation of the overriding importance of democratic governance modes even on a strictly economic plain." Indeed, the greater a worker's educational level and qualifications, the less will he accept working at the behest of another and the more eagerly will he strive to acquire the skills and expertise required to run a firm first-hand.[17]

By the same token, thanks to advancements in communication and knowledge economics, workers are likely to interiorise the conceptual dimensions of their jobs, to join with others in carrying on business independently of capitalists and develop ever more socialised collective working modes.

Whereas this suggests the preliminary conclusion that labour management will be implemented as a matter of course at the same pace that manual labour loses importance and workers gain greater educational and professional qualifications (see, for example, Mandel 1973, p. 349), it remains that confidence in the ultimate advent of democracy at some point in time can by no means be looked upon as a deterministic conception.[18] Adler wrote (1904, p. 198) that it was not inconsistent to speak of a necessary historical course and, at the same time, to assume an ideal purpose behind it. As long as we speak of evolution as governed by necessity, he explained, we are arguing from a purely scientific angle of view, but the moment we assume an ideal goal behind it, we are plunged into the stream of the will and of historical action, which so far had been viewed objectively.

Our confidence in the ultimate success of worker control is explained by our belief that to realise his humanity to the full, a man must be free, i.e. he must not be obliged to act as a lifeless tool for the attainment of other people's aims, but must start obeying his own will and pursue self-conceived goals. A well-known saying by Marx (1867a, p. 284) runs that "what distinguishes the worst architect from the best of bees is that the architect builds the cell in his mind before he constructs it in wax." This means that the human work process is typified by the fact that the result "already existed, i.e. was ideally present, in the imagination of the labourer at its commencement" (*ibid.*). Conversely, as the hired labourer's passive abidance by third-party commands can hardly be described as a genuinely human work process and provided it is true that history is the record of man's stepwise acquisition of ever tighter control over his environment, it is according to reason that workers should be free to conceive and pursue their own aims.

However, our claim that worker management is a necessity must be supported by evidence that ever more people are conceiving an interest in changing the prevailing mode of production. As this is not the place to expatiate on the vast and endless debate on social classes, suffice it to mention that critics of the transition claim that the proletariat, i.e. the working class, has failed to gain in importance. As for Italy, a well-known survey by Sylos Labini showed that in the years from 1881 to 1971 the workforce had increased by about 1 million units in numerical terms, but dropped from 52.2 to 47.8 per cent as a share of the total population (see Sylos Labini 1978, Tables 1.1 and 1.2 on pp. 156–57).

The question now is: is it correct to claim that the class that is pressing most forcefully for the transition from capitalism to a system of democratic firms is actually the proletariat? As argued by Petruccioli (1972, p. 51), during their steady search for the true revolutionary agent – the social group potentially most committed to revolutionary action – Marxists have alternatively adopted the viewpoints of two different, though complementary ideologies, labourism versus proletarianism. As a result, he remarks, at times they have confined the limits of this group to the proletariat only and, at times, they have extended them by including other classes in accordance with the proletarisation formula; but in our estimation it is clear that the basic distinction is between individuals that tend to welcome change and those who tend to oppose it, i.e. between hired workers and those self-employed. And as experience has shown that the former group (blue collars and lower-level clerical workers) has been steadily increasing,[19] we both endorse the widespread belief that the transition would be supported by the majority of the population and Petruccioli's conclusion (see *supra*, pp. 47–48) that the most noticeable change in the social composition of the Italian population has been a drop in self-employment levels and a rising trend in the number of employees. In this connection, Cerroni (1973, p. 22) has remarked that the social status of the intermediate layers of society, specifically intellectuals, technicians and scientists, is progressively seen to level out with that of salaried workers.[20]

An additional argument pointing in the same direction concerns the United States, where Stiglitz (2012, p. 13) notes that "the middle class has become eviscerated as the 'good' middle-class jobs – requiring a moderate level of skills, like autoworkers' jobs – seemed to be disappearing, relative to those at the bottom, requiring few skills, and those at the top, requiring greater skill levels." Indeed, every increase in the polarisation of society exacerbates the contrast between the two main classes and induces the lower class to adopt more radical positions.

Nonetheless, it is evident that many obstacles stand in the way of the establishment of a system of cooperative firms. One of these obstacles is the wide range of income levels and social positions observed within one class, that of hired workers, and the resulting difficulty to bring together different social forces and induce them to join forces (see Magri 1977, p. 84).

At any rate, it is far from easy to anticipate when such a revolution will come about. As is well known, in their day Engels and Marx were persuaded that the times were ripe and that revolution was at hand. Speaking of Engels's lifetime, Henderson (1977, p. 21) reports that "for years, Engels waited for his grim prophecy to come true and for years he waited in vain"; today, in consequence of the failure of the revolutions in Eastern European countries it is absolutely impossible to predict if the transition will be a short- or long-term process.

Class 'in itself' versus class 'for itself'

In the light of these reflections it is possible to attempt a critique of Lenin's claim that the class consciousness that workers develop *from within* is solely economic and trade-unionist in nature, and that true class consciousness can come to workers only *from without*. "However much we may try 'to lend the economic struggle itself a political character' – Lenin wrote in 1902 (p. 115) – "we shall never be able to develop the political consciousness of the workers (to the level of Social-Democratic political consciousness) by keeping within the framework of the economic struggle, for that framework is too narrow." At meetings and conferences attended by workers, he argued, debates are usually focused on economic issues and seldom if ever on subjects such as the conditions of life of individual social classes, the history of the revolutionary movement or the economic trend under way in the country overall. In Lenin's view, it was this unsatisfactory state of affairs that prevented the proletariat from taking the lead of the movement, raising general issues associated with democracy and working towards a change of the existing mode of production. Unlike Lenin, we hold that provided the establishment of a new production mode is made to coincide with the transfer of firm control to workers, it is possible to argue that class consciousness will develop spontaneously from within the working class. As Korsch puts it (1923, p. 79): "the method of Marx and Engels is not that of an abstract materialism, but of a dialectical materialism: it is therefore the only scientific method. For Marxism, pre-scientific, extra-scientific and scientific consciousness no longer exist over and against the natural and (above all) social-historical world. They exist within this world as a real and objective component of it, if also an 'ideal' one."

Having regard to the economic benefits associated with self-management, there is good ground for assuming that the workers may resolve to start a revolution. In addition to this, if workers should successfully bring home the message that firm control by profit-seeking capitalists is an obstacle to the growth of democracy and the general good, they might even win over the middle class to their cause.[21]

Lenin's position is closely associated both with Marx and Engels's claim that each mode of production falls into two distinct stages and with the 'in-itself'/ 'for-itself' distinction that Marx took over from Hegel and reformulated as a distinction between 'class in itself' and 'class for itself.' In Marx, workers under capitalism are said to become a 'class in itself' when they gain an awareness of their true interests, establish a party of their own and develop their own intelligentsia. At that stage, they are ready to start out on a successful battle for improving their conditions right within the existing mode of production. In point of fact, on realising that any strides forward they manage to take are not only far from permanent, but even incompatible with the capitalistic mode of production, their enthusiasm will instantly turn to frustration. This is the rationale behind the claim that on realising that success is at hand, they will also understand that such success must be lasting in time and will resolve to change the existing production mode. It is at this stage that the proletariat becomes 'a class for itself.' And as the belief to be acting in the best interests of society will induce it to join forces with other classes in an effort to suppress capitalism altogether, from a 'class for itself' it will also become 'a class for others.'

As mentioned above, Marx and Engels claimed that a mode of production fell into two distinct phases. At the earlier stage, most workers do not seek revolution since an awareness of the rational relational criteria behind capitalism induces them to accept the system. In due time, however, on realising that these relations are the chains that fetter their progress, they will endeavour to join forces with the middle class in an attempt to revolutionise the existing mode of production. On this point, Engels wrote (1878, p. 137–38): "The connection between distribution and the material conditions of existence of society at any period lies so much in the nature of things that it is always reflected in popular instinct. So long as a mode of production still describes an ascending curve of development, it is enthusiastically welcomed even by those who come off worst from its corresponding mode of distribution. This was the case with the English workers in the beginnings of modern industry. And even while this mode of production remains normal for society, there is, in general, contentment with the distribution, and if objections to it begin to be raised, they come from within the ruling class itself (Saint-Simon, Fourier, Owen) and find no response whatever among the exploited masses. Only when the mode of production in question has described a good part of its descending curve, when it has half outlived its day, when the conditions of its existence have to a large extent disappeared and its successor is already knocking at the door – it is only at this stage that the constantly increasing inequality of distribution appears as unjust, it is only then that appeal is made from the facts which have had their day to so-called eternal justice."

Is the transition a certainty or a conjecture?

Anyone holding Bernstein's view that Marxism is inextricably bound up with the idea of the collapse of capitalism is likely to argue that our transition scenarios are incompatible with Marx's approach.

In fact, there is no such incompatibility. Firstly, all our scenarios start out from the assumption that the worker-capitalist conflict is bound to escalate in time; secondly, at the same pace that workers have access to education and develop the ability to take their lives into their own hands, they will find these contradictions as ever more unbearable – in full harmony with Marx's claim that the prerequisite for a successful transition process is a scientific vision of socialism with specific focus on the laws of motion and inherent contradictions of capitalism. In the estimation of Lukàcs (1923, p. 60), the core idea behind scientific Marxism is the belief that the real driving forces behind history are independent of the degree to which man is (psychologically) aware of them. From our perspective, it is unreasonable to assume that workers should fail to become palpably aware of the fact that the capitalist-worker opposition lies in the nature of things. In this connection, Lukàcs quotes a passage from *Capital*: "Reflection on the forms of human life, hence also scientific analysis of these forms, takes a course directly opposite to their real development. Reflection begins *post festum*, and therefore with the results of the process of development ready to hand. The forms ... already possess the fixed quantity of natural forms of social life before man seeks to give an account, not of their historical character, for in his eyes they are immutable, but of their content and meaning" (Marx 1867a, p. 168). On closer analysis, this passage (which reflects the gist of Marx's historical materialism), tells us clearly that conscience is framed by being, and not vice versa, i.e. that the contrasting views held by men are the effect of real contradictions. "The contradictions of the capitalist system of production" – we read in Lukàcs 1923 (p. 63) – "are reflected in these mutually incompatible accounts of the same object." Marx's argument that the collapse of a production mode is caused by its inherent contradictions runs counter to the typical worldview of the bourgeoisie, which conceives of the organisational forms of the present as obeying natural and, hence, eternal laws. According to J. R. Burke (1981, p. 95), in Marx's writings there is considerable evidence that specific elements of the revolutionary process prepare the working class for its task of self-managing society and exercising social control over means of production and that the revolutionary process itself is triggered by certain tendencies perceived in capitalistic societies.

In this respect, Balibar writes that in Marx's work there is "a progressive line of evolution of modes of production" which "classifies all societies in terms of an intrinsic criterion, *socialisation*, i.e. the capacity of individuals collectively to control their own conditions of existence" (Balibar 1993, p. 131). And there can be little doubt that democratic firm control affords higher levels of socialisation than capitalism.

It is not true, consequently, with reference to what we have said, (to use a phrase of Rosa Luxemburg), that "we have here, in brief, the explanation of the socialist programme by means of 'pure reason.'" In other words, it is not true that "we have here, to use simpler language, an idealist explanation of socialism" and that "the objective necessity of socialism, the explanation of socialism as the result of the material development of society, falls to the ground" (Luxemburg 1913, p. 151).

As mentioned before, all our transition scenarios require of necessity a full awareness of aims and means, and this – let us argue – is fully in keeping with Kant's dictum that the transition must be implemented in accordance with ethical principles. As argued by Staudinger (1899, quoted in Sandkühler 1970, pp. 24–25), when Marx resolved to progress from the scientific analysis of society to a plan for bringing about purposeful changes consistent with his founding principles, he had to refer to Kant; conversely, on realising that finalistic laws stripped of their grounding in the natural laws of real life turn into purely abstract constructs, a student of Kant caring for consistency must necessarily draw on Marx.[22] With regard to this point, therefore, Kant's and Marx's approaches are by no means antithetical since historical materialism "does not deny that men perform their historical deeds themselves and that they do so consciously" (Lukàcs 1923, p. 64).

An argument highlighting both the sound ethical foundations of socialism and a link between Kant and Marx is found in Schmidt (1900, p. 135), who argues that the proletariat demanding revolution is doubtless acting in its own interests, but adds that the realisation that its aspirations fall in with those of people with the best human intentions should give the fighters powerful wings and induce them to act with the spirit of sacrifice that class struggle requires from the members of this class.

Further on, Schmidt (*op. cit.*, p. 138) argues that, while it is true that natural law theorists will describe the goals of socialism as fair, necessary and in full agreement with the *universal law* dictating the duty to work towards meeting the needs of the *community as a whole*, this insight need not be overstated since it naturally flows from the socialist humanitarian ideal. In sum, Schmidt claims that socialists have a 'naturalistic' ethic of their own and can consequently do without Kant's 'metaphysical' ethic (see Woltmann 1900, p. 149).

A different approach to the transition is that of van Parijs and van der Veen (1986, p. 159). According to these authors, Marx nowhere offered any arguments in support of his claim that the growth of the productive forces (as distinct from their use) is fettered by capitalism and that – in line with historical materialism – the substitution of socialism for capitalism is necessitated by this fettering. In other words, these authors maintain that Marx offered no proof of the transition to socialism as a necessary development. An easy way to refute this criticism is to emphasise that the idea of the transition as an unavoidable necessity is a corollary of Marx's claim that capitalism will ultimately collapse due to the inevitable escalation of its typical contradictions.[23]

In point of fact, although the view of a steadily escalating capital-labour conflict is contradicted by the fact that the initial determination of workers to rebel against capitalistic exploitation tends to weaken in consequence of the piecemeal increases in worker incomes recorded in capitalistic countries, there can be little doubt that the degree to which workers experience the capital-labour opposition as an unbearable condition increases in direct proportion to their incomes, access to education and the ability to take their lives into their own hands. Kautsky once argued that two factors which vouchsafed the prospect of a revolution were the narrow-mindedness of the bourgeoisie and the irredeemable conflict sparked off by the fact that economic growth was enabling both capitalists and proletarians to acquire more power.

In the words of van Parijs and van der Veen, "what is politically feasible depends largely on what has been shown to make economic and ethical sense" (1986, p. 156); and it is reasonable to assume that what makes economic and ethical sense will sooner or later come true.

Causation in Marx and Engels, Sowell argues (1985, pp 34), is a matter of interaction, rather than a one-way mechanism. And this, he argues, determines that there is neither pure determinism nor pure change, but a stream of events which reflect both 'accidental' factors and underlying forces whose necessary relations shape the general tendency of these events as a whole.

One point of Marx's approach which is difficult to reconcile with our transition scenarios is his view of the state as the 'lobbying group' of the bourgeoisie. In the awareness that the capitalistic state affords workers scope for gaining strength and ultimately seizing power, we have abstained from describing it as a tool for ensuring class rule; neither have we characterised the socialist state as a tool subservient to the aims of workers only. In our opinion, this line of reasoning reflects an orthodox Kautskian approach, rather than a truly critical idea of Marxism, and this is why we have also avoided to describe the capitalistic state as a tool in the hands of capitalists.

Our train of reasoning suggests the following conclusion: if historical progress is actually a function of the advancement of ideas, democratic firm control is bound to become reality at some point in time because it is the materialisation of a progressive democratic idea. The exact point in time when this will happen is, admittedly, difficult to predict because battles of ideas are of uncertain outcome.[24] In this connection, it is worth emphasising Gramsci's belief that the part that intellectuals are able to play in advancing socialism can hardly be overrated.

Hence, inasmuch as it is true that the power wielded by capital over labour must draw to an end in due time, we cannot but agree with Napoleoni that capitalism will neither collapse mechanically nor evolve to a level where it changes into something different (see Napoleoni 1970, p. lxx). The well-known Italian journalist Eugenio Scalfari put the matter in this way (see Scalfari 2008, p. 1224): "Many people have pinned their hopes of liberation on communism. But now it is time to take off the bandages from their eyes and the plugs from their ears. The reification of individuals, the master-servant confrontation, the refusal to acknowledge the rights of others have been salient traits of our species for millennia and will continue to be so in future." But while the truth of this can hardly be denied, there are reasons to believe that as soon as workers resolve to run firms by themselves and develop the requisite abilities, the master-servant confrontation will become a thing of the past.

Olson's and Buchanan's criticisms of socialism

The transition scenarios we have been sketching may help us refute the reflections on class struggle that Olson (1965) and Buchanan (1979) developed with reference to the free-riding issue. Both these authors start out from the idea that revolution is a public good and that the proletariat is fully aware of this. And as revolution is a costly undertaking which exposes the revolutionaries to a violent backlash from the bourgeoisie – they argue – it will never be followed through since each proletarian will think it convenient to shirk involvement on the assumption that he will nonetheless be able to reap the benefits flowing from the successful efforts of his fellow citizens. In other words, according to these authors, even if revolution is in the best interest of the proletariat despite the fact that every member of the proletariat realises that this is so, so far as its members act rationally, this class will not achieve concerted revolutionary action. This shocking conclusion rests on the assumption that concerted revolutionary action is, for the proletariat, a public good in the technical sense. As is well known, a public good is an object or a condition that can be attained by each member of a group, including those who have not incurred the costs associated with producing it.

In the opinion of Vahabi (2010, p. 691), this theory, unlike Marx's, suggests that the masses fail to make history because rational considerations induce them to opt for political inaction.

The extent to which this view is off the mark will be clearly perceived if we consider that one of our transition scenarios is characterised by state intervention in the economy (which rules out free-riding issues) and that the other envisages a series of strikes, i.e. decisions made jointly by the workers' collective instead of single individuals.

More specifically, Olson's and Buchanan's criticism is not applicable to the hypothesis of strikes proclaimed to press for the transfer of firms to workers for the following reason: although every action geared towards worker control of a firm certainly marks a stride forward in the direction of socialism and, as such, in the interests of the working class at large, it primarily benefits the workers of the firm concerned, since it is these that will stop being hired workers and become their own masters. And while it is impossible to rule out the free-riding hypothesis altogether, we have difficulty believing that many workers will be prepared to face the hatred of their fellow workers for refusing to participate in a strike for the acquisition of democratic worker control that the others deem to be in their best interests.

At the other end of the spectrum is the transition scenario which envisages converting the shares of existing firms into bonds of equal value (and, by the same token, outlawing hired labour to the extent deemed expedient). As is well known, the prerequisite for such a scenario is a parliamentary majority of representatives of the workers or, at any rate, a majority favourable to such a solution, which automatically rules out all free riding risks.

An additional point for further discussion, i.e. Elster and Moene's claim that an inferior mode of production may be stable and a superior one instable (see Elster & Moene 1989, p. 9) may help us outline the present status of the capitalism-versus-socialism debate. Let us assume – they argue – that the majority of the population should be favourable to a system of democratic firms on account of its considerable advantages, but that democratic firms should prove to be less efficient for some reason (for example financing difficulties). Under such circumstances – they argue – individual workers may resolve not to move to self-managed businesses and would hence impede the establishment of the superior production system. In the opinion of Elster and Moene, this is a case where the stability of the inferior mode of production is found to be an obstacle to the establishment of a superior mode.

In our estimation, Elster and Moene's scenario is objectionable for two reasons. Firstly, in strictly Marxian terms it is admissible to characterise as superior a mode of production which is endorsed by the majority of the population. A superior system is one which proves to be at once more productive and more efficient. Secondly, Elster and Moene do not distinguish between the case where the majority pressing for the superior mode is fully familiar with all the aspects of the issue and the case where it is not aware that a superior mode of production, where effectively organised, might prevail over the inferior one. This is why their scenario is to be modified by assuming that democratic firms operating in a capitalistic system are inefficient as long as they are outnumbered by capitalistic firms, but that when they outnumber capitalistic firms and become prevailing, they will outdo all the others in terms of efficiency thanks to the fact that their operating context has been adjusted to their needs. Would the inferior system be as stable as Elster and Moene hold it to be? It is clear that workers who are aware that the few democratic firms in existence are inefficient will hardly think of creating new ones and that the end result would consequently be the stability of the inferior mode.

At this point, we may ask ourselves if the community would be in a position to take action, for instance to pass a majority resolution to the effect of sparking off one of the transition scenarios sketched above. In abstract terms, the answer might be yes, but there is little doubt that advocates of historical materialism would answer this question in the negative. And as they are likely to emphasise the strong conditionings of the economic base on opinions, laws and other elements of the superstructure, they would have every reason to argue that the check that capitalists are able to put on the media would impede the circulation of the necessary information and that the majority of the population, being unaware of the superiority of a system of democratic firms to capitalism, would not work towards its establishment. As far as we can see, the resulting situation paints a precise picture of the circumstances prevailing today.

Conclusion

Such determinism as is observed in Marx is comparable to the worldviews of those, for instance Benedetto Croce and Lord Acton, who believe that history will ultimately head in a given direction. Croce thought that history was the chronicle of the progress of mankind towards freedom; Acton argued, among other things, that universal suffrage would in due time become a reality all over the world. In point of fact, the view of history as heading in a single direction is not incompatible with a major role for the human will in determining the course of events. Far from being the demiurges of history, relations of production are nothing but the background against which progress as a living force driven by man is seen to develop.

Quite appropriately, Rosselli (1930, p. 372) argued that the scenario of dropping income rates determining the progressive impoverishment of the population and the theory of falling rates of profit were not only objectionable in theoretical terms, but had even been proved wrong by history. On closer analysis, however, as it lies in the nature of things that hired workers wish to become their own masters and will therefore battle for abolition of hired labour, this does not rule out the prospect that capitalism will eventually be supplanted by socialism. John Stuart Mill put the matter in this way: "I confess I am not charmed with the ideal of life held out by those who think that the normal state of human beings is that of struggling to get on; that the trampling, crushing, elbowing, and treading on each other's heels, which form the existing type of social life, are the most desirable lot of humankind, or anything but the disagreeable symptoms of one of the phases of industrial progress" (Mill 1871, p. 20). At the same pace that history progresses towards the attainment of ever greater freedom, hired workers will become ever more strongly averse to what Mazzini termed "the slavery of wages" and will make themselves independent. Why should we assume that the automobiles that workers manufacture for the account of Fiat must necessarily be the property of the Agnelli family? Centuries ago, Locke remarked that those who produce goods become the owners of such goods. Inasmuch as it is true that the assumptions for the transition from capitalism to socialism are a turn to awareness on the part of workers and their acceptance of the risks of production, there is good ground for believing that this turn to awareness will in due time become a reality.

Notes

1 Walicki (1969, pp. 158ff.) holds that the salient characteristic of Plechanov's Marxism is his emphasis on determinism.

2 As argued by Panzieri, "no such thing as an 'objective' or hidden factor is inherent in the technological development or planning processes of a modern capitalistic society, which means that nothing can vouchsafe its self-driven transformation or the reversal of the relationships prevailing in it. The new 'technological breakthroughs' worked out in its production systems over time add to the potential of capitalism for further *consolidating* its power. Obviously, this does not mean that the prospects of an ultimate overthrow of the system should not become ever more palpable with the passing of time. Indeed, it is to be expected that workers ever more tightly caught up in its 'wheels' are likely to respond to this state of affairs by stepping up their insubordination" (Panzieri 1961, p. 152; see, also, pp. 155 and 161–62).

3 Panzieri, instead, has pointed to a conflict between Book I of *Capital* and other works by Marx: whereas in *Capital* the opposition between "despotism (planning) in factories and anarchy in society" appears as "the general form of the law of value" (see Panzieri 1964, p. 346), in other works we detect the germs of a different approach (*ibid.*, pp. 346ff. and 362).

4 As Bernstein puts it, production means are owned by individual capitalists who have diverted the output of production activity into their own pockets, whereas the production of commodities has become socialised, i.e. it has become a process which requires the involvement of a great many people seeing to their tasks in accordance with a carefully planned organisational scheme. In Bernstein's opinion, a second antithesis entailed in the first is the opposition between the planned labour organisation models adopted by large-size production concerns and the non-planned way commodities are brought to market (1899a, pp. 42–43).

5 For Kautsky's idea of the capital-labour opposition as the main contradiction of capitalism see, *inter alia*, Panaccione 1974, pp. 10–11 and 16.

6 Quoting Tronti (1962, p. 29): "What really counts is this elementary principle: at a certain stage in the evolution of capitalism, all of its contradictions are but different aspects of the basic contradiction, namely the conflict opposing the whole of the working class to capitalism as a whole."

7 Provided this is true, I cannot subscribe to Foucault's argument that the social extraction of an individual may account for his choice of one system of thought in preference to another, but that the existence of the group concerned is not the precondition for the rise of the relevant system of thought. From my perspective, it cannot be denied that capitalists are stout supporters of capitalism and well-informed workers tend to embrace socialism, but it is no less true that the propensity of workers for democratic firm management arises from teachings they tend to draw from experience (see Foucault 1966, p. 220).

8 In Italy, a 1985 statute known as the Marcora law provided for reliefs and benefits to defaulting enterprises that the workers were willing to take over and run on their own.

9   In Harman (1977) we read that Gramsci often used the battle for power of the bourgeoisie against the feudal class as a metaphor for the battle for power opposing workers to capitalists. In Harman's opinion, this comparison was dangerously flawed for the following reason: whereas the bourgeoisie could use its economic and financial standing to build up its ideological position right within feudalism (the period when commodities production gave rise to capitalistic relations), the same does not apply to the working class, which will not attain economic power unless it manages to gain control of production first. On this point, however, it is Gramsci, not his critic, that is right, because the potential of the cooperative movement for operating successfully even in capitalistic contexts is confirmed both by the existence of thriving cooperatives in capitalistic countries and by the first of the two transition scenarios sketched above.

10 Pérotin (2006, pp. 296–97) reports that many cooperatives were established during periods of social unrest or political change, for instance during the 1930 and 1848 revolutions, after the establishment of the Paris Commune, in the case of the strikes proclaimed in the years 1893–94 and 1905–06, during Popular Front governments in 1936 and in the aftermaths of the two great wars.

11 Anyone believing that the transition to socialism is heralded by declining frictions between opposed classes should give their best attention to the younger Marx's saying (see Rapone 2011, pp. 169–70) that the precondition for class conflict to become an element of progress is that the two opposed actors develop an awareness of their respective roles, as well as the determination to follow them through – and this happens during the phase termed industrial capitalism and not in the decadent phase termed financial capitalism.

12 There is no denying that following the eradication of the misery of the proletarian class in developed capitalistic countries the issue of class consciousness has become an even more urgent one (see Fetscher 1973, p. 227, footnote 17).

13 In Marx's writings, the emergence of the new mode of production is sometimes made to coincide with the point in time when growth is altogether inhibited by the older production mode and sometimes with the moment when the older production mode proves unable to lead to an *optimal* level of growth (for two antithetical opinions on this point, see Elster 1984, p. 42 and Miller 1984).

The Yugoslav Marxists (who joined in the 'Praxis Group' advocated a form of humanistic socialism and self-management), while rejecting determinism, were confident that most socialist principles would be materially implemented at some points in time (see Crocker 1981).

14 As pointed out by Aron (1969, p. 50), it is only liberals and pessimists (who are probably true sages) that tend to advise men against setting themselves tasks which they know they cannot master. From Aron's perspective, Marxists belong to a different family in that they devise their tasks based on their daydreams, not in proportion to their actual abilities. Be that as it may, Marxists resolving to work towards the establishment of worker control are setting themselves a task which is not unrealistic.

15 Quite appropriately, Hobsbawm (1982, p. 32) has argued that the revolutionary climate typifying the 1970s arose from social, rather than economic causes. Hence, there is ground for assuming that the same may be applicable to the democratic revolution discussed in this book.

16 Anyone believing that the transition to socialism is heralded by declining frictions between opposed classes should give their best attention to the younger Marx's saying (see Rapone 2011, pp. 169–70) that the precondition for class conflict to become an element of progress is that the two opposed actors develop an awareness of their respective roles, as well as the determination to follow them through – and this happens during the phase termed industrial capitalism and not in the decadent phase termed financial capitalism.

17 Ben-Ner (1988b, p. 297) is also convinced that skilled and well-educated individuals will find it easier to pool their abilities and establish a firm of their own than to find an external entrepreneur.

18 Unlike Aron, I am agreed that Marxists are probably right in assuming that men tend to raise only those issues they think they can solve, but I think this does not mean (as rightly pointed out by Merleau-Ponty) that society pursues a pre-fixed goal or that human problems always have one and only one solution (see Baczko 1965, pp. 218–19).

19 Concerning Italy's debated class composition, the reader is referred to the revised edition of Sylos Labini's book (Sylos Labini 1984), but also to Carboni (1986), Bagnasco (2008) and Pugliese (2008).

20 The fact that the proportion of the population prepared to welcome an end to capitalism increases as soon as the words 'hired workers' are substituted for 'working class' has also been highlighted by other authors, including Catephores (1989, pp. 221–26).

21 For critical approaches of the views of Lenin just reported, see Magri 1977, pp. 76–77.

22 An attempt to reconcile Kant's criticism and Marx's historical materialism was made within the framework of 'Neokantianism,' a movement which developed within the orbit of German social-democracy in the period between 1895 and 1914 and has remained influential right to this day (see Agazzi 1975).

23 The query whether Marx ever formulated a theory of the collapse of capitalism was answered by Bernstein in the negative in a well-known book (Bernstein 1899a, chap. XV) and by Cunow (1899) in the positive. In later years, the idea that Marx did enunciate a collapse theory was widely shared. With reference to the fall in rates of profit – which he held to be the main cause of the assumed collapse – Marx argued that "this process would entail the rapid breakdown of capitalistic production, if counteracting tendencies were not constantly at work alongside this centripetal force, in direction of decentralization" (Marx 1894, p. 355).

24 "The configuration of socialism" – argues Giuseppe Vacca (1985, p. 38) – "undergoes constant change and the only thing we are able to predict, with respect to this process, is that it extends over a transitional historical time-span during which producers have consistently worked towards securing title to full self-governance."

11 Corporate limited liability as a springboard for socialism

Introduction

There is wide agreement among Marxists that Marx's analyses of joint-stock companies and cooperative firms shed light on the escalating conflict between these organisational forms and the logic of capitalism (see, *inter alia*, Offe 1972b). Their opinion is supported by Schumpeter, who wrote that the modern joint-stock company, "although the product of the capitalistic process, socializes the bourgeois mind" (1954, p. 156). And Keynes, for his part, wrote: "but more interesting than these is the trend of joint-stock institutions, when they have reached a certain age and size, to approximate to the status of public corporations rather than that of individualistic private enterprise. One of the most interesting and unnoticed developments of recent decades has been the tendency of big enterprise to socialise itself. A point arises in the growth of a big institution – particularly a big railway or big public utility enterprise, but also a big bank or a big insurance company – at which the owners of the capital, i.e. its shareholders, are almost entirely dissociated from the management, with the result that the direct personal interest of the latter in the making of great profit becomes quite secondary. When this stage is reached, the general stability and reputation of the institution are the more considered by the management than the maximum of profit for the shareholders" (see Keynes 1926b, p. 75).

Starting out from the quotations from Marx and Keyes reported above, in this chapter we will be arguing that the company limited by shares – the modern-day form of what was once the joint-stock company – is paving the way for a piecemeal democratic transition to socialism.

In this connection, it is worth remarking that a great many commentators have pressed the argument that the fall of the Berlin Wall and globalisation have improved, rather than frustrated, the prospects of an upcoming advent of socialism. Reviewing the changes produced by the globalisation and financiarisation of the economy, the unexpressed, though ever stronger need for community and the "unfulfilled promises of democracy" (Norberto Bobbio), the philosophical thinker Remo Bodei, for example, raised the question (2013, p. 175) whether the world was heading towards one of those far-reaching shifts in historical perspective which due to various – as yet not clearly recognisable – factors may mark a turning point comparable to the dissociation of Humanists from the culture of the Middle Ages or the triumph of the spirit of the Enlightenment over a conventional worldview. In our estimation, the true driving force behind this veritable turnaround is the rapid pace at which the economy – though not yet the political scene – is heading towards a stage where socialism may become a reality.

The origins of the joint-stock company

As is well known, the joint-stock company emerged in the seventeenth century, when the Dutch government granted the East India Company the privilege of corporate limited liability for its debts. In consideration of the financial benefits deriving to governments from the exploitation of the economic resources of the Far East, later on this privilege was also granted to colonial companies in France and Great Britain. At that time, colonial companies were established by Royal Charter. Upon the release of a charter, by way of exception the sovereign would grant the newly established company the privilege of limiting its liability and the right to issue shares in order to distribute such limited liability among a variety of participants in the enterprise. The limited liability doctrine was only applied to enterprises expected to make huge investments in establishing settlements in far-off lands and to initiatives deemed to be made in the interests of the general public.

As a matter of fact, the limited liability principle was not an absolute novelty, since back in Roman times this advantage was enjoyed by a wealth of entrepreneurs operating in association. In Britain and elsewhere, from the 1860s forward capital providers were granted the privilege of limiting their liability under the provisions of several partnership and company laws. By way of example, when limited partnerships were established in Britain, the personal assets of the partners not performing managerial functions were protected in the event of the insolvency of the firm, but this protection was not extended to the partners running the business of the firm. In line with the generalised assumption that businesspeople were to be accountable for the obligations of their enterprise to the whole amount of their personal assets, the general partners were obliged to bear personal responsibility for the firm's liabilities. As a result, the extension of the limited liability regime to all the members of a limited company marked a turning point in the history of capitalism. The right to issue shares and the privilege of corporate limited liability furthered the interests of two social groups within a capitalistic regime which was as yet at its initial stage: the limited liability principle played into the hands of entrepreneurs, whereas the right to issue shares was of benefit to the nobility, the clergy and landowners, who could cash the returns on their investments without engaging in corporate decision-making and were free to sell their shares just as they would do with different personal assets.

After the advent of machinery, the joint-stock company gained more and more ground, in terms that all large-size business enterprises were organised in accordance with this legal model. On closer analysis, however, the proliferation of joint-stock companies was the result "not only, or even primarily, of technological development and growing capital needs as the traditional account would have it, but of the desire of businessmen to eliminate competition" (Ireland 2010, p. 839).

The separate legal personality of companies limited by shares

An additional step forward in the evolution of this corporate model was the granting of a separate legal personality to companies limited by shares. As this further step created the impression that the rights being conferred were privileges granted to an entity other than the natural persons holding shares in the company, its effect was to mask the plain fact that the beneficiaries of such privileges were actually the above-mentioned social groups. As a result, the legal acknowledgment of the status of the limited company as a separate legal entity is not the foundation of the limited liability doctrine; it is a theoretical justification which was fleshed out *ex post* for distinctly ideological purposes at a time when entrepreneurs were pressing for the right to have their liability limited by law. Thanks to the concept of legal person, the limited liability of shareholders ceased to be perceived as a benefit or privilege proper (as it had appeared to be until then). It stopped being a derogation from the overall principle that debtors are to be unlimitedly answerable for their obligations because there was good ground for arguing that members do not assume liability for corporate debts for the obvious reason that they are third-party obligations, i.e. liabilities of a different legal entity (for this line of reasoning, see Galgano 1974, p. 50).

In part, the decision to vest separate legal personality in limited companies was also designed to suggest that the law was intended to protect, not the interests of single individuals, but a *general* interest such as the interest of a firm, which fell in with the superior interest of the community and of the nation to secure efficiency in production. The separate legal personality of the limited company and the resulting ownership-control separation produced a dual effect: on the one hand, there emerged two discrete property forms, the assets, owned wholly by the company, and shares, owned wholly by its shareholders; on the other, the shareholders' accountability to creditors was downgraded to a second-level liability: for the satisfaction of their claims, creditors could not take action directly against the shareholders, but had to seek payment only from the company in its capacity as the owner of the corporate capital assets.

For this reason, it hardly matters to companies who their shareholders are and, by the same token, it hardly matters to shareholders who the other shareholders are. Furthermore, these discrete property forms are treated as distinct in certain respects, for instance with regard to the shareholders' personal responsibility, but not in others, for instance in matters of dividends, since it is understood that managers are expected to run companies in the exclusive interests of shareholders (see Ireland 2010, p. 850). The benefits of this state of affairs are reaped by the latter, in terms that they cash the returns on their investments without bearing responsibility for damages caused by the company's operations, and by financial speculators – with an adverse impact on the stability of the system (Arena 2010, p. 873).[1]

One major implication of the separate personality of limited companies is the possibility to establish holding companies, specifically groups of companies headed by a parent company and constituted of an indifferent number of subsidiaries and affiliates owning in turn subsidiaries and affiliates. The holding company of a business group does not conduct production operations itself. Its corporate mission is managing its share portfolio, viz., running and controlling related businesses. The advantage deriving to capitalists from the status of members of a holding company is that a comparatively modest investment enables them to control a large number of related businesses and, ultimately, a huge amount of third-party capital.

Hence, the Act which vested a separate legal personality in limited companies had a major impact on the notion of property itself. Reviewing a number of decisions made by the Supreme Court of the United States between 1872 and 1897, Commons argued (Commons 1924, p. 173) that its effect was a transition, in the meaning of property, from that of tangible property owned by individuals to that of a going business owned by a going concern to contrast the existing concept of tangible property owned by one or more individuals with the new concept of property owned, not by one or more individuals, but by a business enterprise.

On the separation of ownership and control

The crucial impact of the developments just described, i.e. the separation of ownership from control in limited companies, is examined in numerous theoretical studies.

As is well known, the earliest major theorists of the ownership-control separation were Berle and Means, who held that the transition to managerial capitalism, from which this separation originated, was caused by the dispersion, and resulting weakness, of equity ownership. A few years later, their approach was partly backed and partly elaborated upon by Burnham. Burnham's book, *The Managerial Revolution* (1941), traced the emergence of this late stage of capitalism primarily to the exacting technical and organisational expertise of managers, rather than to shortcomings associated with joint ownership. In 1967, the managerial capitalism theory was once again brought to the forefront of attention by the appearance of Galbraith's *The New Industrial State*, a book intended to argue that over the past thirty-year period power had increasingly been shifted from the owners to the managers of large corporations and that corporate power was actually wielded by managers. In even more recent years, Roe has specified that the empowerment of managers to the detriment of shareholders was not so much the result of economic or technical-organisational factors, as of political choices inspired by the fear that the concentration of economic power might reach excessive levels.

The idea that traditional capitalism, the phase when firms used to be run directly by their owners, evolved into managerial capitalism in the 1930s is far from generally shared. It has been called into question by several authors who hold that managerial capitalism actually arose back in the 1880s. Starting out from the fact that the active participation of shareholders in corporate decision-making was always impeded by a number of different factors, some corporate law specialists have recently gone so far as to contend that the 'primacy of directors' dates as far back as the years when the very first industrial corporations were set up. In point of fact, this view is at odds with the findings of a (nine-volume) study of economic powers performed by the *Temporary National Economic Committee*. Established by the US Congress in 1938, this Committee produced evidence that no fewer than one hundred and forty, out of the two hundred largest US corporations, were controlled by their majority shareholders. Be that as it may, despite major differences between countries and different decades, it is safe to conclude that a great many large concerns in various industrial countries were run in accordance with the managerial capitalism system for over fifty years, from the end of the 1920s through the 1980s.

This historical outline contradicts the widely held assumption that limited companies and the corporate limited liability doctrine are 'nature-given' phenomena arising in connection with efficiency requirements and have nothing to do with a design to protect the interests of one specific class. As argued by Ireland (2010, p. 838), the limited company as it exists today is not a legal form which draws its origin from economic necessity. It is a political construct designed to further the interests of particular groups and has served the needs of finance, in preference to those of industrialists, right to this day. The assumption that joint-stock companies were designed to boost efficiency was strongly denied even by Adam Smith, who argued that the specifics of joint-stock companies, i.e. ownership divorced from control, the pooling of shares in the hands of rentier shareholders hardly interested in the company's business, the existence of inactive shareholders and the fact that managers handled third-person resources were causes of negligence, inefficiency and waste (see Smith 1776, pp. 609–10). As Adam Smith's ideas were very influential, his harsh criticisms were responsible for the unfavourable treatment of joint-stock companies in the economic policies framed throughout the greater part of the nineteenth century.[2]

The idea that joint-stock companies are no 'nature-given' development and the shortcomings ascribed to them have induced numerous economists to press for changes in company law provisions. Some recommend re-enacting the unlimited liability principle on the assumption that the ownership-control separation in limited companies and the limited liability granted to their shareholders may account for the launch of overly risky business operations. From the perspective of confirmed liberalists, both the existence of inactive shareholders cashing returns on investments despite their parasitical conduct and the corporate limited liability doctrine are at odds with the rationale of markets, which expects entrepreneurs to take on full responsibility for their business decisions. Lastly, others think it unjust to oblige managers to administer third-party resources without being able to pursue their own interests (see, *inter alia*, Hansmann & Kraakman 1991).

A much more interesting point is the argument that shareholders who do not perform any management functions acquire a status comparable to that of bondholders (i.e. rentiers proper). As a result, it is argued, in limited companies the distinction between these two security types is becoming unwarranted by the actual situation (see Wood 1928, p. 59) and this poses the need to reform the system in terms of changing shareholders into bondholders.

The current stage of capitalism – an opinion

As is well known, the distinction between industrial and financial capitalism is still widely shared, but in recent years some academics have argued that certain trends currently under way in limited companies point to the inception of a new phase of capitalism.

In the wake of the scandalous financial crashes involving Enron and Parmalat, Luciano Gallino produced an exacting analysis of corporate collapses which were recorded in the 1990s and were variously related to the specifics of limited companies. His book was published in 2005 with the pregnant title *L'impresa irresponsabile* (The 'Irresponsible Company'). The main point of Gallino's book is that the downward spiral in profits recorded in most industrial countries from the 1960s to the 1980s induced capitalists to prioritise bull speculation over the traditional industrial practice of working towards maximising profits from production activities.

According to him, the unprecedented Stock Exchange boom in the 1990s was both an effect and one of the causes of this reversal of trend in industrial practices. Specifically, it was a cause of this evolution since burgeoning stock revenues led capital owners to seek profit by purchasing and selling securities in preference to launching solid industrial initiatives; it was an effect since this newly conceived goal entailed persuading managers to work towards maximising securities prices – and this aim required regaining control of their companies. The main tools owners had available for this end were buying out smaller firms and launching takeover bids on rival companies on the assumption that the dimensional growth produced by new acquisitions would increase the market value of their shares. As is well known, takeovers and buyouts of companies carrying on business in comparable or different sectors were frequent occurrences throughout the 1990s.

From Gallino's perspective, a major aspect of the changes observed in world capitalism over the 1990s was a decline of the managerial capitalism model theorised by Berle and Means and its replacement with 'shareholder-directed managerial capitalism,' a model where managers, though still in charge of corporate governance functions, are obliged to act in accordance with the instructions of the company's majority shareholders and are consequently prevented from adopting the criteria they think most appropriate.

Compared to the present day, Gallino argues, until the end of the 1980s most managers used to adopt more responsible business policies to the advantage of society as a whole, but he also adds that this practice was dictated, not so much by ethical considerations, as by two different reasons. Firstly, in companies run in accordance with the managerial capitalism model the considerable profits flowing from simultaneous increases in labour and capital productivity had allowed managers more freedom of action and attention for the interests of a variety of stakeholders. Secondly, an upward trend in employment and real wage rates, coupled with other social benefits (in the first place more advantageous social security and welfare provisions) had decreed the success of the so-called 'golden age capitalism' model, and this, in turn, had created the perception that the community as a whole would benefit from the efforts of corporate managers.

In the light of the above, it is clear that the main claim of Gallino's book is that the decline of the model of capitalism theorised by Berle and Means was caused by falling industrial profits. In the face of shrinking industrial profit margins – he argues – corporate governance bodies resolved to direct their best efforts towards cashing the gains from surges in securities prices and thereby revived a form of capitalism characterised by shareholder control of business enterprises. To induce managers to work towards boosting the asset values of their shares, he continued, capitalists had no way out but to resume their engagement in the day-to-day running of their business and ended up by stripping managers of the freedom to adopt management criteria of their own choice.

In the opinion of Gallino, this new type of capitalism can still be described as managerial, but as corporate strategies are framed by the owners, it is no longer typified by full freedom of action for the managers. This is why he coined the above-mentioned definition of "shareholder-directed managerial capitalism" to designate this new model of capitalism.

The crucial difference between the older and newer models – let this be re-emphasised – is that under the former managers were free to use their power to meet the interests of a variety of stakeholders (without whom a firm would not be viable), whereas under the latter this power is solely used to maximise manager and shareholder incomes.

In the light of the above, it is clear that Gallino's approach goes to reinforce the conclusion that present-day limited companies are an objectionable corporate form.

Possible solutions

Our reflections so far prompt two main conclusions, both of which have to do with the distinction between the two major phases of capitalism, industrial and financial, and with the idea that the corporate form which is mainly responsible for the rise of financial capitalism is the limited company. Firstly, a historical review of the alternating fortunes of companies allowed to limit their liability is clear evidence that the limited liability doctrine, far from lying in the nature of things, was fleshed out for the purpose of protecting rentiers, rather than increasing business efficiency. Secondly, the combined effect of the limited liability doctrine and of shareholder control is to reverse the principle that every one must be accountable for his actions. Quoting Robertson (1923, p. 98), the 'golden rule' of capitalism is that "where the risk lies, there the control lies also."

The question is: are the shortcomings of limited companies beyond mending?

The first and most obvious solution – making limited companies unlimitedly liable for their obligations – is bound to come up against a number of difficulties. Specifically, if shareholders were obliged to assume unlimited liability for corporate debts, large capital owners might easily exploit a legal loophole offered by the system of cross holdings, i.e. the possibility to create pyramids of companies. To be relieved from their liability they might build a group structure in which all the subsidiaries and affiliates are ultimately controlled by a single holding owned by petty savers. Moreover, since most shareholders are institutions, upon the introduction of a Bill to enforce unlimited liability they might threaten to sell their holdings in order to oblige the issuing companies to hold them harmless against any claims for amounts in excess of the value of their shareholdings; the resulting need for the issuing companies to incur the cost of taking out insurance for this purpose would ultimately produce the effect of pushing up the prices of products. In short, the end result of this move would be to shift onto the community the cost of the unlimited liability principle.

Eventually, upon the re-enforcement of the unlimited liability principle capitalists would prioritise bonds over shares and limited companies would face severer funding difficulties (see Toporowski 2010, p. 890).

In the light of the above, the best solution to the problem is probably the conversion of the shares of limited companies into bonds at their market values: and this takes us back to the idea suggested at the beginning. Limited companies prevented from issuing shares are a contradiction in terms. Upon the ousting of shareholders, the managers of the resulting new company model would become accountable to workers in place of shareholders, with the effect of vesting sovereignty in workers as the ultimate claimants of the company's residual.

In the light of the fact (reported in Arena 2010, p. 883) that even Robertson, Keynes and Sraffa (whose views of limited companies were otherwise diverging) agreed on the need to reform the system with due regard to the interests of hired workers, there seems to be ground for arguing that a call for a law to convert shares into bonds and vest corporate sovereignty in workers is tantamount to a call for changing limited companies into cooperatives.

My reflections so far go to back up my claim that a system of producer cooperatives (with publicly owned production means) is actually a socialist system.

The transition to socialism in a globalised world

In Marxist terms, the type of revolution suggested in this chapter is both topical and feasible. It is feasible because the productivity rates of cooperatives tend to exceed those of capitalistic businesses; it is topical because today capitalistic production relations are not an element of dynamism, but appear like chains impeding a brisk growth of productive forces. In point of fact, considering that a materialistic view dictates the need to prioritise the direction in which history is heading, the globalisation process under way in today's world is a point which requires discussion. From this perspective, it is possible to argue that just as the relentless concentration of capital and the emergence of joint-stock companies, trusts and cartels between 1873 and 1896 induced Engels (in *Anti-Dühring*) to theorise that capitalism would be followed by central planning, and just as the close links between financial capital and the State in late nineteenth-century imperialism induced Lenin to support Engels's view, so globalisation leads us to theorise that market socialism will be the natural outgrowth of the crisis of capitalism.

A few reflections on the trends perceived in capitalistic countries today are necessary before we draw our conclusions.

By globalisation (which Marx was the first to theorise) we mean a world-scale expansion of markets, i.e. an all-embracing process which deprives governments of their traditional powers and a veritable triumph of markets which wipes away central planning and paves the way for the emergence of a system of worker-controlled firms operating in market economies. Moreover, globalisation tends to revitalise democracy in many respects. Democracy furthers the liberalisation of trade, exchanges of goods and services lead to exchanges of ideas and the resulting stimulus to intellectual debate leads to sharper political competition. This means that upward trends in democratisation, combining with advancements in science and the circulation of progressive and revolutionary ideas all over the world, spark off a steady knowledge-building process. In financially open economies, public institutions must be transparent in order to earn the confidence of markets, "and transparency spells doom for autocratic regimes" (see Eichengreen & Leblanc 2008).

But there is more to this. A major determinant both of the advantages vested in worker-controlled firms and the difficulties they come up with is the standard of living of workers. At the same pace that worker incomes rise, workers tend to become less and less averse to risk and to acquire ever greater entrepreneurial abilities;[3] and this is the rationale behind the argument that the higher income levels attained by workers in more advanced social systems may justify the contention that five hundred years after the inception of capitalism the times are ripe for a transition to socialism in richer countries.

This view has been challenged by some authors who object that a revolution providing for the transfer of business control from capital to labour is probably made redundant both by the greater educational qualifications and higher professional expertise levels required by current technological breakthroughs, by the fact that workers no longer experience their status as hired workers as degrading and, last but not least, by the fact that the higher professional qualifications they have acquired will allow them to quit and opt for self-employment.

In point of fact, this objection is anything but convincing. Indeed, the greater a worker's educational level and qualifications, the less will he accept working at the behest of another and the more eagerly will he strive to acquire the skills and expertise required to run a firm first-hand.

The abolition of hired labour in a labour-managed firm system results in an upward movement in democratisation since it ends the coercion to which workers used to be subject at the hands of their employers. And according to Hayek (1960, p. 39), coercion is an evil which turns useful thinking individuals into lifeless tools for the attainment of another's ends. "Poverty" – Mattick writes (1969, p. 152) – "never was and cannot be an element of revolution." Consequently, in the fight for socialism more stress must be laid upon the qualitative, rather than the quantitative needs of workers since "it is just the qualitative needs that capitalism cannot satisfy."

This means we can support the view of some scholars (including Mandel 1973, p. 349) that labour management will take more and more ground at the same pace that manual labour loses importance and workers acquire greater educational and professional qualifications. In other words, proletarians are revolutionaries not because they are poor, but because they draw revolutionary energy from their frustration with the role they have in production, viz., the fact that within the tight limits of the existing mode of production they are unable to develop new production forces.

Accordingly, those holding that workers are following a path which, though tortuous, will ultimately lead up to more freedom, better living standards and higher educational levels can hardly doubt that democratic firm control will in due time become a reality. The author's point, in this chapter, is that this end can be achieved by changing limited companies into cooperatives.

Though widely shared, the objection that the proletariat (the 'midwife' of the new social order according to Marx), is actually declining as a share of the total working population is less convincing than would appear at first sight since no comparable decline is either recorded in the aggregate number of hired workers or in those that would welcome a successful implementation of the transition.

In his latest writings, Engels remarked that ever more people were going to swell the ranks of hired workers and discussed the reasons why ever more members of the middle classes were siding with the proletariat. The more capitalism advances the more economic dependence will increase in the industrial sector, peasants will have to leave their fields and professionals will no longer hope to assert themselves independently of large capitalists. Consequently, it is hardly reasonable to assume that those interested in the suppression of hired work should decline in number over time. In the words of Oskar Negt (1979b, p. 147), the feeling of being divested of their lives and consciences has long spread, with increasing poignancy, from proletariats to classes and social groups whose traditional lifestyles are ever more severely impacted by capitalistic accumulation.[4]

An additional argument pointing in the same direction concerns the United States, where Stiglitz (2012, p. 13) notes that "the middle class has become eviscerated as the 'good' middle-class jobs – requiring a moderate level of skills, like autoworkers' jobs – seemed to be disappearing, relative to those at the bottom, requiring few skills, and those at the top, requiring greater skill levels." Indeed, the more society is polarised, the more the conflict between the main two classes is exacerbated and the more the lower class will be induced to embrace radical positions.[5]

Conclusion

As we have said, Marx's *Capital* includes a great many passages which make it clear that Marx rated a system of producer cooperatives as a new mode of production capable of outperforming capitalism; and in this chapter the author has argued that the limited company can be looked upon as a transitional corporate form in between the capitalistic mode of production and a new mode allowing workers to conduct business in association between them, i.e. as a springboard for the creation of a – fully socialist – system of cooperative firms.

An additional aim of this chapter was to show that Hilferding's and Lenin's distinction between industrial and financial capitalism can be used to shed light on the way the transition from capitalism to a system of democratic firms may come about in practice and realise socialism to the full. The reflections developed so far are clear evidence that financial capitalism, viewed as a necessary offspring of industrial capitalism, magnifies some of the most disastrous aspects of capitalism. The two mainstays of financial capitalism – stock exchanges and speculation – show capitalism at its worst. Indeed, whereas the business of producing goods and services at a profit is worthy of respect, the relentless pursuit of gains through speculation is a conduct which is sure to raise a justifiable storm of protest. Accordingly, the transition to democratic firm control may be viewed as the reaction of the disadvantaged classes to a capitalistic model clearly designed to play into the hands of capitalists only – and a response which gives rise to socialism.

In other words, the view that each step forward in the advancement of capitalism will generate more benefits for an increasing number of people can hardly be shared. In fact, each such step is accelerating the passage from a system for the production of goods and services for the benefit of the community as a whole to a system in which money is used to generate more and money for the exclusive benefit of speculators. Accordingly, there is good ground for arguing that the crucial role securities trading and speculation are acquiring within the contemporary social system is about to spark off a backlash from those classes which do not partake of the relevant benefits and that a system of producer cooperatives is the offshoot of a reaction to a type of capitalism which has failed to perform its main function – the production of commodities for the community as a whole – and will in due time lead to the establishment of a socialist order.

Notes

1 Arena mentions the opinion of Robertson (1923) that the control-ownership separation and the legal personality of limited companies generate growing imbalances in the distribution of industrial power, an ever more marked instability of the system, reduced company flexibility and adaptability, as well as the reduction of industrial operations to routine.

2 For modern opinions on the cogency of Smith's arguments, see Goodacre (2010).

3 Ben-Ner (1988b, p. 297) has argued that skilled and well-educated individuals will find it easier to pool their abilities and establish a firm of their own than to find an external entrepreneur.

4 This line of reasoning is refuted, *inter alia*, by Lowit (1962, p. 84), who emphasises Marx's firm belief that cooperation lacked the inherent dynamic energy that would have been needed to supplant capitalism.

5 At the other end of the spectrum are Marxist authors who think that a revival of nationalism might provide a major impetus for social change (see Munck 1985 and Nimni 1985).

12 The democratic firm and 'passive revolution'

Introduction

The notion of 'passive revolution,' which is usually rated as "one of the richest and most complex concepts" developed in Antonio Gramsci's *Prison Notebooks* (Buci-Glucksmann 1980, p. 314), has recently been the object of intense debate with fairly concordant commentary. Morton (2010, p. 316) defines it as a rupture in society leading to radical changes that are instantly, though only partially, implemented; others describe it as a process producing systematic changes by non-revolutionary means (Callinicos 2010, p. 492) or as a government-directed process of radical changes aimed to perpetuate the existing mode of production (McKay 2010, pp. 363–64); others still explain it as the response of an elite to social unrest and an attempt to oust the masses from transformation processes by strengthening the role of the State (Simon 2010, pp. 430–31) or a 'top-down' bourgeois revolution antithetical to the French Revolution (Davidson 2010, p. 343).

In Gramscian theory, a passive revolution takes place when "a State replaces the local social groups in leading a struggle for renewal," with the clarification that this is "one of the cases in which these groups have the function of 'domination' without that of 'leadership': dictatorship without hegemony" (see Gramsci 1975, vol. III, p. 1823). In short, in Gramsci a 'passive revolution' is described as a bourgeois revolution which is controlled from the top (see Morton 2010, p. 317 and McKay 2010, p. 364) and leads to changes made without the participation of the masses. But is participation to be understood as active or passive? Is there consensus or lack of dissent? And provided there is consensus, is it genuine assent or just resignation? In Gramsci, consensus is often described as 'active' or 'spontaneous' (see Gramsci 1975, vol III, p. 413), and this is an additional point to be revisited further on.[1]

It is often argued that the rationale behind the attitude of the bourgeoisie during a passive revolution runs counter to the very principles of this class. According to Davidson, for instance, this attitude first became clear at the time of the French revolution, when "even the most class-conscious members of the bourgeoisie drew back from the actions necessary to achieve a complete victory over the old regime, paralysed as they were by a fear of the urban plebeians who might push beyond the limits that the former considered acceptable" (Davidson 2010, p. 344).[2]

Analysing the Soviet revolution, Lenin wrote (1956, p. 12): "The specific feature of the present situation in Russia is that the country is passing from the first stage of the revolution – which, owing to the insufficient class-consciousness and organisation of the proletariat, placed power in the hands of the bourgeoisie – to its second stage, which must place power in the hands of the proletariat and the poorest sections of the peasants."

As far as the 1848 revolutions in Europe are concerned, initially the middle classes engaged in reform, but as soon as they perceived the first signs of recovery they swung back to moderatism in an attempt to avert the involvement of the masses and the risk of a turn to more radical policies. In this connection, Engels wrote (1892a, p. 59): "the industrial and commercial middle class had, therefore, not yet succeeded in driving the landed aristocracy completely from political power when another competitor, the working class, appeared on the stage."[3]

In Gramsci's approach, the 'Piedmont conquest' that paved the way for the union of Italy appears as an instance of passive revolution since the dominant classes across Italy, though mostly favourable to a union, did not take the lead of the movement in the awareness that their interests were at odds with those of the working and rural masses. In Gramsci 1975 (vol. III, p. 125) we read that Cavour's chosen strategy proved successful not because it mediated between opposite extremes, but due to the sheer lack of valid political antagonists, and that his policies led to a sectarian structure which could not play an appreciable role on the international scene since at home it was under constant threat from elementary subversive forces – the proletarians whose interests Cavour had deliberately disregarded.

Although it is clear that the notion of passive revolution may add to our understanding of several historical developments recorded over the past two centuries, in this chapter we have resolved to maintain a preferential focus on the fact that it is first and foremost advocates of the transition from capitalism to democratic firm control that will find it particularly rich in valuable insights. As is well known, a system of self-managed firms operates in a market economy which has transferred corporate sovereignty to factory councils, viz., in a system which has vested in the proletariat the main achievements of the French Revolution: free economic initiative and the right to decide what is to be produced. For this reason, the establishment of such a system would amount to a revolution real and proper. Gramsci's approach sheds light on the reasons why no such revolution has come about so far.

Passive revolution and centralised planning

To start with, let us establish if, and to what extent, the concept of passive revolution is applicable to the Soviet revolution. There can be little doubt that the Bolshevik revolution was far from bourgeois in nature, but as soon as the notion of 'passive revolution' is extended to encompass the radical changes made by non-bourgeois agents after the French Revolution (as several authors do), signs of passivity will even be perceived at some steps of the Bolshevik revolution. In an analysis of pre-revolution Russia, Gramsci wrote that the "national forces were inert, passive and receptive, but perhaps precisely for this reason they completely assimilated the foreign influences and the foreigners themselves, Russifying them." In the more recent historical period – he specified – "we find the opposite phenomenon. An élite consisting of some of the most active, energetic, enterprising and disciplined members of society emigrates abroad and assimilates the culture and historical experiences of the most advanced countries of the West, without however losing the most essential characteristics of its own nationality, that is to say without breaking its sentimental and historical links with its own people. Having thus performed its intellectual apprenticeship, it returns to its own country and compels the people to an enforced awakening, skipping historical stages in the process. The difference between this élite and that imported from Germany (by Peter the Great, for example)" – he concluded – "lies in its essentially national-popular character: it could not be assimilated by the inert passivity of the Russian people, because it was itself an energetic reaction of Russia to her own historical inertia" (Gramsci 1975, vol III, p. 1525).

The ultimate implication of this passage, i.e. the claim that the Bolshevik revolution was the feat of a minority in which the masses were not actively involved, is in sync with Noam Chomsky's argument that "the Bolshevik revolution and the ideology of liberal technocrats have in common the firm belief that mass organisations and popular politics have to be suppressed" (Chomsky 2013, p. 69).[4]

The question is: how far does this extend to the events that ensued?

The centrally planned Soviet system has been described as State capitalism, as a system where the proletariat is exploited by a class which, though not the bourgeoisie proper, has much in common with it and, occasionally, as a non-capitalistic system in which a heterogeneous social group acting as a ruling elite reaps the benefits of the surplus generated by the mass of the workers (Simon 2010). The implication here is the widely shared assumption that the turn from capitalism to a centrally planned system is a 'passive revolution' in which the masses do not play an active part.

In point of fact, the phrase 'State capitalism' is not a suitable description for a system in which firms are expected to stick to a plan instead of striving to maximise profits and where the decisions concerning the product mix (viz., the plan) are not freely made by bourgeois operators in competition with rival companies, but by the ruling group in dealings between its various components. In the Soviet system the ruling class does wield political power, and due to the need to retain its power and pass it on to the future generations, it has no option but to monopolise economic power as well. The power position of the ruling elite prevents the emergence of what is termed civil society: in the absence of trade union representation, workers remain an anonymous mass lacking awareness of themselves as a class. In actual fact, occasionally a State does take actions designed to further the interests of the workers, but as these lack class consciousness, the claim that the ruling class exercises a non-authoritarian hegemonic power in Gramsci's definition would be unwarranted.

An additional difference between capitalistic states and the Soviet system is that the former freely engage in international trade and cope with globalisation, while the latter, as a result of the ban on trading freely with foreign firms, finds it hard to entertain international relationships.

Accordingly, it is possible to argue that despite the absence of two antithetical classes and the non-applicability of the State capitalism label, the Soviet system suffers from a basic contradiction which is comparable to that of capitalism: the discrepancy between the efforts of the ruling group to maximise the surplus-generating potential of production activities and the erosion of the actual surplus levels caused by the workers' tendency to minimise the enervation associated with their work inputs. The reason why this conflict of interests was never solved in any of the countries of the so-called Soviet bloc is that all the attempts to put in place the most obvious remedy – vesting decision-making powers in workers or incentivising them to increase their productivity levels – proved abortive because central planning and markets are mutually exclusive institutions (and not, as argued by academics in a long-drawn-out debate, because of the opposition of the ruling classes).

On closer analysis, however, although these reflections are in accord with the widely held view of the Soviet economy as a non-democratic system that failed to involve the masses, in the light of the bourgeois essence of a passive revolution it is hardly appropriate to extend this label to a system in which the bourgeoisie did not take the lead.

The bourgeoisie and passive revolution

Considering that the democratic principles to which the bourgeoisie pays lip service are in stark contrast with the 'one share, one vote' criterion governing decision-making today (see Pateman 1970 and Dahl 1985), we might expect the bourgeoisie to put itself at the head of a transition process intended to establish democratic firm management. As things stand, Lukàcs warns, the mere existence of a scientifically acceptable solution to such a serious problem does not take us very far, since "to accept that solution, even in theory, would be tantamount to observing society from a class standpoint other than that of the bourgeoisie" and "no class can do that unless it is willing to abdicate its power freely" (see Lukàcs 1923, p. 70). Insofar as this is true, we must admit, with Bettelheim (1969), that ever since the victorious revolt of the bourgeoisie against feudal lords the overriding aim of this class has been to prevent workers from attaining power.

The class consciousness of the bourgeoisie, Lukàcs wrote (1923, p. 80) "is cursed by its very nature with the tragic fate of developing an insoluble contradiction at the zenith of its powers and with annihilating itself as a result of this contradiction." This tragedy, he added, "is reflected historically in the fact that even before it had defeated its predecessor, feudalism, its new enemy, the proletariat, had appeared on the scene. Politically, it became evident when, at the moment of victory, the 'freedom' in whose name the bourgeoisie had engaged in its battle against feudalism was transformed into a new repressiveness" which in Lukàcs's mind was capitalistic exploitation, but which we identify with the denial of voting rights to workers in firms.[5]

As argued by Salvadori (1979, p. 290), the intuition that it was the victorious march of socialism that frightened the bourgeoisie into recanting the libertarian ideals of democracy goes back to Kautsky, precisely to Kautsky's argument that when the Prussian bourgeois espoused the cause of the landed nobility, the *Junkertum*, they opted for a reassuring form of authoritarianism.

The extent to which the refusal to grant workers voting rights in firms is antithetical to the very principles of the bourgeoisie has been emphasised by several authors. Carlo Rosselli wrote that all over the world the bourgeoisie had ceased to be liberal-minded and that the more the proletariat managed to assert itself and vindicate its freedom, the more the most reactionary fractions of the bourgeoisie were seen to back away from the discipline entailed in a correct exercise of freedom (see Rosselli 1930, p. 435);[6] and in Thomas Mann's *Confessions of a Nonpolitical Man* we read that "satisfaction reigned supreme in that part of society which had attained political democracy in 1789, that is to say the bourgeoisie, which celebrated its triumph in the belief that there was no need to go any further" (see Mann 1918, p. 62).

The opposition of the bourgeoisie to the introduction of democratic firm control (in contrast with its own principles, as mentioned above) may explain why the nineteenth and twentieth centuries experienced a number of 'passive revolutions.' According to Gramsci, World War I marked a divide in history since all the actions that the bourgeoisie put in place after it were guided by the logic of putting the emerging new class, the proletariat, out of the game.

Though different in many respects, the passive revolutions that took place in Scotland, Canada and Mexico, as well as in Russia and China in more recent times, originated from an attempt of the bourgeoisie to keep the proletariat in check and were consequently defused by the fear that the limits rated as acceptable by the former class should be overstepped.

A somewhat different argument in support of the bourgeois character of passive revolutions is implied in the often-heard remark that the bourgeois class lacks a culture of its own. Lefebvre, for instance (1968, p. 121), argued that, far from creating a culture of their own, the bourgeois had taken over those of precapitalistic and pre-industrial ages and had adjusted them to their own ends. This – he contended – is what is termed 'classicism' and the only additions made to classicism and humanism during the heyday of the bourgeoisie were confutations and refusals.

On closer analysis, all these reflections ultimately suggest that the bourgeoisie refuses to extend to the working class those rights which it succeeded in wresting from the feudal class.

As Karl Korsch puts it, since the principle that all humans are equal and have a right to freedom is not applicable to bourgeois society "for that part which due to its far-reaching implications would be of most concern to workers, i.e. for the part associated with the production of commodities in firms" (see Korsch 1922, p. 112), no liberalist, however well-meaning, will ever be able to fully appraise the benefits that would flow from the liberation of workers. When Gramsci's writings for *Ordine Nuovo* fired the minds of the members of the movement for workers' councils during Italy's so-called 'red biennium,' Luigi Einaudi argued that one of the burning issues of his day was restoring the 'pleasure' that workers drew from their work until it was utterly destroyed in large industrial concerns (Einaudi 1920a, p. 848). The worker – he wrote – would like to regain control of his work input; he would like to know why and how he engages in production, and he would expect to be given a voice in decisions concerning the distribution of the output of industry. "This typically human aspiration – he concluded – "may lead to moral elevation and is the transposition to industry of a principle which is acknowledged by the governments of all modern nations" (Einaudi 1920a, p. 849).

The transfer of corporate decision powers to workers would generate benefits for society as a whole. By way of example, the disempowerment of capitalists in a worker-controlled firm system (especially one mainly formed of LMF-type cooperatives – see Vanek 1971a and 1971b, Jossa & Cuomo 1997, pp. 162–63 and Jossa 2005b, chap. III) would afford major steps in the direction of full democracy. And from our perspective, this is probably the most important of all the advantages associated with a democratic firm system.[7] As capital is the all-dominating economic power of bourgeois society – Marx wrote (1857–58) – stripping capitalists of their power would be a major step forward in the direction of greater freedom for all. This point will be discussed in greater depth in the next section.

Passive revolution and democracy in the firm

Introducing the notion of passive revolution, Gramsci wrote: "Speaking of the revolution that took place in Italy in response to the Napoleonic wars, Vincenzo Cuoco used the phrase 'passive revolution.' From my perspective, this concept is correct not only for Italy, but also for other countries which modernized the state through a series of reforms or national wars, but without going through a political revolution of a radical-Jacobin type" (Gramsci 1975, p. 504).

Whereas the term radical-Jacobin revolution may designate (a) a violent revolution and (b) the overthrow of the existing mode of production (the French Revolution put an end to feudalism), in the passage quoted above (which, admittedly, allows of various interpretations) it clearly designates a radical change in historical conditions which is not violently revolutionary in the manner theorised by Marx, but leads to the establishment of a new mode of production by non-violent means. In addition to this, as the passage from Gramsci is related to the 'Piedmont conquest' of Italy, it evidently refers to a passive revolution which does not involve the masses.

Further on, trying to establish a parallel between Cuoco's 'passive revolution' and Quinet's 'revolution-restoration,' Gramsci argues that both these notions "express the historical fact that popular initiative is absent from the whole course of Italian history, as well as the fact that progress occurs as the response of the ruling classes to the sporadic and inconsistent rebelliousness of the popular masses – a response consisting of 'restorations' that grant some part of the popular demands and are therefore 'progressive restorations' or 'revolution-restorations'" (see Gramsci 1975, p. 957).

Besides confirming that a passive revolution is characterised by the non-involvement of the masses, this passage tells us that such a revolution cannot take the form of an insurrection intended to establish a superior mode of production through the use of violence.[8]

Taken together, the passages quoted suggest that a passive revolution, though, admittedly, a radical change in historical circumstances, differs from a Marxian revolution because of aspects typical of a restoration and may acquire all the connotations of a real and proper restoration, viz. a return to an earlier mode of production (as happened in post-1989 Russia).

If this is a correct interpretation of Gramsci's thought, the core element behind his notion of passive revolution is the idea (suggested by Lukàcs, as mentioned above) that following the considerable growth of the working class in the years after the French Revolution and, even more so, ever since the advent of the proletariat to power during the Bolshevik revolution, the bourgeoisie has failed to make radical changes involving the popular masses for fear that the proletariat should call for unacceptable solutions – specifically the establishment of a socialist society and the disempowerment of the bourgeoisie. Accordingly, the bourgeoisie has blatantly acted against its own principles since the privileges it refuses to extend to workers are those which it conquered for itself during the French Revolution.

At this point we may ask ourselves if the phrase 'passive revolution' reflects a theoretical or historical notion, i.e. if it designates revolutionary processes in general or revolutions which actually took place in given historical periods. What is sure is that notwithstanding changes and refinements to the original idea made by Gramsci himself and other authors (see Callinicos 2010), it merely describes bourgeois 'revolutions' since the bourgeoisie is an intermediate class which conceives the fear of a subsequent proletarian revolution when still engaged in its own revolution against feudalism.[9]

Our reflections so far back up our initial claim that Gramsci's concept of passive revolutions sounds both more significant and more relevant if the revolution we have in mind is one that puts an end to capitalism through the establishment of a democratic firm system. Indeed, in self-managed firms choices related to the product mix are invariably made in accordance with democratic and non-plutocratic procedures, i.e. in full harmony with the principles of the French Revolution. Consequently, anyone endorsing the revolution we have in mind will find it singularly evident that the refusal of the bourgeoisie to pass on to the working class those privileges which it gained during the French Revolution runs counter to its distinctive values.

Let us repeat that no such claim can be advanced by advocates of a revolution aimed to establish a centrally planned system, since the substitution of planning for markets is unrelated to the principles of the French Revolution. The opposition of the bourgeoisie to centralised planning does not conflict with its principles because such a system does not envisage the extension of free economic initiative to the working class. And as free economic initiative, the farthest-reaching of all the rights ever attained by the bourgeoisie, has no currency in a centrally planned system, it can hardly come as a surprise that the bourgeoisie is inimical to centralised planning.

This is the rationale behind our argument that a Gramscian-type passive revolution makes more sense for an advocate of the establishment of worker control. Not for nothing was this notion fleshed out by a theoretician of factory councils such as Gramsci and not by an advocate of centralised planning.

Eventually, let us mention that the implication of a reactionary involution of the bourgeoisie that is perceived behind Gramsci's concept of passive revolution confirms that Lenin was absolutely right when he diagnosed the capitalistic nature of early twentieth-century Russia and insisted on a revolutionary strategy founded on an alliance between workers and peasants (for an exhaustive discussion of this point, see Howard & King 1989).

Passive revolution and hegemony

Now it is time to raise the question if a non-hegemonic position of the bourgeoisie is a precondition for describing a revolution as 'passive.' The idea that a passive revolution rules out a hegemonic position of the bourgeoisie is spelt out both in a Gramscian passage quoted above and in an additional one which runs as follows:

"Piedmont had a function which can, from certain aspects, be compared to that of a party, i.e. of the leading personnel of a social group (and in fact people always spoke of the 'Piedmont party'), with the additional qualification that it was in fact a State, with an army, a diplomatic service, etc. This fact is of the greatest importance for the concept of 'passive revolution' – the fact, that is, that what was involved was not a social group which 'led' other groups, but a State which, even though it had limitations as a power, 'led' the group which should have been 'leading' and was able to put at the latter's disposal an army and a politico-diplomatic strength" (Gramsci 1975, vol III, pp. 1822–23).[10]

Although this view is widely shared (see, *inter alia*, Buci-Glucksmann 1979, p. 217), some authors object that the distinction between active participation and passive consent (or consensus and lack of dissent) is much too hazy and suggest describing passive revolutions as typified by the predominance of force over consent, rather than by lack of hegemony (see Bruff 2010, pp. 412–13). From our perspective, it is the definitions of 'passive revolution' and 'hegemony' themselves that rule out a hegemonic position of the bourgeoisie during passive revolutions.

Since hegemony originates from the ability to grasp the dynamics of events and identify those social forces which are capable of expediting feasible developments and since it requires the ability to gain the consensus of the majority of the workers concerning the choices lying ahead, what remains to be established is what kind of consensus is to be gained.

Gramsci himself emphasised that "hegemony presupposes that account be taken of the interests and the tendencies of the groups over which hegemony is to be exercised and that a certain compromise equilibrium should be found – in other words, that the leading group should make sacrifices of an economic-corporate kind," but he also warned that "such sacrifices and such compromise cannot touch the essential" (Gramsci 1975, vol. III, p. 1591). As a result, there is little doubt that Gramsci's notion of hegemony fits within a worldview which conceives of the conquest of power as a process characterised by frictions between base and superstructure and of social evolution as proceeding 'from the bottom to the top.'[11]

Inasmuch as the precondition for the acquisition of hegemony is the consent of the majority of the workers concerning necessary choices, it is clear that so long as the bourgeoisie strives to hold back the masses it will not be able to attain a hegemonic position. And this conclusion is in full sync with the above-mentioned claim that the refusal of the bourgeoisie to pass on its own privileges to the working class runs counter to its very principles.

According to Norberto Bobbio, Gramsci's numerous in-depth analyses of the base-superstructure opposition are clear evidence that – unlike Marx – he thought of civil society as part of the superstructure, rather than the base (see Bobbio 1969 and Prestipino 1990, pp. 36–59 and 65)[12] and looked upon hegemony as the result of the influence of the superstructure on the base.[13] In Gramsci's own words, "What we can do, for the moment, is to fix two major superstructural 'levels,' the one that can be called 'civil society,' that is the ensemble of organisms commonly called 'private,' and that of 'political society' or 'the State.' These two levels correspond [...] to the function of 'hegemony' which the dominant group exercises throughout society" (Gramsci 1975, p. 1518; see, also, pp. 1020 and 1590–2302).[14]

In Gramsci, the notion of hegemony fits within a worldview in which the conquest of power appears as a process associated with frictions between the base and the superstructure[15] and social evolution is perceived as a 'bottom-up' process that detractors tend to characterise as highly subjective (see Riechers 1970, p. 202).[16]

Gramsci held that a revolution will only come about when the working class manages to persuade the majority of the people, i.e. the amorphous middle class, intellectuals and peasants, that its immediate and future interests fall in with those of the majority" (Gramsci 1919–20, p. 144).

Insofar as is true that the bourgeoisie will not attain hegemony unless it wins the consent of the majority of the workers concerning the choices lying ahead, it is clear that a passive revolution rules out a hegemonic position of the bourgeoisie just as it rules out the involvement of the popular classes. Although there is general agreement on this point (see, *inter alia*, Buci-Glucksmann 1979, p. 217), it is hard to deny that the distinction between active participation and passive consent or consent and lack of dissent is rather hazy and that a passive revolution is mainly characterised by the predominance of force over consensus, rather than lack of hegemony (see Bruff 2010, pp. 412–13).

Marx on the divide between civil society and the State under capitalism

With reference to political democracy as the main strong point of firm control, in the *Contribution to the Critique of Hegel's Philosophy of Right* the young Marx spoke of a divide between civil society and the State which was unknown in feudal times and emerged in the modern age. In medieval society, he wrote, "man was political; the material content of the stage was fixed by reason of its form; every private sphere had a political character or was a political sphere, [...] the landowner was also sovereign within the political sphere, whereas those who were servants in civil society were also bereft of political rights" (1843, p. 44). "In the Middle Age, popular life and State [...] were identical. Man was the actual principle of the state, but he was *unfree man*. It was therefore the *democracy of unfreedom*, accomplished alienation. The abstract, reflected opposition [...] belongs only to modern times" (*ibid.*). In Marx's view, it was only in post-Renaissance times that towns experiencing industrial growth wrested themselves free from the feudal organisation, so that the inception of the slow process resulting in the separation of civil society from political society dates from that time and the growing distance between the State and social life is a basic characteristic of modern society. In the modern world – he also wrote (*op. cit.*, p. 62) – "the distinction between State and civil society is established. The State does not reside within civil society, but outside it." In other words, whereas at one time the State was a totality of political and social aspects, in modern society the State has – regrettably – distanced itself from society. "The abstraction of the State as such belongs only to modern times because the abstraction of private life belongs only to modern times" (Marx 1843, p. 43).

The divide between civil society and the State was not only a key notion of Hegel's approach to the philosophy of right, but had also been analysed in depth by Saint-Simon. As Saint-Simon's thought had gained wide currency at that time, it is from him that Marx took over this notion in order to claim that the State, faced with the advancement of civil society, had put up its defence by retaining older social organisational forms such as monarchy, putting in place an oppressive bureaucracy and vesting political power in the landed aristocracy. "As taught by Saint-Simon, political power and bureaucracy are not coeval with civil society, but remnants of feudal times!" (Ansart 1969, p. 374).

Marx and Hegel firmly believed that the gulf between civil society and the modern State is responsible for a major discrepancy: whereas civil society is the sphere where private individual interests play themselves out in a *bellum omnium contra omnes*, the aim of the State is to meet the general interest (according to Hegel) or the interests of the bourgeoisie (according to Marx). And as people acting in the status of private members pursue egotistic ends, whereas in the status of citizens of the state they are expected to work towards the general interest, this discrepancy extends from society as a whole to single individuals. In this connection, it is worth bearing in mind that in Hegel's approach private interests are not negated, but superseded and, hence, retained, whereas Marx held them to be antithetical to the general interest, but constantly prioritised over the latter.

In contrast with Hegel's position, he spelt out in bold letters that the economy prevails over politics and that private interests are always being pursued in preference to the public interest. As a result, the 1843 version of the *Criticism of Hegel's Philosophy of Right* can be said to contain the seeds of Marx's later theory of historical materialism (see Della Volpe 1969a, p. 8).

The question to be raised at this point is whether the gap between civil society and political society can be bridged.

The passage from Marx printed below tells us that the remedy is democracy. "In democracy" – Marx argued – "the constitution itself appears only as one determination and indeed as the self-determination of the people," and "the formal principle is simultaneously the material principle [...] democracy is the first true unity of the universal and the particular" (Marx 1843, p. 42). "For all their complexity" – Petrucciani (2009, p. 34) remarks on this point – "these reflections reveal an embryonic insight which will influence all the subsequent development of Marx's political thought: the conviction, that is, that true democracy, understood as the people's self-determination, requires superseding the separation between the domain of politics and other social spheres."

The claim that worker control furthers political democracy by acting as a link between economics and politics takes us back to the central point of this book, in terms that this link is the strongly democratic connotations that both these spheres acquire thanks to the disempowerment of capital and the substitution of the democratic 'one head, one vote' principle for the plutocratic 'one share, one vote' principle.

From our perspective, however, the decisive factor is and remains democratic firm control, while centralised planning, though also narrowing the gap between the two spheres concerned, is incapable of enhancing democracy since it is founded on the subordination of economics to politics.[17]

Conclusion

According to Kautsky (1906, p. 90), the French revolution "gave the bourgeoisie the essence of what they wanted," but it also revealed "social forces which wanted to go further than themselves." Since the bourgeois rated those forces as even "more dangerous than the relics of the deposed old" it is possible to argue, with Bettelheim, that ever since its victorious revolt against the feudal lords, the overriding aim of the bourgeoisie has been to bar the workers' path to power (see Bettelheim 1969).

On closer analysis, this argument receives further confirmation from Gramsci's description of all post-French Revolution revolts as 'passive revolutions.'

In the light of Gransci's approach, we have argued that (a) confining democracy to the political sphere runs counter the principles of the French Revolution which are the foundation of all bourgeois revolutions; that (b) the extension of democracy to economic life magnifies political democracy; and that (c) Gramsci's notion of 'passive revolution' sheds meaningful light on these points.

Simone Weil wrote that "there is democracy to the extent that it is simultaneously political and economic" (see Weil 1959, p. 177); and there can be little doubt that "s'il est un point qui distingue le socialisme du liberalisme, c'est bien le pouvoir de l'homme d'agir par la raison sur l'organisation sociale" (Denizet 1981, p 6). Provided this is true, it is possible to argue that all those liberals who speak out for democracy but refuse to accept democratic firm control act against their own principles and do not place any trust in human reason.

If we try to identify a single element of Marx's approach that can be rated as his main contribution to science we are faced with an embarrassing array of options to choose from: the labour theory of value, the materialistic conception of history, the notion of modes of production or the historical method, just to mention a few. In the opinion of many, this issue is ill posed since Marx's farthest-reaching contribution to science is his global theoretical edifice, a complex compound including both parts which narrowly come short of spanning the entire domain of human knowledge and, in contrast, worn-out notions no longer acceptable today. Unlike these authors, we hold that Marx's theoretical approach revolves around one core idea from which all the others are seen to branch out. This key concept is the description of capitalism as a mode of production which asserted itself at a certain stage of history, whose mechanisms are governed by a set of rules (always basically the same) which shape the political and ideological superstructure and whose internal dynamic irredeemably leads to its erosion and ultimate replacement with a different mode of production.

Marx's claim that this new mode of production is the communist society he himself theorised is far from convincing, nor do we believe that the keys for a correct understanding of the working of capitalism are Marx's value and exploitation theory. One central notion of Marxism is the materialist conception of history in a strictly scientific form, not in the version that even some non-Marxists would be prepared to accept.

The reflections developed in this chapter underscore the need to flesh out a new interpretative approach to Marx's work and bring it into line with the new revolutionary scenario that is taking shape. Irrespective of opinions to the contrary advanced by some Marxists today (see, *inter alia*, Carandini 2005, Introduction), it is a fact that Marx was not only a critic of capitalism, but a theoretician of revolution who predicted the ultimate replacement of capitalism by a new mode of production which he indifferently named socialism or communism and vaguely divided into a set of stages. And from our perspective a theory envisaging the right of producers in association to keep the output of their work for themselves can be rated as truly radical and revolutionary (see, *inter alia*, Marcovic 1969, p. 143).

The need to rethink Marx's theoretical work is imposed by the different revolutionary scenario that appears feasible today, as mentioned above. As a stout enemy of markets, Marx took it for granted that a communistic society would in due time suppress markets, but since he failed to draw a clear-cut distinction between socialism and communism, the assumption that he contrasted socialism and communism in terms of thinking of the former as a post-capitalistic production mode retaining the characteristics of a market economy and the latter as a production mode without markets is unwarranted (see, *inter alia*, Brunetta 2014, p. 61).

If Marx's theoretical approach is 'rethought' in line with the recommendations of modern market socialists, the emerging 'new Marx' and the resulting revisited version of Marxism would have to be described as *critical of capitalism but not inimical to markets*.

Notes

1 Concerning the events of Brumaire 18th, Marx wrote: bourgeois revolutions "storm more swiftly from success to success, their dramatic effects outdo each other, men and things seem set in sparkling diamonds; ecstasy is the order of the day – but they are short-lived. Soon they reach their zenith, and a long Katzenjammer [cat's winge] takes hold of society before it learns to assimilate the results of its storm-and-stress period soberly" (Marx 1852c, p. 491).

2 In this connection, in Schorske (1979, p. 110) we read: "In the late nineteenth century, the policies enforced by the Liberal government ran counter the interests of the upper classes and led to the turbulent emergence of the lower classes. In point of fact, the political energies of the masses that the policies of the Liberals had unleashed turned against the Liberals themselves, rather than the traditional enemies of the proletariat."

3 By general agreement, the popular masses remained on the margin of warfare even at the time of the Paris Commune (see, *inter alia*, Cortesi 2010, p. 75).

4 On the assumption that "the salient characteristic of any revolution is the active involvement of the masses," Sartori goes so far as to contend that the movement led by Lenin and his successors was no genuine revolution at all (see Sartori 2015, p. 34).

5 As argued by Paul Lafargue, when the bourgeois were struggling against the nobility and the clergy mobilised in their support, they "hoisted the flag of free thought and atheism, but once they had triumphed, they changed their tone and manner" (see Lafargue 1880, p. 23).

6 In this connection, Bloch quoted the wise old saying that people on an empty stomach speak differently. Prior to coming to power – he argued – the bourgeoisie acted more humanely than any other group had done before it. It acted as a champion of freedom and spoke out for the sons of the nations and for universal human values (Bloch 1968, p. 73).

7 This means I unconditionally endorse Gould's claim (see Gould 1985, p. 204) that "Rawls fails to take clearly into account that equality with respect to certain social and economic conditions is necessary for political freedom."

8 Years before, faced with the positions taken by the socialist parliamentary group regarding certain matters, Gramsci had dubbed those socialists "cowardly souls of democratic troglodytes" striving to oust the proletariat from the active stream of events (Gramsci 1918a).

9 In a study explaining modernity as the result and major driving force of accelerated historical progress (see Fusaro 2010), such acceleration is said to have been fuelled by the Industrial and French Revolutions, but as Fusaro does not mention the concept of passive revolution, he fails to specify that the progress of history is slowed down by the fear of proletarian revolutions.

10 The earliest definition of the notion of passive revolution dates back to Lenin. According to Lenin – Gruppi writes (1970, p. 64) – "the dialectical analysis of economic processes and class relations indicates that the Russian revolution of 1915, though undeniably bourgeois in nature and, as such, designed to expedite the advancement of capitalism in Russia, was not bourgeois in the classical sense of this word since it occurred at a historical stage at which the bourgeoisie could no longer take the lead."

11 The frictions between base and superstructure mentioned by Gramsci account for the dialectical essence of Marxism and conflict with the mechanistic and positivistic view of Marxism prevailing within the Italian Socialist Party in those days. In a positivistic logic, the second term of the base-superstructure relation was practically cancelled in consequence of the postulate that the base mechanistically creates the superstructure and the result was a one-way relation between the two terms. The superstructure was deprived of its autonomy and the dialectical nature of the historical process was consequently neutralised (see Bonomi 1973, pp. 25–31).

12 Unlike Marx, Gramsci held that civil society was the aggregate of a rich web of ideological-cultural relations only and not of all existing material relations. For an analysis of the different notions of civil society theorised by Gramsci, see Badaloni (1990, pp. 16–18).

13 Compared to Marx's approach, in Gramsci the interrelations between institutions and ideology are reversed, in terms that ideologies are the primary historical phenomena, while institutions are the secondary ones (see Bobbio 1969, vol. I, p. 91).

14 According to Anderson, a passage from the *Notebooks* (which he quotes – see Anderson 2002, p. 8, note 2) makes it clear that Gramsci looked upon hegemony as a combination of force and consent in varying proportions, but that in certain situations, for example when the hegemonic function is hard to exercise or the use of force is too risky, he did not rule out the use of corruption/fraud, the intermediate form between consent and force which "consists in procuring the demoralisation and paralysis of the antagonist (or antagonists)" (see Gramsci 1975, vol. III, p. 1638).

15 As Prestipino puts it, to account for Bobbio's controversial classification of Gramsci's 'civil society' as a component of the superstructure it is worth bearing in mind that Gransci looked upon civil society as the arena where the struggle for the attainment of hegemony acts itself out (see Prestipino 1990, p. 38).

16 As the base-superstructure frictions theorised by Gramsci underscore the dialectical essence of Marxism, they go to refute the mechanistic and positivistic understanding of Marxism which prevailed within the Italian Socialist Party in those days. The effect of this misleading view was to cancel the second term of the base-superstructure relation by creating the impression that the base was mechanistically created by the superstructure. What remained was a one-way relation between the two terms, with the cancellation of the autonomous status of the superstructure and the dialectical essence of the historical process (see Bonomi 1973, pp. 25–31).

17 The fact that the roots of Gramsci's notion of passive revolution are in Marx is clearly revealed by the roles assigned to the bourgeoisie and the proletariat in social processes (see Johnson 1983).

13 A few reflections on the reasons why cooperative firms have failed to gain a firm foothold

Introduction

After the inception of the cooperative movement in the mid-nineteenth century, it was widely held that capital-managed enterprises would soon be replaced by a system of worker-controlled firms and a wealth of political agendas called for a major impulse to cooperation in later years also. Shortly after the establishment of the Rochdale Society of Equitable Pioneers (which is rated as the true prototype of the modern cooperative), John Stuart Mill argued that the form of association which would eventually prevail was "not that which can exist between a capitalist as chief, and work-people without a voice in the management, but the association of the labourers themselves on terms of equality, collectively owning the capital with which they carry on their operations, and working under managers elected and removable by themselves" (see Mill 1871, pp. 720 and 723). A comparable view is perceived behind Marshall's claim that no serious obstacles stand in the way of the growth of the cooperative movement and that its ultimate assertion is consequently just a question of time.[1]

All the same, the defeating, but undeniable fact that cooperation has been lagging behind is right before our eyes and the tentative explanations proposed by some scholars can hardly be rated as exhaustive or fully convincing. Mandel, for instance, has simply argued that labour management is sure to make headway at the same pace that manual labour loses importance and workers acquire greater educational and professional qualifications (see Mandel 1973, p. 349).

Specifically, employee management specialists are unable to account for the fact that the policy proposal to introduce democratic firm control still carries little consensus despite the collapse of the Soviet model of communism. In other words, I wonder why democratic firm management is still receiving little attention from scholars and why few of them are prepared to bet on its final success.

Two different, though closely linked issues acquire relevance in this connection: (a) the reason why cooperatives have failed to supplant capitalistic companies by degrees; (b) the true rationale behind the lukewarm support of cooperation by economists and, generally, intellectuals. Considering the numerous advantages of firm control discussed in the economic literature and the huge step it would mark in the direction of economic democracy – an obvious complement of political democracy – it must come as a surprise that few economists specialising in employee management have suggested the introduction of worker control on a large scale.[2]

Ideas, interests and unaided growth

The belief that anything benefiting the community will come about unaided and that whatever deserves to make headway should be left to do so through natural or cultural selection is a corollary of the axiom that individual behaviour is rational and of neoclassical economic theorems postulating that those allowed to see to their personal interests will ultimately help maximise the community's well-being. An additional core notion behind rational action theory is that markets can do without institutions. Indeed, the argument runs, whenever a step towards increasing the community's well-being is dependent on institutional changes, it will be taken on condition that there is a political majority prepared to vote for such changes. It is on this particular point that conflict is strongest: on the one hand are those who believe that progress is a function of ideas (and that positive ideas will always assert themselves); on the other are those claiming that the rise of institutions working towards the social good is impeded by vested interests. As is well known, liberalists believe in the power of ideas and tend to assume that mass propaganda will not spark off any appreciable political breakthroughs unless it succeeds in achieving its primary aim – persuading intellectuals (see, *inter alia*, Hayek 1983, pp. 192–93).[3] At the other end of the spectrum are Marxists, who denounce the noxious power of vested interests.[4]

Accordingly, it is necessary to raise the question if the establishment of democratic firm control is actually hampered by specific vested interests or ideologically biased assumptions.

The ruling classes and high-income individuals all over the world are the stoutest enemies of democratic firm control. As the prevailing circumstances play into their hands, they are inimical to change; and as they look upon economic democracy as a revolution designed to assert equality, they oppose any schemes for the establishment of a different social order.

As mentioned above, liberalists reject economic democracy because of their confidence in spontaneous evolution and uncritical acceptance of the idea that whatever is good and viable will come about as a matter of course. On the assumption of the superiority of capitalism, they are averse to the very idea of revolution (even to a democratic one implemented through a parliamentary vote).

A less obvious finding is that enemies of democratic firm control include trade unions, most of which are ill-disposed towards allowing workers to run firms on their own. The rationale behind their attitude is the risk that economic democracy should make workers 'their own masters' and allow them to do without the services of organisations for the protection of workers. Economic democracy would sweep away class divisions and the traditional confrontation between associations of employers and unions of workers defending the interests of their respective members. These reflections are, in themselves, enough to explain why trade unions are inimical to such a prospect (see Moene & Wallerstein 1993, pp. 148–49, Kester & Pinaud 1996 and George 1997, pp. 59–60).

Quite appropriately, Raniero Panzieri wrote (1960, p. 116): "Taking roots within and outside the factory is not a question of distributing tasks and existing (union) officials more effectively. The decisive factor is an innovation process sparked off right within the factory at the cost of calling into question the role, and even the very existence of trade unions. Only a trade union organisation boldly offering collaboration in this direction is likely to play a major role in a true innovation process."

Many authors hold that trade unionists oppose democratic firm control on the assumption that their members are not prepared to take business risks. Palmiro Togliatti, for instance, wrote that industrialists tend to be less inimical to economic democracy than workers. When Italian businessmen announce their intention to turn capitalistic businesses into cooperatives – he claimed – their true design is to turn the current shareholders into creditors of the cooperative firms. This done, they will stop running the production, marketing and other business of those firms and, without sparing a thought for the fate of the industrial sector as a whole, will be satisfied with cashing the fixed interest accruing on their claims (Togliatti 1920, p. 183). Others have argued that – far from making workers free – industrial democracy would produce the awkward effect of obliging them to adopt the uncongenial rationale of capitalistic businessmen committed to maximising their profits (Tornquist 1973, p. 393).

The idea that workers do not wish to become 'their own masters' is widely shared. In point of fact, to establish if this is true workers should be polled following awareness-building programmes illustrating the latest findings on modern economic theory – and as far as we know this has never been done. As mentioned by Hansmann (1996, p. 45), empirical observation has shown that corporate governance researchers tend to overrate the role of risk-takers in the day-to-day running of firms.

Moreover, those workers who do declare themselves hostile to democratic firm control are doubtless influenced by trade union officials, i.e. by those whom they hold to represent their interests.

One reason behind the lukewarm support of cooperation by the Left is the fear that the rise of two organisations for the protection of worker interests might result in a split within the working class. This is what the historian Gaetano Salvemini suggested in the years when Italy was ruled by Cabinets presided over by Giolitti. As the cooperative movement had gained a firm foothold in central and northern Italy, but not in the South (much like today), he argued that its leaders were actively securing government contracts in the exclusive interests of northern versus southern workers and that this strategy had been chosen to please Giolitti (see Salvemini 1993, pp. 356–58 and 359–83).

To account for the half-hearted support of trade unions (rather than opposition proper), Braverman points to issues such as technological progress and labour productivity. "The unionized working class" – he writes (1974, p. 10) – "intimidated by the size and complexity of capitalistic production, and weakened in its original revolutionary impetus by the gains afforded by the rapid increase in productivity, increasingly lost the will and ambition to wrest control of production from capitalistic hands and turned ever more to bargaining over labor's share in the product. This labor movement formed the immediate environment of Marxism; and Marxists were, in varying degrees, compelled to adapt themselves to it."

Lastly, democratic firm management is opposed by the traditional Left, especially by Marxists, due to the fear that the market economy in which an all-cooperatives system is intended to operate would envisage far less state intervention in the economy than there is today (see, *inter alia*, Adler-Karlsson 1986, pp. 46–47). Indeed, the propelling force which might correct the dysfunctions of the system and drive on a market economy is democratic firm management, rather than state intervention. Considering that workers in an economic democracy are held to become 'their own capitalists' (Mill 1871, p. 739 and Dubravcic 1970), there is ground for arguing that cooperation would help workers acquire a role which used to be monopolised by capitalistic businessmen and corporate governance executives. Hence, the scant concern of some Leftist groups with economic democracy arises in connection with three main reasons: a mistrust of markets, statist leanings and a traditional aversion to entrepreneurs (though this seems to be a thing of the past). In 1888, André Gide (p. 66) suggested that the distance between workers' parties and cooperative ideals was to be traced to a more than centennial influence of socialist, specifically collectivist ideas.

As Gide himself acknowledges further on in his essay (1888, p. 68), this finding may strike us as surprising since socialism and cooperation claim descent from Robert Owen in Britain and Charles Fourier in France and are consequently akin by origin.[5]

Concluding this section, let me mention that my approach is disclaimed by a great many authors who think that role of ideology in hampering the growth of the cooperative movement has been at most tangential (see, *inter alia*, Hansmann 1996, pp. 87–88).

Corporate governance and economic democracy

A variety of different forces, besides antithetical ideologies and interests, stand in the way of the transition – albeit slow and gradual – from capitalism to economic democracy.

Firstly, today economic activity is conducted within a legal framework which is structured in such a way as to favour the growth of capitalism and extend it in time. As is well known, Marx distinguished between the economic base and the superstructure, i.e. between the economic structure of society and its legal, political and other aspects, and held the latter to be conditioned by the former.[6] In point of fact, this view is also shared by a large number of non-Marxist economists. There is little denying that laws and institutions which play into the hands of capitalistic businesses are antithetical to those that would expedite the growth of democratic firms. Over the centuries, the laws and institutions of capitalistic society have been fleshed out in a manner conducive to the creation of an environment consistent with its requirements, and the main beneficiaries of this state of affairs are doubtless capitalistic businesses, rather than democratic firms.[7] Several authors (see Putterman 1982 and 1984, Hodgson 1993, pp. 91–93 and Gunn 2000, pp. 451–55) have argued that within a different context, with different institutions, democratic firms would probably outnumber capitalistic businesses. In other words, in accordance with a typical hysteresis process the economic growth pattern of the past ensures that those systems that have gained the upper hand for whatever reason will generate institutions and an environment that will help them trounce competition from others (see Arthur 1989, North 1990 and Pagano 1991a and 1991b).[8] In the opinion of Vanek (1971a, p. 171), producer cooperatives and other democratic firm types fail to gain a firm foothold since they operate within an extraneous environment.

From the perspective of a well-known law expert, throughout this century, the legislatures have been pursuing a clever design: instead of repressing the cooperative movement, they have manoeuvred to 'sabotage' it from within, i.e. they have introduced the capitalistic logic of profit into cooperatives in an attempt to win over their members to this logic (Galgano 1974, p. 163).[9]

One aspect of this issue is the theory that traces firm control to the specificity of its resources and emphasises the tendency of economic systems to self-perpetuate themselves. The theorists concerned hold that business firms arise when a group of producers uses team-specific resources, i.e. resources which would suffer a decline in value if they were moved to a different team. From this basic idea, it follows that control will usually be vested in the most significant firm-specific factor. In capitalistic systems, this factor is usually capital. At this point, one may wonder if – in a vicious circle of sorts – there is a mechanism capable of determining that just as capitalistic firms are mainly connoted by capital, so democratic firms would be mainly connoted by labour.

It is well known that ownership titles vest in the owners of goods the right to prohibit others from using such goods, and although it is inappropriate to use the term ownership title when speaking of a business enterprise (see Ellerman 1990 and 1992), it is possible that the factor resolving to take over the control of a firm may do so in an effort to avoid being ousted from it. Thanks to the awareness that they cannot be ousted, those in control of firms will probably increase their investments in 'human capital' and this will further increase the specificity of the firms they control.

In other words, the relation between the ownership title in resources and the specifics of such resources can be said to evolve in either direction. Marx held relations of production and ownership rights to be determined by the level of growth of the productive forces, but he also emphasised the opposite causal link when he demonstrated that the effect of capitalistic ownership relations is to multiply obsessively repetitious jobs that can do without specialised skills.

A causality link between ownership rights and the characteristics of the resources used has recently been emphasised by some radical economists who have reversed the links highlighted by neoinstitutionalists. From the starting assumption that control is either vested in firm-specific resources or in resources that are difficult to monitor, they have deduced that most of the workers employed in capitalistic businesses are both 'easily monitored' and 'non-firm-specific' since the owners of such businesses select them with this end in mind and will barely think of adding to the qualifications of workers not bound to their firms by permanent ties. As is well known, an investor in human capital is not entitled to cash the (future) earnings of the individuals concerned. Consequently, a firm investing in staff qualification programmes is at risk of wasting the relevant expenditure due to the fact that nothing can prevent its workers from leaving the firm upon completing their training programme. In other words, from the perspective of radical theorists, difficult control of resources and their greater or lesser specificity are the effects, not the cause, of the existing structure of property rights (see Braverman 1974, Marglin 1974, Edwards 1979; Bowles 1985, Pagano 1991a, 1991b, 1992a and 1992b and Marginson 1993, pp. 149–53).

In even more general terms, it is possible to argue that growth obeys the same mechanism in democratic and capitalistic businesses: conditions favourable to their growth are more likely to arise in situations where firms of the category concerned outnumber other forms of business enterprise (see Bowles & Gintis 1993a, p. 31; see, also, Levine & Tyson 1990).

The costs of democracy

It is a fact that the costs entailed in the exercise of democracy are an additional explanation for the limited success of the cooperative movement. Discussing the costs of democracy as a drag on the assertion of cooperation, in a well-known monograph Hansmann remarks that such costs: (a) are low in capitalistic businesses because capital holders consistently pursue the same goal – maximising return on capital – and measure their respective inputs by reference to a single parameter – the amount of capital resources contributed by each of them; (b) are much higher in self-managed firms, and even more so when their members have different professional qualifications and diverging interests. In Hansmann's estimation, there is a basic issue which has received far too little attention: what might be termed the internal policies of the firm or, in more abstract terms, the costs of collective decision making, have a critical bearing on the patterns of ownership that we observe and the ways in which firms are structured internally (see Hansmann 1996, p. 2); and his conclusion is that the costs of democracy are the primary explanation for the relative paucity of democratic firms.

It is well known that one of the main costs of democracy stems from the fact that a majority and an opposition may engage in a head-on clash. In capitalistic companies, where workers have no decision powers, they only have the option, as it were, to 'vote with their feet,' i.e. to give up their jobs and leave the firm. As long as they stay, being deprived of decision powers they are 'voiceless'; the workers of a capitalistic business have no way out but to stick to their jobs and put up with a systematic disregard for their needs.

At the other end of the spectrum, workers in democratic firms do have 'a voice,' but may have to endure the bitter experience of being in a minority and having their 'voice' silenced by the majority. In such a situation, the minority members may oppose the decisions of a majority which they feel is refusing to listen and abusing its power position. The 'costs' of the resulting split in the workforce and rise of two hostile factions may be a head-on confrontation, the refusal of minority workers to collaborate and manoeuvres designed to reverse the resolutions passed.[10] These costs may spike to a tremendous high if – as often happens – a particularly active and able minority group, using to advantage the disinterest of many and a better familiarity with the circumstances of the case, should succeed in imposing its will on the majority.

Additional major costs of democracy include the time and effort required for collective decision-making. To meet the wishes of the greatest possible number of members, the decision-makers will have to determine the preferences of possible participants in an initiative and then proceed to call meetings, exchange opinions and put alternative options to the vote. As different individuals are known to have different preferences and there is never just one possible option, the more such preferences diverge, the more will decision-making prove difficult and require cyclical polls. Occasionally, during such cyclical decision-making processes some workers may even be tempted to trade votes (see Weingast & Marshall 1988, p. 32 and Hansmann 1996, pp. 41–42).

A way out of this deadlock is delegating decision powers to third parties, for instance committees, and instructing them to analyse a set of options or pass resolutions that will be binding on all the members, but Hansmann warns that power delegation may result in difficult relationships between principals and agents.

An additional cost stems from the egalitarian ideology by which democracy is connoted, especially from the tendency of democratic firms to level out payroll rates and, at times, assign the same pay rate to all the members. Hansmann remarks (see *op cit.*, p. 93) that in some types of firm, for instance cooperative law firms, the individual productivity levels of the members are fairly easy to monitor and hence he finds it stupefying (p. 93) that such a firm should resolve to adopt equal pay policies and thereby renounce the benefits that might flow from the powerful incentive of some members to increase their inputs in an effort to boost their incomes (*supra*, p. 93). His conclusion is that democratic firms are likely to gain ground only in sectors of activity with fairly similar job descriptions or easily measured productivity levels, for instance among cab drivers.[11]

On the subject of homogeneous job descriptions, Hansmann argues that "the viability of employee ownership is severely compromised when the employees who share ownership play diverse roles within the firm" (see *op. cit.*, p. 92) and concludes that "homogeneity of interest is one of the major factors determining the costs of ownership that a given class of patrons can bear." In his opinion, this is one of the reasons why self-managed firms have failed to gain a firm foothold despite the major efficiency gains they ensure (see *op. cit.*, p. 288).

Hansmann gives credit to the widely held view that egalitarianism is a by-product of collective decision-making. In other words, he holds that distributive inequalities are less pronounced in cooperative firms because the members have equal decision powers (see *op. cit.*, p. 95) and notes that this explanation supports the argument that democratic firms will gain ground only in sectors where the members have roughly the same qualifications and preferences.[12]

The homogeneous-personnel requirement is closely associated with the argument that cooperatives are 'weak' firms operating in 'weak' markets and may help explain the particularly slow progress of the cooperative movement in the South of Italy. Surveys have shown that the workforces of cooperatives in northern Italy include higher percentages of women workers than those in southern Italy, while over 60 per cent of the cooperatives operating in Southern Italy are owned by women (see Battilani & Bertagnoni 2007, p. 24).

To refute this argument, suffice it to mention that it is based on existing cooperatives and not on the model recommended by economists today. In the author's opinion, the main plus points of cooperation are the disempowerment of capital, a fundamental contribution to political democracy and the suppression of 'classical' and 'Keynesian' unemployment (see Jossa 2001, Jossa 2009b and Jossa 2014a, chap. VIII), rather than the empowerment of workers. In other words, departing from the traditional model, modern economic theorists think that the powers of the workers' collective should be confined to passing a limited number of resolutions such as electing and revoking managers.

This adjustment to the traditional organisational model should be viewed in combination with an additional one. Inasmuch as it is true – as we think it is – that the model deserving to be prioritised is the medium-large cooperative, it will hardly appear reasonable to vest in workers the power to make important business decisions. These will draw adequate satisfaction from the sovereign rights (albeit confined to appointing and revoking managers) which are vested in them, from the awareness that their jobs are stable and safe and, above all, from the shares of the residual they are entitled to cash.

On several occasions, Luigi Einaudi argued that democracy was detrimental to business performance and that self-managed firms were bound to face serious financing difficulties on account of inefficiences inherent in economic democracy. "Today" – he wrote – "capital is a submissive, inarticulate servant granted to persons who are deemed to be trustworthy and have made a name for themselves for major organisational skills. … In the eyes of capitalists, giving *carte blanche* to the entrepreneur or tradesman, i.e. to one man, is a prerequisite for the success of any enterprise" (Einaudi 1920b, p. 849).

Our main objection to this is that Einaudi did not consider that the members of a cooperative are free to delegate all their powers to a manager of their choice. In the estimation of Putterman (1990, p. 169), the management and leadership delegation hypothesis entails that decision-making in worker-controlled firms does not necessarily require the involvement of a large number of people; and at any rate, he adds, final decision-makers in worker-controlled firms do not necessarily outnumber the shareholders performing this role in a capitalistic firm such as a limited company (see Putterman 1990, p. 169).

Luigi Einaudi's argument that "able proactive managers will be leaving the enterprise as soon as a workers' council is established" (see Einaudi 1920b, p. 688) was later refuted in theoretical contributions published within the framework of the long-drawn-out debate on Alchian and Demsetz's 1972 paper (see, *inter alia*, Eswaran & Kotwal 1989, pp. 162–63 and Dahl 1989, p. 331).[13] Indeed, there is no evidence that managers working in the interests of workers are less efficient than those working in the interests of – mostly absentee – capitalists.

At first sight, the idea that business decision-making powers should be solely vested in managers would appear to nullify the main advantage of a cooperative system, its democratic essence. On closer analysis, instead, democratic governance is doubtless the most significant characteristic of cooperatives, but has nothing to do with empowering the members to run the day-to-day business of their firm. It is worth mentioning that the principal advantages of economic democracy are (a) the disempowerment of capital and (b) a leap forward in the direction of political democracy with the resulting eradication of plutocracy. This does not mean one should endorse the view of the State as the lobbying group of the bourgeois class. It simply means that – given the strong impact of economics on politics – no political system can be rated as fully democratic if it fails to introduce democracy into its economic system.[14]

An additional thorny aspect of democratic firm management is that difficult decision-making may both accelerate the disappearance of cooperatives and the degeneration process that will be discussed below. The most proactive members of a cooperative and those interested in rapid and efficient decision-making may be tempted to gain full control of the firm by ousting the other members one by one.

Concluding this section, let me emphasise that the main advantage of self-management, democratic firm governance, is often rated as its main defect (see, *inter alia*, Webb & Webb 1921, p. 133, Hodgson 1982–83 and 1987, pp. 137–38, Benham & Keefer 1991 and Klein 1991, pp. 219–20).

Startup problems

Obstacles standing in the way of the establishment of cooperatives are an additional reason why the cooperative movement has lost out to competition from capitalistic businesses. In this connection, Marshall argued that a wealth of activities which in due time might have made a valuable contribution to society are seen to languish and die away because of inequitable starting conditions. This, he added, is especially true of a number of activities that might have been carried on in cooperation (see Marshall 1898, p. 205) and can be traced to the fact that propertied individuals, rather than pooling their capital resources with those of prospective partners, are likely to opt for the establishment of a capital-owned enterprise employing hired personnel.

Additional reflections acquire relevance in this connection.

Before a cooperative can be established a group of individuals with equal powers will have to come together and reach an agreement covering all the main aspects of a business project. There is little denying that such an agreement is far from easy to reach. The same is not applicable to capitalistic businesses, whose founders are simply required to enter into bilateral agreements, i.e. to conduct negotiations with one person at a time in two-way interviews during which third parties have no voice. In other words, whereas the precondition for the birth of a democratic firm is a multilateral contract unanimously executed by a number of different stakeholders, the capitalistic business enterprise arises following the execution of bilateral contracts through which the instigator secures the collaboration of third parties – and bilateral contracts are much more easy to negotiate.[15]

Some theorists think that the difficulties associated with the execution of multilateral contracts are usually overstated. As a rule, they argue, the model firm is established on the initiative of a single individual and where the firm concerned is intended to become a cooperative, the relevant ownership rights and management functions are apportioned among a plurality of individuals only after the establishment of the firm. Examples of this procedure include a number of forest cooperatives in the Pacific Northwest, which were originally set up by single promoters (see Hansmann 1996, p. 145). On closer analysis, the above objection is not fully overruled by this argument. While it is true that some cooperatives are established on the initiative of single individuals, it remains that businessmen setting up firms will opt for hired personnel in preference to sharing powers with third parties in a cooperative. Consequently, the startup problems just discussed are an additional explanation for the relatively small number of cooperatives in existence.

The situation is less complex when it comes to changing an existing firm, for example a limited company, into a cooperative. Indeed, in such a case the business structure, organisation chart and payroll arrangements of the pre-existing enterprise can often be transferred to the new firm without any appreciable changes.[16]

The part played by startup difficulties in impeding the unaided growth of the cooperative movement is confirmed by the experience that most existing cooperatives were established by groups of partners with comparable qualifications and skills. Typical cases are cooperatives joining professionals with the same qualifications, for instance law firms, which will take on hired staff exclusively for jobs which require qualifications different from theirs, for example typists or personnel assigned for janitoring services (see Hansmann 1996, pp. 91–92). Experience seems to support the view that people with non-homogeneous qualifications and preferences will have difficulty reaching the agreement needed to establish a cooperative firm (see Hart & Moore 1990).

Things stand differently when existing firms, for example limited companies, are to be turned into cooperatives. More often than not, in such cases the existing business structure, organisation chart and payroll arrangements can be transferred from the pre-existing company to the new firm without appreciable changes. And limited companies turned into cooperatives become oft very efficient.

The 'degeneration' of the democratic firm

Most cooperation theorists ascribe to cooperative firms a 'dual nature': on the one hand, they argue, these firms build on the democratic 'one head, one vote' principle, apportion the surplus among all their members and show a concern with the advancement of the community as a whole; on the other, they operate in a market economy and tend to adopt the typical business methods of capital-managed enterprises. Put differently, a cooperative is both a business enterprise and a democratic association, a 'Janus-faced entity' of sorts in which the 'realistic' members embrace the logic of markets and put cooperative principles behind them, while the 'idealistic' members stick to the noblest principles of cooperation at the cost of undermining the firm's sound management. This dual nature is held to be responsible for the degeneration of the cooperative movement.

It is widely held that cooperative firms are established by individuals who set out to put into practice the democratic principles of cooperation and are then gradually won over to the typical management modes of capitalistic firms. Very often, it is argued, this process is one of straightforward regression which sees the members distance themselves from cooperative values and adopt capitalistic management modes. Some theorists put the blame on the cooperators themselves, i.e. on the fact that due to their scant familiarity with the requirements of markets they prevent their managers from adopting efficient business strategies or furthering the firm's technological advancement. In contrast, others trace it to the straightforward abandonment of cooperative principles. The latter is a process of degeneration proper and is said to occur when the firm's decision powers are transferred from the members of the firm to its managers.

From individual cooperative firms, this malady extends to the system as a whole and this – the authors concerned argue – is what explains the scant success of the movement as a whole. From their perspective, its most deleterious implication is the resulting reduced role of those social forces that might have worked towards the assertion of the values of democracy, furthered the circulation of innovative ideas and paved the way for the emergence of a different mode of production.

To avert this risk, they argue, it takes a concerted effort to infuse fresh life into the cooperative movement and shield it from marginalisation. Specifically, it is the members of cooperatives that are to be persuaded not to consign the values of cooperation to oblivion.[17]

In point of fact, the critique of the cooperative movement just expounded in this section has little bearing on our line of reasoning because the organisational model recommended in this book will enable cooperatives to secure maximum efficiency and trounce the competition of capitalistic enterprises.

The principle that the main corporate powers of a producer cooperative are to be vested in the working partners in line of the 'one head, one vote' criterion is not applicable to medium-large size enterprises, in which the partners are expected to elect managers and instruct them to run the firm in ways that will maximise efficiency. Given the need to fight off competition from capital-managed enterprises, cooperatives are called upon to outperform their capitalistic rivals in terms of efficiency – which means they cannot afford neglecting such an overriding goal as efficiency. And while it is true that cooperatives are free to reduce both the working hours and work paces of the labour force, in consequence of the cuts on worker incomes that such a strategy would entail it is safe to assume that the management modes of cooperatives will not appreciably depart from those of capital-managed enterprises.

The first theorist to raise the issue of a possible 'degeneration' of cooperative firms was Beatrice Webb. The more a cooperative moves ahead, she argued, the more will it tend to 'degenerate' into a capitalistic firm, in terms that its members will find it convenient not to share the firm's earnings with other members. Since then, several authors have suggested that the majority members of a cooperative will consider the replacement of minority members with hired workers every time the residual is to be distributed (hired workers have no title to distributions). At that point, they argue, the members left will form a new majority which will once again consider the possibility of ousting minority members and replacing them with hired staff (or, alternatively, depriving them of their voting and participation rights and, hence, changing them into hired employees). As the transformation of the cooperative into a capitalistic business is accelerated by each new hire, there is good ground for arguing that a successful cooperative wishing to increase its workforce will tend to use hired personnel (see Potter 1893, Webb & Webb 1921 and 1923, Ben-Ner 1984 and 1988a, Leete-Guy 1991, pp. 66–67, White 1991, pp. 83–84, Gunn 2000, pp. 451–55; on the contrary, the 'degeneration' process is understated in Hansmann 1996, pp. 81–84).

In my opinion, to read this aspect of the degeneration thesis as a criticism of self-management would be a mistake. The most obvious objection here is that a democratic firm must not be turned into a mixed business and must consequently abstain from taking on hired personnel. In other words, the prerequisite for the final success of a system of democratic firms is the enforcement of laws which prohibit cooperatives from employing more than a certain percentage of hired personnel.[18]

In Egan 1990 (pp. 74–75), we read that Marx had in mind three institutional mechanisms that might have prevented or hindered the transformation of cooperatives into capitalistic enterprises. Firstly, it is workers that could be expected to prevent such transformation by pressing for the issuance of a law prohibiting the use of hired labour in cooperatives. Secondly, instead of remaining isolated and engaging in competition against each other, they should be merged into groups and create a nationwide organisation. Thirdly, a portion of the surplus earned by cooperatives should be allocated to a provision to be used for setting up new cooperatives. In point of fact, the short passages from Marx's works reported by Egan in support of his reflections would rather suggest that Marx did not have in mind a well fleshed-out strategy intended to ensure that cooperatives would outperform capitalistic enterprises in the long run.

The approach of Gregory K. Dow

At this point, it is worth examining a book-length study in which Gregory K. Dow discusses the reasons why capitalistic businesses outnumber employee-controlled firms. From Dow's perspective, the crucial point is the contrast between alienable and inalienable labour, i.e. the fact that capital can be sold, while labour cannot be purchased, but only hired by capital. As far as this antithesis is concerned, he presents it as a unifying factor common to a large number of possible explanations for the relative paucity of cooperatives, but is forced to admit that it is of little help when it comes to refuting other explanations.

A capitalistic company resolving to upgrade its plant, he argues, does so in the awareness that its capital goods cannot be appropriated by third parties. Conversely, a cooperative in the same situation knows all too well that the member-workers who develop sophisticated qualifications or skills are free to move to other firms prepared to offer them higher pay rates. Secondly, whereas an able entrepreneur who sets up a capitalistic firm or takes over a cooperative can keep for himself the whole of the income he is able to earn thanks to a successful business concept developed by him, individuals joining to form a cooperative or taking over a capitalistic business will have to share their earnings with others. Thirdly, but most importantly, a high-income capitalist who takes over a firm is free to run its operations as he deems best, whereas the management of a cooperative firm is conditioned by the above-mentioned constraints associated with collective control. In more general terms, while capitalistic businesses are mostly run by a comparatively small number of like-minded directors, the control group of a cooperative is always the workers' collective, i.e. a larger group.

In Dow's estimation, three main arguments determine which factor will be taking over control: the sense of purpose that those entitled to take over control are able to develop, the size and heterogeneity of the control group and the existence of a market for control positions; and the differences between capitalistic and worker-controlled firms with respect to these factors are caused by the alienable capital/inalienable labour contrast (see Dow 2003, chap. 11).

On closer analysis, however, Dow's approach is far from convincing. The argument that the progress of self-management is impeded by the contrast between alienable capital and inalienable labour does not add much to our understanding and we also doubt that Dow's approach actually includes elements common to other explanations for the paucity of worker-controlled firms. For example, even assuming that the funding problems of cooperatives are as material as he holds them to be, it remains that they have nothing to do with the alienable capital/inalienable labour antithesis. In actual fact, they are caused by the inability of workers to lodge all such security as is generally given to lenders by capitalists.

In our opinion, an additional reason why Dow's approach is objectionable is his failure to mention the option of delegating decision powers to a manager – an option which effectively refutes the assumption that the control group of a capitalistic business is more efficient since it consists of fewer members. At any rate, its most serious shortcoming is that Dow fails to mention lack of support from intellectuals as a cause of the paucity of cooperatives in existence. In point of fact, the limited scale of the cooperative movement is to be traced to inadequate awareness of the advantages of cooperation and, therefore, to insufficient government incentives. Regardless of the reasons why cooperatives are far from firmly established, there can be little doubt that the moment their nature as merit goods is understood to the full, they will start moving ahead and ultimately fight off the competition of capitalist-managed enterprises.

Dow thinks that cases such as the Mondragon Group in Spain and Italian cooperatives are clear evidence of the importance of an institutional mechanism supporting the establishment of new cooperatives and/or the conversion of capitalistic businesses into employee-controlled firms. Hence, he correctly concludes that governments should enforce suitable laws and financial aid systems to encourage the rise of a large-scale cooperative sector, but erroneously adds (*op. cit.*, p. 75) that sceptics have good ground for arguing that the social benefits flowing from a large-size cooperative sector are barely such as to justify the requisite expenditure. Considering the nature of Dow's approach, it comes as no surprise that he fails to emphasise the paucity of government support compared to the considerable social benefits of a system of cooperatives – which in our estimation is the crucial point.

Conclusion

In this chapter we have emphasised the idea that progress in the direction of a generalised system of cooperative firms would amount to a considerable improvement over capitalism, but will hardly be made without the effective contribution of intellectuals and political parties. Consistently with our own line of reasoning, Dahl (1989, p. 331) has remarked that both at the national and corporate levels democracy requires favourable circumstances, i.e. conditions which do not lie in the nature of things and will therefore not arise as a matter of course.

Considering the importance that is generally attached to democracy, there are reasons to argue that political parties should stop waiting for a worker-controlled firm system to grow in its own right and should make it their task to support its emergence by framing platforms envisaging suitable forms of public intervention. In Ramsey (1983), the struggles for worker control in firms are described as a cyclical, rather than continuous process. In particular, the cyclical attempts of workers to seize factories spanned the years 1917–21, 1935–37 and 1968–83 (see Visser 1989, pp. 171–76) and were sparked off not only by the political circumstances prevailing from time to time, but also by advancements in economic theory. More than in any other field, in the area of cooperation a major breakthrough can only be achieved through the combined action of spontaneous evolution, the recommendations of economic theorists and focused political programmes.

To conclude this chapter, let me mention the well-known theorist of social democracy Georges Sorel, specifically his argument that the crisis of European socialism can be traced to an excessive level of consumerism and the even more convincing claim that the ultimate cause of this crisis is the equation of socialism with centralised planning. As is well known, Bernstein's reformist approach was developed on the assumption that the main obstacle to the establishment of a socialist order was not so much the need to lead the proletariat to power, as the difficulties involved in rapidly organising production in keeping with the principles of a planned economy.

In contrast, the transition from capitalism to self-management socialism can take place by degrees and without appreciable organisational problems.

To dispel the doubt that this prospect is barely realistic Amartya Sen wrote that pessimism about the ability of society to redress inequality is only justified if we cling to the wrong assumption that human beings are exclusively concerned with maximising narrow personal concerns (see Sen 2015, p. 50).

From my perspective, this argument is far from convincing. Inasmuch as it is true that self-employment is preferable to hired work, from two of the advantages discussed in Chapter 5 above – the remote bankruptcy risks faced by worker-controlled firms and the higher income levels they afford – it follows that the advancement of society towards socialism is a realistic prospect even though the workers should have exclusive regard to their personal interest.

The issue of the transition from capitalism to socialism will be discussed below.

Notes

1 In this connection, also see, for instance, Oakeshott 1978, Cornforth *et al.* 1988, Ellerman 1990, chap. 7, and Bardhan & Roemer 1993).

2 The *Poor Man's Guardian* (Sept. 1833) reported that the delegates from all over the country that had been convened for a meeting of the First International had conceived the aim, "the sublimest that can be conceived – to establish for the productive classes a complete domination over the fruits of their own industry" (Cole 1953a, p. 91). But following the advent of Marxism, socialism ceased being identified with worker control of firms.

3 Nevertheless, even Hayek was compelled to admit that most rules had been fleshed out by reference to the views and interests of one class, so that positive ideas were often prevented from asserting themselves in their own right (see Hayek 1982, p. 115).

4 Schumpeter, one of those who placed no trust in the power of ideas, wrote (1954, p. 140): "Political criticism cannot be met effectively by rational argument. From the fact that the criticism of the capitalist order proceeds from a critical attitude of mind, i.e., from an attitude which spurns allegiance to extra-rational values, it does not follow that rational refutation will be accepted. Such refutation may tear the rational gart of attack but can never reach the extra-rational driving power that always lurks behind it."

5 Fabbri also (see Fabbri 1981, p. 829) described cooperation as the 'brother german' of trade unions.

6 In *German Ideology* and elsewhere, Marx ed Engels wrote that the ideas of the ruling class are in every epoch the ruling ideas, i.e. that the class which is the ruling *material* force of society is at the same time the ruling *intellectual* force (see Marx and Engels 1845–46, pp. 35–36).

7 In this connection, Perotin has argued (2006, p. 299) that "as the number of organizations of a given form grows, the form is regarded as more legitimate and this legitimacy in turn results in more organizations of the same king being created."

8 With regard to the conservative essence of institutions, see, also, Veblen 1899, pp. 190–98.

9 In point of fact, this argument is rated as fairly negligible by other authors (including Hansmann 1996, pp. 85–86).

10 The smaller the firm, Panebianco (2004, p. 83) argued, the greater the risk that a majority group may coerce a minority group.

11 In an essay dating from 1996, Hart and Moore provided evidence that cooperatives with homogeneous member preferences may reach first-best equilibrium, whereas business enterprises managed by capitalists may turn out to operate inefficiently.

12 Kollock (1998) and Huberman & Glance (1998) have remarked that peer monitoring among members, far from being a simple practice, may give rise to paradoxical situations.

13 For criticisms of the *free riding* issue raised in Alchian and Demsetz (1972), see Putterman (1984, pp. 172–75), Eswaran and Kotwal (1989, p. 163), Faccioli and Scarpa (1998, pp. 70–72), Bruni and Zamagni (2004) and Jossa (2005b, vol II, pp. 3–9).

14 According to Touraine, the main characteristic of capitalism is the suppression of all social, political and other checks on the actions of economic actors: whenever these are freed from control, they impose their will on all other institutions, in terms that the latter will always have to act in accordance with the interests of those controlling the economy. This power, he adds, is the true cornerstone of capitalism (Touraine 2004).

15 In the opinion of Ben-Ner (1987), one of the causes of the relative paucity of cooperatives is the fact that an able entrepreneur does not deem it in his interests to share the prospective earnings from a newly founded firm with third parties – as would be the case in a cooperative. In point of fact, the different distribution patterns of cooperatives versus capitalistic businesses arise in connection with a variety of different reasons (see, *inter alia*, Dow, 2003, p. 17, Gunn, 2006, p. 346, Pérotin 2006). However, in Pérotin (2006, p. 296) we read that the average entry rate for cooperatives in France in the years 1979–2002 was 15 per cent, i.e. considerably higher than the corresponding average recorded for conventional businesses in the same period (12 per cent). See, also, Steinherr & Vanek (1976, p. 340).

16 The democratic essence of the firm may weaken managers in terms of depriving them of authority in their relations with the members by whom they are elected. And this may in turn pose a serious threat to efficiency (see Jensen & Meckling 1979). In this connection, Bernstein (1899a, p. 159) argued that where the disempowerment of the capitalistic owners, "the true reference point of all corporate governance organs" should not be accompanied by the thorough transformation of the organisation as a whole, it would automatically lead to the prompt dissolution of such organs. For an in-depth analysis of the involvement of the members in decision-making processes and the powers of managers in self-managed firms, see Obradovic and Dunn (1978).

17 The ideas just expressed are expounded, *inter alia*, in Meister (1974 and 1984), Birchall (1997), Cornforth *et al.* (1988), Chaddad (2012) and Diamantopoulos (2012).

18 Producer cooperatives tend to take on hired personnel whenever this is not prohibited by law. In this connection, it is interesting to note that C. Gide, one of the most convinced and authoritative nineteenth-century advocates of cooperation, observed that the future of cooperation lay in consumers', rather than producers' cooperatives. The reason for this prediction was that many French cooperatives were employing hired workers and had consequently been turned, in practice, into associations of petty masters using hired personnel working at their orders and for their account (see Gide 1888, p. 101).

14 Democratic firm management and the role of the State in capitalism versus socialism

Introduction

A contentious issue on which no clear consensus has been reached is the proper role of economic State interventionism. Besides discussing some of the most controversial points associated with this issue, in this chapter I wish to lay in the claim that within a genuinely socialist system the State would be in a position to perform the role that was vested in it by Hegel, i.e. to serve the interests of the community at large.

The State in the estimation of Marx and Engels

Inasmuch as it is true that Marx's pre-1857 works are just preparatory steps in the development of his system (see, *inter alia*, Luporini 1966), the passage from the *Manifesto* in which Marx and Engels maintain that the ultimate goal of a revolution is to allow the proletariat to secure political supremacy and use it in "centralising all the instruments of production in the hands of the State" (see Marx & Engels 1848, p. 87) is of minor consequence.

In the framework of a tentative reconstruction of the successive steps in the evolution of Marx's thought on this specific point, it is worth noting that until the establishment of the Paris Commune Marx and Engels thought that the precondition for realising socialism was centralising all powers firmly in the hands of the State. The Paris Commune induced them to reconsider this view and to come to conceive of socialism as mainly connoted by democratic production processes (see Screpanti 2007a, pp. 145–46), but in later years, the *Inaugural Address* (1864) marked an end to their "infatuation with the utopianism of the Paris Commune" (Lichtheim 1965, p. 228).

To clarify Marx and Engels's definition of the role of the State in capitalism it is possible to start out from a statement by Engels (1884, p. 170):

"The State is [...] by no means a power imposed on society from the outside; just as little is it 'the reality of the ethical idea' or 'the image and reality of reason,' as Hegel maintains. Rather, it is a product of society at a certain stage of development; it is the admission that this society has become entangled in an insoluble contradiction, that it has split into irreconcilable antagonisms which it is powerless to dispel. But in order that these antagonisms and classes with conflicting economic interests might not consume themselves and society in fruitless struggle, it became necessary to have a power seemingly standing above society that would alleviate the conflict, and keep it within the bounds of 'order'; and this power, arisen out of society but placing itself out of it, and alienating itself more and more from it, is the State."

The interest of this passage lies in the fact that, far from categorising the State as 'the lobbying group of the bourgeoisie' (as Marxists often do), it highlights its positive – though ultimately pro-bourgeois – function of striving to damp down those conflicts which would otherwise destroy society before it has run its necessary course. Further on (*ibid.*, p. 172), Engels remarked that, by way of exception, "periods occur in which the warring classes balance each other so nearly that the State power, as ostensible mediator, acquires, for the moment, a certain degree of independence of both."

In this connection, Merker (2010, pp. 198–99) contends that Engels's call for a consensus-driven effort of the masses to stand up for legality and democracy was ultimately intended to underscore the need for a constitutional State founded on the principle of the supremacy of the rule of law, but that this call was bound to remain unrealised as long as the State was looked upon as the legal tool enabling one class to hold sway over the others.

Time and again, Engels argued that even in systems which had enforced the principle of universal suffrage the State was still basically a tool in the service of a single class.

The Austromarxists Karl Renner, Otto Bauer, Max Adler and Rudolf Hilferding were the first leftist thinkers to challenge the view of the State as consistently concerned with promoting the interests of the bourgeoisie. Renner suggested that the State's increasing concern with the interests of the proletariat was digging a gulf between the State apparatus and the business community; Bauer laid stress on the fact that state power was actually wielded by the classes; Adler held that the 'dictatorship of the proletariat' could be exercised as part of political democracy and Hilferding emphasised the need to rethink Marxist political theories, specifically to proceed from anarchism to statism by abandoning the base-superstructure distinction and acknowledging the far-reaching influence of the organised forces of the proletariat on the superstructure. A non-Marxist such as Kelsen pressed the need for a transition from Marx to Lassalle, i.e. for admitting that nothing prevented the State from operating democratically and with due attention to the needs of the proletariat (see Marramao 1980).

In the *Critique of Hegel's Philosophy of Right* (1843) and again in *The 18th Brumaire of Lous Bonaparte* (1851), Marx argued that a State bureaucracy could exercise its decision-making authority independently of the class in power because there was a division of labour between capitalists and public officials and the latter were not typical members of their respective classes. At a later stage, instead, he strongly endorsed the theory of the State as a 'class-based power structure'[1] and lobbying group of the bourgeoisie which was subsequently developed by Lenin both in *State and Revolution* and in *The Proletarian Revolution and the Renegade Kautsky* and was eventuallty taken over by the Marxist movement at large.[2]

This theory has lately been challenged by quite a lot of Marxists on fairly good grounds.

The view of Marxism as a non-statist approach is principally based on an reading of the *Economic and Philosophical Manuscripts* of 1844. Unfortunately, the integral text of this major work was published in its original German version as late as 1932, which means that the classics who established the canon for a statist interpretation of Marx's socialism (Kautsky, Plekhanov, Lassalle, Gramsci and Lenin) could have no knowledge of it.

As mentioned before, an additional work supporting a non-statist reading of Marx's approach is *The Civil War in France*, which was written under the strong impression of the experience of the Paris Commune: instead of centralising means of production in the hands of the State, the Commune espoused Proudhon's and Bakunin's idea of a 'slimming State.' The radical change of course on major issues suggested by Marx's line of reasoning in that work and his prediction of a non-authoritarian future for society have induced some authors to categorise this pamphlet as 'anti-Marxist' straightaway (see Lehning 1969, p. 431). In the *Civil War* Marx made it absolutely clear that the primary goal of the Commune – which he evidently endorsed – was to create a system of self-governing producers and have it coordinated by a federation of autonomous municipalities.

As mentioned above, the classics of Marxism had a fragmentary knowledge of the actual evolution of Marx's thought because they had had no access to major texts: in the opinion of Schaff (1965, p. 11), this would have misled even the greatest of all geniuses.[3]

In the estimation of well-known authors including Bigo (1953) and Orfei (1970), though not Althusser, the picture of Marx emerging from the *Manuscripts of 1844* is that of a humanist, and there can be little doubt that a socialist system with democratically managed firms is more cognate with humanism than with statism.[4]

The traditional Marxist view of the role of the State in capitalistic systems

In years nearer to us, Marx's mature approach was praised by Offe (1972b) and Ferrajoli (1978), both of whom are now classed as orthodox Marxists.

From Offe's perspective, a State can be categorised as a class-based power structure when its institutional mechanisms provide scope for its apparatus to perform a selectivity function designed to generate given events and exclude others. The underlying assumption, here, is that the bourgeoisie uses the State apparatus for the purpose of pursuing interests which is unable to attain autonomously.

Consequently, the primary criterion against which the class character of a State is to be measured is the extent to which the goal selection process performed by its apparatus is designed to identify and further the "overall interests of capital" even *in defiance* of individual aggregations of capitalists or lobbying groups (Offe 1972b, p. 133).

Actions to protect capital from the attacks of anti-capitalists constitute an equally far-reaching selectivity function. In other words, selectivity comes in two forms: negative when it is designed to generate events and forestall erroneous moves from capitalists, positive when it is intended to protect capital from its enemies by averting events or producing "non-events." Offe defines four institutional selection mechanisms: structure, ideology, process and repression. Structural selectivity, which is exemplified by the protection of private property, is exercised *de facto* in full accordance with the rule of law and is the process which governs the gleaning of goals eligible for inclusion in the government's policy agenda. The process which is termed ideological selectivity, i.e. the choice of goals which reflect the dominant cultural-ideological patterns, is also used to restrict the range of feasible State policies. Still another selection mechanism is used to identify and implement policy goals which play into the hands of certain lobbies to the detriment of other groups. Lastly, a major role is played by repression, i.e. the action of the State's police, military and criminal justice systems. The combined action of these mechanisms accounts for the fact that capitalistic systems fail to satisfy a vast array of needs (*ibid.*, chap. V).[5]

It is these selection mechanisms that explain the permanent disregard for, and repression of needs which might endanger the system (*ibid.*, p. 41) and the protection of the interests of capital overall, not of specific groups of capitalists.

In Offe's estimation, therefore, the class bias of the capitalistic State is not a contingent feature, but a structural characteristic because neither the State as such nor individual members of the government are expressly 'retained' to serve as instruments for furthering the interests of one class in preference to another.

According to Ferrajoli, ever since the State made it its task to protect and further the interests of capital it has growingly drifted apart from its social basis. Ferrajoli's stance is antipodal to the belief of social democratic reformists that the State may change course and resolve to govern the system in the interests of the working class. Indeed, the core idea behind reformism is that the State is "in the hands" of capitalists who use its apparatus as a tool to protect their interests and that this necessitates bringing to power a class with a distinct resolve to protect the interests of workers in preference to those of capital. In turn, this idea is founded on the – clearly non-Marxist – idea of the primacy of politics.

With the passing of time – Ferrajoli adds – deflecting from its original function as the outside guarantor of capitalistic development the State turned into its internal guarantor. The reason behind this turn-around, he clarifies, is the noticeable increase in economic State intervention caused by the transition from the competition-based model of capitalism to monopoly capitalism. "Only apparently is it a paradox" – he argues (Ferrajoli 1978, p. 53) – "that the high-water mark of economic State intervention and, hence, of State control over individual capital stocks should coincide with its ultimate subjugation and even enslavement to the logic behind capitalism." In line with this logic, the State intervenes in the economy in the attempt to reverse adverse business cycles, damp down social conflict, support firms in distress and provide subsistence aid to those unemployed, but due to the structural characteristic highlighted above, even in the absence of outside pressure it will never endorse any moves designed to overthrow capitalism. The system's efforts at self-defence, he argues (*ibid.*, pp. 55–59), stretch so far as to lead to the enforcement of emergency laws which suspend or cancel constitutional guarantees at the cost of jeopardising the rule of law of the constitutional State and such liberal principles as the need to ensure equal starting opportunities for all (dubbed as 'luxuries' that the system cannot afford). The co-optation of social democratic parties into the government is a move which helps bring home the message that the decision-making processes under way reflect the will of the masses.

Ferrajoli shares Offe's idea that democracy and political liberties tend to be undermined when capitalism enters its mature phase. "Regardless of the political or social forces by which it is exercised" – he argues – "power is inescapably a sign and the expression of social inequality and has a natural tendency to wrest itself free from the rule of law and degenerate into absolutism" (*ibid.*, p. 64). In this connection, it is worth noting that the stout defence of democracy by the working class, the traditional mission of leftist parties, is not at odds with what has been said above. In part, the above-mentioned separation of the State from its social basis is caused by the tendency of major parties (and trade union organisations) to form public-private corporations in which specialised professional apparatuses inhibit democratic processes and any decisions made end up by reflecting the choices of a top management formed of bureaucratic oligarchies (Zolo 1978, p. 80).

To secure permanence of tenure, these party and union oligarchies co-opt members from all classes of society and thereby contribute to the depoliticisation of the masses and their apathy towards politics.

From an orthodox Marxist angle of view, before ending this section it is worth adding that as soon as the basic institutions of the modern capitalistic State have been firmly established, capitalists realise that the class structure of the State and the privileges of their class are dependent on these institutions and consistently strive to extend them in time as best they can. "The uninhibited operation of the economic institutions will continue to bestow power, wealth and prestige upon the capitalists" (Edwards & McEwan 1970, p. 359).

A critique of traditional Marxist thinking

Instrumentalism, the idea of a class-oriented State[6] acting as a tool in the hands of the ruling class, has long come under increasing criticism even from Marxists and is consequently no longer viewed as acceptable (see Block 1977).

Unlike the State, which is not necessarily bourgeoisie-oriented, in capitalistic systems economic activity doubtless is and remains the exclusive domain of one class and has a pervasive impact on politics even when power is wielded by the representatives of the working class. Rather than an agent of the bourgeoisie, a capitalistic State ruled by the representatives of the workers must be looked upon as an agent of the working class whose action is conditioned and, hence, inhibited by the power of capital.

This means I reject the view that any political forces acquiring autonomy in today's society are always and exclusively moved on by the resolve to further the class interests of the bourgeoisie (Galli 2010, p. 43).

Specifically, as soon as socialism is equated with worker management of firms, it is no longer possible to think of the State as the lobbying group of the bourgeoisie during the decline of capitalism. As worker management cannot be lawfully opposed by the State, a parliamentary majority of working class representatives would be able to further the establishment of cooperatives by enforcing tax benefits and credit facilities in their favour and to back up strikes proclaimed with the aim of pressing for the transfer of management powers to the workers – in short, to start a peaceful transition to socialism.[7]

This necessitates rejecting the argument that "parliamentarism is far from being an absolute product of democratic development, of the progress of the human species, and of such nice things. It is, rather, the historical determined form of the class rule of the bourgeoisie" (see Luxemburg 1899, p. 189). "State and class" – Pizzorno argues (1966, p. 254) – "are solidarity systems engaging in actions designed to protect the values upheld by the system of vested interests; on the other hand, inasmuch as their actions are the expression of solidarity, they do produce the effect of silencing particular interests."

In the light of the above reflections and, especially, of the equation of socialism with worker management of firms, the assumption that the state exclusively and permanently acts as the 'lobbying group of the bourgeoisie' will barely hold.

Engels and centralised planning

The question to be raised at this point is why it has long been assumed that the substitution of central planning for the working of markets is a necessary requirement for the establishment of a Marxian-type socialist system. The fact that Marxism asserted itself and was codified well before the appearance of a number of writings which clarify the evolution of Marx's thought is doubtless the main factor, but the part played by Engels is far from negligible.[8] For a long time, the main compendium and handbook of socialism was Engels's *Antidühring*, which was published between 1877 and 1878 and describes socialism as a system founded on planned production and the suppression of the division of labour.[9] Upon the takeover of means of production by society – Engels wrote (1878, p. 307) – "the production of commodities is done away with" and "the social anarchy of production gives place to a social regulation of production upon a definite plan."

There is general agreement that orthodoxy produces the effect of substituting dogmatism for critical thought. "What is known as orthodoxy" – Gerratana wrote (1968, p. XIII) – "ultimately smuggles in the eclectic approach to Marxism that revisionist movements overtly endorse and develop in different directions." Moreover, although in *Antidühring* Engels presented himself as the authorised spokesman of Marx, his views diverged from those of Marx on several points.[10]

As mentioned before, the shaping principle of the Paris Commune that Marx praised in *The Civil War* was the criterion that factories were to be run by their workers, i.e. the self-government of producers. In the *Foreword* to the 1891 edition of this work, Engels adopted a train of reasoning which closely re-echoes Marx. For instance, discussing the notion of the dictatorship of the proletariat (p. 28), he remarked that whoever wished to know what this dictatorship was like had to look at the Paris Commune.

This statement helps clarify Engels's actual stance with respect to the central planning issue. The planning model he had in mind was not intended to turn the State into an oppressive power. In his estimation, it was to be a form of social organisation whose ultimate goal was stopping the bourgeoisie from establishing capitalistic enterprises. The planning function he vested in the State was to be exercised in full synch with the sentiment of the working class and – with the necessary exception of the enforcement of a ban on the establishment of capital-owned factories – without recourse to authoritarianism. Engels clarified that the oppressive power of the capitalistic State had to fall everywhere (Engels 1891b, p. 25) and (taking the cue from Marx's *Civil War*) that all state deputies and officials, without exception, were to be subject to recall at any moment.

Concerning the society imagined by Dühring, Engels argued that the place of the capitalist would be taken by the community and that much like modern theorists Dühring was convinced that society was in a position to take over all the means of production without being obliged to revolutionise the old method of production from top to bottom or abolish the old division of labour (Engels 1891a, p. 317). In stark contrast to such approaches, Engels argued that a self-managed firm system which fails to suppress the division of labour would ultimately perpetuate the division of society into classes (*ibid.*, p. 300).

To this day, many socialists have found it difficult to account for Engels's dissatisfaction with such a promising prospect as the handover of firms to workers. Among them, Gerratana (1968, p. xxxvi) described Engels as overdemanding and "unimpressed by the noblest of intentions." For my part, I rather think that far from being excessively demanding, those Marxists who are still following in Engels's steps are wanting in realism. What chances are there for a socialist system to trounce the tough competition of capitalistic enterprises if it resolves to take a leap in the dark by suppressing the division of labour almost overnight upon seizing political power?

The need to retain markets and the division of labour at the earliest State of the post-revolutionary period was even acknowledged by a revolutionary such as Bucharin. In an analysis of the NEP, for instance, this author remarked that backward economic concerns were being integrated into the burgeoning economic apparatus of the State in a variety of different ways, but principally *via the market* (see Bucharin 1925, p. 160) and that the long-held idea that the victorious proletariat would have to do away with markets *instantly after* the seizure of power, break up the capitalistic economic apparatus almost overnight and introduce planning as soon as possible was actually a misconception (*ibid.*, p. 161).

All the same, the belief that markets and the division of labour must be swept away on the very day after the completion of a revolution is still held by a great many Marxists and constitutes the main weak point of their theoretical approaches. A centrally planned system without markets cannot function properly because it is unable to deal with a number of problems: the 'information issue' (the governance of a modern economy is too complex a task for any planning agency to master), the 'motivation issue' (in the absence of the profit motive, the main driving force of a market economy, people lack the incentive to work hard); the 'innovation problem' (see, *inter alia*, Li, p. 2011). This is why it is interesting to note that Marx was prepared to accept the retention of the division of labour and performance-based pay scales at the early post-revolutionary stage (see his *Critique of the Gotha Programme*).

In the light of this, it is possible to argue that where the Bolsheviks had taken up Lenin's above-mentioned ideas on a system of worker-controlled firms (see Lenin 1923a) or such a system had been established at any other stage in the evolution of the Soviet Union, the tragic degeneration of that country into a dictatorship might have been averted. As suggested by Anweiler in his well-documented history of the Soviets, there are no means of establishing if centralised planning was necessitated by the backwardness of Russian society or if the opposite choice, i.e. the creation of a democratic firm system, might have proved successful in that country. The attempt to establish a socialist market economy founded on worker-run factories in Yugoslavia and comparable experiments made in Poland would appear to support the view that the establishment of a democracy founded on the self-government of the producers in post-1917 Russia would not necessarily have been doomed to failure (Anweiler 1958, p. 472).

Should State aid be used to further a revolution?

At this point, it is worth raising an additional question: is it appropriate for a Marxist to think that a revolution can be furthered by means of State aid?

In the *Inaugural Address* of 1864 Marx spelt out that "co-operative labour ought to be developed to national dimensions, and, consequently, to be fostered by national means." Conversely, in the *Critique of the Gotha Programme* he criticised both Lassalle's idea of the State and his belief that the emancipation of the working class could be attained through the establishment of a state-subsidised system of producer cooperatives. The social programme framed in the Gotha Programme envisaged the use of State aid for the establishment of producer cooperatives and their democratic control by the workers employed in them. Marx's objection (1875a, pp. 93–94) was that "the workers' desire to establish the conditions for co-operative production on a social scale, and first of all on a national scale, in their own country, only means that they are working to revolutionise the present conditions of production, and it has nothing to do with the foundation of co-operative societies with state aid." Otherwise – Marx argued – socialism would come about thanks to the action of the State, in contrast with the central idea behind scientific socialism that it is workers themselves that must achieve their emancipation. A worker movement requiring State aid to support its revolutionary action and putting such demands to the State would thereby reveal "its full consciousness that it neither rules nor is ripe for ruling!" (*ibid.*, p. 93).

Marx's line of reasoning on this point can be summed up as follows: the prerequisite for inducing the State to further the growth of the cooperative movement on a national scale is, quite obviously, the *transfer of political power* to the enemies of capitalism. In Marx's view, a political pro-worker majority would be fully entitled to frame subsidising policies to support the growth of the cooperative movement. The far-ranging social changes needed to convert social production into a large and harmonious system for free and co-operative labour – he wrote – can only be brought about through the transfer of all State power from capitalists and landlords to the producers themselves.[11] And Engels, for his part, held that the apparatus of the capitalistic state was to be suppressed by the proletariat upon taking over the power of the State (see Negt 1978, p. 140). In Marx's view, the primary task of the working class was taking possession of political power.[12]

This necessitates the conclusion that Marx did envisage a gradual growth of the cooperative movement "fostered by national means," though he made it dependent on the rise to power of a pro-worker majority and the framing of a peaceful parliamentary strategy designed to attain this aim.

In point of fact, few if any Marxists will be prepared to endorse this conclusion because the idea that stepwise changes in the political structure of society should be brought upon by alternative economic and social institutions right within capitalism is anathema to most of them (see Thomas 1985, p. 872). For my part, I am inclined to think they doubt the ability of a parliamentary pro-worker majority to revolutionise the legal mechanisms of the State and take it for granted that any such attempt would be doomed to failure in consequence of the predictable resistance of capitalists and massive outflows of capital from the country concerned (for a more detailed analysis of possible objections, see Jossa 2010b, pp. 282–85).

State intervention in a system of producer cooperatives

Before I draw my conclusions, let me discuss the possible role of economic inter-ventionism in a system of worker-controlled firms.

Arrow has recently re-emphasised the incompatibility of markets with govern-ment in any form, and an analysis of industrial countries published by Barro in 1996 has provided evidence that the increase in redistributive state intervention caused by each piecemeal extension of democracy, though geared towards such a basic goal and component of democracy as greater equality, is ultimately at odds with the achievement of efficiency.

The view that state intervention in the form of higher taxation is an obstacle to the achievement of a Pareto optimum is endorsed by other laissez-faire liberalists. Specifically, experiential data reported by Barro in support of liberalist theoretical approaches (see Barro *op. cit.*) point to a surprising link between slow growth and political freedom that may justify the decision to scale back state intervention: a political freedom index (ranging between 0 and 1) determined based on the 1960–90 data of about 100 countries shows that growth was slowest in countries with an index value above 0.5.

As the approaches of Arrow, Barro and other laissez-faire liberalists are well-argued, they can be used to pinpoint some of the advantages of a system of producer cooperatives.

The idea that a perfect-competition system achieves a Pareto optimum is doubtless one of the most important findings of economic science. As is well known, however, a Pareto optimum is a situation that maximises well-being only with respect to a specific initial distribution of economic resources and within a system to which the 'survival assumption' is found to apply. As a result, if we take as a starting point a Pareto-optimal situation, a new situation with a better initial income distribution will improve the well-being of a community. Indeed, this is the reason why governments attempt to improve income distribution.

These reflections suggest an important argument in support of a cooperative system. It is common knowledge – John Stuart Mill remarked – that production activities obey mechanical rules while income distribution is socially determined. Insomuch as this is true, such choices as are needed to bring about fairer income distribution patterns can either be made through tax bracket adjustments (at the cost of inhibiting the free working of markets and preventing the attainment of Pareto optimums), or by enforcing laws capable of ensuring equal access opportunities to the more lucrative professions. Hence there is scope for arguing that a democratic firm system stripping capital of its power and control rights can bring about a fairer income allocation structure even in the absence of changes to the tax system or actions interfering with the smooth working of markets. Options open to governments include a reform of the educational system, well-organised systems of employment by competitive examination or the enforcement of a well-orchestrated succession tax regime, i.e. options with a negligible impact on market mechanisms. In overall terms, governments can be expected to shape focused and goal-specific strategies providing for a selection of State intervention policies capable of improving income distribution without hampering the free working of market mechanisms.[13]

State intervention is designed to pursue the dual aim of re-distributing incomes and scaling down the adverse effects of what are known as 'market failures.'

Especially in a globalised world, the working of the invisible hand is sure to spark off unwanted economic crises as long as there are markets,[14] but despite the obvious implication that downturns in the economy will be a material risk even in markets where capitalists have been ousted from power, there are reasons to assume that such undesirable turns of events would be less frequent than they are in capitalistic systems. Indeed, in a system freed from the control of capitalists the state will find it easier to intervene in the economy for the purpose of fending off crises. The multitude acts either as one or as many, and becomes a political agent either through the unity of the will or through the workings of the invisible hand. But the unity of the will that is expressed through political majority resolutions is much less forcefully counteracted by the action of markets (the invisible hand) if the markets concerned are no longer conditioned by the requirements of capital.

Moreover, whereas a comparative analysis of such antipodal systems as a pure capitalistic market economy and one where the State strives to correct malfunctions may prompt the *prima facie* conclusion that problems can be readily handled if 'market failures' are rare and can be confined to a minimum throuth the action of the State, today there is general agreement that market failures are the rule and that the inefficiencies likely to be generated by the massive intervention of a state bureaucracy would probably be grimmer than those self-generated by the market.

This poses a need to establish if, and to what extent, a system of producer cooperatives can outperform capitalistic markets in terms of averting, or at least remedying, the typical failures of a system driven by the private profit motive only. Experience has taught that many issues likely to degenerate into classical market or state failures (destaffing, excessive or ineffectual work input control, environment-averse actions, etc.) can be effectively tackled by communities. As communities have available a large quantity of crucial information on the needs and abilities of their members to which neither markets nor the state have access (see Bowles & Gintis 2002, pp. 425–26), near-community organisations such as producer cooperatives can take the place of the State or supplement its action in a wide range of situations and thereby reduce the need for public intervention.

In overall terms, a democratic firm system in which capitalists have been deprived of their power is able to tackle the causes of most market failures without the need for economic state intervention. Insofar as this is true, in a system of democratic firms the State would still have to play an active role, but its intervention in the economy would be less pervasive than it tends to – and must – be under the circumstances prevailing today.

Concluding, a considerable advantage of a cooperative firm system is its potential for furthering the smooth working of markets thanks to a reduced need for State action.

One further drawback is worth considering here.

As argued by the renowned Italian theorist of the cooperative movement Valenti (1902, p. 526), "for my part, I think it at odds with the very nature of the producer cooperative and of any other cooperative firm model that such a firm should be granted any benefits or competitive edge because the costs of such a provision would ultimately have to be paid by taxpayers or consumers."

Is this objection well-grounded?

The claim that democratic institutions foster growth is backed up by a considerable body of empirical evidence. One such piece of evidence is that democracy acts as an enabler of growth for a number of reasons, for instance because it reduces uncertainty and makes the general public aware of the need and effectiveness of State intervention under given circumstances, but also because democracy eases the accumulation of social capital. Specifically, it tends to develop civic virtues by favouring a correct appreciation of the general interest and inducing the general public to work towards its achievement. The third reason is a potential for reducing inequality, which acts as an additional impulse to the flourishing of civic virtues (see Hall & Jones 1999, Acemoglu *et al.* 2002, Rodrik *et al.* 2002 and Zamagni 2008).

An advocate of the abolition of capitalism, Raniero Panzieri, argued that 'cognitive' participation was a necessary, though not sufficient prerequisite for efficient labour management. In his opinion, such a goal called for a concerted action designed to revolutionise and streamline business hierarchies and the associated power relations; and its impact would transcend the level of the firm. As its prime aim was to eradicate the pervasive effects of the 'despotism' of capital felt at every level throughout the social pyramid, he added, its range of action was not confined to the firm and it required awareness-building actions capable of mobilising the working class into overthrowing the system as a whole (see Panzieri 1975, p. 168).

These are strong arguments in support of the idea that the State is called upon to help cooperative firms trounce competition from their rival capital-managed enterprises.

In the *Manifesto of the Communist Party*, Marx and Engels wrote: "When, in the course of development, class distinctions have disappeared, and all production has been concentrated in the hands of a vast association of the whole nation, the public power will lose its political character. Political power, properly so called, is merely the organised power of one class for oppressing another" (Marx & Engels 1848, p. 505).

Marx and Engels's radical interpretation of State power as exclusively intended to serve the interests of the ruling class and oppress other classes of society is fully consistent with my own conclusion: a system of producer cooperatives which virtually abolishes class distinctions would empty State power of its political essence and, concomitantly, reduce economic State interventionism by divesting it of part of the reason for its existence.

Further reflections on economic State interventionism in a system of producer cooperatives

Marx's argument that the precondition for a successful revolution was suppressing the State was strongly endorsed by Lenin in *The State and Revolution* (1917a), but subsequently dropped by most Marxists. Finelli, for instance (2007, p. 130), dismissed it as "the well-known, though bizarre Marxist-Leninist theory of the extinction of the State."

There can be little doubt that refuting the theory of the extinction of the State requires rejecting "the popular belief, which is rightly shared by the working class in its entirety, that the State is the enemy and the master" (see Tronti 1978, p. 24), i.e. the description of the State as the spokesman for a single class which has been criticised in this book.[15]

As is well known, the stoutest critics of the State today are not Marxists, but liberalists, who have traditionally been pressing the view that markets are inherently efficient and that there is no need for the State to intervene and correct its dysfunctions. On closer analysis, even a liberalist such as Friedman did not hesitate to acknowledge the need to retain the State as long as there are markets in which individuals make their exchanges.

Developing the traditional liberalist stances of the Right to extreme, neo-liberalists today have gone so far as to argue that the citizens of the modern world no longer need the State which past generations used to rate as an absolute necessity. Thanks to increasing education and income levels, the citizens have come to conceive the wish to pursue their goals autonomously, by making the most of impersonal market mechanisms. As argued by Hardin (2000), evidence of this is provided by the growing depoliticisation of the citizens.

As said above, in parliamentary systems the State may either protect the interests of the bourgeoisie or those of the proletariat, but it may also act in the general interest, depending on the circumstances prevailing from time to time. Consequently, there is scope for arguing that in a democratic firm system the State will concomitantly exercise its traditional administrative and political powers,[16] and perform the function that was vested in it by Hegel, that is to say working towards the attainment of the general interest.

A system of democratic firms will neither cancel conflicts of interests, especially those between rich and poor, nor the unfair income distribution patterns likely to result from the working of market mechanisms. As a result, the State will have to make it its task to counteract the economic crises that markets inevitably generate and to provide public services. The great liberal philosopher John Dewey (1935, p. 11) effectively refuted the idea that economic laws only are genuine natural laws, and that the rest are man-made laws whose ranges of action should be restricted as far as possible. Contrasts of opinion between free market liberals and statists advocating State intervention are no less likely to occur.

In point of fact, there can be little doubt that interest groups will continue to oppose State intervention, that large-scale concerns will still be able to put pressure on the State and that injustice will barely be swept away, but it is difficult to deny that the erosion of the power of capital and the resulting impulse to full democracy would make it easier for the State to perform its functions to the full.

Incidentally, it is worth refuting the assumption that the strong impulse to full employment generated by a self-managed firm system would accelerate inflation. As argued in Chapter 5, in a system without hired labour the Phillips curve das not exist, in terms that decreasing levels of unemployment do not drive up wages and, hence, inflation. On closer analysis, the non-applicability of the Phillips curve is one of the greatest advantages of democratic firm management. Moreover, in a system of democratic firms the role of the State as 'employer of last resort' would no longer be opposed or hindered as it tends to be in capitalistic systems.

Even more importantly, let me re-emphasise that the State will be able to act in full accordance with the dictates of Hegel, i.e. as "the actuality of the ethical idea."

Conclusion

In an attempt to criticise Marx and Engels's view of State power, in this Chapter I have argued that even in capitalistic systems the State might well be able to further and force through a stepwise transition to socialism by peaceful means.

Moreover, since I dissent from Marx and Engels's argument that socialism necessitates suppressing the State apparatus, instead of endorsing the thesis that the precondition for the establishment of socialism is disempowering the State, I have laid stress on the assumption that within a system of democratic firms the State would be given more scope for serving the general interest. Thanks to the virtual abolition of class distinctions, in a system of cooperatives this prospect is anything but unrealistic since the purpose of economic State intervention would be to correct market failures and, overall, further the interests of the community at large.

Notes

1 Stedman Jones (1978, pp. 340–42) holds that the definition of the State as a class-based power structure was suggested by Engels well before Marx and represents one of Engels's main contributions to the materialist conception of history. As argued by McGovern (1970, pp. 430–31), it was not until 1845 that Marx fully accepted the idea that the capitalistic State was a tool in the hands of the bourgeoisie.

2 Bobbio (1986, p. 114) called attention to the fact that Rousseau's description of the historical State (not the State theorised in the *Social Contract*) as generated by violence and fraud predates Marx's pessimistic view of the antagonism between governors and those governed.

3 In part, the growing consensus in favour of a non-statist reading of Marx's system can be explained by the retreat of many Marxists from their one-time dogmatic stances. It is widely held that "the tragedy of Marxism" is that "ideologies have been in the ascendancy for so long that the Marxist system as an analysis has been perverted by dogma" (see de Schweinitz Jr. 1962, p. 49). It was the excessive dogmatism of Marxists (and their scant familiarity with Marx's writings, see Robinson 1973, *Foreword*) that led Keynes to argue (Keynes 1925, p. 231): "How can I accept a doctrine which sets up as its bible, above and beyond criticism, an obsolete economic textbook which I know to be not only erroneous, but without interest or application for the modern world?"

4 Bearing in mind the positive role vested in the bourgeoisie in Marx's works, Marx has rightly been described as the heir of the ideals of the French Revolution and a theorist wishing to pass on to the proletariat all the privileges that the bourgeois class had been able to conquer for itself. (The place of radical socialism in Marx's educational background is discussed in some of his biographies, for instance Mehring 1918, pp. 75–80 and Merker 2010, chap. III).

5 G.D.H. Cole (1919, p. 4) is just one of many who argue that no government will ever dare to adopt policies that might prove detrimental to the interests of magnates in business and industry.

6 As is well known, in the opinion of Bobbio the reason why the workers' movement has no theory of the State is that Marx never formulated such a theory (see Bobbio 1976 and, for a discussion of Bobbio's argument, AA.VV. 1976). Unlike Bobbio, Tronti (1977, p. 67) holds that Marx's political thought, though, admittedly, not constituting a theory of the State proper, was actually "developed in writings other than *Capital* and the *Grundrisse* and is therefore not part of his critique of political economy."

7 Instead of categorising the State as the power structure of one class, Lelio Basso highlights its function as a mediator and, as it were, "clearing house of contradictory energies" (see Basso 1969, pp. 165–66). For a convincing explanation of the reasons why the capitalistic State cannot be downsized to a tool in the service of capital and, overall, capitalistic relations worldwide, see Bieler, Bruff and Morton's critique of *Open Marxism* (2010). This theoretical movement sees capitalistic relations as the sole

enablers of human activity and, by extension, of historical growth throughout the world. On closer analysis, though, it has so far proved unable to account for the fact that changing State-capital relations have given rise to different State models. In the estimation of *Open Marxists*, capital becomes the founding stone of all State models – a stance which is evidently unacceptable.

8 The socialism = central planning equation is closely associated with the theoretical approaches of Engels and Lenin and made headway thanks to the success of the Bolshevik revolution.

Several authors (including Yudt 2012, p. 193) have emphasised that the circulation of this idea among the general public was also furthered by the publication of an influential book by Kolakowsky (1979).

9 For an analysis of Engels's influence on the evolution of Marxist thought see, *inter alia*, Lichtheim (1962, chap. 3). In this connection, it is worth mentioning that the earliest attempts at systematising the theoretical edifice of Marxism date from the 1970s (Negt 1979b, p. 109).

10 "Marxism was created by Engels," but "Marx is one thing and Marxism is quite another." Inasmuch as this is true, as I am personally inclined to hold, as soon as we clear the field of the supposed all-importance of planning, it is possible to put Marx's theoretical edifice in its right perspective and "make it no longer appear obsolete or irrelevant, but topical and full of relevance for our days" (Rockmore 2005, pp. 154–55).

11 This is the gist of a passage from Thomas (1985, p. 275).

12 In the *Manifesto* we read that "the first step in the revolution of the working class is to raise the proletariat to the position of ruling class, to win the battle of democracy."

13 In the awareness that the legal 'superstructure' of the bourgeois state was a historical necessity, Marx went so far as to argue that even at the earliest stages of the communist system it would hardly be outperformed by any alternative formal criterion for the distribution of property (see Zolo 1974, p. 47). In this connection, G. Della Volpe has argued: "As long as a state – albeit a democratic one such as a socialist state – does exist, and as long as there is a social order structured in line with the criterion of the distinction between governors and governed, there is no way of deflecting from the basic principle that a limit is to be placed on the power that the state is allowed to wield over the citizens" (Della Volpe 1964, p. 47).

14 This is true notwithstanding the creation of the Group of Eight following the epoch-making admission of China and India as additional members.

15 Elster and Screpanti have described this idea as both naïve and at odds with the very principles of democracy. Insofar as it is true, they argue, that public choices are translated into administrative policies and should therefore be made in line with efficiency criteria, democratic firm management becomes redundant (see Elster 1985, p. 458; Screpanti 2007a, p. 133).

16 A Marxist such as Wolff (2012, p. 162) shares the view that economic State intervention would be more massive in a self-managed firm system than it is under capitalism, but does not trace the assumed lower intervention levels of capitalistic States to the opposition of firms.

References

A.I.S.S.E.C., 1993, Associazione italiana per lo studio dei sistemi economici comparati, *preprints* of the proceedings of the 9th Scientific Convention.

AA.VV., 1968, *Cent'anni dopo il Capitale*, Ital. transl., Samonà e Savelli, Rome, 1970.

AA.VV., 1969, *Neocapitalismo e sinistra europea*, Laterza, Bari.

AA.VV., 1969a, *Marx vivo*, Mondadori, Milan.

AA.VV., 1969b, *Sviluppo economico e rivoluzione*, De Donato, Bari.

AA.VV., 1970a, *Il controllo operaio*, Samonà e Savelli, Rome.

AA.VV., 1970b, *Marxismo ed etica*, Ital. transl., Feltrinelli, Milan.

AA.VV., 1970c, *Gramsci e la cultura contemporanea*, Editori Riuniti, Rome.

AA.VV., 1971, *Anarchici ed anarchia nel mondo contemporaneo*, Atti del convegno promosso dalla Fondazione Luigi Einaudi, Einaudi, Turin.

AA.VV., 1974, *Classe, consigli, partito*, Alfani edtore, Rome.

AA.VV., 1975a, *L'autogestione in Italia; realtà e funzione della cooperazione* De Donato, Bari.

AA.VV., 1975b, *Teoria economica ed economia socialista*, Savelli, Rome.

AA.VV., 1977, *Classe, consigli, partito*, Alfani edtore, Rome.

AA.VV., 1978, *Operaismo e centralità operaia*, Editori Riuniti, Rome.

AA.VV., 1982, *Storia del marxismo*, Einaudi, Turin.

AA.VV., 1986, *Cooperare e competere*, Feltrinelli, Milan.

AA.VV., 1990, *Gramsci e il marxismo contemporaneo*, ed. by B. Muscatello, Editori Riuniti, Rome.

AA.VV., 2008, *Sinistra senza sinistra*, Feltrinelli, Milan.

Abbagnano N., 2006, *Storia della filosofia*, vol. 9, Gruppo editoriale l'Espresso, Rome.

Abendroth W., 1958, Il marxismo è 'superato'?, in Abendroth 1967.

Abendroth W., 1967, *Socialismo e marxismo da Weimar alla Germania Federale*, trad. ital., Florence, La Nuova Italia, 1978.

Acemoglu D., Johnson S., Robinson J., 2002, Reversal of Fortune: Geography and Development in the Making of Modern World Income Distribution, in *Quarterly Journal of Economics*, vol. 117.

Acton H. B., 1955, *The Illusion of an Epoch*, Cohen & West, London.

Adams J. S., 1963, Toward an Understanding of Inequity, in *Journal of Abnormal and Social Psychology*, vol. 67.

Adler M., 1904, Kant e il socialismo, in Agazzi 1975.

Adler M., 1919, *Democrazia e consigli operai*, Ital. transl., De Donato, Bari, 1970.

Adler-Karlsson G., 1986, Il socialismo 'minimale' e il dilemma delle uova, in AA.VV. 1986.

Adorno T. W., 1968, Is Marx Obsolete?, in *Diogenes*, no. 64.

Agazzi E., 1975, *Marxismo ed etica*, Feltrinelli, Milan.

Albanese M., 2003, Le difficoltà di finanziamento delle LMF ed il finanziamento del credito, in *Economia politica*, vol. 20, no. 3.

Albert M., 2003, *L'economia partecipativa*, Datanews, Rome.

Alchian A. A., Demsetz H., 1972, Production, Information Costs and Economic Organization, in *American Economic Review*, vol. 62, December.

Alesina A., Danninger S., Rostagno M., 2001, Redistribution through Public Employment: The Case of Italy, in *IMF Staff Papers*, vol. 48.

Althusser L., 1965a, *Per Marx*, Ital. transl., Editori Riuniti, Rome, 1969.

Althusser L., 1965b, L'oggetto del capitale, in Althusser & Balibar, 1965.

Althusser L., 1969 and 1995, *Sur la reproduction*, Presses universitaires de France, Paris.

Althusser L., 1972, Risposta a John Louis, in Althusser 2005.

Althusser L. 1995, *Sur la reproduction*, Paris, Presses Universitaires de France.

Althusser L., 2005, *I marxisti non parlano mai al vento*, ed. by L. Tomasetta, Mimesis, Milan.

Althusser L., Balibar E., 1965, *Leggere il Capitale*, Ital. transl., Feltrinelli, Milan, 1968.

Altvater E., 1982, La teoria del capitalismo monopolistico di Stato e le nuove forme di socializzazione capitalistica, in Hobsbawm *et al.* 1978–1982, vol. IV.

Amirante C., 2008, *Dalla forma Stato alla forma mercato*, Giappichelli, Turin.

Anderson P., 1976, *Il dibattito sul marxismo occidentale*, Ital. transl. Bari, Laterza, 1977.

Anderson P., 1980, *Arguments within English Marxism*, Verso, London.

Anderson P., 2002, Force and Consent, in *New Left Review*, vol. 17, September–October.

Andreani T., 2001a, Market Socialism: Problems and Models, in Bidet and Kouvelakis 2001.

Andreani T., 2001b, *Le Socialisme est (a) venir*, Parigi, Syllepse.

Andreani T., 2008, Market Socialism: Problems and Models, in Bidet & Kouvelakis 2008.

Ansart P., 1967, *La sociologia di Proudhon*, Ital. transl., Il Saggiatore, Milan, 1972.

Ansart P., 1969, *Marx e l'anarchismo*, Ital. transl., Il Mulino, Bologna, 1972.

Ansart P., 1978, *P. J. Proudhon*, La Pietra, Milan.

Antoni C., 1952, *Dallo storicismo alla sociologia*, La Nuova Italia, Florence.

Anweiler O., 1958, *Storia dei soviet, 1905–1921*, Ital. transl., Laterza, Bari, 1972.

Arena R., 2010, Corporate Limited Liability and Cambridge Economics in the Inter-war Period: Robertson, Keynes and Sraffa, in *Cambridge Journal of Economics*, vol. 3, no. 5, September.

Arena R., Salvadori N. O., eds., 2004, *Money, Credit and the Role of the State*, Ashgate, New York.

Argeri D., 1988, *La teoria della democrazia nel pensiero di J. A. Schumpeter*, Esi, Napoli.

Arnason J. P., 1982, Prospettive e problemi del marxismo critico nell'Est europeo, in Hobsbawn *et al.* 1978–1982.

Aron R., 1955, *L'oppio degli intellettuali*, Ital. transl., Cappelli, Bologna, 1958.

Aron R., 1965, The Impact of Marxism in the Twentieth Century, in Drachkovitch, 1965.

Aron R., 1969, Equivoco e inesauribile, in AA.VV. 1969a.

Aron R., 1970, *Marxismi immaginari; da una sacra famiglia all'altra*, Ital. transl., F. Angeli, Milan, 1977.

Arrighi G., 1994, *Il lungo XX secolo*, Il Saggiatore, Milan, 1996.

Arrighi G., 2007, *Adam Smith a Pechino*, Feltrinelli, Milan.

Arthur W. B., 1989, Competing Technologies, Increasing Returns and Lock-in by Historical Events, in *Economic Journal*, vol. 99, no. 1.

Artoni R., ed., 1981, *Teoria economica e analisi delle istituzioni*, Il Mulino, Bologna.

Asor Rosa A., 1964, Fine della battaglia culturale, in Vacca 1972.

Aspromourgos T., 2000, Is an Employer-of-Last-Resort Policy Sustainable? A Review Article, in *Review of Political Economy*, vol. 12, no. 2.

Atkinson A. B., ed., 1993, *Alternatives to Capitalism: The Economics of Partnership*, Macmillan, London.

Avineri S., 1968, *The Social and Political Thought of Karl Marx* Cambridge University Press, London.

Backhouse R. E., Bateman B. W., 2013, Inside Out: Keynes's Use of the Public Sphere, in Mata & Medema 2013.
Baczko B., 1965, Marx e l'idea di universalità dell'uomo, in Fromm 1965.
Badaloni N., 1990, Marxismo e teoria politica in Gramsci, in Muscatello 1990.
Baglioni G., 1995, *Democrazia impossibile?*, Il Mulino, Bologna.
Bagnasco A., 2008, *Ceto medio*, Il Mulino, Bologna.
Bagnoli L., ed., 2010, *La funzione sociale della cooperazione*, Carocci, Rome.
Bahro R., 1977, *Eine Dokumentation*, Europäische Verlagsanstalt, Frankfurt am Maino.
Bakunin M., 1871, *La théologie politique de Mazzini et l'Internationale*, G. Guillame Fils, Neuchâtel.
Balibar E., 1965, Sui concetti fondamentali del materialismo storico, in Althusser & Balibar 1965.
Balibar E., 1974, *Cinque studi di materialismo storico*, Ital. transl., De Donato, Bari, 1976.
Balibar E., 1993, *La filosofia di Marx*, Ital. transl., manifestolibri, Rome, 1994.
Ball T., Farr J., eds., 1984, *After Marx*, Cambridge University Press, Cambridge.
Baranzini R., 2001, Léon Walras: il singolare socialismo di un marginalista atipico, in Guidi & Michelini 2001.
Baratta G., 1999, Gramsci tra noi: Hall, Said, Balibar, in Baratta & Liguori 1999.
Baratta G., Liguori G., eds., 1999, *Gramsci. da un secolo all'altro*, Editori Riuniti, Rome.
Bardhan P., Roemer J. E., eds., 1993, *Market Socialism: The Current Debate*, Oxford Economic Press, New York.
Barone E., 1908, Il Ministro della produzione in uno stato collettivista, in *Giornale degli econo*misti, vol. 34.
Barro R. J., 1996, Democracy and Growth, in *Journal of Economic Growth*, vol. 1, March.
Bartlett W., Cable J., Estrin S., Derek C., Smith S., 1992, Labour-Managed versus Private Firms: An Empirical Comparison of Cooperatives and Private Firms in Central Italy, in *Industrial and Labour Relations Review*, vol. 46.
Bascetta M., 2004, *La libertà dei postmoderni*, manifestolibri, Rome.
Basso L., 1969, Appunti sulla teoria rivoluzionaria in Marx ed Engels, in AA.VV. 1969b.
Basso L., 2008, *Socialità e isolamento: la singolarità in Marx*, Carocci, Rome.
Bataille G., 1996, *Il limite dell'utile*, Ital. transl., Adelphi, Milan, 2000.
Battilani P., Bertagnoni G., eds., 2007, *Competizione e valorizzazione del lavoro. La rete cooperativa del Consorzio nazionale dei servizi*, Il Mulino, Bologna.
Bauer O., 1920, Bolscevismo o socialdemocrazia, in Marramao 1977.
Bauer R., 1963, Presente e futuro dell'impresa cooperativa, in Briganti 1982, vol. III.
Baum J. A. C., ed., 2002, *The Blackwell Companion to Organizations*, Blackwell, Oxford.
Baumol W. J., 1953–54, Firms with Limited Money Capital, in *Kyklos*, vol. 6, no. 2.
Becattini G., 1989, Mercato e comunismo nel pensiero di Alfred Marshall, in Jossa 1989.
Becker J. F., 1977, *Marxian Political Economy; an Outline*, Cambridge University Press, Cambridge.
Bellas C., 1972, *Industrial Democracy and Worker-Owned Firm: A Study of Twenty-one Plywood Companies in the Pacific Northwest*, Praeger, New York.
Bellofiore R., ed., 1998, *Marxian Economics; a Reappraisal,* Palgrave Macmillan, New York.
Bellofiore R., 2007, *Da Marx a Marx?*, manifestolibri, Rome.
Ben-Ner A., 1984, On the Stability of the Cooperative Type of Organization, in *Journal of Comparative Economics*, vol. 8, no. 3, September.
Ben-Ner A., 1987, Producer Cooperatives: Why Do They Exist in Market Economies?, in Powell 1987.
Ben-Ner A., 1988a, Comparative Empirical Observation on Worker-owned and Capitalist Firms, in *International Journal of Industrial Organization*, vol. 6, no. 1.

Ben-Ner A., 1988b, The Life-Cycle of Worker-owned Firms in Market Economies: A Theoretical Analysis, in *Journal of Economic Behavior and Organization*, vol. 10, no. 3.
Ben-Ner A., Jones D. C., 1995, Employee Participation, Ownership and Productivity: A Theoretical Framework, in *Industrial Relations*, vol. 34, no. 4, October.
Ben-Ner A., T. Han, Jones D. C., 1996, The Productivity Effects of Employee Participation in Control and in Economic Returns: A Review of Empirical Evidence, in Pagano & Rowthorn 1996.
Ben-Ner A., Ellman M., 2013, The Contribution of Behavioural Economics to Understanding and Advancing the Sustainability of Worker Cooperatives, in *Journal of Entrepreneurial and Organizational Diversity*, vol. II, no. 1.
Benham L., Keefer P., 1991, Voting in Firms: The Role of Agenda Control, Size, and Voter Homogeneity, in *Economic Inquiry*, vol. 29, no. 4, October.
Bensaïd D., 2002, *Marx for Our Times*, Verso, London.
Bensaïd D., 2009, *Marx, istruzioni per l'uso*, Ital. transl., Ponte alle Grazie, 2010, Milan.
Berle A., 1932, For Whom Corporate Managers Are Trustees, in *Harvard Law Review*, vol. 45.
Berle A., Means G., 1932, *Modern Corporation and Private Property*, Harcourt Brace & World, New York, 1967.
Berlin I., 1963, *Marx*, Ital. transl., La Nuova Italia, Florence, 1967.
Berman K. V., Berman M. D., 1989, An Empirical Test of the Theory of the Labour-managed Firm, in *Journal of Comparative Economics*, vol. 13, no. 2, June.
Berman M. D., 1977, Short Run Efficiency in the Labour-managed Firm, in *Journal of Comparative Economics*, vol. 1, no. 3.
Bernstein E., 1899a, *Evolutionary Socialism. A Criticism and Affirmation*, Shocken Books, New York, 1961.
Bernstein E., 1899b, *I presupposti del socialismo e i compiti della socialdemocrazia*, Ital. transl., Laterza, Bari, 1969.
Bernstein E., 1901, *Zur Geschichte und Theorie des Sozialismus*, Akademischer Verlag für Soziale Wissenschaft, Berlino.
Besley T. F., Coate S. T., 1998, Sources of Inefficiency in a Representative Democracy: A Dynamic Analysis, in *American Economic Review*, vol. 88.
Bettelheim C., 1969, Sulla transizione tra capitalismo e socialismo, in *Monthly Review*, Ital. ed., March–April.
Bettelheim C., 1971, Ancora sulla società di transizione, in *Monthly Review*, Ital. ed., March.
Bettilani P., Bertagnoni G., eds., 2007a, *Competizione e valorizzazione del lavoro. La rete cooperativa del Consorzio nazionale dei servizi*, Il Mulino, Bologna.
Bettilani P., Bertagnoni G., 2007b, Introduction to Bettilani & Bertagnoni 2007a.
Bidet J., 1990, La teoria del modo di produzione capitalistico, in AA.VV. 1990.
Bidet J., 2004, *'Il Capitale', spiegazione e ricostruzione*, Ital. transl., manifesto-libri, Rome, 2010.
Bidet J., Kouvelakis S., eds., 2001, *Dictionnaire Marx Contemporain*, Presses Universitaires de France, Paris.
Bidet J., Kouvelakis S., eds., 2008, *Critical Companion to Contemporary Marxism*, Brill, Leideno.
Bieler A., Bruff I., Morton A. D., 2010, *Acorns and Fruit: From Totalization to Periodization in the Critique of Capitalism*, University College, Dublin.
Bigo P., 1953, *Marxismo e umanismo*, Ital. transl., Bompiani, Milan, 1963.
Birchall J., 1997, The International Cooperative Movement, University of British Columbia Press, Vancouver.
Blackledge P., 2004, *Perry Anderson, Marxism and the New Left*, The Merlin Press, London.
Blinder A., ed., 1990, *Paying for Productivity*, The Brookings Institutions, Washington D.C.

Bloch E., 1968, *Karl Marx*, Ital. transl., Il Mulino, Bologna, 1972.

Block F., 1977, The Ruling Class Does Not Rule: Notes on the Marxist Theory of the State, reprinted in Roemer 1994a.

Bloom S. F., 1943, Man of His Century: A Reconsideration of the Historical Significance of Karl Marx, in Wood 1988.

Blumberg P. 1968. *Industrial Democracy. The Sociology of Participationo.* Constable, London.

Bobbio N., 1969, Gramsci e la concezione della società civile, in AA. VV., 1969, *Gramsci e la cultura contemporanea*, Editori Riuniti, Rome.

Bobbio N., 1976, Gramsci e il PCI; intervista con Norberto Bobbio, reprinted in AA.VV. 1977.

Bobbio N., 1984, *Il futuro della democrazia*, Einaudi, Turin.

Bobbio N., 1985, *Stato, governo, società; frammenti di un dizionario politico*, 2nd ed., Einaudi, Turin, 1995.

Bobbio N., 1986, Marx, lo Stato e i classici, in Mancina 1986.

Bobbio N., 1990, *L'età dei diritti*, Einaudi, Turin.

Bodei R., 2013, *Immaginare altre vite. realtà, progetti, desideri*, Feltrinelli, Milan.

Boffa G., Martinet G., 1976, *Dialogo sullo stalinismo*, Laterza, Bari.

Böhle E., Sauer O., 1975, Intensivierung der Arbeit und staatliche Sozialpolitik, in *Leviathan*, vol. III, no.1.

Bonazzi G., 2002, Perché i sociologi italiani del lavoro e dell'organizzazione, pur essendo pro-labour, non sono post-bravermaniani e meno ancora foucaultiani, in *Sociologia del lavoro*, fasc. II e III, no. 86–87.

Bondarcuk V., 1970, Psicologia sociale e storia in Gramsci, in AA.VV. 1970c.

Bonin, J. P., Jones D. C., Putterman L., 1993, Theoretical and Empirical Studies of Producer Cooperatives: Will the Twain Ever Meet?, in *Journal of Economic Literature*, vol. 31.

Bonomi G., 1973, *Partito e rivoluzione in Gramsci*, Feltrinelli, Milan.

Borzaga C., Depedri S., Tortia E. C., 2011, Organizational Varieties in Marker Economies and the Role of Co-operatives and Social Enterprises: A Plea for Organizational Pluralism, in *Journal of Cooperative Studies*, vol. 44, no. 1.

Bowles S., 1985, The Production Process in a Competitive Economy: Walrasian, Neo-Hobbesian and Marxian Models, in *American Economic Review*, vol. 75, no. 1, March.

Bowles S., Edwards R., eds., 1990, *Radical Political Economy*, vol. I, E. Elgar, Aldershot.

Bowles S., Gintis H., 1986, *Democracy and Capitalism*, Basic Books, New York.

Bowles S., Gintis H., 1993a, Post-Walrasian Political Economy, in Bowles, Gintis & Gustaffson 1993.

Bowles S., Gintis H., 1993b, The Democratic Firms: An Agency Theoretic Evaluation, in Bowles, Gintis & Gustafsson 1993.

Bowles S., Gintis H., 1994, Credit Market Imperfections and the Incidence of Worker-Owned Firms, in *Metroeconomica*, vol. 45, no.3.

Bowles S., Gintis H., 1996, The Distribution of Wealth and the Viability of the Democratic Firm, in Pagano & Rowthorn 1996.

Bowles S., Gintis H., 2002, Social Capital and Community Governance, in *Economic Journal*, vol. 112.

Bowles S., Gintis H., 2011, *A Cooperative Species: Human Reciprocity and its Evolution*, Princeton University Press, Princeton, NJ.

Bowles S., Gintis H., Gustafsson B., eds., 1993, *Markets and Democracy: Participation, Accountability and Efficiency*, Cambridge University Press, Cambridge.

Bradley K., Gelb A., 1980, The Radical Potential of Cash Nexus Breaks, in *British Journal of Sociology*, June.

Branco M. C., 2012, Economics against Democracy, in *Review of Radical Political Economics*, vol. 44, no. 1.

Braudel F., 1977, *Afterthoughts on Material Civilization and Capitalism*, Johns Hopkins University Press, Baltimore.

Braverman H., 1974, *Labour and Monopoly Capital*, Monthly Review Press, New York.

Brenner R., 1986, The Social Basis of Economic Development, in Roemer 1986.

Brewer A. A., Browning M. J., 1982, On the Employment Decision of a Labour-Managed Firm, in *Economica*, vol. 49, no. 194.

Bricianer S., 1969, *Pannekoek e i consigli operai*, Ital. transl., Musolini editore, Turin, 1975.

Briganti W., ed., 1982, *Il movimento cooperativo in Italia. Scritti e documenti, dal 1854 al 1980*, Editrice cooperativa, Rome.

Bronfenbrenner M., 1970, The Vicissitudes of Marxian Economics, in Wood 1988, vol. III.

Bruff I., 2010, Germany's Agenda 2010 Reforms: Passive Revolution at the Crossroads, in *Capital & Class*, vol. 34, no. 3.

Brunetta R., 2014, *La mia utopia*, Mondadori, Milan.

Bruni L., 2006, *Reciprocità*, B. Mondadori, Milan.

Bruni L., Zamagni S., 2004, *Economia civile*, Il Mulino, Bologna.

Buchanan A., 1979, Revolution, Motivation and Rationality, in *Philosophy and Public Affairs*, vol. 9, no. 1.

Buchanan A. E., 1982, *Marx and Justice; the Radical Critique of Liberalism*, Rowman & Allanheld, Totowa, New Jersey.

Bucharin N., 1925, La nuova politica economica e i nostri compiti, in Bucharin & Preobrazenskij 1969.

Bucharin N., Preobrazenskij Y. A., 1969, *L'accumulazione socialista*, ed. by L. Foa, Editori Riuniti, Rome.

Buci-Glucksmann C., 1979. *State, Transition and Passive Revolution*, in Mouffe 2010.

Buci-Glucksmann C., 1980, *Gramsci and the State*, Lawrence & Wishart, London.

Bulgarelli M., Viviani M., eds., 2006, *La promozione cooperativa; Copfond tra mercato e solidarietà*, Il Mulino, Bologna.

Bull M., 2006, On Agency, in *New Left Review*, vol. 40, July–August.

Burczak T., 2006, *Socialism after Hayek*, University of Michigan Press, Ann Arbor.

Buonocore V., Jossa B., eds., 2003, *Organizzazioni economiche non capitalistiche*, Il Mulino, Bologna.

Burgio A., ed., 2007, *Dialettica, tradizioni, problemi, sviluppi*, Quodlibet Studio, Macerata.

Burke J. P., ed., 1981, The Necessity of Revolution, in Burke, Crocker & Legters 1981.

Burke J. P., Crocker L., Legters L. H., eds., 1981, *Marxism, the Good Society*, Cambridge University Press, Cambridge.

Burnham J., 1941, *La rivoluzione dei tecnici*, Ital. transl., Mondadori, Milan, 1947.

Bush P. D., 2009, The Neoistitutionalist Theory of Value, in *Journal of Economic Issues*, vol. XLIII, no. 2.

Buzgalin A. V. & Kolganov A. I., 2013, Marx re-loaded: il dibattito russo, in *Il Ponte*, a. LXIX, nos 5–6.

Callinicos A., 2005, I contorni del marxismo anglosassone, in Musto 2005.

Callinicos A., 2010, The Limits of Passive Revolution, in *Capital & Class*, vol. 34, no. 3.

Calvo E., Murillo M. V., 2004, Who Delivers? Partisan Clients in the Argentine Electoral Market, in *American Journal of Political Science*, vol. 48.

Campbell M., Reuten G., eds., 2002, *The Culmination of Capital; Essays on Volume III of Marx's Capital*, Palgrave, London.

Capo G., 2003, Spunti di riflessione da una teoria economica della cooperazione, in Buonocore & Jossa 2003.

Carandini G., 2005, *Un altro Marx. Lo scienziato liberato dall'utopia*, Laterza, Bari.

Carboni C., ed., 1986, *Classi e movimenti in Italia, 1970–1985*, Laterza, Bari-Rome.

Carling A., 1995, Rational Choice Marxism, in Carver & Thomas 1995.

Carver T., 1984, Marxism as Method, in Ball & Farr 1984.

Carver T., Thomas P., eds., 1995, *Rational Choice Marxism*, Macmillan, London.

Castoriadis C., 1975, *L'institution imaginaire de la société*, Le Seuil, Parigi.

Castronovo V., 1987, Dal dopoguerra ad oggi, in Zangheri, Galasso & Castronovo 1987.

Catephores G., 1989, *An Introduction to Marxist Economics*, Macmillan, London.

Cattabrini F., 2010, Assemblea costituente: il dibattito sulla cooperazione, in Bagnoli 2010.

Cerroni U., 1973, *Teoria politica e socialismo*, Editori Riuniti, Rome.

Chaddad F., 2012, Advancing in the Theory of the Cooperative Organization: The Cooperative as True Hybrid, in *Annals of Public and Cooperative Economics*, vol. 83, no. 4.

Chattopadhyay P., 2010, The Myth of Twentieth-Century Socialism and the Continuing Relevance of Karl Marx, in *Socialism and Democracy*, vol. 24, no. 3.

Checov A., 1894a, Il monaco nero, Ital. transl., in Checov 1894b.

Checov A., 1894b, *Racconti*, vol. III, Einaudi, Turin, 1974.

Cheung S., 1987, Economic Organization and Transaction Costs, in Eatwell, Milgate & Newman 1987.

Cheung S., 1992, On the New Institutional Economics, in Werin & Wijkander 1992.

Chilosi A., ed., 1992a, *L'economia del periodo di transizione; dal modello di tipo sovietico all'economia di mercato*, Il Mulino, Bologna.

Chilosi A., 1992b, Il socialismo di mercato: modelli e problemi, in Chilosi 1992a.

Chomsky N., 1971, *Conoscenza e libertà*, Ital. transl., Il Saggiatore, Milan, 2010.

Chomsky N., 2009, Un mondo ingiusto, in *Internazionale*, vol. 16, no. 816.

Chomsky N., 2013, *I padroni dell'umanità*, Ital. transl., Salani, Milan, 2014.

Chubb J., 1982, *Patronage, Power and Poverty in South Italy: A Tale of Two Cities*, Cambridge University Press, Cambridge.

Clarke P., Mearman A., 2003, Why Marxist Economics Should Be Thought, but Probably Wont't Be!, in *Capital & Class*, no. 79, Spring.

Clayre A., ed., 1980, *The Political Economy of Cooperation and Participation: A Third Sector*, Oxford Economic Press, Oxford.

Coase R. H., 1937, The Nature of the Firm, in *Economica*, vol. 4, no.4.

Cohen G. A., 1978 and 2000, *Karl Marx's Theory of History: A Defence*, Clarendon Press, Oxford.

Cohen G. A., 1983, Forces and Relations of Production, in Roemer 1994a, vol. II.

Cohen J., 1982, Review Article of G. A. Cohen, *Karl Marx's Theory of History: A Defence*, in Roemer 1994a.

Cohen J. E., Rogers J., 1983, *On Democracy: Toward a Transformation of American Society*, Penguin, London.

Cohen S. H., 1973, *Bucharin e la rivoluzuione bolscevica*, Ital. transl., Feltrinelli, Milan, 1975.

Cole G. D. H., 1919, Self-Government in Industry, Hutchinson, London, 1972.

Cole G. D. H., 1953a, *Attempts at General Union*, Macmillan, London.

Cole G. D. H., 1953b, *Socialist Thought*, vol. I, *The Forerunners (1789–1850)*, Macmillan, London.

Cole G. D. H., 1954, *Socialist Thought*, vol. II, *Marxism and Anarchism 1850–1890)*, Macmillan, London.

Colletti L., 1974, *Intervista politico-filosofica*, Laterza, Bari.

Colletti L., 1979, *Tra marxismo e no*, Laterza, Bari.

Colombatto E., 2002, Towards a Quasi-Lamarckian Theory of Institutional Change, ICER, Working paper no. 26/2002.

Colombo A., ed., 1994, *Crollo del Comunismo sovietico e ripresa dell'utopia*, Edizioni Dedalo, Bari.

Commons J. R., 1924, *Legal Foundations of Capitalism*, University of Wisconsin Press, Milwaukee, 1968.

Commons J. R., 1934, *Institutional Economics; its Place in Political Economy*, Macmillan, New York.

Conte M. A., 1982, Participation and Performance in U.S. Labour-managed Firms, in Jones & Svejnar 1982.

Cook M. L., Chaddad F. R., Iliopoulos C., 2003, Advances in Cooperative Theory since 1990: A Review of Agricultural Economics Literature, in Hendrikse 2003.

Copeland M. A., 1931, Economic Theory and the Natural Science Point of View, in *American Economic Review*, vol. 21, no. 1, March.

Copeland M. A., 1936, Common's Institutionalism in Relation to the Problem of Social Evolution and Economic Planning, in *Quarterly Journal of Economics*, vol. 50, no. 2, February.

Coppellotti F., 1972, *Marx e la rivoluzione*, Feltrinelli, Milan.

Cornforth C., 1989, Worker Cooperatives in U. K.: Temporary Phenomenon or Growing Trend?, in Lammers & Széll 1989.

Cornforth C., Thomas A., Lewis J., Spear R., 1988, *Developing Successful Worker Cooperatives*, Sage, London.

Cornu A., 1948, *Karl Marx e il pensiero moderno*, Ital. transl., Turin, 1949.

Cornu A., 1955, *Marx e Engels dal liberalismo al comunismo*, Ital. transl., Milan, 1962.

Corradi C., 2007, Storia dei marxismi in Italia: un tentativo di sintesi, in Bellofiore 2007.

Corrigan P., Ramsay H., Sawyer D., 1978, *Socialist Construction and Marxist Theory*, Monthly Review Press, New York.

Cortesi L., 2010, *Storia del comunismo; da utopia al Termidoro sovietico*, manifestolibri, Rome.

Craig B., Pencavel I., 1995, Participation and Productivity: A Comparison of Worker Cooperatives and Conventional Firms in the Plywood Industry, *Brookings Papers: Microeconomics* I.

Croce B., 1896, Sulla forma scientifica del materialismo storico, in Croce 1968.

Croce B., 1899, *Materialismo storico ed economia marxista*, Laterza, Bari, 1968.

Croce B., 1968, *Materialismo storico ed economia socialista*, Laterza, Bari.

Crocker D. A., 1981, Markovic on Social Theory and Human Nature, in Burke, Crocker & Legters 1981.

Crouch C., 2003, *Postdemocracy*, Cambridge UK, Polity Press.

Crouch C., Heller F., eds., 1989, *International Yearbook of Organizational Democracy*, Wiley, Chichester.

Cunningham F., 1987, *Teoria della democrazia e socialismo*, Ital. transl., Editori Riuniti, Rome, 1991.

Cunow H., 1899, Zur Zusammenbruchsheorie, in *Die neue Zeit*, vol. XVII.

Cuomo G., 1997, Sottoinvestimento, diritti di proprietà ed orizzonte temporale nelle imprese autogestite, in Jossa & Pagano 1997.

Cuomo G., 2003, La cooperativa di produzione italiana e i modelli teorici di riferimento, in Buonocore & Jossa 2003.

Cuomo G., 2004, Il finanziamento esterno delle imprese gestite dai lavoratori, in Jossa 2004a.

Cuomo G., 2010, *Microeconomia dell'impresa cooperativa di produzione*, Giappichelli, Turin.

Cuomo G., 2016, Impresa cooperativa e democrazia economica, in *Studi Economici*, fortcoming.

D'Andrea Tyson L., 1979, Incentives, Income Sharing, and Institutional Innovation in the Yugoslav Self-Managed Firm, in *Journal of Comparative Economics*, vol. 3, no. 3, September.

D'Iorio P., 2013, Ontologia e genealogia nell'estate del 1881. La svolta costruttivista di Nietzsche, in *Il Ponte*, a. lxix, August–September.

Dahl R. A., 1985, *A Preface to Economic Democracy*, Polity Press, Cambridge.

Dahl R. A., 1989, *Democracy and its Critics*, Yale University Press, New Haveno.

Dahl R. A., 1997, Procedural Democracy, in Goodin & Pettit 1997.

Danielson P., ed., 1998, Modelling Rationality, Morality and Evolution, Oxford University Press, Oxford.

Danner P. L., 2002, *The Economic Person*, Rowman & Littlefield Publishers, Lanham, MD.

Davidson N. O., 2010, Scotland: Birthplace of Passive Revolution?, in *Capital & Class*, vol. 34, no. 3.

Dawkins R., 1992, *Il gene egoista*, Ital. transl., Oscar Mondadori, Milan, 1995.

De Giovanni B., 1976, *La teoria politica delle classi nel 'Capitale'*, De Donato, Bari.

De Giovanni B., Gerratana V. & Paggi L., eds., 1977, *Egemonia, stato, partito in Gramsci*, Editori Riuniti, Rome.

De Gregory T. R., 2003, Vitalism versus Hamiltonian Matter-of Fact Knowledge, in *Journal of Economic Issues*, vol. XXXVII, no. 1, March.

de Schweinitz K. jr., 1962, On the Determinism of the Marxian System, in *Social Research*, vol. 29, April.

Defourny J., 1992, Comparative Measures of Technical Efficiency for 500 French Workers' Cooperatives, in Jones & Svejnar 1992.

Defourny J., Estrin S., Jones D. C., 1985, The Effects of Workers' Participation on Enterprise Performance, in *International Journal of Industrial Organization*, vol. 3, no. 2.

Della Volpe G., 1964 (4th editn), *Rousseau e Marx*, Editori Riuniti, Rome.

Della Volpe G., 1969a, Avvertenza alla seconda edizione di Marx, 1843, in Marx 1969.

Della Volpe G., 1969b, *Logica come scienza storica*, Editori Riuniti, Rome.

Denizet J., 1981, Equilibre économique et équilibre sociale chez Walras, in *Économie Appliquée*, vol. 34, no. 1.

Derrida J., 1993, *Spettri di Marx*, Ital. transl., Raffaello Cortina, Milan, 1994.

Deutscher I., 1970, *Lenin; frammento di una vita e altri saggi*, Ital. transl., Laterza, Bari, 1970.

Dewey J., 1935, *Liberalismo e azione sociale*, Ital. transl., La Nuova Italia, Florence, 1967.

Di Giacomo E., 1991, *Economia e democrazia*, Lalli Editore, Poggibonsi.

Di Quattro A., 1976, Market Socialism and Socialist Value, in *Review of Political Economy*, vol. 8, Winter.

Di Siena G., 1972, Biologia, darwinismo sociale e marxismo, supplement to *Critica marxista*, no. 4, 1972.

Diamantopoulos M., 2012, Breaking out of Cooperation's 'Iron-Cage': From Movement Degeneration to Building a Developmental Movement, in *Annals of Public and Cooperative Economics*, vol. 83, no. 2.

Dinerstein, A. C. (2005) A Call for Emancipatory Reflection: Introduction to the Forum, *Capital and Class*, 85, pp. 13–17.

Dobb M., 1933a, Economic Theory and the Problems of a Socialist Economy, reprinted in Dobb 1955b.

Dobb M., 1933b, La teoria economica e i problemi di un' economia socialista, in Dobb 1955b.

Dobb M., 1939, Gli economisti e la teoria economica del socialismo, in Dobb 1955b.

Dobb M., 1953, Rassegna della discussione riguardante il calcolo economico in un'economia socialista, in Dobb 1955b.

Dobb M., 1955a, *On Economic Theory and Socialism: Collected Papers*, Routledge & Kegan, London.

Dobb M., 1955b, *Teoria economica e socialismo*, Ital. transl., Editori Riuniti, Rome, 1974.

Dobb M., 1969, *Economia del benessere ed economia socialista*, Ital. transl., Editori Riuniti, Rome, 1972.

Dobb M., 1970, *Le ragioni del socialismo*, Ital. transl., Editori Riuniti, Rome, 1973.

Dodd E. M., 1932, For Whom Corporate Managers are Trustees?, in *Harvard Law Review*, vol. 45.

Dodd E. M., 1941, The Modern Corporation, Private Property and the Recent Federal Legislation, in *Harvard Law Review*, vol. 54.

Domar E. D., 1966, The Soviet Collective Farm as a Producer Cooperative, in *American Economic Review*, vol. 56, no. 4.

Donahue J. D., 1989, *The Privatization Decision*, Basic Books, New York.

Donnaruma C., Partyka N., 2012, Challenging the Presumption in Favor of Markets, in *Review of Radical Political Economics*, vol. 44, no.1.

Doucouliagos C., 1995, Worker Participation and Productivity in Labor-Managed and Participatory Capitalist Firms: A Meta-Analysis, in *Industrial and Labour Relations Review*, vol. 49, no. 1.

Dow G., 2003, *Governing the Firm; Workers' Control in Theory and Practice*, Cambridge University Press, Cambridge.

Drachkovitch M. M., ed., 1965, *Marxism in the Modern World*, Oxford University Press, London.

Dreyfus M., 2012, La cooperazione di produzione in Francia dalle origini alla Grande guerra, in *Il Ponte*, a. 68, nos 5–6.

Drèze J. H., 1976, Some Theory of Labour Management and Participation, in *Econometrica*, vol. 44, no. 6.

Drèze J. H., 1985, Labor Management and General Equilibrium, in Jones & Svejnar 1985.

Drèze J. H., 1989, *Labour-Management, Contracts and Capital Markets. A General Equilibrium Approach*, Basil Blackwell, Oxford.

Drèze J. H., 1993, Self-Management and Economic Theory: Efficiency, Funding and Employment, in Bardhan & Roemer 1993.

Dubravcic D., 1970, Labor as an Entrepreneurial Input; an Essay on the Theory of the Producer Cooperative Economy, in *Economica*, vol. 37, no. 147.

Duffield J., 1970, The Value Concept in Capital in Light of Recent Criticism, reprinted in Wood 1988.

Dugger W. M., 2003, David Hamilton: A Radical Institutionalist, in *Journal of Economic Issues*, vol. XXXVII, no. 1, March.

Dunayevskaya R., 1951, The Cooperative Form of Labor vs. Abstract Labor, available at www.marxists.org/archive/dunayevskaya/works/1951/labor.htm.

Dunayevskaya R., 1988, *Marxism and Freedom: From 1776 until Today*, Columbia University Press, New York.

Dunlap L. A., 1979, Social Production in Karl Marx, in *Review of Social Economy*, vol. 37, no. 3.

Dunn J., 2005, *Il mito degli uguali. La lunga storia della democrazia*, Ital. transl., Egea, Milan, 2006.

Durkheim E., 1928, *Socialism and Saint-Simon*, Engl. transl., Routledge & Kegan Paul, London, 1959.

Dussel E., 1999, *Un Marx sconosciuto*, manifestolibri, Rome.

Eatwell J., Milgate M., Newman P., eds., 1987, *The New Palgrave: A Dictionary of Economics*, Macmillan, London.

Edwards R., 1979, *Contested Terrain; the Transformation of the Workplace in the Twentieth Century*, Basic Books, New York.

Edwards R., McEwan A., *et al.*, 1970, A Radical Approach to Economics, in *American Economic Review*, vol. 60, no. 2.

Efferson C., 2012, Book review feature: two book reviews of *A Cooperative Species: Human Reciprocity and Its Evolution*, in *Economic Journal*, vol. 122, no. 562.

Egan D., 1990, Towards a Marxist Theory of Labour-Managed Firms: Breaking the Degeneration Thesis, in *Review of Radical Political Economy*, vol. 22, no. 4.

Eichengreen B., Leblanc D., 2008, Democracy and Globalization, in *Economics and Politics*, vol. 20, no. 3.

Einaudi L., 1920a, Il significato del controllo operaio, in Einaudi 1966.

Einaudi L., 1920b, Partecipazione degli operai alla gestione e socializzazione, in Einaudi 1966.

Einaudi L., 1966, *Cronache economiche e politiche di un trentennio*, vol. V, Einaudi, Turin.

Ekins P., Max-Neef M., eds., 1992, *Real-Life Economics. Understanding Wealth Creation*, Routledge, London.

Ellerman D. P., 1990, *The Democratic Worker-Owned Firm*, Unwin Hyman, Boston.

Ellerman D. P., 1992, *Property and Contract in Economics*, Blackwell, Oxford.

Elster J., 1984, Historical Materialism and Economic Backwardness, in Ball & Farr 1984.

Elster J., 1985, *Making Sense of Marx*, Cambridge University Press, Cambridge.

Elster J., ed., 1998, *Deliberating Democracy*, Cambridge University Press, Cambridge.

Elster J., Moene K. O., 1989, *Alternatives to Capitalism*, Cambridge University Press, Cambridge.

Engels F., 1845, Due discorsi a Eberfeld, in Marx & Engels, *Opere complete*, vol. 4.

Engels F., 1847, Principles of Communism, in Marx & Engels, 1975–2001, *Collected Works*, vol. 6.

Engels F., 1859a, Review of *Per la critica dell'economia politica*, in Marx 1859a.

Engels F., 1859b, Lettera a Marx del 12 dicembre, in Marx & Engels 1972.

Engels F., 1872, Lettera a Cuno del 24 gennaio, in Marx & Engels 1966

Engels F., 1875, *Lettera a Bebel*, del 18 (28) marzo, in Marx & Engels 1966.

Engels F., 1878, *Antidühring*, Ital. transl., Editori Riuniti, Rome, 1968.

Engels F., 1882, *Socialism, Utopian and Scientific*, Foreign Languages Publishing House, Moskow, 1976.

Engels F., 1884, *L'origine della famiglia, della proprietà privata e dello stato*, Rinascita, Rome, 1950.

Engels F., 1886, Lettera a Edward Pease, del 27 January, in Marx & Engels, *Opere complete*, vol. 36.

Engels F., 1890–91, In the Case of Brentano versus Marx. Regarding Alleged Falsifications of Quotations, in Marx & Engels, 1975–2001, *Collected Works*, vol. 27.

Engels F., 1890, Farewell Letter to the Readers of the Sozialdemokrat, in Marx & Engels *Collected Works*, vol. 27.

Engels F., 1891a, A Critique of the Draft Social–democratic Programme, in Marx & Engels, 1975–2001, *Collected Works*, vol. 27.

Engels F., 1891b, Introduzione all'edizione tedesca del 1891, in Marx 1871a.

Engels F., 1892a, *L'evoluzione del socialismo dall'utopia alla scienza*, Ital. transl., Editori Riuniti, Rome, 1976.

Engels F., 1892b, Lettera a Lafargue, 12/XI, in Marx & Engels, *Opere complete*, vol. 38.

Engels F., 1894, On Authority, reprinted in Engels 1959.

Engels F., 1895, Introduction to Karl Marx's *The Class Struggle in France, 1848 to 1850*, in Marx & Engels, *Collected Works*, vol. 27.

Engels F., 1959, *Basic Writings in Political and Philosophy*, ed. by L. Feuer, Doubleday, Garden City, New York.

Estrin S., 1991, Some Reflections on Self-Management, Social Choice and Reform in Eastern Europe, in *Journal of Comparative Economics*, vol. 15, no. 2, June.

Estrin S., Jones D. C., Svejnar J., 1987, The Productivity Effects of Worker Participation: Producer Cooperatives in Western Europe, in *Journal of Comparative Economics*, vol. 11, no. 1.

Estrin S., Jones D. C., 1992, The Viability of Employee-Owned Firms: Evidence from France, in *Industrial and Labor Relations Review*, vol. 45, no. 2.

Eswaran M., Kotwal A., 1989, Why Are Capitalists the Bosses?, in *Economic Journal*, vol. 99, no. 394, March.

Etzioni A., 1990, Concorrenza incapsulata, in Magatti 1990.

Etzioni A., 1991, Beyond Self-Interest, in Weimer 1991.

Etzioni A., 1992, The I & We Paradigm, in Ekins & Max-Neef 1992.

Etzioni A., ed., 1995, *New Communitarian Thinking*, University Press of Virginia, Charlottesville and London.

Etzioni A., 1999, *Essays in Socio-Economics*, Springer, Berlin.

Fabbri F., 1981, La cooperazione: 1945–1956, in Ilardi & Accornero 1981.

Faccioli D. & Fiorentini G., 1998, Un'analisi di efficienza comparata tra imprese cooperative e for profit, in Fiorentini & Scarpa 1998.

Faccioli D. & Scarpa C., 1998, Il vantaggio comparato delle imprese cooperative: aspetti teorici, in Fiorentini & Scarpa 1998.

Fearon J. D., 1998, Deliberation as Discussion, in Elster 1998.

Ferrajoli L, 1978, Esiste una democrazia rappresentativa?, in Ferrajoli & Zolo 1978.

Ferrajoli L. & Zolo D., 1978, *Democrazia autoritaria e capitalismo maturo*, Feltrinelli, Milan.

Fetscher I., 1973, Karl Marx and Human Nature, in Wood 1988, vol. I.

Fetscher I., 1979, Bernstein e la sfida all'ortodossia, in AA. VV. 1982.

Finan F. & Schechter L., 2012, Vote-Buying and Reciprocity, in *Econometrica*, vol. 80.

Finelli R., 2004, *Un parricidio mancato. Hegel e il giovane Marx*, Bollati Boringhieri, Turin.

Finelli R., 2007, Un marxismo 'senza Capitale', in Bellofiore 2007.

Fineschi R., ed., 2005, *Karl Marx: Rivisitazioni e prospettive*, Mimesis, Milan.

Fineschi R., 2006, *Marx e Hegel*, Carocci, Rome.

Fineschi R., 2007, Attualità e praticabilità di una teoria dialettica del 'Capitale' (ovvero: Marx è un ferrovecchio?), in Burgio 2007.

Fineschi R., 2008, *Un nuovo Marx; filologia e interpretazione dopo la nuova edizione storico-critica (MEGA2)*, Carocci, Rome.

Finocchiaro M. A., 1988, *Gramsci and the History of Dialectical Thought*, Cambridge University Press, Cambridge.

Fiorentini G., Scarpa C., eds., 1998a, *Cooperative e mercato*, Carocci, Rome.

Fischer L., 1964, *Vita di Lenin*, Ital. transl., Il Saggiatore, Milan, 1967.

Fitoussi J. P., 1995, *Le débat interdit*, Arléa, Paris.

Fitoussi J. P., 2004, *La démocratie et le marché*, Grasset, Paris.

Fitzroy F. R., Kraft K., 1987, Cooperation, Productivity and Profit Sharing, in *Quarterly Journal of Economics*, vol. 102.

Fleetwood S., 2006, Rethinking Labour Market: A Critical-Realist-Socioeconomic Perspective, in *Capital & Class*, vol. 89, Summer.

Foa V., 1962, Lotte operaie nello sviluppo capitalistico, in *Quaderni rossi*, n. 1, ristampa, Sapere, Milano-Roma, 1974.

Ford E. C., 2000, The Development of Cooperative Ideology: From Social Transformation to Organisational Survival, University of Brunswick, *mimeo*.

Forgacs D., 1995, Gramsci in Gran Bretagna, in Hobsbawn 1995.

Foucault M., 1966, *Le parole e le cose*, Ital. transl., Rizzoli, Milan, 1967.

Freeman A., 2010, Marxism without Marx: A Note towards a Critique, in *Capital & Class*, vol. 34, no. 1, February.

Freeman A., Carchedi G., 1996, *Marx and Non-equilibrium Economics*, E. Elgar, Cheltenham.

Fromm E., 1961, *Marx's Concept of Man*, Frederick Ungar, New York.

Fromm E., 1962, *Marx e Freud*, Ital. transl., Il Saggiatore, Milan, 1968.

Fromm E., 1965, *L'umanesimo marxista*, Ital. transl., Dedalo libri, Bari, 1971.

Frowen S. F., ed., 1997, *Hayek: Economist and Social Philosopher*, Macmillan, London.

Fukuyama F., 1989, The End of History?, in *The National Interest*, Summer.

Fukuyama F., 1992, *La fine della storia e l'ultimo uomo*, Ital. transl., Rizzoli, Milan, 1992.

Furubotn E. G., 1971, Toward a Dynamic Model of the Yugoslav Firm, in *The Canadian Journal of Economics*, vol. 4, no. 2.

Furubotn E. G., 1976, The Long-Run Analysis of the Labor-Managed Firm: An Alternative Interpretation, in *American Economic Review*, vol. 66, no. 1.

Furubotn E. G., 1980, The Socialist Labor-Managed Firm and Bank-Financed Investment: Some Theoretical Issues, in *Journal of Comparative Economics*, vol. 4, no. 2.

Furubotn E. G., Pejovich S., 1970, Tax Policy and Investment Decision of the Yugoslav Firm, in *National Tax Journal*, vol. 23, no. 3.

Furubotn E. G., Pejovich S., 1972, Property Rights and Economic Theory: A Survey of Recent Literature, in *Journal of Economic Literature*, vol. 10, no. 4.

Furubotn E. G., Pejovich S., 1973, Property Rights, Economic Decentralization and the Evolution of the Yugoslav Firm, 1965–1972, in *Journal of Law and Economics*, vol. 16.

Fusaro D., 2010, *Essere senza tempo; accelerazione della storia e della vita*, Bompiani, Milan.

Galasso G., 2013, *Liberalismo e democrazia*, Salerno editrice, Rome.

Galbraith J. K., 1967, *Il nuovo stato industriale*, Ital. transl., Einaudi, Turin, 1968.

Galgano P., 1974, *Le istituzioni dell'economia capitalistica*, Zanichelli, Bologna.

Galli C., 2010, *Genealogia della politica*, Il Mulino, Bologna.

Gallino L., 2005, *L'impresa irresponsabile*, Einaudi, Turin.

Garaudy R., undated, *L'alternativa; cambiare il mondo e la vita*, Ital. transl., Cittadella editrice, Assisi, 1972.

Garson G. D., 1973, Beyond Collective Bargaining, in Hunnius, Garson & Case 1973.

Geary R. J., 1974, Difesa e deformazione del marxismo in Kautsky, in Istituto Giangiacomo Feltrinelli 1974.

Genovese R., 2007, L'utopia non può finire, in *Il Ponte*, vol. LXIII, no. 5–6.

Gentile G., 1974, *La filosofia di Marx*, Sansoni, Florence.

George, D. A. R., 1997, Self-Management and Ideology, in *Review of Political Economy*, vol. 9, no.1, January.

Gerratana V., 1968, Introduction to Engels 1878.

Gerratana V., 1977, Stato, partito, strumenti ed istituti dell'egemonia nei 'Quaderni del carcere', in De Giovanni, Gerratana & Paggi 1977.

Gibson-Graham J. K., 2003, Enabling Ethical Economies: Cooperativism and Class, in *Critical Sociology*, vol. 29, no. 2.

Giddens A., 1981, *A Contemporary Critique of Historical Materialism*, University of California Press, Berkeley.

Gide C., 1888, L'avenir de la cooperation, in Gide 1900.

Gide C., 1900, *La cooperation: conferences de propagande*, Larousse Forces, Paris.

Gimpelson V., Treisman D., 2002, Fiscal Games and Public Employment, in *World Politics*, vol. 54.

Gintis H., 1976, The Nature of Labor Exchange and the Theory of Capitalistic Production, in *Review of Radical Political Economics*, vol. 8, no. 2.

Gobetti P., 1924, *La rivoluzione liberale*, Einaudi, Turin, 1965.

Godelier M., 1966, Sistema, struttura e contraddizione nel *Capitale*, Ital. transl., in Godelier & Seve 1970.

Godelier M., 1975, *Rapporti di produzione, miti, società*, Ital. transl., Feltrinelli, Milan, 1976.

Godelier M., 1982, Il marxismo e le scienze dell'uomo, in Hobsbawm *et al.*1978–1982.

Godelier M., Sève L., 1970, *Marxismo e strutturalismo*, Einaudi, Turin.

Goldstein A., Bonaglia F., 2010, Come sta cambiando la governance dell'economia mondiale?, in Quadrio Curzio & Marseguerra 2010.

Goldstein W. S., ed., 2006, *Marx, Critical Theory and Religion*, Leiden, Brill.

Gonnard R., 1930, *Histoire des doctrines économiques*, Valois, Paris.

Goodacre H., 2010, Limited Liability and the Wealth of 'Uncivilised Nations': Adam Smith and the Limits of European Enlightenment, in *Cambridge Journal of Economics*, vol. 3, no. 5, September.

Goodin R., Pettit P., eds., 1997, *Contemporary Political Philosophy*, Blackwell, Oxford.

Goodman P. S., 1974, An Examinations of Referents Used in the Evaluation of Pay, in *Organizational Behavior and Human Performance*, vol. 12.

Gordon D. M., 1976, Efficienza capitalistica ed efficienza socialista, in *Monthly Review*, Ital. ed., September.

Gould C. C., 1985, *Rethinking Democracy*, Cambridge University Press, Cambridge.

Gramsci A., 1918a, Individualismo e collettivismo, in Gramsci 1958a.

Gramsci A., 1918b, *L'intransigenza italiana e la storia di classe*, in *Grido del Popolo*, 18 maggio, reprinted in Gramsci 1984.

Gramsci A., 1918c, La rivoluzione contro 'Il Capitale', in Gramsci 1958a.

Gramsci A., 1919–20, *L'ordine nuovo*, Einaudi, Turin, 1954.

Gramsci A., 1921, Inganni, in Gramsci 1971.

Gramsci A., 1923–26, *La costruzione del partito socialista*, Einaudi, Turin, 1971.

Gramsci A., 1958a, *Scritti giovanili (1914–18)*, Einaudi, Turin.

Gramsci A., 1958b, *Sotto la mole*, Einaudi, Turin.

Gramsci A., 1964a, *Il materialismo storico e la filosofia di Benedetto Croce*, Einaudi, Turin.

Gramsci A., 1964b, *Il Risorgimento*, Einaudi, Turin.

Gramsci A., 1967, *Scritti Politici*, Editori Riuniti, Rome.

Gramsci A., 1971, *Socialismo e fascismo; l'Ordine Nuovo, 1921–1922*, Einaudi, Turin.

Gramsci A., 1972, *L'Ordine Nuovo, 1919–1922*, Einaudi, Turin.

Gramsci A., 1975, *Quaderni del carcere*, ed. by V. Gerratana, Einaudi, Turin.

Gramsci A., 1984, *Il nostro Marx, 1918–1919*, ed. by S. Caprioglio, Einaudi, Turin.

Grossman S. J., Hart O. D., 1986, The Costs and Benefits of Ownership: A Theory of Vertical and Lateral Integration, in *Journal of Political Economy*, vol. 94, no. 4, August.

Gruppi L., 1970, *Il pensiero di Lenin*, Editori Riuniti, Rome.

Gruppi L., 1972, *Il concetto di egemonia in Gramsci*, Editori Riuniti, Rome.

Guerin D., 1971, Le marxisme libertaire, in AA.VV. 1971.

Gui B., 1982, Imprese gestite dal lavoro e diritti patrimoniali dei membri: una trattazione economica, in *Ricerche economiche*, vol. 36, no. 3.

Gui B., 1985, Limits to External Financing: A Model and an Application to Labour-Managed Firm, in Jones & Svejnar 1985.

Gui B., 1993, The Chances for Success of Worker Managed Firm Organization: An Overview, in A.I.S.S.E.C. 1993.

Gui B., 1996, Is there a Chance for the Worker-managed Form of Organization?, in Pagano & Rowthorn 1996.

Guidi M. E. L., Michelini L., eds., 2001, *Marginalismo e socialismo nell'Italia liberale, 1870–1925*, Feltrinelli, Milan.

Gunn C. E., 2000, Markets Against Economic Democracy, in *Review of Radical Political Economics*, vol. 32, no. 3, September.

Gunn C. E., 2006, Cooperatives and Market Failure: Workers' Cooperatives and System Mismatch, in *Review of Radical Political Economics*, vol. 38, no. 3, Summer.

Gunn C. E., 2011, Workers' Participation in Management, Workers' Control in Production, in *Review of Radical Political Economics*, vol. 43, no. 3.

Gunn C. E., 2012, Introduction to the Special Issue on Economic Democracy, in *Review of Radical Political Economics*, vol. 44, no. 1.

Gurley J. G., 1984, Marx's Contribution and their Relevance Today, in *American Economic Review*, vol. 74, May.

Gustafsson Bo, 1974, Capitalismo e socialismo nel pensiero di Bernstein, in Istituto Giangiacomo Fertrinelli 1974.

Habermas J., 1969, La tecnica e la scienza come ideologie, in AA.VV. 1969a.

Habermas J., 1975, *Legitimation Crisis*, transl. by Thomas McCarthy, Beacon Press, Boston.

Hahn F. H., 1993, Il futuro del capitalismo: segni premonitori, in *Rivista milanese di economia*, no. 46, April–June.

Hall R., Jones C., 1999, Why Do Some Countries Produce So Much More Output for Workers Than Others, in *Quarterly Journal of Economics*, vol. CXIV, no 1, February.

Hamilton D., 1999, *Evolutionary Economics; a Study of Change in Economic Thought*, Transaction Publishers, New Brunswick.

Hamilton D., 2003, Technology Is Not Ancillary: The Dramatic and Prosaic in Economic Theory, in *Journal of Economic Issues*, vol. XXXVII, no. 1, March.

Hansmann H., 1996, *The Ownership of Enterprise*, Belknap Press of the Harvard University Press, Cambridge, MA.

Hansmann H., Kraakman R., 1991, Toward Unlimited Stockholder Liability for Corporate Torts, in *Yale Law Journal*, vol. 100.

Hardin R., 2000, The Public Trust, in Pharr & Putnam 2000.

Harman C., 1977, Gramsci versus Eurocommunism, Part 2. International Socialism, 1999, available at www.marxists.anu.edu.au.

Hart O., Moore J., 1990, Property Rights and the Nature of the Firm, in *Journal of Political Economy*, vol. 98, no. 6.

Hart O., Moore J., 1996, The Governance of Exchanges: Members' Cooperatives versus Outside Ownership, *working paper*, available at http//ssrno.com/abstract=60039.

Harvey D., 2005, *A Brief History of Neoliberalism*, Oxford University Press, Oxford.

Haupt G., 1978a, Marx e il marxismo, in Hobsbawn *et al.* 1978–82, vol. I.

Haupt G., 1978b, *L'internazionale socialista dalla Comune a Lenin*, Einaudi, Turin.

Hausman D. M., ed., 1994, *The Philosophy of Economics: An Anthology*, 2nd editn, Cambridge University Press, Cambridge.

Hayek F. A., 1960, *The Constitution of Liberty*, University of Chicago Press, London.

Hayek F. A., 1982, *Legge, legislazione e libertà*, Ital. transl., Il Saggiatore, Milan, 1986.

Hayek F. A., 1983, The Rediscovery of Liberty; Personal Recollections, in Hayek 1992.

Hayek F. A., 1992, *The Fortunes and the Ideal of Freedom*, Routledge & Kegan, London.

Hegedüs A., 1980, La costruzione del socialismo in Russia: il ruolo dei sindacati, la questione contadina, la Nuova politica economica, in Hobsbawm *et al.* 1978–82, vol. III.

Heller A., 1969, Il posto dell'etica nel marxismo, in AA.VV. 1969a.

Heller A., 1980, *Per cambiare la vita*; intervista di Ferdinando Adornato, Editori Riuniti, Rome.

Henderson W. O., 1977, *The Life of Friedrich Engels*, Cass, London.

Hendrikse G., ed., 2003, *Restructuring Agricultural Cooperatives*, Drukkerij Haveka, Alblasserdam.

Hicks J. R., 1969, *A Theory of Economic History*, Oxford University Press, Oxford.

Hilferding R., 1910, *Il capitale finanziario*, Ital. transl., Feltrinelli, Milan, 1961.

Hinden R., ed., 1964, *The Radical Tradition*, Pantheon Books, New York.

Hirsch F., 1976, *The Social Limits to Growth*, Harvard University Press, Cambridge, MA.

Hirschmam A. O., 1982, Rival Interpretations of Market Society: Civilizing, Destructive or Feeble?, in *Journal of Economic Literature*, vol. 20, no. 4.

Hobsbawm E. J., 1982, Il marxismo, oggi: un bilancio aperto, in Hobsbawm *et al.* 1978–1982, vol. IV, 1982.

Hobsbawm E. J., ed., 1995, *Gramsci in Europa e in America*, Laterza, Roma-Bari.

Hobsbawm E. J., Haupt G., Marek F., Ragionieri E., Strada V., Vivanti C., eds., 1978–1982, *Storia del marxismo*, 5 vols., Einaudi, Turin.

Hodges D. C., 1965, The Value Judgement in Capital, reprinted in Wood 1988.

Hodges D. C., 1970, Marx's Concept of Value and Critique of Value Fetishism, reprinted in Wood 1988.

Hodges D., Gandy R., 1982, Marx and Economic Determinism, in *Review of Radical Political Economy*, vol. 14, no. 1, Spring.

Hodgson G. M., 1982–83, Worker Participation and Macroeconomic Efficiency, in *Journal of Post-Keynesian Economics*, vol. 5, no. 2.

Hodgson G. M., 1987, Economic Pluralism and Self-Management, in Jones & Svejnar 1987.

Hodgson G. M., 1993, Transaction Costs and the Evolution of the Firm, in Pitelis 1993.

Hodgson G. M., 1995, The Political Economy of Utopia, in *Review of Social Economy*, vol. 53, no. 2.

Hodgson G. M., 1996, Organizational Form and Economic Evolution, in Pagano & Rowthorn 1996.

Hodgson G. M., 1999, *Economics and Utopia*, Routledge, London.

Hodgson G. M., 2000, What is the Essence of Institutional Economics?, in *Journal of Economic Issues*, vol. 34, no. 2.

Hodgson G. M., 2003, Darwinism and Institutional Economics, in *Journal of Economic Issues*, vol. 37, no. 1, March.

Hollas D., Stansell S., 1988, An Examination of the Effect of Ownership Form on Price Efficiency: Proprietary, Cooperative, and Municipal Electric Utilities, in *Southern Economic Journal*, vol. 50.

Holloway J., 2005, *Change the World Without Taking the Power: The Meaning of Revolution Today*, 2nd editn, Pluto Press, London.

Holt R. P. F., Pressman S., eds., 1988, *Economics and its Discontents.* Twentieth Century Dissenting Economists, Elgar, Cheltenham.

Horkheimer M., 1972, *Studi di filosofia della società*, Ital. transl, Einaudi, Turin, 1981.

Horvat B., 1975, On the Theory of the Labor-managed Firm, reprinted in Prychitko & Vanek 1996.

Horvat B., 1976, *The Yugoslav Economic System*, M. E. Sharpe, New York.

Horvat B., 2000, Social Ownership, 10th Conference of IAFEP, Trient, 6–8 July.

Horvat B., Markovic M., Supek R., eds., 1975, *Self-governing Socialism: A Reader*, International Arts and Science Press, New York.

Houston D. B., 1983, Capitalism without Capitalists: A Comment on "Classes in Marxian Theory", in *Review of Radical Political Economics*, vol. 15, no. 1, Spring.

Howard M. C., King J. E., 1989, *A History of Marxian Economics: Vol. I, 1883–1920*, Macmillan, London.

Huberman B. A., Glance NO. S., 1998, Belief and Cooperation, in Danielson 1998.

Huberman L., Sweezy P. M., 1968, Introduzione al socialismo, Ital. transl., Savelli, Rome, 1978.

Hume D., 1877a, *Essays*, Macmillan, London.

Hume D., 1877b, Enquiry Concerning the Principles of Morals, in *Essays*, vol. 2.

Hunnius G., Garson G. D., Case J., eds., 1973, *Workers' Control; A Reader on Labor and Social Change*, Vintage Books, New York.

ICA (International Cooperative Alliance), 1937, The Present Application of the Rochdale Principles of Cooperation, available at www.coop.org/coop/1937-04.html.

ICA, 1966, Report of the ICA Commission on Cooperation Principles, available at www .ICA.coop/coop/1966.html.

ICA, 1995, Report of the Proceedings of the Centennial Congress of Manchester, available at www.wisc.edu/UWCC/.

Ilardi M., Accornero A., eds., 1981, *Il Partito Comunista Italiano. Struttura e storia dell'organizzazione. 1921/1979*, Annali della Fondazione Giangiacomo Feltrinelli, Milan.

Ireland P., 2010, Limited Liability, Shareholder Rights and the Problem of Corporate Irresponsability, in *Cambridge Journal of Economics*, vol. 34, no. 5, September.

Istituto Giangiacomo Feltrinelli, 1974 and 1975, *Storia del marxismo contemporaneo*, Feltrinelli, Milan.

Istituto Gramsci, 1972, *Il marxismo italiano degli anni sessanta e la formazione teorico-politica delle nuove generazioni*, Editori Riuniti, Rome.

Jacobsson F., Johannesson M., Borgquist L., 2007, Is Altruism Paternalistic?, in *Economic Journal*, vol. 117.

Jacoby R., 1987, *The Last Intellectuals*, Basic Books, New York.

Jaspers K., 1958, *Max Weber politico, scienziato, filosofo*, Ital. transl., Morano editore, 1969, Napoli.

Jensen A., Patmore G., Tortia E., eds., 2015, *Cooperatives Enterprises in Australia and Italy*; *Comparative Analysis and Theoretical Insigths*, Firenze University Press, Florence.

Jensen M. C., Meckling, W. J., 1979, Rights and Production Functions: An Application to Labor-managed Firms and Codetermination, in *Journal of Business*, vol. 52, no. 4.

Johnson C., 1983, Philosophy and Revolution in the Young Marx, in Wood 1988.

Johnstone M., 1980, Lenin e la rivoluzione, in Hobsbawn *et al.* 1978–1982.

Jones D. C., Backus D. K., 1977, British Producer Cooperatives in the Footwear Industry: An Empirical Evaluation of the Theory of Financing, in *Economic Journal*, vol. 87, September.

Jones D. C., Pliskin J., 1991, The Effects of Worker Participation, Employee Ownership and Profit Sharing on Economic Performance: A Partial Review, in Russel & Rus 1991.

Jones D. C., Svejnar J., eds., 1982, *Participatory and Self-Managed Firms: Evaluating Economic Performance*, Lexington, Heath.

Jones D. C., Svejnar J., eds., 1985, *Advances in The Economic Analysis of Participatory and Labor-Managed Firms*, Jai Press, Greenwich, Ct.

Jones D. C., Svejnar J., eds., 1987, *Advances in the Economic Analysis of Participatory and Labor-Managed Firms*, vol. II, JAI Press, Greenwich, CT.

Jones D. C., Svejnar J., eds., 1992, *Advances in the Economic Analysis of Participatory and Labor-Managed Firms*, vol. IV, Greenwich, CT: JAI Press.

Jossa B., 1978, *Socialismo e mercato*, Etas Libri, Milan.

Jossa B., 1986, Considerazioni su di un'tipo ideale' di cooperative di produzione, in *Studi Economici*, vol. 41, no. 28, reprinted in Jossa 1999.

Jossa B., ed., 1989, *Teoria dei sistemi economici*, UTET, Turin.

Jossa B., 1998, *Mercato, socialismo e autogestione*, Carocci, Rome.

Jossa B., 1999, *La democrazia nell'impresa*, Edizioni Scientifiche, Naples.

Jossa B., 2001, L'impresa gestita dai lavoratori e la disoccupazione classica e Keynesiana, in *Rivista italiana degli economisti*, vol. VI, no. 1, April.

Jossa B., 2003, Cooperativismo e teoria economica, in Buonocore & Jossa 2003.

Jossa B., ed., 2004a, *Il futuro del capitalismo*, Il Mulino, Bologna.

Jossa B., 2004b, La possibile fine del capitalismo, in Jossa 2004a.

Jossa B., 2004c, The Cooperative as a Public Good, in Arena & Salvadori 2004.

Jossa B., 2004d, The Democratic Firm as a Public Good, in Arena & Salvadori 2004.

Jossa B., 2005a, Marx, Marxism and the Cooperative Movement, in *Cambridge Journal of Economics*, vol. 29, no.1, January.

Jossa B., 2005b, *La teoria economica delle cooperative di produzione e la possibile fine del capitalismo*, Giappichelli, Turin.

Jossa B., 2005c, La nuova fase del capitalismo secondo Gallino, in *Studi Economici*, no. 87.

Jossa B., 2007, Qualche considerazione sul perché le imprese democratiche non si affermano, in *Economia Politica*, vol. XXIV, no. 3.

Jossa B., 2008, *L'impresa democratica*, Carocci, Rome.

Jossa B., 2009a, Alchian and Demsetz's Critique of the Cooperative Firm; Thirty-Six Years After, in *Metroeconomica*, vol. 60, no. 4.

Jossa B., 2009b, Unemployment in a System of Labour-managed Firms, in Salvadori & Opocher 2009.

Jossa B., 2010a, A Few Advantages of Cooperative Firms, in *Studi Economici*, no. 65.

Jossa B., 2010b, *Esiste un'alternativa al capitalismo?*, manifestolibri, Rome.

Jossa B., 2010c, Investment Funding: The Main Problem Facing Labor-Managed Firms?, in *Economia e Politica Industriale*, 2010, vol. 37, no. 2.

Jossa B., 2011, Le contraddizioni del capitalismo e il loro possibile superamento, in *Studi e Note di Economia*, vol. XVI, no. 1.

Jossa B., 2012a, *Il marxismo e le sfide della globalizzazione*, manifestolibri, Rome.

Jossa B., 2012b, Cooperative Firms as a New Production Mode, in *Review of Political Economy*, vol. 24, no. 3.

Jossa B., 2012c, A System of Self-managed Firms as a New Perspective on Marxism, in *Cambridge Journal of Economics*, vol. 36, no. 4.

Jossa B., 2012d, *Cooperativismo, capitalismo e socialismo*, Novalogos, Aprilia.

Jossa B., 2012e, Alienation and the Self-Managed Firm System, in *Review of Radical Political Economics*, 2013, vol. 46, no. 2.

Jossa B., 2012f, Sulla definizione del socialismo, in *Rivista di politica economica*, vol. I–III, January–March.

Jossa B., 2014a, *A System of Cooperative Firms as a New Mode of Production*, Routledge, London.

Jossa B., 2014b, Marx, Lenin and the Cooperative Movement, in *Review of Political Economy*, 2014, vol. 26, no. 2.

Jossa B., 2014c, The Key Contradiction in Capitalism, in *Review of Radical Political Economics*, vol. 46, Issue 1, March 2014.

Jossa B., 2014d, The Joint-Stock Company as a Springboard for Socialism, in *Rivista internazionale di Scienze Sociali*, vol. CXXII, gennaio-marzo.

Jossa B., 2015, *Un socialismo possibile*, Il Mulino, Bologna, 2015.

Jossa B., Casavola R., 1986, The Problem of Under-Investment in Firms Managed by Workers, in Atkinson 1993.

Jossa B., Casavola P., 1993, The Problem of Under-Investment in Firms Managed by Workers, in Atkinson 1993.

Jossa B., Cuomo G., 1997, *The Economic Theory of Socialism and the Labour-Managed Firm*, E. Elgar, Cheltenham.

Jossa B., Lunghini G., eds., 2006, *Marxismo oggi*, Il Ponte Editore, Florence.

Jossa B., Pagano U., eds., 1997, *Economia di mercato ed efficienza dei diritti di proprietà*, Giappichelli, Turin.

Kahneman D., 2011, *Pensieri lenti e veloci*, Ital. transl., Mondadori, Milan, 2013.

Kalecki M., 1937, The Principle of Increasing Risk, in *Economica*, vol. 3, November.

Kalecki M., 1943, *Gli aspetti politici della piena occupazione*, in Kalecki 1975.

Kalecki M., 1975, *Sulla dinamica dell'economia capitalistica. Saggi scelti, 1933–1970*, Einaudi, Turin.

Kant I., 1784, Idea per una storia universale dal punto di vista cosmopolitico, in Kant 1956.

Kant I., 1798, Se il genere umano sia in costante progresso verso il meglio, in Kant 1956.

Kant I., 1956, *Scritti politici e di filosofia della storia e del diritto*, UTET, Turin.

Karst S., 1974, *Teoria e politica: Louis Althusser*, Ital. transl., Dedalo libri, Bari, 1976.

Kautsky K., 1892, *Introduzione al pensiero economico di Marx*, Ital. transl., Laterza, Bari, 1972.

Kautsky K., 1899, *Bernstein und das sozialdemokratische Programm. Eine Antikritik*, Dietz, Stuttgart.

Kautsky K., 1902, Che cosa è una rivoluzione sociale, in Mills 1962.

Kautsky K., 1906, *Etica e concezione materialistica della storia*, Ital. transl., Feltrinelli, Milan, 1975.

Kautsky K., 1960, *Erinnerungen und Erörterungen*, Gravenhage, Berlin.

Kaysen C., 1957, The Social Significance of Modern Corporation, in *American Economic Review*, vol. 57.

Kellner D., 1995, The Obsolescence of Marxism?, in Magnus & Cullenberg 1995.

Kester G., Pinaud H., 1996, *Trade Unions and Democratic Participation: A Scenario for the 21st Century*, Averbury, Aldershot.

Keynes J. M., 1925, Breve sguardo alla Russia, in Keynes 1931.

Keynes J. M., 1926a, *Esortazioni e profezie*, Il Saggiatore, Milan.
Keynes J. M., 1926b, La fine del *laissez-faire*, in Keynes 1926a.
Keynes J. M., 1931, *Esortazioni e profezie*, Ital. transl., Il Saggiatore, Milan, 1968.
Keynes J. M., 1933, The Distinction Between a Cooperative Economy and an Entrepreneur Economy, in Keynes 1979.
Keynes J. M., 1936, *Occupazione, interesse, moneta. Teoria Generale*, Ital. transl., Utet, Turin, 1959.
Keynes J. M., 1966, *Scritti politici*, Ital. transl., Sansoni, Florence.
Keynes J. M., 1979, *The Collected Writings of John Maynard Keynes*, Macmillan, London.
Khalil E. L., Boulding K. E., eds., 1996, *Evolution, Order and Complexity*, Routledge, London.
Kicillof A., Starosta G., 2007, Value Form and Class Struggle: A Critique of the Autonomist Theory of Value, in *Capital & Class*, no. 92, Summer.
Kirchgassner G., 1989, On the Political Economy of Economic Policy, in *Economia delle scelte pubbliche*, Ybk VII, nos. 1–2.
Kitschelt H., Wilkinson S. I., eds., 2007, *Patrons, Clients and Policies: Patterns of Economic Accountability and Political Competition*, Cambridge University Press, Cambridge.
Klein B., 1991, Vertical Integration as Organizational Ownership: The Fisher Body-General Motors Relationship Revisited, in Williamson & Winter 1991.
Klein M., 2014, *This Changes Everything. Capitalismus vs. the Climate*, Klein Lewis Production Ldt., New York.
Kliman A. J., 1998, Value, Exchange Value and the Internal Consistency of Volume III of Capital: A Refutation of Refutations, in Bellofiore 1998.
Kliman A. J., 2010, The Disintegration of the Marxian School, in *Capital & Class*, vol. 34, no. 1.
Kolakowsky L., 1976–77, *Nascita, sviluppo, dissoluzione del marxismo*, Ital. transl., Sugarco, Milan, 1980.
Kolakowsky L., 1979, *Nascita, sviluppo, dissoluzione del marxismo*, Ital. transl., SugarCo, Milan, 1980.
Kollock P., 1998, Transforming Social Dilemmas: Group Identity and Cooperation, in Danielson 1998.
Kornai J., 1971, *Anti-equilibrium*, North Holland, Amsterdam.
Kornai J., 1980, *Economics of Shortage*, North-Holland, Amsterdam.
Kornai J., 1994, 2nd editn, *Overcentralization in Economic Administration*, Oxford University Press, Oxford.
Korsch K., 1891, *Il programma di Erfurt*, Ital. transl., Samonà e Savelli, Rome, 1971.
Korsch K., 1922, *Consigli di fabbrica e socializzazione*, Ital. transl., Laterza, Bari, 1970.
Korsch K., 1923, *Marxismo e filosofia*, Ital. transl., Sugar Editore, 1966, Milan.
Korsch K., 1938, *Karl Marx*, Ital. transl., Laterza, Bari, 1968.
Kouvelakis S., 2005, Marx e la critica della politica, in Musto 2005.
Krugman P., 2007, *La coscienza di un liberal*, Ital. transl., Laterza, Bari, 2008.
Krugman P., 2009, How Did Economists Get it so Wrong?, in *New York Times*, 2 Sept. 1991.
La Grassa G., 1972, Alcune note sull'*Introduzione del '57*, in La Grassa 1973.
La Grassa G., 1973, *Stuttura economica e società*, Editori Riuniti, Rome.
Labriola A., 1895, In memoria del *Manifesto dei Comunisti*, in Labriola 1965.
Labriola A., 1902, *Discorrendo di socialismo e di filosofia*, reprinted in Edizioni Millennium, Bologna, 2006.
Labriola A., 1942, *La concezione materialistica della storia*, Laterza, Bari.
Labriola A., 1965, *La concezione materialistica della storia*, ed. by E. Garin, Laterza, Bari.
Labriola A., 1970, *Scritti politici (1886–1904)*, ed. by V. Gerratana, Laterza, Bari.
Lafargue P., 1880, *Il diritto all'ozio*, Ital. transl., Il Ponte editore, 2015.

Laibman D., 2006, The Future Within the Present: Seven Theses for a Robust Twenty-First-Century Socialism, in *Review of Radical Political Economics*, vol. 18, no. 3, Summer.

Lammers C. J., Széll G., eds., 1989, *International Handbook of Participation in Organization*; vol. I, *Organizational Democracy: Taking Stock*, Oxford University Press, Oxford.

Landauer C., 1959, *European Socialism: A History of Ideas and Movements*, University of California Press, Berkeley and Los Angeles.

Lange O., 1932, Il ruolo dello Stato nel capitalismo monopolistico, in Lange 1970.

Lange O., 1935, Marxian Economics and Modern Economic Theory, in *Review of Economic Studies*, vol. 2, no. 3, June.

Lange O., 1936–37, Sulla teoria economica del socialismo, Ital. transl., in AA.VV. 1975b.

Lange O., 1957, Alcuni problemi riguardanti la via polacca al socialismo, in Lange 1966.

Lange O., 1958a, *Economia politica*, Ital. transl., Editori Riuniti, Rome, 1962.

Lange O., 1958b, Marxismo ed economia borghese, in Lange 1966.

Lange O., 1966, *Socialismo ed economia socialista*, Ital. transl., La Nuova Italia, Florence, 1975.

Lange O., 1970, *Teoria marxista, economia politica e socialismo; scritti di economia e sociologia*, Ital. transl., F. Angeli, Milan, 1975.

Lasch C., 1995, *La ribellione delle élite*, Ital. transl., Feltrinelli, Milan, 2001.

Laski H. J., 1947, *Le origini del liberalismo europeo*, Ital. transl., La Nuova Italia, Florence, 1962.

Lazonick W., 1978, The Subjection of Labour to Capital: The Rise of the Capitalist System, in *Review of Radical Political Economics*, vol. 10, no. 1, Spring, reprinted in Bowles & Edwards 1990.

Lee F. and Harley S., 1999, Peer Review, Research Assessment Exercise and the Demise of Non-Mainstream Economics, in *Capital & Class*, no. 66.

Leete-Guy F., 1991, Federal Structure and the Viability of Labour-Managed Firms in Mixed Economies, in Russel & Rus 1991.

Lefebvre H., 1968, Bilancio di un secolo e di due mezzi secoli (1867–1917–1967), in AA.VV. 1968.

Lega Nazionale Cooperative e Mutue, 1982, *L'impresa cooperativa degli anni '80*, De Donato, Bari.

Lehning A., 1969, Anarchisme et bolscevisme, in AA.VV. 1971.

Leibman D., 2013, Market Socialism: Design, Prerequisites, Transition, in *Review of Radical Political Economics*, vol. 45, no. 4.

Lenin V. I., 1902, *Che fare?*, Editori Riuniti, Rome, 1974.

Lenin V. I., 1913, Tre fonti e tre parti integranti del marxismo, in Lenin 1965.

Lenin V. I., 1917, *L'imperialismo, fase suprema del capitalismo*, Ital. transl., Editori Riuniti, Rome, 1969.

Lenin V. I., 1917a, *Stato e rivoluzione*, Editori Riuniti, Rome, 1974.

Lenin V. I., 1917b, Come organizzare l'emulazione, in Lenin 1965.

Lenin V. I., 1917c, La catastrofe imminente e come lottare contro di essa, in Lenin 1957–70, *Opere complete*, vol. XXII.

Lenin V. I., 1918, *La rivoluzione proletaria e il rinnegato Kautsky*, in Lenin 1965.

Lenin V. I., 1921a, La nuova politica economica, in Lenin 1972.

Lenin V. I., 1921b, Rapporto sulla sostituzione dei prelevamenti alle eccedenze con l'imposta in natura, in Lenin 1957–70, vol. XXXII.

Lenin V. I., 1921c, Per il quarto anniversario della rivoluzione d'Ottobre, in Lenin 1957–70, vol. 33.

Lenin V. I., 1921d, Ancora sull'imposta in natura, in Lenin 1972.

Lenin V. I., 1922a, Cinque anni di rivoluzione russa e le prospettive della rivoluzione mondiale, in Lenin 1965.

Lenin V. I., 1922b, La funzione e i compiti dei sindacati nelle condizioni della Nuova politica economica, in Lenin 1965.
Lenin V. I., 1923a, Sulla cooperazione, in Lenin 1965.
Lenin V. I., 1923b, Meglio meno, ma meglio, in Lenin 1972.
Lenin V. I., 1956, *La rivoluzione d'ottobre*, Rinascita, Rome.
Lenin V. I., 1957–70, *Opere complete*, Editori Riuniti, Rome.
Lenin V., 1958, *Oeuvres*, Paris-Moscou, t. XXIV.
Lenin V. I., 1965, *Opere scelte*, Editori Riuniti, Rome.
Lenin V. I., 1972, *La costruzione del socialismo*, Editori Riuniti, Rome.
Lepage H., 1978, *Autogestion et capitalisme*, Masson, Paris.
Lerner A. P., 1938, Theory and Practice in Socialist Economics, in *Review of Economic Studies*, vol. 6, no. 1.
Leube K. R., 1988, Social Policy: Hayek and Schmoller Compared, in *International Journal of Social Economics*, vol. 15, nos 9–11.
Lévi-Strauss C., 1962, *Il pensiero selvaggio*, Ital. transl., Il Saggiatore, Milan, 1964.
Levine A., 1984 and 1988, *Arguing for Socialism*, Verso, London.
Levine D. J., Tyson d'Andrea L., 1990, Participation, Productivity and the Firm's Environment, in Blinder 1990.
Levine D. J., 1995, *Reinventing the Workplace. How Business and Employees Can Both Win*, Washington D.C., Brookings Institution.
Li M., 2011, The 21st Century Crisis: Climate Catastrophe or Socialism, in *Review of Radical Political Economics*, vol. 43, no. 3, Summer.
Libertini L., Panieri R., 1958, Sette tesi sulla questione del controllo operaio, in *Mondo operaio*, February.
Lichtheim G., 1962, *Marxism; an Historical and Critical Study*, F. A. Praeger, New York.
Lichtheim G., 1965, *Marxism*, 2nd ed., F. A. Praeger, New York.
Liguori G., 1996, *Gramsci conteso; Storia di un dibattito, 1923–1996*, Editori Riuniti, Rome.
Lindbeck A., 1993, *Unemployment and Macroeconomics*, MIT Press, Cambridge, MA.
Lindblom C., 1977, *Politica e mercato*, Ital. transl., Etas Libri, Milan, 1979.
Lindsey J. K., 1983, Classes in Marxist Theory, in *Review of Radical Political Economics*, vol. 15, no. 1, Spring.
Lippi M., 1976, *Marx; il valore come costo sociale reale*, Etas Libri, Milan.
Lippincott B. E., ed., 1938, *On the Economic Theory of Socialism*, University of Minnesota Press, Philadelphia.
Liss S. B., 1984, *Marxist Thought in Latin America*, University of California Press, Berkeley and Los Angeles.
Livorsi F., 2009, Il mistero del comunismo nella storia, in *Il Ponte*, a. LXV, no. 9.
Lockwood D., 1964, Social Integration and System Integration, in Zollshan & Hirsch 1964.
Longo G. O., 2005, Cosa intendiamo quando parliamo di 'cultura', in Snow 1959 and 1963.
Longxi Z., 1995, Marxism: From Scientific to Utopian, in Magnus and Cullenberg, 1995.
Lorenz R., 1974, La costruzione del socialismo in Lenin, in Istituto Giangiacomo Feltrinelli, 1974.
Losurdo D., 2005, Marxismo, globalizzazione e bilancio storico del socialismo, in Musto 2005.
Lowit T., 1962, Marx et le mouvement cooperatif, in *Cahiers de l'institut de science èconomique appliquée*, no. 129, September.
Löwy M., 2005, To Change the World we Need Revolutionary Democracy, in *Capital and Class*, vol. 85.
Lukàcs G., 1922, *Geschichte und Klassenbewusstsein*, Literaturverlag, Luchterhand, 1988.
Lukàcs G., 1923, *Storia e coscienza di classe*, Ital. transl., Sugarco Edizioni, 1974, Milan.
Lukàcs G., 1924, *Lenin*, Ital. transl., Einaudi, Turin, 1970.
Lukàcs G., 1968, *Scritti politici giovanili, 1919–1928*, Laterza, Bari.

Lukàcs G., 1971, Vecchia kultur e nuova kultur, in *Quaderni Piacentini*, April.

Lukàcs G., 1972, *L'uomo e la rivoluzione*, Ital. transl., Editori Riuniti, Rome, 1973.

Luporini C., 1966, Realtà e storicità: economia e dialettica nel marxismo, in Luporini 1974.

Luporini C., 1974, *Dialettica e materialismo*, Editori Riuniti, Rome.

Lutz M. A., 1997, The Mondragon Cooperative Complex: An Application of Kantian Ethics to Social Economies, in *Journal of Social Economy*, vol. 24.

Luxemburg R., 1899, Riforme sociali o rivoluzione, in Luxemburg 1970.

Luxemburg R., 1904, Problemi di organizzazione nella socialdemocrazia russa, in Luxemburg 1967.

Luxemburg R., 1913, *L'accumulazione del capitale*, Ital. transl., Einaudi, Turin, 1960.

Luxemburg R., 1918, Discorso sul programma, in Luxemburg 1967.

Luxemburg R., 1948, La rivoluzione russa, in Luxemburg 1967.

Luxemburg R., 1967, *Scritti politici*, ed. by L. Basso, Editori Riuniti, Rome.

Luxemburg R., 1970, *Lo sciopero spontaneo di massa*, Musolini editore, Turin.

Macchioro A., 2001, Lineamenti per una storia epistemologica dell'economia politica italiana, 1900–1950, in Guidi & Michelini 2001.

Macciocchi M. A., 1974, *Per Gramsci*, Il Mulino, Bologna.

MacPherson C. B., 1984, Democracy: Utopian and Scientific, in Ball & Farr 1984.

Magatti M., ed., 1990, *Azione economica come azione sociale*, F. Angeli, Milan.

Magnus B., Cullenberg S., 1995, *Whither Marxism?*, Routledge, New York.

Magri L., 1967, A cinquant'anni da 'Stato e Rivoluzione', in AA.VV. 1974.

Magri L., 1977, 'Via italiana' e strategia consiliare, in AA.VV. 1974.

Maitan L., 1995, La crisi attuale, in Colombo 1994.

Makoto I., 2006, Marx's Economic Theory and the Prospect for Socialism, in Uchida 2006.

Mancina C., 1986, ed., *Marx e il mondo contemporaneo*, Editori Riuniti, Rome.

Mandel E., 1973, The Debate on Workers' Control, in Hunnius, Garson & Case 1973.

Mann T., 1918, *Considerazioni di un impolitico*, Adelphi, Milan, 1997.

Marcovic M., 1969, Marx e il pensiero critico-scientifico, in AA.VV. 1969.

Marcuse H., 1932, Nuove fonti per la fondazione del materialismo storico, in Marcuse 1975.

Marcuse H., 1954, *Ragione e rivoluzione*, Ital. transl., Il Mulino, Bologna, 1966.

Marcuse H., 1964, *One-Dimensional Man*, Beacon Press, Boston.

Marcuse H., 1967, *La fine dell'utopia*, Ital. transl., Laterza, Bari, 1968.

Marcuse H., 1969, Un riesame del concetto di rivoluzione, in AA.VV. 1969.

Marcuse H., 1970, Prospettive del socialismo nella società industriale avanzata, in Coppellotti 1972.

Marcuse H., 1975, *Marxismo e rivoluzione; studi 1929–32*, Einaudi, Turin.

Marcuse P., 2015, Cooperatives on the Path to Socialism?, in *Monthly Review*, vol. 66, no. 9.

Marek F., 1982, Teorie della rivoluzione e fasi della transizione, in Hosbawm et al. 1978–82, vol. IV.

Marga A., 1995, The Modern World and the Individuals, in Magnus & Cullenberg 1995.

Marginson P., 1993, Power and Efficiency in the Firm: Understanding the Employment Relationship, in Pitelis 1993.

Marglin S., 1974, What Do the Bosses Do?, in *Review of Radical Political Economics*, vol. 6, no. 2, Summer.

Markus G., 1966, *Marxismo e antropologia*, Ital. transl., Liguori Editore, Naples 1978.

Marramao G., 1977, *Austromarxismo e socialismo di sinistra tra le due guerre*, La Pietra, Milan.

Marramao G., 1980, Tra bolscevismo e socialdemocrazia: Otto Bauer e la cultura politica dell'austromarxismo, in Hobsbawm et al. 1978–82.

Marshall A., Paley Marshall M., 1881, *The Economics of Industry*, 2nd editn, Macmillan, London.

Marshall A., Paley Marshall M., 1920, *Economia della produzione*, Ital. transl., Isedi, Milan, 1975.

Marshall A., 1873, The Future of the Working Classes, in Marshall 1925.

Marshall A., 1889, Cooperation, reprinted in Marshall 1925.

Marshall A., 1890, *Principles of Economics*, Macmillan, London.

Marshall A., 1897, The Old Generation of Economists and the New, in Marshall 1925.

Marshall A., 1898, La gestione dell'impresa. Domanda e offerta in relazione a capitale, potere economico e organizzazione industriale, in Marshall 2014.

Marshall A., 1925, *Memorials of Alfred Marshall*, edited by A. C. Pigou, Macmillan, London.

Marshall A., 2014, *Scritti sull'economia cooperativa*, a cura di A. Zanotti, Il Mulino, Bologna.

Marx K., 1841, Difference Between the Democritean and Epicurean Philosophy of Nature, in Marx & Engels 1975–2001, *Collected Works*, vol. I.

Marx K., 1843, Critica della filosofia hegeliana del diritto pubblico, in Marx & Engels 1966.

Marx K., 1844a, *Economic and Philosophical Manuscripts of 1844*, Foreign Languages Publishing House, Moscow, 1960.

Marx K., 1844b, Kritische Randglossen zu dem Artikel 'Der König von Preussen …', in Marx & Engels, Werke.

Marx K., 1845, Theses on Feuerbach, in Marx & Engels, 1975–2001, *Collected Works*, vol. 5.

Marx K., 1847, *Miseria della filosofia*, Ital. transl., Editori Riuniti, Rome, 1969.

Marx K., 1849, *Lavoro salariato e capitale*, Ital. transl., Editori Riuniti, Rome, 1971.

Marx K., 1851–52, *Il 18 Brumaio di Luigi Bonaparte*, Editori Riuniti, Rome, 1997.

Marx K., 1852a, Article in New York Times issue of 21 August.

Marx K., 1852b, *Il 18 brumaio di Luigi Napoleone*, in Marx & Engels 1966.

Marx K., 1852c, The Eighteenth Brumaire of Louis Bonaparte, in Marx & Engels 1975–2001, *Collected Works*, vol. 11.

Marx K., 1857–58, *Grundrisse: Introduction to the Critique of Political Economy*, Pelican Books, London.

Marx K., 1859a, *Per la critica dell'economia politica*, Ital. transl., Editori Riuniti, Rome, 1969.

Marx K., 1859b, Outline of the Critique of Political Economy, in Marx & Engels, *Collected Works*, vol. 29.

Marx K., 1860, letter to Engels of 19 December, in Marx & Engels, 1975–2001, *Collected Works*, vol. 30.

Marx K., 1861, letter to Lassalle of 16 January, in Marx & Engels, 1975–2001 *Collected Works*, vol. 30.

Marx K., 1862–63, *Storia delle teorie economiche*, Einaudi, Turin, 1958.

Marx K., 1863–66, *Il Capitale: libro I, Chapter VI inedito*, La Nuova Italia, Florence, 1969.

Marx K., 1864, Inaugural Address of the Working Men's International Association, in Marx & Engels 1975–2001, *Collected Works*, vol. 20.

Marx K., 1865, *Salario, prezzo e profitto*, Ital. transl., Editori Riuniti, Rome, 1961.

Marx K., 1867a, *Capital*, vol. I, Penguin Books, Harmondsworth, 1986.

Marx K., 1867b, letter to Engels of 7 December in Marx & Engels 1975–2001, *Collected Works*, vol. 5.

Marx K., 1869, Letter to Laura and Paul Lafargue of 15 February, in Marx & Engels 1975–2001, *Collected Works*, vol. 1.

Marx K., 1871a, *La Guerra civile in Francia*, Ital. transl., Editori Riuniti, Rome, 1974.

Marx K., 1871b, Lettera a Kugelmann del 12 aprile, in Marx & Engels, *Opere complete*, vol. 44.

Marx K., 1875a, Critique of the Gotha Programme, in Marx & Engels 1975–2001, *Collected Works*, vol. 24.

Marx K., 1875b, Letter to Peter Lavrov dated 12–17 November, in Marx & Engels 1975–2001, *Collected Works*, vol. 24.

Marx K., 1877, Letter of end 1877 to the editor's office of the *Otecestvennye Zapinski*, in Marx & Engels 1965.

Marx K., 1894, *Capital*, vol. III, Penguin Books, Harmondsworth, 1981.

Marx K., 1969, *Opere filosofiche giovanili*, ed. by G. della Volpe, Editori Riuniti, Rome.

Marx K., Engels F., 1845–1846, *L'ideologia tedesca*, Ital. transl., Editori Riuniti, Rome, 1969.

Marx K., Engels F., 1845, *La sacra famiglia*, Ital. transl., Editori Riuniti, Rome, 1969.

Marx K., Engels F., 1848, Manifesto of the Communist Party, in Marx & Engels 1975–2001, *Collected Works*, vol. 6.

Marx K., Engels F., 1850, Indirizzo al Comitato centrale della Lega dei comunisti del marzo 1850, in Marx & Engels 1978.

Marx K., Engels F., 1942, *Selected Correspondence, 1846–95*, International Publisher, New York.

Marx K., Engels F., 1965, *India, Cina, Russia*, Ital. transl., Il Saggiatore, Milan.

Marx K., Engels F., 1966, *Opere Scelte*, ed. by L. Gruppi, Editori Riuniti, Rome.

Marx K., Engels F., 1972, *Carteggio Marx-Engels*, vols. I–VI, Editori Riuniti, Rome.

Marx K., Engels F., 1975–2001, *Collected Works*, vols. 1–49, Lawrence and Wishart, London.

Marx K., Engels F., 1978, *Proletariato e comunismo*, ed. by G. M. Bravo, Editori Riuniti, Rome.

Marx K., Engels F., *Opere complete*, Editori Riuniti, Rome.

Marx K., Engels F., *Werke*, Dietz Verlag, Berlin.

Marzano F., 1997, Complementarietà di piano e mercato, in Schiavone 1997.

Massari R., 1974, *Le teorie dell'autogestione*, Jaca Book, Milan.

Mata T., Medema S. G., eds., 2013, *The Economist as Public Intellectual*, Duke University Press, Durham and London.

Mattick P., 1969, Il nuovo capitalismo e la vecchia lotta di classe, in AA.VV. 1969b.

Mattick P., 2002, Class, Capital and Crisis, in Campbell and Reuten 2002.

Mayer T., 1994, *Anaytical Marxism*, Sage Publications, London.

Mazzini G., 1935, *Scritti editi e inediti*, P. Galeati, Imola.

McKay I. G., 2010, The Canadian Passive Revolution, 1840–1950, in *Capital & Class*, vol. 34, no. 3.

McCain R. A., 1992, Transaction Costs, Labor Management, and Codetermination, in Jones & Svejnar 1992.

McGovern A. F., 1970, The Young Marx on the State, in *Science and Society*, vol. 34, no. 4.

McMurtry J. J., 2004, Social Economy as a Social Practice, in International Journal of Social Economics, vol. 31, nos. 9, 10.

McQuarie D., Amburgey T., 1978, Marx and Modern Systems Theory, in Wood 1988, vol. IV.

Meade J. E., 1972, The Theory of Labour-Managed Firms and of Profit Sharing, in *Economic Journal*, vol. 82, March, Supplement.

Meade J. E., 1979, The Adjustment Processes of Labor Cooperatives with Constant Returns to Scale and Perfect Competition, in *Economic Journal*, vol. 89, December.

Meade J. E., 1980, Labour Cooperatives, Participation and Value-Added Sharing, in Clayre 1980.

Megginson W. L., Nash R. C., van Randenborgh M., 1994, The Financial and Operating Performance of Newly Privatized Firms: An International Empirical Analysis, in *Journal of Finance*, vol. XLIX.

Mehring F., 1918, *Vita di Marx*, Ital. transl., Editori Riuniti, Rome, 1966.

Meister A., 1974, *La partecipation dans les associations*, Editions Ouvrières, Paris.

Meister A., 1984, *Participation, Associations, Development and Change*, Transaction Books, New York.

Mellor M., Hannah J. E., Stirling J., 1988, *Worker Cooperative in Theory a Practice*, Open University Press, Philadelphia.

Melnyk G., 1985, *The Search for Community: From Utopia to a Cooperative Society*, Blackrose Books, Montreal.

Merker NO., 2010, *Karl Marx; vita e opere*, Laterza, Rome-Bari.

Merleau Ponty M., 1955, *Le avventure della dialettica*, Ital. transl., Sugar, Milan, 1965.

Mészàros I., 1970, *Marx's Theory of Alienation*, The Merlin Press, London.

Mészàros I., 1995, *Beyond Capital*, Merlin Press, London.

Meyer A. G., 1957, *Il leninismo*, Ital. transl., Edizioni di Comunità, Milan, 1965.

Mileikovsky A., 1969, Marx e la pianificazione sconomica, in AA.VV. 1969a.

Mill J. S., 1871, *Principi di economia politica*, III ediz., Ital. transl., UTET, Turin, 1953.

Miller D., 1989, *Market, States and Community*, Clarendon Press, Oxford.

Miller E. S., 2002, Economics in a Public Interest: Remark upon Receiving the Veblen-Commons Award, in *Journal of Economic Issues*, vol. XXXVI, no. 2, June.

Miller E. S., 2003, Evolution and Stasis: The Institutional Economics of David Hamilton, in *Journal of Economic Issues*, vol. XXXVII, no. 1, March.

Miller M., Modigliani F., 1958, The Cost of Capital, Corporation Finance and the Theory of Investment, in *American Economic Review*, vol., 48, no. 3.

Miller R. W., 1984, Producing Change: Work, Technology, and Power in Marx's Theory of History, in Ball & Farr 1984.

Mills C. W., 1956, *L'élite del potere*, Ital. transl., Feltrinelli, Milan, 1959.

Mills C. W., 1962, *I marxisti*, Ital. transl., Feltrinelli, Milan, 1969.

Miyazaki H., Neary H. NO., 1983, The Illyrian Firm Revisited, in *Bell Journal of Economics*, vol. 14, no. 1.

Moene K. O., Wallerstein I., 1993, Unions versus Cooperatives, in Bowles, Gintis & Gustafsson 1993.

Mondolfo R., 1909, Feuerbach e Marx, in Mondolfo 1968.

Mondolfo R., 1923, *Sulle orme di Marx*, Cappelli, Bologna.

Mondolfo R., 1962, La concezione dell'uomo in Marx, in Mondolfo 1968.

Mondolfo R., 1968, *Umanismo di Marx. Studi filosofici, 1908–1966*, Einaudi, Turin.

Montias J. M., 1976, *The Structure of Economics Systems*, Yale University Press, New Haven.

Morris J., 1966, Commodity Fetishism and the Value Concept: Some Contrasting Point of View, reprinted in Wood 1988.

Morton A. D., 2010, The Continuum of Passive Revolution, in *Capital & Class*, vol. 34, no. 3.

Mouffe C., ed., 2010, *Gramsci and Marxian Theory*, Routledge & Kegan Paul, London.

Mueller D. C., 1989, *Public Choice II*, Cambridge University Press, Cambridge.

Mueller D. C., 1992, The Corporation and the Economist, in Hausman 1994.

Munck R., 1985, Otto Bauer: Towards a Marxist Theory of Nationalism, in *Capital & Class*, vol. 34, no. 1.

Murray P., 2002, The Illusion of Economic: The Trinity Formula and the 'Religion of Everyday Life', in Campbell and Reuten 2002.

Musgrave R. A., 1958, On Merit Goods, in Musgrave 1986.

Musgrave R. A., 1986, *Public Finance in a Democratic Society, Collected Papers of Richard A. Musgrave*, Wheatsheaf Books, Brighton.

Musto M., ed., 2005, *Sulle tracce di un fantasma*, manifestolibri, Rome.

Musto M., 2011, *Ripensare Marx e i marxismi; studi e saggi*, Carocci, Rome.

Mygind N., 1997, Employee Ownership in Baltic Countries, in Uvalic & Vaughan-Whitehead 1997.

Napoleoni C., 1970, Su alcuni problemi del marxismo, in Sweezy *et al.* 1970.

Napoleoni C., 1985, Dalla scienza all'utopia, in Napoleoni 1992.
Napoleoni C., 1992, *Dalla scienza all'utopia: saggi scelti, 1961–1988*, ed. L. Vaccarino, Bollati Boringhieri, Turin.
Nassisi A. M., ed., 1987, *Marx e il mondo contemporaneo*, Editori Riuniti, Rome.
Natoli S., 2008, Felicità, in AA.VV. 2008.
Negri A., 1979, *Marx oltre Marx. Quaderno di lavoro sui 'Grundrisse'*, Feltrinelli, Milan.
Negt O., 1978, *L'ultimo Engels*, in Hobsbawn *et al.* 1978–1982, vol. II.
Negt O., 1979a, Il marxismo e la teoria della rivoluzione nell'ultimo Engels, in Hobsbawm *et al.* 1978–82.
Negt O., 1979b, L'ultimo Engels, in Hobsbawm *et al.* 1978–82, vol. II.
Nimmi E., 1985, Great Historical Failures: Marxist Theories of Nationalism, in *Capital & Class*, vol. 34, no. 1.
Noble J., 1984, Marxian Functionalism, in Ball & Farr 1984.
Nordhal R. A., 1982, Marx on the Use of History in the Analysis of Capitalism, in Wood 1988, vol. I.
North D., 1990, *Institutions, Institutional Change and Economic Performance*, Cambridge University Press, Cambridge.
Nove A., Thatcher I. D., eds., 1994, *Markets and Socialism*, Elgar, Aldershot.
Nozick R., 1974, *Anarchy, State and Utopia*, Basil Blackwell, Oxford.
Nuti D. M., 1985, The Economics of Participation, in Eminent Scholars Lecture Series of IRTI-Jeddah, no.11.
Nuti D. M., 1992, Il socialismo di mercato. Il modello che avrebbe potuto esserci, ma che non c'è mai stato, in Chilosi 1992a.
Nuti D. M., 2001, I sistemi economici della transizione postcomunista, *mimeo.*
Oakeshott R., 1978, *The Case for Workers' Co-ops*, Routledge and Kegan Paul, London.
Obradovic J., Dunn W., eds., 1978, Workers' Self Management and Organizational Power in Yugoslavia, Centre for International Studies, University of Pittsburgh.
Offe C., Lenhardt G., 1979, *Teoria dello stato e politica sociale*, Ital. transl., Feltrinelli, Milan.
Offe C., 1958, The Future of Labour Market, in Offe 1985.
Offe C., 1972a, Il capitalismo maturo. Un tentativo di definizione, in Offe 1977.
Offe C., 1972b, *Lo Stato nel capitalismo maturo*, Ital. transl., Etas Libri, Milan, 1977.
Offe C., 1985, *Disorganised Capitalism*, Polity, Cambridge.
Ojzerman T. I., 1969, Il materialismo storico di Marx e alcuni problemi dello sviluppo sociale contemporaneo, in AA.VV. 1969, vol. I.
Ollman B., 2003. *Dance of the Dialectic; Steps in Marx's Method*, University of Illinois Press, Chicago.
Olson M., 1965, *The Logic of Collective Action*, Harvard University Press, Cambridge.
Olson M., 1982, *The Rise and Decline of Nations*, Yale University, New Haven.
Orfei R., 1970, *Marxismo e umanismo*, Coines Edizioni, Rome.
Pagano U., 1991a, Property Rights, Asset Specificity, and the Division of Labour under Alternative Capitalist Relations, in *Cambridge Journal of Economics*, vol. 15, no. 3.
Pagano U., 1991b, Imprese, tecnologia e diritti di proprietà, in Artoni 1981.
Pagano U., 1992a, Organizational Equilibria and Production Efficiency, in *Metroeconomica*, nos 1–2.
Pagano U., 1992b, Democrazia economica e diritti di proprietà, in *Politica ed economia*, September.
Pagano U., Rowthorn R., eds., 1996, *Democracy and Efficiency in the Economic Enterprise*, Routledge, London.
Paggi L., 1974, La teoria generale del marxismo in Gramsci, in *Storia del marxismo contemporaneo*, Feltrinelli, Milan.
Panaccione A., 1974, L'analisi del capitalismo in Kautsky, in Istituto Giangiacomo Feltrinelli 1974.

Panayotakis C., 2009, Individual Differences and the Potential Tradeoffs Between the Value of a Participatory Economy, in *Review of Radical Political Economics*, vol. 41, no. 1.

Panebianco A., 2004, *Il potere, lo stato, la libertà*, Il Mulino, Bologna.

Pannekoek A., 1950, L'idea dei consigli, in Bricianer 1969.

Panzieri R., 1960, Intervento sui temi per il Congresso della CGIL, in Panzieri 1975.

Panzieri R., 1961, Sull'uso capitalistico delle macchine nel neocapitalismo, in Panzieri 1975.

Panzieri R., 1962, Capitale sociale e lotta di classe, in Panzieri 1975.

Panzieri R., 1964, Plusvalore e pianificazione, in Panzieri 1975.

Panzieri R., 1975, *La ripresa del marxismo leninismo in Italia*, Sapere Edizioni, Milan.

Pateman C., 1970, *Participation and Economic Theory*, Cambridge University Press, Cambridge.

Pejovich S., 1966, *The Market Planned Economy of Yugoslavia*, University of Minnesota Press, Minneapolis.

Pejovich S., 1975, The Firm, Monetary Policy and Property Rights in a Planned Economy, in Horvat, Markovic & Supek 1975.

Pejovich S., 1982, Karl Marx, Property Rights and the Process of Social Change, in *Kyklos*, vol. 35, no. 3, reprinted in Wood 1988.

Pellicani L., 1976, Socialismo ed economia di mercato, in *Mondoperaio*, June.

Pérotin V., 2004, Early Cooperative Survival: The Liability of Adolescence, in *Advances in the Economic Analysis of Participatory and Labor-managed Firms*, vol. 8.

Perotin V., 2006, Entry, Exit, and the Business Cycle: Are Cooperatives Different?, in *Journal of Comparative Economics*, vol. 34, no. 2.

Perri S., 1998, *Prodotto netto e sovrappiù*, UTET, Turin.

Pesciarelli E., 1981, *Un nuovo modo di produrre: la cooperazione nel pensiero degli economisti classici da Smith a Cairnes*, Editrice CLUA, Ancona.

Petrucciani S., 2009, *Marx*, Carocci, Rome.

Petruccioli C., 1972, Su alcuni aspetti del rapporto tra stratificazione sociale e orientamenti ideologici, in Istituto Gramsci 1972.

Peyrelavade J., 2005, *Le Capitalisme Total*, Seuil-La République des Idées, Paris.

Pharr S. J., Putnam R. D., eds., 2000, *Disaffected Democracies: What's Troubling the Trilateral Countries?*, Princeton UP, Princeton.

Piff, P., *et al.*, 2012, Reply to Francis in *Proceedings of the National Academy of Sciences*, no. 109, 25.

Piketty T., 2013, *Capital in the Twenty-First Century*, Harvard University Press, Cambridge, MA.

Pitelis C., ed., 1993, *Transactions Costs, Markets and Hierarchies*, Blackwell, Oxford.

Pittatore S., Turati G., 2000, A Map of Property Rights in Italy and the Case of Cooperatives: An Empirical Analysis of Hansmann's Theory, in *Economic Analysis*, vol. 3, no. 1.

Pivetti M., 2006, Marx e lo sviluppo dell'economia critica, in Jossa & Lunghini 2006.

Pizzorno A., 1966, Introduzione allo studio della partecipazione politica, in *Quaderni di Sociologia*, nos. 2–4, July–December.

Plamenatz J., 1963, *Man and Society*, McGraw-Hill, New York.

Plechanov G. V., 1895, *La concezione materialistica della storia*, Samonà e Savelli, La Nuova sinistra, Rome, 1970.

Plechanov G. V., 1911, *Anarchismo e socialismo*, 3rd editn, Ital. transl., Samonà e Savelli, Rome, 1971.

Potter B., 1893, *The Cooperative Movement in Great Britain*, Swan Sonnershein, London.

Poulantzas N., 1974, *Classi sociali e capitalismo oggi*, Ital. transl., Etas Libri, Milan, 1975.

Powell W., ed., 1987, *The Non Profit Sector: A Research Handbook*, Yale University, New Haven, CT.

Prandergast C., 1999, The Provisions of Incentives on Firms, in *Journal of Economic Literature*, vol. 37.

Prestipino G., 1973, *Natura e società*, Editori Riuniti, Rome.
Prestipino G., 1990, Presenza di Gramsci filosofo della politica, in Muscatello B., ed., 1990, *Gramsci e il marxismo contemporaneo*, Editori Riuniti, Rome.
Proudhon, P. J., 1851, *Idea generale della rivoluzione nel XIX secolo*, partial transl. printed in Ansart 1978.
Proudhon P. J., 1960, *Carnets*, M. Rivière, Paris.
Prychitko D. L, Vanek J., eds., 1996, *Producer Cooperatives and Labor-managed Systems*, E. Elgar, Cheltenham.
Pugliese E., 2008, Le trasformazioni delle classi sociali in Italia negli ultimi decenni, in *Economia italiana*, no. 3.
Putterman L., 1982, Some Behavioural Perspectives on the Dominance of Hierarchical over Democratic Forms of Enterprise, in *Journal of Economic Behaviour and Organization*, vol. III.
Putterman L., 1984, On Some Explanations of Why Capital Hires Labor, in *Economic Inquiry*, vol. 22, no. 2, April.
Putterman L., 1990, *Division of Labor and Welfare; An Introduction to Economic Systems*, Oxford University Press, Oxford.
Putterman, L., Roemer, J. E., Silvestre J., 1998, Does Egalitarianism Have A Future?, in *Journal of Economic Literature*, vol. 36, no. 2.
Quadrio Curzio A., Marseguerra G., eds., 2008, Democracy, Institutions and Social Justice, Libri Scheiwiller, Milan.
Quadrio Curzio A., Marseguerra G., 2010, *Values and Rules for a New Model of Development*, Libri Scheiwiller, Milan.
Quarter J., 1992, *Canada's Social Economy*, J. Lorimer & Co, Toronto.
Ragionieri E., 1965, Il marxismo e la Prima Internazionale, in Ragionieri 1968.
Ragionieri E., 1966, Alle origini del marxismo della Seconda Internazionale, in Ragionieri 1968.
Ragionieri E., 1968, *Il marxismo e l'Internazionale*, Editori Riuniti, Rome.
Ramos-Martinez A., Rodriguez-Herrera A., 1996, The Transformation of Values into Prices of Production: A Different Reading of Marx's Text, in Freeman & Carchedi 1996.
Ramsey H., 1983, Evolution or Cycle? Worker Participation in the 1970s, in Crouch & Heller 1983.
Rapone L., 2011, *Cinque anni che paiono secoli; Antonio Gramsci dal socialismo al comunismo (1914–1919)*, Carocci Editore, Rome.
Ratner C., 2013, Cooperation, Community and Co-ops in a Global Era, Springer Publishers, New York.
Rawls J., 1958, Giustizia come equità, Ital. transl., in *Biblioteca Della Libertà*, nos 164–65, May–August, 2002.
Rawls J., 1971, *A Theory of Justice*, Harvard Economic Press, Cambridge, MA.
Rawls J., 2000, *Lezioni di storia della filosofia morale*, Ital. transl., Feltrinelli, Milan, 2004.
Reich M., 1981, Economic Theory and Class Conflict, reprinted in Bowles & Edwards 1990.
Reich M., Devine J., 1981, The Microeconomics of Conflict and Hierarchy in Capitalist Production, in *Review of Radical Political Economics*, vol. 13.
Resnick S., Wolff R. D., 1982, Classes in Marxian Theory, in *Review of Radical Political Economics*, vol. 13, no. 4, Winter.
Rider C., 1998, Oskar Lange's Dissent from Market Capitalism and State Socialism, in Holt & Pressman 1998.
Riechers C., 1970, *Antonio Gramsci, il Marxismo in Italia*, Ital. transl., Thelèma, Naples, 1975.
Rifkin J., 2009, *Civiltà ed empatia*, Ital. transl., Mondadori, Milan, 2011.
Rigi J., 2013, Peer Production and Marxian Communism: Contours of a New Emerging Mode of Productioon, in *Capital & Class*, vol. 37, no 3.
Robbins L., 1952, *La base economica dei conflitti di classe*, Italian transl., La Nuova Italia, 1952.

Roberts W. C., 2006, The Origin of Political Economy and the Descent of Marx, in Goldstein 2006.
Robertson D. H, 1923, *The Control of Industry*, Cambridge University Press, Cambridge, 1928.
Robinson J., 1942, *Marx e la scienza economica*, Ital. transl., La Nuova Italia, Firenze, 1951.
Robinson J., 1973, *After Keynes*, New York.
Robinson J. A., Verdier T., 2013, The Political Economy of Clientelism, in *Scandinavian Journal of Economics*, vol. 115, no 2.
Rockmore T., 2005, Lukàcs tra Marx e il marxismo, in Fineschi 2005.
Rodinson M., 1969, Sociologia marxista e ideologia marxista, in AA.VV. 1969.
Rodotà S., 2012, *Il diritto di avere diritti*, Laterza, Bari.
Rodrik D., Subramanian A., Trebbi F., 2002, Institutions Rule: The Primacy of Institutions over Geography and Integration in Economic Development, NBER, no. 9305, November.
Roemer J. E., 1982, *A General Theory of Exploitation and Class*, Harvard University Press, Cambridge.
Roemer J. E., ed., 1986, *Analytical Marxism*, Cambridge University Press, Cambridge.
Roemer J. E., 1988, *Free to Lose: An Introduction to Marxist Economic Philosophy*, Harvard University Press, Cambridge.
Roemer J. E., 1993, Can there Be Socialism after Communism?, in Bardhan & Roemer 1993.
Roemer J. E., ed., 1994a, *Foundations of Analytical Marxism*, E. Elgar, Aldershot.
Roemer J. E., 1994b, *Un futuro per il socialismo*, Ital. transl., 1966, Feltrinelli, Milan.
Roncaglia A., 2004, Cooperative e riformismo sociale, in Jossa 2004a.
Roncaglia A., 2008, Il socialismo liberale di Paolo Sylos Labini, in Roncaglia, Rossi & Salvadori 2008.
Roncaglia A., Rossi P., Salvadori M., 2008, *Libertà. giustizia, laicità; in ricordo di Paolo Sylos Labini*, Laterza, Bari.
Rosanvallon P., 1976, *L'age de l'autogestion*, Seuil/Politique, Paris.
Rosselli C., 1930, *Socialismo liberale*, Einaudi, Turin, 1973.
Rothschild K. W., 1986, Capitalist and Entrepreneurs: Prototypes and Roles, in Wagener & Drukke 1986.
Rubel M., 1974, La légende de Marx ou Engels fondateur, in M. Rubel., *Marx critique du marxisme. Essais*, Payot, Paris.
Rubin I. I., 1928, *Saggi sulla teoria del valore di Marx*, Ital. transl., Feltrinelli, Milan, 1976.
Russel B., 1935, *Storia delle idee del secolo XIX*, Ital. transl., Mondadori, Milan, 1970.
Russel R., Rus V., eds., 1991, in *International Handbook of Participation in Organizations*, Oxford University Press, Oxford.
Sacchetti S., Tortia E., 2015, The Silver Lining of Cooperation: Self-defined Rules, Common Resources, Motivations and Incentives in Co-operative Firms, in Jensen, Patmore & Tortia 2015.
Salvadori M. L., 1976, Gramsci e il Pci: due concezioni dell'egemonia, reprinted in Salvadori 1978.
Salvadori M. L., 1978, *Eurocomunismo e socialismo sovietico*, Einaudi, Turin.
Salvadori M. L., 1979, Kautsky tra ortodossia e revisionismo, in Hobsbawm *et al.* 1978–1982.
Salvadori N., Opocher A., *Long-run Growth, Social Institution and Living Standard*, Edward Elgar, Cheltenham, 2009.
Salvemini G., 1993, *Movimento socialista e questione meridionale*, ed. by Arfè G., Feltrinelli, Milan.
Sandkühler H. J., 1970, Kant, il socialismo neokantiano e il revisionismo. Per le origini dell'ideologia del socialismo democratico, in Agazzi 1975.
Sapelli G., 1982, *Necessità di una teoria dell'impresa cooperativa*, in Lega Nazionale Cooperative e Mutue 1982.
Sapelli G., 2006, *Coop: il futuro dell'impresa cooperativa*, Einaudi, Turin.

Sartori G., 1969, *Democrazia e definizioni*, 3rd editn, Il Mulino, Bologna.
Sartori G., 2015, *La corsa verso il nulla*, Mondadori, Milan.
Sartre J. P., 1960, *Critica della ragione dialettica*, Ital. transl., Il Saggiatore, Milan, 1963.
Scalfari E., 1995, Alla ricerca della morale perduta, in Scalfari 2012.
Scalfari E., 2008, L'uomo che non credeva in Dio, in Scalfari 2012.
Scalfari E., 2012, *La passione dell'etica; scritti 1963–2012*, Mondadori, Milan.
Scalfari E., 2013, La fragile armonia di una politica ambigua, in *La Repubblica*, 27 October.
Schaff A., 1965, *Il marxismo e la persona umana*, Ital. transl., Feltrinelli, Milan, 1966.
Schaff A., 1971, Sulla traduzione francese della VI tesi di Marx su Feuerbach, Ital. transl., in Schaff & Séve 1975.
Schaff A., Séve L., 1975, *Marxismo e umanesimo*, Dedalo Libri, Bari.
Schiavone G., ed., 1997, *La democrazia diretta*, Edizioni Dedalo Libri, Bari.
Schlicht E., Von Weizsäcker C. C., 1977, Risk Financing in Labour Managed Economies: The Commitment Problem, in *Zeitschrift für die Gesamte Staatswissenschaft*, special number.
Schmidt C., 1900, Il socialismo e l'etica, in Agazzi 1975.
Schorske C. E., 1979, *Vienna fin de siècle*, Bompiani, Milan, 1991.
Schumpeter J. A., 1941, An Economic Interpretation of Our Time: The Lowell Lectures, in Schumpeter 1991.
Schumpeter J. A., 1942, *Capitalismo, socialismo e democrazia*, Ital. transl., Edizioni di Comunità, Milan, 1964.
Schumpeter J. A., 1954, *History of economic analysis*, Oxford University Press, London.
Schumpeter J. A., 1991, *The Economics and Sociology of Capitalism*, ed. by R. Swedberg, Princeton University Press, Princeton.
Schweickart D., 1992, Socialism, Democracy, Market Planning: Putting the Pieces Together, in *Review of Radical Political Economics*, vol. 24, nos 3–4.
Schweickart D., 1993, *Against Capitalism*, University Press, Chicago.
Schweickart D., 2002, *After Capitalism*, Rowman & Littlefield Publishers, Inc., Lanham.
Screpanti E., 2001, *The Fundamental Institutions of Capitalism*, Routledge, London.
Screpanti E., 2003, Value and Exploration: A Counterfactual Approach, in *Review of Political Economy*, no. 1.
Screpanti E., 2007a, *Comunismo libertario*, manifestolibri, Rome.
Screpanti E., 2007b, Democrazia redicale e lotta di classe: alcune precisazioni, in *Il Ponte*, a. LXIII, nos 8–9.
Screpanti E., 2013, *Marx dalla libertà alla moltitudine (1841–1843)*, II edit., Petit plaisance, Pistoia.
Sen A. K., 1966, Labour Allocation in a Cooperative Enterprise, in *Review of Economic Studies*, vol. 33, October.
Sen A., 2015, *La libertà individuale come impegno sociale*, Laterza, Bari.
Sertel M. R., 1982, *Workers and Incentives*, North-Holland, Amsterdam.
Settembrini D., 1973, *Due ipotesi per il socialismo in Marx ed Engels*, Laterza, Bari.
Sève L., 1967, Metodo strutturale e metodo dialettico, in Godelier & Sève 1970.
Sève L., 1970, Lucien Sève a Giulio Einaudi, in Godelier & Sève 1970.
Sève L., 1996, Le communisme, in Texier *et al.*, *Congrès Marx International. Cent ans de marxisme*, PUF, Paris.
Sève L., 2004, *Penser avec Marx aujourd'hui*, Tome I, *Marx et nous*, La Dispute, Paris.
Severino E., 2012, *Capitalismo senza futuro*, Rizzoli, Milan.
Shaw W. H., 1984, Marxism, Revolution, and Rationality, in Ball & Farr 1984.
Sherman H., 1995, *Reinventing Marxism*, Johns Hopkins University Press, London.
Sidoti F., 1987, Parlamento e governo in Marx. Alcune 'verità sociologiche' di un centenario, in Nassisi 1987.
Simon R., 2010, Passive Revolution, Perestroika, and the Emergence of the New Russia, in *Capital & Class*, vol. 34, no. 3.
Singer P., 1980, *Marx*, Oxford University Press, London.

Smith A., 1776, *Indagine sulla natura e le cause della ricchezza delle nazioni*, Ital. transl., ISEDI, Milan, 1973.

Smith A., 1790, *Teoria dei sentimenti morali* (VI edition), Ital. transl., Rizzoli, Milan, 2001.

Smith S. B., 1984, Considerations on Marx's Base and Superstructure, reprinted in Wood 1988.

Snow C. P., 1959 e 1963b, *Le due culture*, Ital. transl., Marsilio Editori, Venice, 2005.

Sobel R., 2008, Travail et justice dans la société communiste chez Marx. Un commentaire à propos de quelques ambiguïtés naturalistes de 'l'etage du bas' de la 'phase superieure' du communisme, in *Economies et Sociétés*, vol. 40, no. 5.

Solari S., 2012, The 'Pratical Reason' of Reformers: Proudhon vs. Istitutionalism, in *Journal of Economic Issues*, vol. XLVI, no.1.

Sombart W., 1894, Zur Kritik des oekonomischen Systems von Karl Marx, in *Archiv für Soziale Gesetzgebung und Statistik*, vol. VII, no. 4.

Sombart W., 1902 and 1916, *Il capitalismo moderno*, Ital. transl., UTET, Turin, 1967.

Sowell T., 1985, *Marxism; Philosophy and Economics*, Quill William Morris, New York.

Spriano P., 1967, Introduzione a Gramsci, in Gramsci 1967.

Sraffa P., 1922, The Bank Crisis in Italy, in *Economic Journal*, vol. 32, no. 126, June.

Sraffa P., 1960, *Produzione di merci a mezzo di merci*, Einaudi, Torino.

Srinivasan R., Phansalkar S. J., 2003, Residual Claims in Cooperatives: Design Issues, in *Annals of Public and Cooperative Economics*, vol. 74, no. 3, September.

Staber U., 1989, Age-dependence and Historical Effects on the Failure Rates of Worker Cooperatives; an Event-history Analysis, in *Economic and Industrial Democracy*, vol. 10, no. 1.

Stalin J., 1938, *Del materialismo dialettico e del materialismo storico*, in Stalin 1973.

Stalin J., 1940, *Questioni del leninismo*, Edizioni in lingue straniere, Moscow.

Stalin J., 1973, *Opere scelte*, Edizioni del movimento studentesco, Milan.

Stauber L. G., 1977, A Proposal For a Democratic Market Economy, in *Journal of Comparative Economics*, vol. I, no. 3, September.

Stauber L. G. 1987, Capitalism and Socialism: Some General Issues and the Relevance of Austrian Experience, reprinted in Nove & Thatcher 1994.

Stauber L. G., 1989, Age-dependence and Historical Effects on the Failure Rates of Worker Cooperatives. An Event-history Analysis, in *Economic and Industrial Democracy*, vol. 10, no. 1.

Stedman Jones G., 1978, Ritratto di Engels, in Hobsbawm *et al.* 1978–82, vol. I.

Steedman I., 1977, *Marx after Sraffa*, New Left Books, London.

Stefanelli R., 1975, Un'interpretazione, in AA.VV. 1975.

Steinherr A., 1975, Profit-maximizing vs. Labor-managed Firms: A Comparison of Market Structure and Firm Behavior, in *Journal of Industrial Economics*, vol. 24.

Steinherr A., Thisse J. F., 1979a, Are Labour-Managers Really Perverse?, in *Economic Letters*, vol. 2.

Steinherr A., Thisse J. F., 1979b, Is There a Negatively-Sloped Supply Curve in The Labour-Managed Firm?, in *Economic Analysis and Workers' Management*, vol. 13.

Steinherr A., Vanek J., 1976, Labour-managed Firms and Imperfect Competition, in *Economic Journal*, vol. 86, no. 342, June.

Sterner T., 1990, Ownership, Technology and Efficiency: An Empirical Study of Cooperatives, Multinationals, and Domestic Enterprises in the Mexican Cement Industry, in *Journal of Comparative Economics*, vol. 14, no. 2.

Stiglitz J. E., 1969, A Re-examination of the Modigliani-Miller Theorem, in *American Economic Review*, vol. 59, December.

Stiglitz J. E., 1994, *Whither Socialism?*, MIT Press, Cambridge, MA.

Stiglitz J. E., 2012, *Il prezzo della diseguaglianza*, Ital. transl., Einaudi, Turin, 2013.

Stone B., 1998, Why Marxism Isn't Dead (Because Capitalism Isn't Dead): The Case for Cooperative Socialism, 20th World Congress of Philosophy, Boston, in *Paideia Archiv, Social Philosophy*, 1999.

Strada V., 1979, La polemica tra bolscevichi e menscevichi sulla rivoluzione del 1905, in Hobsbawm *et al.* 1978–82.

Strada V., 1980, Lenin e Trockij, in Hobsbaswm *et al.* 1978–1982, vol. III.

Strang D., Sine, W. D., 2002, Interorganizational Institutions, in Baum 2002.

Streit M. E., 1997, Constitutional Ignorance, Spontaneous Order and Rule-Orientation: Hayekian Paradigms from a Policy Perspective, in Frowen 1997.

Struve P., 1899, La théorie marxienne de l'évolution sociale, reprinted in *Cahiers de l'Institut de science économique appliquée*, 129, September, 1962.

Sumner W. G., 1906, *Folkways*, Ginn & Co, Boston.

Sweezy P. M., 1963, Communism as an Ideal, in *Monthly Review*, October.

Sweezy P. M., 1967, Marx and the Proletariat, in Wood 1988, vol. IV.

Sweezy P. M., 1968, Cecoslovacchia, capitalismo e socialismo, *Monthly Review*, Ital. ed., November.

Sweezy P. M., 1971, Sulla teoria del capitalismo monopolistico, in Sweezy 1972.

Sweezy P. M., 1972, *Il capitalismo moderno*, Ital. transl., Liguori, Naples, 1975.

Sweezy P. M., 1981, *Il marxismo e il futuro*, Ital. transl., Einaudi, Turin, 1983.

Sweezy P. M. *et al.*, 1970, *Teoria dello sviluppo capitalistico*, ed. by C. Napoleoni, Turin, Boringhieri.

Sylos Labini P., 1978, *Saggio sulle classi sociali*, Laterza, Bari.

Sylos Labini P., 1984, *Le classi sociali negli anni '80*, Laterza, Bari-Rome.

Sylos Labini P., 2006, Perché gli economisti debbono fare i conti con Marx, in Jossa & Lunghini 2006.

Tabellini G., 2008, The Scope of Cooperation, in *Quarterly Journal of Economics*, vol. CXXIII, no. 3.

Tawney R. H., 1918, *The Conditions of Economic Liberty*, in Hinden 1964.

Therborn G., 1971, *Critica e rivoluzione; la Scuola di Francoforte*, Ital. transl., Laterza, Bari, 1972.

Thomas H., Logan C., 1982, *Mondragon, an Economic Analysis*, George Allen & Unwin, London.

Thomas P, 1985, *Karl Marx and the Anarchists*, Routledge and Kegan, London.

Thompson W., 1827, *Labour Rewarded: The Claims of Labour and Capital Conciliated by One of the Idle Classes, or, How to Secure to Labour the Whole Products of its Exertions*, A. M. Kelley, 1969, New York.

Togliatti P., 1920, Cooperative o schiavitù, reprinted in Togliatti 1967.

Togliatti P., 1967, *Opere*, ed. by Ernesto Ragionieri, Editori Riuniti, Rome.

Tomba M., 2013, Accumulation and Time: Marx's Historiography from the *Grundrisse* to *Capital*, in *Capital and Class*, vol. 37, no. 3.

Tonini V., 1967, *Che cosa ha veramente detto Lenin*, Ubaldini Editore, Rome.

Tool M. R., 1995, *Pricing, Valuation and Systems*, Elgar, Aldershot.

Toporowski J., 2010, Corporate Limited Liability and the Financial Liability of Firms, in *Cambridge Journal of Economics*, vol. 3, no. 5, September.

Tornquist D., 1973, Workers' Management: The Intrinsic Issues, in Hunnius, Garson & Case 1973.

Tortia E., 2007, Self-financing in LMFs: Individual Capital Accounts and Bonds, in *Advances in the Economic Analysis of Participatory and Labour-Managed Firms*, vol. 10.

Tortia E. 2008a, *Le determinanti dello sforzo lavorativo nelle imprese sociali*, University of Trent, Trent.

Tortia E., 2008b, Dal contratto di lavoro al contratto di associazione nelle cooperative di lavoro, in *Il Ponte*, vol. 64, no. 10.

Tortia E., Knox Haly M., Jensen A., 2015, From Neoliberal to Participatory Firm: Employee Participation Through Industial Relations and Governance in Australia and Italy, in Jensen, Patmore & Tortia 2015.

Touraine A., 2004, *La globalizzazione e la fine del sociale*, Ital. transl., Il Saggiatore, Milan.

Tronti M., 1962, La fabbrica e la società, in *Quaderni Rossi*, II, reprint, Sapere, Milan-Rome, 1974.

Tronti M., 1966, *Operai e capitale*, Einaudi, Turin.

Tronti M., 1977, *Sull'autonomia del politico*, Feltrinelli, Milan.

Tronti M., 1978, Operaismo e centralità operaia, in AA.VV. 1978.

Trotsky L. D., 1933, *Soviet Economy in Danger*, New York.

Trower C., 1973, Collective Bargaining and Industrial Democracy, in Hunnius, Garson & Case 1973.

Tseo G. K. Y., Hou Gui Sheng, Zhang Peng-Zhu, Zang Libain, 2004, Employee Ownership and Profit Sharing as Positive Factors in the Reform of Chinese State-Owned Enterprises, in *Economic and Industrial Democracy*, vol. 25, no.1.

Tsuru S., 1969, Marx e l'analisi del capitalismo. Un nuovo studio della contraddizione fondamentale?, in AA.VV. 1969a.

Tucidide, 4th cent. B.C., *La guerra del Peloponneso*, Ital. transl., Garzanti, Milan, 2003.

Tucker R. C., 1965, *Philosophy and Myth in Karl Marx*, Cambridge University Press, Cambridge.

Tucker R. C., 1969, *The Marxian Revolutionary Idea*, W. W. Norton, New York.

Turati, F., 1897, Il miraggio delle cooperative, in *Critica sociale*, 1 August, 16 August and 1 September.

Uchida H., ed., 2006, *Marx for the 21st Century*, Routledge, London.

Ureña E. M., 1977, Marx and Darwin, reprinted in Wood 1988, vol. IV.

Uvalic M., Vaughan-Whitehead D., eds., 1997, *Privatization Surprises in Transition Economies: Employee Ownership in Central and Eastern Europe*, E. Elgar, Cheltenham.

Vacca G., 1967a, Lettura di *L'uomo a una dimensione*, in Vacca 1969b.

Vacca G., 1967b, Tecnologia e rapporti sociali: Dahrendolf, Marcuse, Mallet, in Vacca 1969b.

Vacca G., 1969a, *Lukàcs o Korsch?* De Donato, Bari.

Vacca G., 1969b, *Marxismo e analîsi sociale*, De Donato, Bari.

Vacca G., 1972, *Politica e teoria nel marxismo italiano 1959 1969*, De Donato, Bari.

Vacca G., 1985, *Il marxismo e gli intellettuali*, Editori Riuniti, Rome.

Vahabi M., 2010, Integrating Social Conflict into Economic Theory, in *Cambridge Journal of Economics*, vol. 34, no. 4, July.

Valenti G., 1901, L'associazione cooperativa e la distribuzione della ricchezza. Contributo alla teoria economica della cooperazione, in *Archivio giuridico 'Filippo Serafini'*, terza serie, vol. VIII.

Valenti G., 1902, *L'associazione cooperativa e la distribuzione della ricchezza. Contributo alla teoria economica della cooperazione*, con un'appendice intorno alla legislazione sulle società cooperative, in *Archivio giuridico 'Filippo Serafini'*, Nuova serie, Mucchi editore, Modena.

Van Parijs P., 1984, Marxism's Central Puzzle, in Ball & Farr 1984.

Van Parijs P., 1993, *Marxism Recycled*, Cambridge University Press, Cambridge.

Van Parijs P., van der Veen R. J., 1986, A Capitalist Road to Communism, in van Parijs 1993.

Vanek J., 1969. Decentralization under Workers' Management: A Theoretical Appraisal, in *American Economic Review*, vol. 59.

Vanek J., 1970, *The General Theory of Labor-Managed Market Economies*, Cornell University Press, Ithaca.

Vanek J., 1971a, Some Fundamental Considerations on Financing and The Form of Ownership under Labour Management, reprinted in Vanek 1977a.

Vanek J., 1971b, The Basic Theory of Financing of Participatory Firms, reprinted in Vanek 1977a.

Vanek J., 1971c, The Participatory Economy: An Evolutionary Hypothesis on a Strategy for Development, Cornell University Press, Ithaca.

Vanek J., ed., 1975a, *Self-Management: Economic Liberation of Man*, Penguin Books, Baltimore.

Vanek J., 1975b, Introduction to Vanek 1975a.

Vanek J., 1977a, *The Labor Managed Economy: Essays by J. Vanek*, Cornell University Press, Ithaca.

Vanek J., 1977b, Educazione alla pratica dell'autogestione, in Vanek 1985.

Vanek J., 1978, La cooperativa di lavoro al crocevia della storia, Ital. transl., in Vanek 1985.

Vanek J., 1985, *Imprese senza padrone nelle economie di mercato*, Edizioni Lavoro, Rome.

Vanek J., 1993, From Partnership with Paper to Partnership among Human Beings, in Atkinson 1993.

Vanek J., 2006. The Future, Dynamics and Fundamental Principles of Growth of Economic Democracy, *mimeo*.

Vaughan-Whitehead D., 1999, Employee Ownership on the Policy Agenda: Lessons from Central and Eastern Europe, in *Economic Analysis*, vol. 2, February.

Veblen T. B., 1899, *The Theory of the Leisure Class*, reprint, August M. Kelley, New York, 1965.

Veblen T. B., 1904, *The Theory of Business Enterprise*, Reprints of classics, Augustus M. Kelley, New York, 1965.

Veblen T. B., 1964, *What Veblen Thought*, Augustus M. Kelley, New York.

Vernon R., Aharoni Y., eds., 1981, *State Owned Enterprise in Western Economies*, Croom Helm, London.

Vining A., Boardman A., 1992, Ownership vs. Competition: Efficiency in Public Enterprise, in *Public Choice*, vol. LXXIII.

Visser J. C., 1989, Factory Occupation and Industrial Democracy, in Lammers & Széll 1989.

Von Siemens F. A., 2011, Heterogeneous Social Preferences, Screening, and Employment Contracts, in *Oxford Economic Papers*, vol. 63, no. 3.

Vorländer C., 1911, Kant e Marx, in AA.VV. 1970.

Vygodskij V. S., 1967, *Introduzione ai 'Grundrisse' di Marx*, Ital. transl., La Nuova Italia, Florence, 1974.

Wagener H. J., Drukker J. W., 1986, *The Economic Law of Motion of Modern Society*, Cambridge University Press, Cambridge.

Walicki A., 1969, *The Controversy over Capitalism*, Oxford University Press, Oxford.

Wallerstein I., 2000, *Alla scoperta del sistema mondo*, Ital. transl., manifestolibri, 2003, Rome.

Wallerstein I., 2002, New Revolts against the System, in *New Left Review*, November–December.

Wallerstein I., 2003, *Il declino dell'America*, Ital. transl, Feltrinelli, Milan, 2004.

Walras L., 1865, *Les associations populaires*, Dentu, Paris.

Walras L., 1868, Recherche de l'idéal social, in Walras 1990.

Walras L., 1990a, Socialisme et libéralisme. Lettres à M. Scherer, in Walras 1990c.

Walras L., 1990b, *Etudes d'économie social*, in Walras 1990c, vol IX.

Walras L., 1990c, *Œuvres économiques complètes d'Auguste et Léon Walras*, Economica, 1866–1867.

Walzer M., 1995, The Communitarian Critique of Liberalism, in Etzioni 1995.

Ward B., 1958, The Firm in Illyria: Market Syndacalism, in *American Economic Review*, vol. 48, no. 4, September.

Watkins W. P., 1986, *Cooperative Principles Today and Tomorrow*, Holyoake Books, Manchester.

Webb B., 1891, *The Cooperative Movement in Great Britain*, Swan Sonnenschein & Co, London.
Webb S., Webb B., 1921, *A Constitution for the Socialist Commonwealth of Great Britain*, Longmans, London.
Webb S., Webb B., 1923, *The Decay of Capitalistic Civilization*, Allen & Unwin, London.
Weber M., 1918, La nuova Germania, in M. Weber, *Scritti politici*, Donzelli, Rome, 1998.
Weber M., 1961, *Il metodo delle scienze storico-sociali*, Einaudi, Turin.
Weber Marianne, 1984, *Max Weber, una biografia*, Ital. transl., Il Mulino, Bologna, 1995.
Wedderburn B., 2004, *The Future of Corporate Law*, IER, London.
Weil S., 1955, *Riflessioni sulle cause della libertà e dell'oppressione sociale*, Ital. transl., RCS Quotidiani, 2010.
Weil S., 1959, *Lezioni di filosofia*, Ital. transl., Adelphi, Milan, 2012.
Weimer D., 1991, *Policy Analysis and Economics. Developments, Tensions, Prospects*, Kluver, Dordrecht.
Weingast B. R., Marshall W. J., 1988, The Industrial Organization of Congress; or, Why Legislatures, like Firms, are Not Organized as Markets, in *Journal of Political Economy*, vol. 96, February.
Weisskopf T. E., 1992, Toward a Socialism for Future, in the Wake of the Demise of the Socialism of the Past, in *Review of Radical Political Economics*, vol. 24, nos 3–4.
Weitzman M., Kruse D. L., 1990, Profit Sharing and Productivity, in Blinder 1990.
Weitzman M. L., 1984, *L'economia della partecipazione*, Ital. transl., Laterza, Bari, 1985.
Wennerlind C., 2002, The Labor Theory of Value and the Strategic Role of Alienation, in *Capital and Class*, no. 77, primavera.
Werin L., Wijkander H., eds., 1992, *Contract Economics*, Basil Blackwell, New York.
West E. G., 1969, *The Political Economy of Alienation: Karl Marx and Adam Smith*, reprinted in Wood 1988.
Westra R., 2002, Marxian Economic Theory and an Ontology of Socialism: A Japanese Intervention, in *Capital and Class*, no. 78, Autumn.
Wetter G. A., 1948, *Il materialismo dialettico sovietico*, Einaudi, Turin.
Wheeler G. S., 1973, *Le contraddizioni del socialismo*, Ital. transl., Coines edizioni, Rome, 1976.
White F., 1991, Learning from Mondragon, in Russel & Rus 1991.
Wiles P., 1962, *The Political Economy of Communism*, Harvard University Press, Cambridge, MA.
Williamson O. E., 1975, *Markets and Hierarchies: Analysis and Anti-trust implications*, Free Press, New York.
Williamson O. E., 1980, The Organization of Work: A Comparative Institutional Assessment, in *Journal of Economic Behavior and Organization*, vol. 1, no. 1.
Williamson O. E., 1985, *The Economic Institutions of Capitalism*, New York, Free Press.
Williamson O. E., Winter S., eds., 1991, *The Nature of the Firm; Origins, Evolution and Development*, Oxford University Press, New York.
Wilson E. O., 1998, *L'armonia meravigliosa*, Ital. transl., Mondadori, Milan, 1999.
Wilson J. Q., 1961, The Economics of Patronage, in *Journal of Political Economy*, vol. 69.
Winn J., 2013, Notes towards a Critique of 'Labour Managed Firms', available at http://josswinn.org/2013/07.
Wolff R., 2012, *Democracy at Work: A Cure for Capitalism*, Haymarket Books, Chicago.
Wolff R., Resnick S., 1982, Classes in Marxian Theory, in *Review of Radical Political Economics*, vol. 14, Winter.
Wolff R., Resnick S., 1983, Reply to Houston and Lindsey, in *Review of Radical Political Economics*, vol. 15, no. 1, Spring.
Woltmann L., 1900, La fondazione della morale, in Agazzi 1975.
Wood F. S., 1928, The Status of Management Stockholders, in *Yale Law Journal*, vol. 38.

Wood G., 1969, *Creation of the America Republic*, The University of North Carolina Press, Chapel Hill.

Wood J. C., ed., 1988, *Karl Marx's Economics: Critical Assessments*, Croom Helm, New South Wales.

Wright E. O., 1995, What is Analytical Marxism?, in Carver & Thomas 1995.

Yudt T., 2012, *Novecento; il ruolo degli intellettuali e della politica*, Ital. transl., Laterza, Roma-Bari.

Yunker J. A., 1992, *Socialism Revised and Modernised*, Praeger, New York.

Yunker J. A., 1995, Post-Lange Market Socialism: An Evolution of Profit Oriented Proposals, in *Journal of Economics Issues*, vol. 29, no. 3, September.

Zafiris N., 1986, The Sharing of the Firm's Risks Between Capital and Labour, in *Annals of Public And Cooperative Economics*, vol. 57, no. 1.

Zagari E., 2000, *L'economia politica dal mercantilismo ai giorni nostri*, Giappichelli, Turin.

Zagari E., 2011, Nota sull'alternativa al capitalismo proposta da Bruno Jossa, in *Studi economici*, fasc. 104.

Zagrebelsky G., 2014, *Contro la dittatura del presente. Perché è necessario un discorso sui fini*, Laterza, Bari-Rome.

Zamagni S., 2005, Per una teoria economico-civile dell'impresa cooperativa, Università di Bologna, sede di Forlì, Working paper no. 10.

Zamagni S., 2006, Promozione cooperativa e civilizzazione del mercato, in Bulgarelli & Viviani 2006.

Zamagni S., 2008, Sul nesso causale tra economia e sviluppo economico, in Quadrio Curzio & Marseguerra 2008.

Zamagni S., Zamagni V., 2008, *La cooperazione*, Il Mulino, Bologna.

Zangheri R., Galasso G., Castronuovo V., 1987, *Storia del movimento cooperativo in Italia*, Einaudi, Turin.

Zanone V., 2002, Il liberalismo di Franco Romani, in *Biblioteca della libertà*, no. 164–65, May–August.

Zanotti A., 2014, *Introduction* to Marshall 2014.

Zevi A., 1982, *The Performance of Italian Producer Cooperatives*, in Jones & Svesnar 1982.

Zollshan G. K., Hirsch W., eds., 1964, *Explorations in Social Change*, Houghton Mifflin, Boston.

Zolo D., 1974, *La teoria comunista dell'estinzione dello Stato*, De Donato, Bari.

Zolo D., 1978, Democrazia corporativa, produzione del consenso, socialismo, in Ferrajoli & Zolo 1978.

Index